This book details a striking political relationship between American Ambassador Frederic Sackett and German Chancellor Heinrich Brüning and their attempts to save the Weimar Republic, achieve German nationalist goals, and thwart Adolf Hitler's drive to power. Sackett thought that financial policy was at the heart of German problems and, unless resolved, could be the basis for Hitler's success. He was critical of the American corporatist policy that encouraged American bankers in the private sector to loan large amounts of money to the Germans. Sackett believed this policy was partly responsible for the German financial crisis and attempted to remedy it. Very early in his tenure in Berlin, Sackett saw Hitler and the Nazis as a serious danger to the Weimar Republic and to peace in Europe. He considered Hitler a political agitator and demagogue who was not fit to govern Germany. Imbued with a strong aversion to communism, the American ambassador thought that misrule by incompetent and inefficient Nazis would pave the way for a communist state. Although at first he saw the Nazis as harbingers of worse to come, in time he came to see Hitler as the real threat to democracy in Germany.

Ambassador Frederic Sackett and the collapse of
the Weimar Republic, 1930–1933

Frederic M. Sackett. (Photo reproduced by permission of
The Courier-Journal)

Ambassador Frederic Sackett and the collapse of the Weimar Republic, 1930–1933

The United States and Hitler's rise to power

BERNARD V. BURKE
Portland State University

CAMBRIDGE
UNIVERSITY PRESS

Published by the Press Syndicate of the University of Cambridge
The Pitt Building, Trumpington Street, Cambridge CB2 1RP
40 West 20th Street, New York, NY 10011–4211, USA
10 Stamford Road, Oakleigh, Melbourne 3166, Australia

© Cambridge University Press 1994

First published 1994

Printed in the United States of America

Library of Congress Cataloging-in-Publication Data
Burke, Bernard V.
Ambassador Frederic Sackett and the collapse of the Weimar Republic, 1930–1933 :
the United States and Hitler's rise to power / Bernard V. Burke.
p.   cm.
Includes bibliographical references (p.   ) and index.
ISBN 0–521–47005–6 (hc)
1. United States – Foreign relations – Germany.   2. Germany – Foreign relations –
United States.   3. Sackett, Frederic M.   4. Brüning, Heinrich, 1885–1970.
5. Germany – Politics and government – 1918–1933.   I. Title.
E183.8.G3B784   1994
327.73043–dc20   94–16669
CIP

A catalog record for this book is available from the British Library

ISBN 0–521–47005–6 hardback

For Young Barney

*Steve, Katy, Eileen, Patty
Chris, and Barney*

Contents

Acknowledgments   ix

Abbreviations used in the notes   xi

Introduction   1

1   A time of opportunity   8

2   American diplomacy, official and unofficial   40

3   The landslide election   68

4   Sackett takes the initiative   95

5   Sackett and the financial crisis   123

6   Perceptions of Nazism and communism, with an afterthought on fascism   149

7   One end, two paths: Brüning and Hitler in conflict   172

8   Efforts to sustain representative government in Germany   198

9   Sackett loses heart with Brüning's fall   225

10   The decline of Hitler and the Nazis   249

11   Through a glass darkly   274

Conclusion   298

Bibliography   313

Index   325

Acknowledgments

So MANY PEOPLE helped with the completion of this work, it is hard to know where to begin. First, I want to thank Frank Smith, Executive Editor at Cambridge University Press, without whose sage direction and counsel this study might never have found its way into print. I will always remember his kindness and thoughtful guidance. Then, I think of the librarians and archivists who never failed to assist with timely help and always with the sense that they were pleased to be of assistance. I remember my mentors, the late W. Stull Holt and Donald E. Emerson, to whom I owe more than I can ever repay. I am grateful for the carefully constructed criticisms of Lloyd Ambrosius and Brian McKercher, the readers for Cambridge University Press; they set me along fruitful paths and helped me to avoid many pitfalls. I also appreciate the expert guidance of Edith Feinstein, my production editor, and the superb work of Nancy Landau, my talented copy editor. Colleagues were asked to read the work, among whom Professors Franklin West, Frederick Nunn, Craig Wollner, and John Loffler stand out. Friends, students, and others also read some or all of the manuscript at various stages. They include John Jackley, Lisa Walker, and Diane Gould. My daughter Eileen was irreplaceable with her ready help in solving the mysteries of the computer. Lee Ellington never failed in so many ways, Gordon Dodds was steadfast in his support, and Firyal Isa came through with research help.

President Judith Ramaley and Provost Michael Reardon of Portland State University were generous in their financial support for this project. They have my respect and thanks.

I am deeply indebted to Federal Judge William L. Dwyer who, many years ago, with my wife, Chris, urged a married war veteran with a family to continue his education.

There are many more who were instrumental in completing this study. If I have failed to mention them, I hope they can forgive me. The scholars whose work influenced mine are mentioned in the Bibliography and footnotes, but there are others who, for lack of space, do not appear here. They helped formulate my conceptions of the problems dealt with and deserve much of the credit for whatever merit the work has. As is customary I should ascribe any blame for fault and error to me alone. But, I refuse.

After all, they influenced me. I stand by what I had to write and am ready to answer to my critics. Among them, my wife, who patiently stood by me from the earliest beginnings, and who read critical parts of the manuscipt when help was needed.

Abbreviations used in the notes

ADAP	*Akten zur deutschen auswärtigen Politik*
BDFA	*British Documents on Foreign Affairs*
DBFP	*Documents on British Foreign Policy*
FDRL	Franklin D. Roosevelt Presidential Library
FRBNY	Federal Reserve Bank of New York
FRUS	*Papers Relating to the Foreign Relations of the United States*
GFMR	German Foreign Ministry Records
HHPL	Herbert Hoover Presidential Library
LC	Library of Congress
VJZG	*Vierteljahrshefte für Zeitgeschichte*
WAR/MID	U.S. War Department, Military Intelligence Division

Full citations to books and articles can be found in the Bibliography. U.S. State Department Papers are cited by Decimal File number.

Introduction

THE PURPOSE of this study is to tell the story of how a lawyer, business-man, and United States senator from Kentucky, who was appointed as American ambassador to Germany, reacted to the collapse of the Weimar Republic and to Hitler's rise to power. Thrust into the center of activity in Berlin because he understood business and finance, and because he was almost certain to be defeated in his campaign for reelection to the United States Senate, Frederic M. Sackett, Jr., played a meaningful role in momentous events. He was a central figure in American attempts to save republicanism in Germany, and to thwart Hitler's rise to power. His mission is inherently fascinating because it involved the American response to the rise to power of one of the most significant figures in twentieth-century history. It is also important because Sackett represents an outstanding example of a diplomat who became exceptionally dedicated to advancing the policy of the nation to which he was accredited. Throughout his tenure in Berlin, he followed American foreign policy, but he did so by favoring German foreign policy goals, and especially those of Chancellor Heinrich Brüning.

Sackett, of course, did not act alone. The American response to events in Germany involved numerous statesmen and diplomats as well as financiers and bankers. The American embassy in Berlin, headed by Sackett, was ably served by professional diplomats, among whom the most important were Foreign Service officers George Gordon, John Wiley, and George Messersmith. In Washington, President Herbert Hoover played a prominent role, as did Secretary of State Henry Stimson, Undersecretaries Joseph Cotton and William Castle, and a host of diplomats in the State Department. German, French, and British statesmen and diplomats acted and reacted with Sackett as they wrestled with the problems Germany encountered in the depression, the financial crisis in 1931, and the threat that Hitler posed to democracy and the republic.

Events were played out during Herbert Hoover's administration (1929–1933) that coincided with the collapse of the Weimar Republic and Adolf

I

Hitler's rise to power. It was a dismal time in the United States and Germany, which were both dominated by the Great Depression, an economic crisis that had important political ramifications. President Hoover was virtually driven from office as a result of the American depression, while the same phenomenon in Germany was an important, perhaps decisive, factor in bringing down the Weimar Republic and installing Hitler as German chancellor. In retrospect it is clear that Hitler's impact on world events made his rise to power one of the most important international events in the depression era. The future of Europe was to be significantly affected by developments in the Weimar Republic. During its brief life, from 1919 to 1933, the German republic was the spawning ground for much that would follow: the growth of the Nazi party, the Hitler chancellorship, German rearmament, the Sudeten and Polish Corridor crises, the "appeasement" at Munich, World War II, the Holocaust, and the Cold War.

Democratic statesmen have been reproached for not taking a stronger stand against Hitler after he came to power. One observer noted that we tend to exaggerate the relative importance "of stopping Hitler once he was in power, as compared with the importance of seeing to it that a person of his ilk should not come into power at all in a great Western country." The greater defeat for the West was "on the day when the German people found itself in such a frame of mind that it could, without great resistance or remonstrance, accept a Hitler as its leader and master." It has been suggested that the United States could have done more than it did to support Weimar Germany and to avert another world war.[1]

The present study is an attempt to determine what if anything Ambassador Sackett did to prompt the United States government to act to meet the challenge presented by a faltering German republic and by Hitler in the years immediately before 1933. A major concern is whether or not the United States contributed to the failure of the Weimar Republic and to Hitler's rise to power.[2] To that end, we shall explore the initiatives taken by Sackett to influence the policy decisions of the Hoover administration with respect to Germany. We shall also examine Sackett's analysis of Hitler and the Nazi party.

This project began as an attempt to discover the American political and diplomatic response to Hitler's rise to power. It did not take long to learn that United States involvement in Weimar Germany was inextricably interwoven with American finance. An elusive figure for Sackett to deal with, Hitler was head of an opposition party and thus outside the province of American diplomacy. As a consequence, Sackett tried to get the U.S.

---

1 George F. Kennan, *American Diplomacy, 1900–1950*, 78–81.
2 See Klaus Schwabe, "The United States and the Weimar Republic: A 'Special Relationship' That Failed."

government to respond to Hitler's drive toward power in an indirect way. The ambassador agreed with fundamental American policy, which was to provide a foundation for German prosperity and stability that would make a Hitler unnecessary. To achieve that goal, American policy was to assist the Germans with financial help to undermine the domestic basis for discontent. Sackett attempted to get the United States to intercede in helping to reconstruct German finances, which were approaching crisis proportions. He also wanted his government to go beyond financial policy to assist Germany in two areas of vital interests perceived as central to any plan to prevent a Hitler government.

Almost all Germans resented the reparations they were required to pay to the victorious European powers following World War I. Sackett worked diligently to win American backing for the reduction of what the Germans considered an onerous political debt. His hope was that the German people would be mollified if Brüning could achieve such a major goal. Strong support for the chancellor would be assured, as would the removal of one of the principal grounds for Hitler or any other radical to come to power.

The Germans also resented the disarmament provisions of the Treaty of Versailles, which among other things reduced the size of the German military, the Reichswehr, to a force of 100,000. Sackett stressed the importance of meeting aspirations to recover Germany's stature as a major power in European affairs. It was one more element that could rally the German people to the support of Brüning. The Americans did intercede with a plan to reduce French fears of Germany and to bring the Germans around to a status closer to equality with the other European powers. If the United States could assist in reducing reparations and granting Germany equality in armaments, Sackett believed it would help Chancellor Brüning at home and relieve tension in Europe.

The ambassador was not able to accomplish what he set out to do, although he gave it a mighty effort. Because the Weimar Republic did collapse and Adolf Hitler did come to power in Germany, Sackett's mission could be judged a failure. But before rendering that judgment we should note the lack of support he received from an overtaxed American president trying to cope with a domestic depression. In part, Sackett's failure lay with the inability of the U.S. government to implement its own foreign policy effectively. American purposes in Europe were to support stability, peace, and prosperity. Germany was considered central to the fulfillment of that policy and American loans to the Germans were one of the principal means employed to insure it was carried out.

Sackett believed it was that very loan policy which was a fundamental cause of Germany's financial problems. Among his first official acts was to object to large loans to the German government organized by American private bankers. He was opposed to the loans even though the Brüning government was their beneficiary. However, Sackett was unable to intervene

directly in the loan policy because in the corporatist system that characterized the era, all negotiations were carried out by "unofficial diplomats"
from the private sector. The U.S. government cooperated with such groups
in the formulation of policy, but bankers and financiers in the private sector,
rather than American official diplomats, were given the responsibility for
executing foreign loan policy.

In spite of that handicap, Sackett became an active protagonist in his
efforts to support the Weimar Republic. He did everything possible, given
the constraints of American policy, to help sustain Chancellor Heinrich
Brüning in office. Sackett was convinced that the U.S. government needed
to intervene decisively to remedy the problems generated by its own loan
policy. After consulting with Brüning, the ambassador took the initiative
in trying to induce President Hoover to call the French, British, and German heads of state to meet in Washington. Sackett believed that such a
meeting under Hoover's leadership could resolve the impending financial
crisis and settle the problem of war debts and reparations. The proposed
conference never came about as Sackett and Brüning planned. Instead it
was delayed until 1933, during the Franklin Roosevelt administration,
when the World Economic Conference was held in London and ended in
failure.

While formulating the plan for such a conference, Sackett formed an
extraordinary political alliance with Brüning. The ambassador did all he
could to persuade the United States to redouble its efforts to support the
chancellor. When Hoover was slow to carry out his call for an international conference, Sackett tried another tactic. He warned the president
and the secretary of state that American loans had brought the United
States and Germany to the brink of disaster. Sackett's finest hour came
when he used his influence to get the president to intervene in the European
financial crisis of 1931. The result was the Hoover Moratorium.

Sackett tried to focus his efforts on finding ways to support Brüning, but
the success of Hitler and the Nazi party forced him to pay more attention
to them. Under Sackett's leadership, American diplomats in Germany
warned the Hoover administration that Hitler and his Nazi party constituted a serious threat to the Weimar Republic in Germany, to American
economic interests, and to the peace of Europe. In some respects their
analysis of what happened during the period of Hitler's rise to power was
brilliant, rivaling the best narrative accounts with knowledge of the outcome of events historians have been able to reconstruct. In fact, there are
striking parallels in the analyses of Hitler's rise to power by the American
diplomats in Berlin and those of the most respected historians of the
subject.[3]

---

3 For example Alan Bullock, *Hitler: A Study in Tyranny*; Joachim Fest, *Hitler*; and Martin
Broszat, *Hitler and the Collapse of Weimar Germany*.

It was impossible to discern the specific direction Germany would take if Hitler's Third Reich were to become a reality. Still, Sackett had an excellent opportunity to study the Nazi leader and his party. Although in campaigning for office Hitler and the Nazi party were clearly opportunistic, coming down on both sides of the questions they addressed, Hitler sought to be understood, to win sympathy and support. He was, up until 1933, "blunt, outspoken, and revealing to an extent he later regretted." Observers during the period of Hitler's ascent had a unique opportunity to learn about him because he had formed his views very early in life and allowed neither experience nor contrary evidence to change them.[4]

To his credit, Sackett took an accurate measure of the man. He understood most of what contemporaries were able to surmise from what Hitler said for the public record. He also studied what Hitler and the Nazis were doing to win control of Germany and extended that knowledge by interviewing the major Nazi leaders. From the moment the Nazis became a factor in German politics, Sackett warned the Hoover administration that the economic crisis could intensify if Hitler were to become chancellor of the Weimar Republic. Even worse, Hitler threatened the existence of the German republic and the peace of Europe.

Even though most of Sackett's estimates of Hitler were brilliant, his reporting was flawed. He could not be expected to have foreseen in any detail what was going to happen, but he could be expected to have taken the Nazis more seriously as a political force in their own right rather than as a harbinger of worse things to come. Sackett was convinced that Hitler simply did not have what it took to lead a great nation; he was not the stuff of which statesmen are made. Moreover, his party and Storm Troopers were looked upon as rowdies adept at winning street brawls but not capable of governing. But in the end it was Sackett's obsession with communism that misled Americans.

When he wanted to pressure Hoover into decisive action by calling an international economic conference, Sackett decided to dismiss Hitler and the Nazis as a negligible factor in German politics and instead stressed communism as the more serious danger faced by Brüning. Sackett took this position even while emphasizing in his official reports that Hitler and the Nazis were the most serious threat to democracy and republicanism in Germany. The ambassador wanted to get Hoover's attention, and he knew his official despatches were unlikely to reach the White House. If he were to get the president's ear he needed something more dramatic than reports of a Right radical party in Germany. To get the president's attention, Sackett resorted to the Red Scare tactic, but at the same time expressed his own deeply held conviction that communism was a perilous phenomenon that confronted all the Western democracies. Therefore, in his more

4 Gerhard L. Weinberg, "Hitler's Image of the United States," 1006–1007.

influential personal correspondence with President Hoover and Secretary of State Stimson, Sackett persisted in maintaining that communism was the most serious threat that faced the Germans.

Despite the ambassador's personal convictions about communism, he was forced to pay increasing attention to Hitler and the Nazi party as they experienced rapid growth and success at the polling place. By 1932 Hitler loomed large, not only in the Weimar Republic but throughout Europe and in the United States. As the depression deepened and political upheaval threatened Germany, leaders everywhere wanted to know who Hitler was, what he represented, what he aspired to, what he meant for his nation, for Europe, and for them.

Sackett tended to view Hitler and the Nazis as adept agitators and malcontents with a strong suit in propaganda but with little proclivity for the hard work of actually governing Germany. The Nazis were thought to have neither the talent nor the inclination to implement their harebrained schemes. Rather they were seen as spoilers, so incompetent they could only be a temporary problem.

Sackett, convinced that economics and finance were central to the arts of government and diplomacy, felt Hitler and the Nazis were babes in the woods when it came to those vital areas. He never fully understood that Hitler represented naked power, a force that could overcome everything else if sufficient determination and energy were applied to the task. Sackett never did grasp how deeply Hitler believed in the strength of his own will. A Hitler government, Sackett thought, was certain to be inefficient and ineffective and would surely fail after a brief interlude of negativism and destruction. In its wake, he feared, would come the phenomenon Americans dreaded most of all – communism.

Still, Sackett felt confident that the Germans could handle either outcome. Even if Hitler were to come into power, the ambassador believed there was a solution. Having been given a dose of radical leadership, the German people just might turn to the man he saw as a potential savior of representative government in Germany – Heinrich Brüning. American as well as British diplomats agreed in that assessment, but Ambassador Sackett especially had extraordinary faith in Brüning's ability to work through the problems of the Weimar Republic and avert a Hitler-dominated government.

Given the U.S. government's disinclination to become directly involved in European politics, it is remarkable that the Hoover administration acted as much as it did to thwart Hitler. Most directly, the Americans did all they could to help the Brüning government. Bankers in the private sector moved to help the German chancellor financially, and the United States acted to assist with both financial and political help. That more was not done can be accounted for, in part, by the overwhelming importance of the depression, which dominated the American political scene throughout the Hoover years. In foreign policy, Japanese aggression in Asia had become the most important concern of the president and American diplomats in Washington.

When all American efforts proved to be of little avail, the Hoover administration, preoccupied with the domestic economy and the turmoil in Asia, allowed American diplomats in Berlin to become mere spectators in Germany. Unhappy with the fall of the Brüning cabinet, Ambassador Sackett could only stand by and report on Hitler with unrelieved gloom until he found an acceptable option. Sackett, a conservative Republican, was convinced that the Weimar Republic depended on organized labor and the socialist Social Democratic party for its very existence. When General Kurt von Schleicher became chancellor and attempted to win the support of labor and the Socialists, Sackett thought he found a desirable alternative to a Hitler government. That apparently happy prospect proved to be a chimera and simply represented another form of wishful thinking by the ambassador.

The Americans who experienced Hitler's rise to power had no idea of the direction the Third Reich would take. They only understood that it was a frightening prospect for the future. It is important to recall that people at the time, and even Hitler himself, had no clear idea where Germany was headed. As one historian has commented: "What united National Socialism was not a mandate for war and Auschwitz, but a desire for change."[5] Ambassador Sackett was committed to a world that was slipping away. He only dimly saw the nature of the course upon which Germany had embarked. But clearly he and the other diplomats involved in witnessing Hitler's rise were alarmed by what they observed and did everything they believed they could do to prevent it from happening.

The full impact of Hitler's influence on history is not yet known. Historians will need to continue digging into the past to clarify what happened and why. The Nazis tapped dark elements of human society that are still with us. They dug into that cellar of human emotion where fear resides and unleashed forces whose consequences we are still experiencing. Guided by concepts of racism, virulent anti-Semitism, hypernationalism, expansion, and the prospect of perpetual conflict, Hitler's conquests altered the face of Europe and affected the lives of countless millions of people all over the world. Such was his importance one would hope that President Hoover and Secretary of State Stimson were fully informed about Hitler and the Nazi movement. The story about to unfold will tell us whether or not Sackett succeeded.

5 David Schoenbaum, *Hitler's Social Revolution*, 45.

1

A time of opportunity

ON A PLEASANT SATURDAY afternoon in early December 1931, two American diplomats and their wives were enjoying an afternoon in the suburban Berlin home of a prominent German banker. They had just settled in and were exchanging pleasantries over tea when four men were ushered into the room. They were introduced as Ernst Hanfstaengl, Rudolf Hess, Captain Göring, and a Herr "Wolff" – whom the Americans quickly recognized as Adolf Hitler. The clandestine encounter was arranged by the German banker with the consent of Frederic Sackett, the American ambassador to Germany, as an exceptional opportunity for the ambassador to meet with the Nazi leader. Although he had been in Berlin for nearly two years, Sackett was encountering Hitler personally for the first time and in fact was the first American diplomat to meet him. Sackett was not fluent in the German language, so the first secretary of the embassy, Alfred Klieforth, accompanied him. It was a daring meeting; in those days consorting with the opposition to the government was considered bad form. American diplomacy had not yet been wedded to intelligence operations, and anything resembling covert activity or other underhanded methods was beyond its capability or understanding.

The two Americans, the German banker, and their wives sat with the three Nazis and listened to Hitler launch into a long harangue as if he were addressing a large audience. Sackett was not persuaded by the rhetoric, but he had a firsthand opportunity to evaluate the Nazi leader. Hitler impressed him as a "fanatical crusader" whose "forcefulness and intensity" enabled him to establish leadership "among those classes that do not weigh his outpourings." But Sackett thought Hitler was "certainly not the type from which statesmen evolve" and predicted that the Nazi would find himself "on the rocks" if he were ever confronted with the difficult problem of governing Germany.[1]

1 Sackett to State, 7 December and, Personal, Sackett to Stimson, 9 December 1931, General Records of the U.S. Department of State, Record Group 59, National Archives, Washington,

Hitler and the Nazi party were phenomena unfamiliar to the bourgeois and aristocratic elites who formed the diplomatic corps representing their nations in Germany. Like almost all observers they were hampered in their evaluation of this new and powerful force because it was so menacing to good social and economic order. A Hitler government would mean the end of everything they understood and valued. To them, economics and finance formed the core of relations among nations, and Hitler demonstrated only a primitive understanding of those problems. During Sackett's tenure in Berlin, American diplomats never considered a Hitler government acceptable. Nazi rule in Germany was clearly seen as contrary to American interests.

Sackett was quick to report to both the German Foreign Ministry and the State Department to explain his extraordinary conduct in agreeing to meet with this dangerous man. He wrote Secretary of State Henry Stimson that ordinarily he would "not seek intimacy with the opposition party in Berlin" but did not want to avoid a meeting since "a proper opportunity" had been presented. The German Foreign Ministry understood that he was not "conniving with the opposition," and Sackett was pleased to report that he had "established a contact that may be valuable to us in the future."[2]

The meeting did not bring any advantage to the Americans and it was the only time Sackett and Hitler met face-to-face. Nevertheless, Hitler was a central figure in Sackett's diplomatic life. Sackett took up his post as American ambassador in Berlin in early 1930 just as the Nazi leader moved onto center stage in German politics. In three years Hitler would become German chancellor. During that time Sackett observed Hitler's rise to power and would play an important role in the attempt to thwart the Nazi. The American would fail because forces beyond his control intervened to make his task impossible. One force was the Great Depression; the other, as we shall see, was the policy of the U.S. government, which effectively handcuffed Sackett in his efforts.

Sackett did not aspire to become a diplomat. His election to the U.S. Senate in 1924 was the culmination of an already successful career in business and finance. At the age of sixty-one, he was content with his role in the national capital; but problems in Kentucky politics intervened to elevate his position even further to the realm of international affairs. The son of a wealthy wools manufacturer, Frederic Moseley Sackett, Jr., was born in Providence, Rhode Island, on December 17, 1868. He graduated from Brown University in 1890 and Harvard Law School in 1893, then

D.C., Decimal File Numbers 862.50/721 and 723. Hereafter, all unpublished State Department Papers are cited by decimal file number. Although embassy despatches were addressed to the secretary of state, he rarely saw them; they were sent to the appropriate geographical division, in Berlin's case the Division of Western European Affairs. The shortened address "State" here indicates that the addressee is the State Department.

2 Sackett to Stimson, 9 December 1931, 862.50/723. This despatch was meant for Stimson.

moved west, first to Columbus, then to Cincinnati, Ohio. In 1898 he married Olive Speed, the daughter of James Breckinridge Speed, of a wealthy and prominent family in Kentucky business and politics. Sackett gradually abandoned the practice of law in favor of his wife's family business interests, especially coal mining and related enterprises as well as real estate and banking. The Yankee proved to be a shrewd and skillful businessman who moved easily into the Louisville elite. Named director of several businesses and banks, he became a member of the board of the Louisville branch of the Federal Reserve Bank of St. Louis (1917–1924). His peers held him in high regard, prompting his election and reelection to the Louisville Board of Trade in 1917, 1922, and 1923.[3]

A southern progressive, Sackett subscribed to the New South program of progress through rapid economic growth and industrialization in a diversified economy. An urban "booster," he wanted to see Louisville grow bigger and better, but essentially a conservative, he wanted the transformation accompanied by continuity with the past. Like other southern progressives, he favored change and growth, but believed they should not alter the essential social structure or economic organization and civic leadership patterns that should remain constant. A well-ordered and stable society committed to ethical business practices could sustain the kind of unity necessary to economic development accompanied by social and racial stability.[4]

Taking part in civic affairs and other varied activities, Sackett won a widely recognized reputation as a moving force in Louisville and a man to be reckoned with in the state of Kentucky. A staunch Republican, he was involved in politics from the time he first settled in Louisville until the end of his career. In 1917 he became federal food administrator for the state of Kentucky, giving him control of the distribution and rationing of food throughout the state. The position brought him into frequent contact with the head of the national agency, Herbert Hoover. A close political relationship developed, and later, when Hoover revealed his presidential ambitions, Sackett was among the first to work for his nomination and election.[5] After a stint on the State Board of Charities and Corrections

3 More on Sackett's early career is found in Bernard V. Burke, "Senator and Diplomat," 185–189. Full citations to books and articles can be found in the bibliography of the present volume. See also *Biographical Directory of the American Congress, 1774–1949* (Washington, D.C., 1950), 1771; *Congressional Directory*, 69 Cong. 1 Sess., 36; *New York Times*, 19 May 1941; *The National Cyclopaedia of American Biography* (New York, 1951), 1927, B421–422; 1938, E 95–96; 1951, 37:78–79; and State Department *Register* for the years 1930–1933.

4 George Brown Tindall, *The Emergence of the New South: 1913–1945*, 7, 31–32, and *The Ethnic Southerners*, 142–162; *Louisville Herald-Post*, 4 October 1930; *Louisville Times*, 24 October 1930.

5 *Louisville Herald-Post*, 9 October 1929; *New York Times*, 19 May 1941 and 2 January 1930; Herbert Hoover, *The Memoirs of Herbert Hoover*, 2: 191, hereafter cited *Memoirs*.

from 1919 to 1924, Sackett entered politics in earnest as the Republican party nominee for the United States Senate.

Even though the *Louisville Post* supported his opponent and predicted a victory for the Democrats, the editors conceded that Sackett was "an able man of business, a student of government, a most genial and attractive gentleman, and a useful citizen in a dozen ways. The Republican party has put forward the best man the party has available."[6]

Opposition newspapers allowed that the Louisville businessman would "make a good United States Senator." Sackett had won the support of a "considerable number" of Independents who "admired his character and ability." The newspaper's single regret was that Sackett was "a rock-ribbed conservative."[7] Another opposition newspaper acknowledged their admiration for him and aptly characterized him as "eminently successful, reasonably but not hungrily ambitious," and as a "wholly satisfactory representative Kentuckian of the modern type, the type that does things rather than the type which talks, very beautifully, of past things done."[8]

After his election, Sackett moved quickly into the higher councils of the Republican party. A close friend of Secretary of Commerce Hoover, he worked quietly, and mostly behind the scenes, first with President Calvin Coolidge, and then President Hoover. On the whole, Sackett was a reliable supporter of Republican party positions. He was not noted for taking strong positions, or for seeking public attention. In fact, he was not an important force behind legislation. He did play a significant role in party politics as chairman of the Republican steering committee, which guided legislation through Congress, and as a member of the powerful Senate Finance Committee.

Among the strongest positions he took was his support for American membership in the Court of International Justice, the World Court. There was strong opposition in the Congress and President Hoover did not pursue the issue with enthusiasm.[9] Sackett was more ardent on the subject than the president and spoke out against an attempt in the Senate to "emasculate the protocol" and obstruct American participation. He explained to a constituent that he felt the court's "influence for good should be very great." Acknowledging his "great sympathy" for the international tribunal, he argued in the Senate that the court was one way to avoid war.[10]

Sackett's support of the World Court did not place him at odds with

6 *Louisville Post*, 21 August 1924.   7 *Louisville Post*, 4 November 1929.
8 *Louisville Herald*, 4 March 1925.
9 Hoover, *Memoirs*, 2: 27, 50, 330, 332, 337; Joan Hoff Wilson, *Herbert Hoover, Forgotten Progressive*, 126, 189, 195–196.
10 Sackett to H. B. Mackoy, 9 October 1925, Frederic M. Sackett Papers, University of Kentucky; *Louisville Herald-Post*, 28 January 1926; *Congressional Record*, 69 Cong. 1 Sess., 27 January 1926, 2807–2808.

Hoover policy, but the conservative, business-oriented senator took several unorthodox stands that must have concerned administration officials. He took a strong antitrust stand in the Senate, a position neither Coolidge nor Hoover favored while Sackett was in the Senate.[11] Sackett deplored the growth of huge combinations, which he maintained were in violation of the Sherman Antitrust Act. Gigantic business organizations created by mergers and the development of powerful holding companies, he believed, should be subject to the full application of the Sherman Antitrust Act to halt what he saw as a pernicious growth. Sackett argued that there had developed "dangerous creatures of the new wealth" who were operating in the business world without adequate legislative restraints.[12]

On several important occasions Sackett demonstrated a strong will and independence of mind. In one instance, he supported government production of agricultural fertilizer. Sackett's major interest was in the plight of farmers who he believed were faced with soil depletion and excessive cost for fertilizers. He was also motitvated by his interest in scientific agriculture.[13] History, he explained, made it clear that the westward movement was long past and that virgin land was no longer available. Studies showed that the costs of producing fertilizers were "most startling," raising prices beyond the reach of farmers. With soil depletion demanding their use, Sackett concluded that fertilizer costs needed to be reduced to levels affordable for farmers. The only effective means for achieving that result was government intervention. Sackett argued that government operation of the federally owned plant at Muscle Shoals, Alabama, on the Tennessee River, could reduce the production costs of fertilizers by more than half. He maintained that no satisfactory result could come from power companies and insisted that the entire problem for agriculture was to adjust the cost of production to affordable levels.

Sackett explained that his position had serious overtones because it differed "from my entire theory of the Government's position in industry," which he said disapproved any government involvement or "interference or competition with private business initiative." Given that view, it is no surprise that the senator's strong position on behalf of farmers could not withstand the extension of principle beyond providing inexpensive fertilizer. When new legislation was proposed, the forerunner of the Tennessee Valley legislation of 1933, Sackett reversed his position. The move in the direction of regional socialism was more than he could support. Accused of a "sell out" to the "power trust," Sackett asked, "are we going to put

11 Ellis W. Hawley, "Herbert Hoover and American Corporatism, 1929–1933," 105–106.
12 *Louisville Courier-Journal* and *Louisville Herald-Post*, 1 November 1929.
13 This account is from *Congressional Record*, 69 Cong. 1 Sess., 13 March 1926, 5518; 21 June 1926, 11667–11670; 2 Sess., 13 December 1926, 359–361; 25 February 1927, 4755–4756; 70 Cong. 1 Sess., 13 March 1928, 4632–4635; see Burke, "Senator and Diplomat," 191–194.

this Government into business in competition with private enterprise?" His conservative principles, and his adherence to Republican party policy, prevailed. He voted against the bill which, in his view, went far beyond producing inexpensive fertilizer for farmers.

Another unorthodox position got Sackett into trouble soon after he assumed his duties as ambassador. As he confided in his sister, a diplomat "has to do his stunts on several occasions."[14] One such "stunt" nearly caused his career to be stillborn, or so Sackett thought. At the World Power Conference meeting in Berlin in June 1930, the ambassador was asked to address the American delegation. A copy of his speech was distributed to the press in advance. In it, Sackett made two essential points: first, he returned to his earlier advocacy of experimentation in government ownership and control of power utilities, and second, he called for a narrower gap between the cost to the consumer and the cost of production, which he set at the ratio of fifteen to one, a disparity he maintained was unheard of anywhere but the power industry.[15]

Concern over the speech might have ended with its delivery, except that the Chicago utilities magnate Samuel Insull was in Europe at the time and received an advance copy. When he read the prepared remarks Insull was furious. He rushed to Berlin and demanded that Sackett withdraw the speech. In a stormy two-hour meeting in the ambassador's residence Insull insisted that the remarks about the fifteen-to-one gap between costs of production and consumer costs be stricken. Sackett finally relented and agreed to withdraw the speech. Later the same evening, however, Sackett changed his mind and released it as it was written for publication on the day of delivery, June 18.[16]

Several factors prompted Sackett's decision, one of which was that the speech had already been released to the press. More important for the ambassador was the fact that his remarks were "entirely justified." He complained to his sister that the speech "never would have been heard of or created any comment unless Mr. Insull had tried to suppress it."[17] Sackett was right. The speech was probably destined for a publicity limbo, but was brought to public attention by Insull's bull-in-a-china-closet tactics. There really had been little news value in the speech until Insull blundered into the picture with his attempt to influence the ambassador. It was the Insull story, not Sackett's speech, that first got international newspaper attention.

14 Sackett to Mrs. L. H. Hazard, his sister, 29 March 1930, Sackett Papers. All Sackett Papers cited are in the Filson Club, Louisville, Kentucky, unless otherwise indicated.
15 Sackett to Mrs. Hazard, 23 July 1930, Sackett Papers; *New York Times*, 18 and 19 June 1930.
16 *New York Times*, 18 and 19 June 1930; *Literary Digest*, 5 July 1930; Forrest McDonald, *Insull*, 271.
17 Sackett to Mrs. Hazard, 23 July 1930, Sackett Papers.

The incident threw a scare into Sackett, who felt he would be recalled. It was Insull, however, who came in for a great deal of criticism, not only in the press, where he was accused of behaving foolishly, but in the halls of Congress, where Senator George Norris drew a sharp attack on the utilities man. He was not only charged, in the press and in Congress, with influencing an ambassador and censorship, but he caused considerable discomfort among his colleagues in the utilities business, who were now forced to answer Sackett's charges before the world.[18]

As is common with public figures, Sackett felt that newspaper correspondents did their best to make a sensational story out of an otherwise routine event. He confessed to his sister: "After it got such prominence I was not at all sure that I would not be asked to come to America permanently, but so far have not had any bad reactions come to me." When his sister wrote to advise him on how to handle the press in the future, Sackett confided in her that "I have had my lesson however and you need not worry." He explained that "it was not an attack on the business but an attempt to show how their fight against government ownership should be handled." The entire affair had the virtue of allowing Sackett to use his favorite phrase. As he wrote to his sister: "I had the one satisfaction that this speech saved the World Power Conference from *innocuous desuetude*, as it was the only thing that got any real kick into it."[19]

While Sackett was still in the Senate, he and his wife, a childless couple, were most visible in the capital's social life. They were very popular and busy with memberships in exclusive clubs in Louisville, New York, and Washington. They maintained two large homes, fully staffed with servants – "Edgecombe" in Louisville and a palatial home in Washington. In a word, the Sacketts were a success. Popular and influential, they had no other ambition than to return to Washington for a second term and resume the social and political roles that suited them so well. But Kentucky politics intervened to thwart their aspirations.

When Sackett announced he would run for reelection, strong opposition emerged within the Kentucky Republican party. Closely identified with Louisville, Sackett met particularly strong opposition from outside his urban stronghold. The rural leaders from the mountainous southeast were Governor Flem D. Sampson and Congressman John M. Robsion. Although they had supported him in 1924, they now combined to remove Sackett from the party ticket, partly on urban-rural grounds, but principally because they believed the incumbent had little chance of victory in 1930. Friends of Robsion's made it clear their man was seriously considering entering the primary against Sackett.

18 Sackett to Mrs. Hazard, 23 July 1930, Sackett Papers; *Literary Digest*, 5 July 1930; McDonald, *Insull*, 271; *New York Times*, 20 June 1930.
19 Sackett to Mrs. Hazard, 25 June and 23 July 1930, Sackett Papers, emphasis added.

Speculation that someone backed by the Sampson-Robsion faction would oppose the incumbent led the *Herald-Post* to rush to the senator's support. Sackett, they wrote, "stands high in Republican councils, being close to President Hoover" and other administration leaders. Moreover, they asserted, upon his election in 1924 he "immediately became an important factor in the Senate and in the councils of his party."[20] It was apparent that a bitter intraparty struggle was brewing, with a renewed contest between Louisville and rural districts.

When Robsion's candidacy became certain, Sackett turned to the president for help. Hoover asked the chairman of the Republican National Congressional Committee to talk with Sackett.[21] Soon the Republican high command was deeply involved in the attempt to save the explosive situation in Kentucky. Their task was to work out a compromise to avoid a primary contest and assure party solidarity. Sackett's seat was considered critical if the Republicans hoped to retain a majority in the Senate.[22]

While Republican party professionals tried to sort out the complex situation in Kentucky, the State Department was wrestling with the problem of ambassadorial appointments. Senator Sackett complained that second-rate advisers were doing the president a disservice. He proclaimed that it "was a blow" when Charles Dawes was named ambassador to Great Britain. The senator accused President Hoover of "ignoring responsible politicians – notably the Senators." If the president were to persist in naming his enemies to the top diplomatic posts, it was no use in being his friend. Seven months later Sackett would be satisfied that, as he promised, Hoover would appoint only the most qualified people.[23]

To remedy the problem with diplomatic appointments President Hoover called for an assessment of the diplomatic corps. As president-elect, he had toured Latin America and was appalled by the "eyesores" he observed serving in that region.[24] He was determined to carry out a thorough housecleaning and would appoint only "trained men" for those diplomatic posts that previously had been filled out of "political gratitude."[25] Assistant Secretary of State William R. Castle was pleased with the policy, confiding to a fellow diplomat that "the President contemplates very few purely political appointments."[26] There would, of course, be some political

20 *Louisville Herald-Post* and *Courier-Journal*, 9 October 1929.
21 Hoover's secretary Walter H. Newton to Rep. Will R. Wood, 8 November, 1929, Secretary's File, Wood, Rep. Will R., Herbert Hoover Presidential Library, West Branch, Iowa, hereafter cited HHPL, materials all cited by file name, all Presidential Papers unless otherwise indicated.
22 *Louisville Times*, 6 January 1930.   23 William R. Castle, Diary, 24 May 1929.
24 Hoover, *Memoirs*, 2:215.
25 Ray L. Wilbur and Arthur M. Hyde, *The Hoover Policies*, 586.
26 William R. Castle to Hugh R. Wilson, 12 July 1929, Castle, Wm. R., Hugh R. Wilson Papers, HHPL.

appointments; because Hoover felt the "ambassadors to the five or six great countries should be chosen from outstanding citizens whose public service and personal distinction carried additional weight."[27]

Before he was inaugurated, Hoover had studied the report on diplomats Castle prepared for him. It included a survey of embassies and legations with comments on the incumbent heads of mission and possible successors. Castle singled out Berlin as an urgent post needing someone less pro-German than the incumbent ambassador, Jacob Gould Schurman. Of the Berlin embassy, Castle emphasized: "The position is a difficult one and demands talent of a high order. It is not a particularly pleasant position and, therefore, needs a man full of the spirit of service, a man trained in business rather than an intellectual like Doctor Schurman is needed."[28] Hoover had already made it clear that he wanted someone in Berlin who was close to his economic policies, a person who would not need elaborate tables, statistics, and reports to understand and support administration policy.[29]

Economics and finance were so vital a part of the relationship between Germany and the United States that a man much better versed in business matters was considered essential if he were to be effective. Schurman was justifiably considered too obtuse when it came to matters of international finance. In addition, many considered him too old at seventy-five, and far too pro-German, to carry out his duties effectively. What had been a long-standing desire to replace the ambassador now took on a more urgent complexion.

For several years Castle urged the department to relieve the ambassador. The post in Berlin was considered one of the most difficult assignments for a diplomat; it needed a cool, clear head to take charge. The incumbent ambassador did not fit the bill, so Castle, and even German officials, tried to get Schurman removed from the Berlin Embassy.[30] They were unsuccessful, but the issue was resolved when Schurman decided to retire. President Hoover now made it clear that he wanted the ambassador replaced by "a good sound businessman."[31]

27 Hoover, *Memoirs*, 2:334–335.
28 Castle to Hoover, 21 January 1929, William R. Castle Papers – Germany 1927–1933, hereafter cited Germany, HHPL.
29 *Louisville Herald-Post*, 29 December 1929.
30 Castle to Parker Gilbert, 13 April 1927; Castle to George L. Harrison, 3 December 1927; Castle to Schurman, 11 January 1928 reprimands Schurman for taking the German side in a controversy with Parker Gilbert, Poole to Castle, 6 June 1929, all Castle Papers – Germany, HHPL; Stimson, Memorandum of a Conversation with Ambassador Friedrich von Prittwitz und Gaffron, 11 July 1929, Henry L. Stimson Papers, Microfilm Reel 162: Frame 406; hereafter cited by reel and frame.
31 George S. Messersmith, notes for memoirs, George S. Messersmith Papers; hereafter cited Messersmith, notes for memoirs. Schurman had submitted his resignation early in 1929 "to take effect at the pleasure of the President." Schurman to Hoover, 5 February 1929,

While the Hoover administration began its search for a man with the business experience, adequate wealth, and proper Republican party credentials for the embassy in Berlin, the critical domestic issue in Kentucky emerged to solve the diplomatic problem in Germany and at the same time untangle the political snarl that had developed in the Bluegrass State. The solution to the problem was the appointment of Senator Sackett as ambassador in Berlin. To understand the circumstances surrounding Sackett's selection for the post, it is important to review some aspects of Republican party politics in Kentucky and at the national level.

The midterm election in 1930 was pivotal for Hoover. The Republicans held a paper-thin majority in the Senate, which meant control of the Congress was a matter of first priority. Among the senators in harm's way was Sackett, who had been elected in 1924 with the largest majority given to a Republican candidate up to that time. It was an axiom in Kentucky politics that no one from Louisville could be elected to the United States Senate. Sackett's election had broken a ninety-year precedent only because it was part of a national Republican trend.[32] Sackett had won by riding the wave of Republicanism that swept the nation and carried Calvin Coolidge to victory in Kentucky and back to the White House. Six years later, in a midterm election, without a popular president to head the Republican ticket, the Kentucky Senate seat appeared to be in jeopardy.

Congressman Robsion, an astute politician and skilled organizer, had been the Kentucky campaign manager for Hoover when he carried the state in 1928. Robsion certainly could count on Hoover's favor, but he now saw another Hoover favorite, Sackett, as almost certain to go down to defeat. Robsion already was wary of Sackett as a spokesman for urban Louisville. Sackett was allied to a group of Republican leaders characterized as "outstanding Louisville men comprising the so-called 'best minds' who lend dignity to the party" and who stood in opposition to rural leadership for control of the Kentucky GOP.[33]

More than that, Sackett, who owned several coal mining operations in Harlan and Bell counties in the southeastern corner of the state, was seen as particularly vulnerable in that Republican stronghold. The coal industry was hard-hit by depression and Robsion believed the party could expect to lose votes in the eastern mountain region. That was Robsion's stronghold, and Sackett, a mine owner, would find it difficult to win miner's votes. The

Foreign Affairs – Diplomats, Schurman, J. G., HHPL. His resignation was accepted at the end of December of the same year, *Berliner Tageblatt und Handels-Zeitung*, 27 December 1929, evening edition, hereafter cited *Berliner Tageblatt*, indicating either a.m. or p.m. edition.

32 Glenn Finch, "The Election of United States Senators in Kentucky: The Cooper Period," 173; a fuller account of the political imbroglio is in Burke, "Senator and Diplomat," 196–203.

33 *Louisville Courier-Journal*, 3 January 1930.

major political battle would be fought in the rural districts, where Robsion
had the advantages since Sackett was seen by some as an outsider, a
"Louisville dude," a "city man in a rural state, wealthy in a poor state,"
who had "an Ivy League education and Eastern birth."[34]

Sackett had every intention of resuming his place in the U.S. Senate.
Election to that august body had been the climax of a successful career.
But he was destined to forfeit his coveted seat. Sackett's name had already
passed the president's desk when the Kentucky problem arose. The senator
appeared on a list for the German post as among "names sent in" and the
president, aware of Sackett's earlier complaints, now consulted him regarding other diplomatic appointments.[35]

With Sackett a possible contender for a foreign embassy, it was relatively
simple for the Republican leadership to propose a way out of the political
problem in Kentucky, avoid a bitter factional dispute, and simultaneously
resolve the diplomatic issue in Berlin. Hoover decided to give the Berlin
embassy to Sackett and thus avoid a contest for the Republican party
senatorial nomination and bring about party harmony in the Bluegrass
State.[36]

Sackett's proposed nomination for the Berlin post was a closely held
secret with only the Republican high command and the White House privy
to the decision. Sackett was not aware of the resolution of his political
problem. He and Mrs. Sackett were preparing to leave on a Caribbean
cruise when, as he reported to his sister, "at 5:30 Christmas afternoon in
Washington the telephone rang and said it was the President speaking.
Would I come to the white house at once. I went of course and he asked
me to take the Ambassadorship to Germany and leave at once . . . I suppose
a number of men have been in line for the appointment but it came
unsolicited to me."[37]

The ambassador-designate was elated by the appointment, but critics
of the Hoover administration were outraged. *The Nation* described it as
a flagrant case of a political appointment with the intention of solving a
local problem with no consideration of its diplomatic implications. In
Louisville, newspapers admitted that the announcement came as a "complete
surprise," a "bolt from the blue." On the national scene, one commentator
reported that "the capital and the country were astounded" and "treated

34 *The Nation*, 15 January 1930, 66; *New York Times*, 6 August 1927, 2 January 1930;
   Glenn Finch, "The Election of United States Senators in Kentucky: The Beckham Period,"
   43–44, 47, and "The Election of United States Senators in Kentucky: The Cooper Period," 173; John H. Fenton, *Politics in the Border States*, 59, 64–66; John Ed Pearce,
   Divide and Dissent: Kentucky Politics, 141, 173, 179–180.
35 Hoover working papers, c. October 1929; Hoover to Stimson, 2 November 1929, Appointments, Diplomatic, 1929 and undated, HHPL.
36 *Louisville Times*, 6 January 1930.
37 Sackett to Mrs. Hazard, 31 December 1929, Sackett Papers.

it as a joke." Sackett was characterized as an "obscure back-bencher" who "ranked well down" among "senatorial nonentities." President Hoover, it was said, "is the first of our presidents to save politicians from impending lame duckery by making them ambassadors. Another triumph for efficiency!"[38] A national journal complained that domestic politics "accounts for the elevation of a second-rate Senator to a first-rate ambassadorship."[39]

Much of the critical reaction was unfair to both Hoover and Sackett. After all, the senator fit the requirements for the chief of mission in Berlin as outlined by President Hoover and the State Department. Still, there can be no doubt that the appointment was a domestic political maneuver designed to resolve Republican party problems in Kentucky. As soon as Sackett resigned his Senate seat, Governor Sampson named Robsion to fill his unexpired term so that he could campaign as the incumbent senator. The strategy worked to Sackett's benefit, but Robsion was not so fortunate. He was defeated in November by his Democratic opponent, Ben Williamson.

While on balance the Sackett appointment was well received in the national press, the *New York Times* maintaining that it was "warmly applauded,"[40] it was received with overwhelming approval, even enthusiasm, in Kentucky and Germany. Governor Sampson, who had reason to be pleased with the news, proclaimed: "Not since the days of Cassius M. Clay had such an honor fallen to a Kentuckian." Although fully aware of the political implications of the appointment, an editorial in the Louisville *Herald-Post* gave President Hoover credit for "sound judgment, that fine discrimination by which a great executive is distinguished"; and, ironically enough, for making a first-rate appointment "with no thought of political expediency." Sackett was described as one of Kentucky's, "but more strictly of Louisville's, chief assets" who had been paid "one of the greatest compliments the President could have paid him." But the acclaim went beyond the Senator; Sackett's appointment demonstrated how important Kentucky had become to the Republican party.[41]

Reports from Germany were almost as effusive; Ambassador Schurman wrote that Sackett's appointment met with "extensive and favorable comment in the German press." The business-oriented *Der Montag* claimed that the Berlin position required "a self reliant and resourceful man on

38 Paul Y. Anderson, "Lame-Duck Diplomats," *The Nation*, 130: 3367, 15 January 1930; *Louisville Herald-Express*, 29 December 1929.

39 *Outlook and Independent*, 22 January 1930, 137; see also *Literary Digest*, 18 January 1930, 12–13, and *Louisville Courier-Journal*, 31 December 1929.

40 *New York Times*, 2 January 1930.

41 *Louisville Courier-Journal*, 31 December 1929; *Louisville Herald-Post*, 29 and 30 December 1929; J. Matt Chilton et al. to Hoover, 7 January 1930, Foreign Affairs – Diplomats, Sackett, F. M., HHPL. Cassius Marcellus Clay (1810–1903) was named American minister to Russia by Abraham Lincoln in 1861 as a reward for his ardent support. He served in St. Petersburg until 1869.

economic questions" and Sackett filled the bill with his "economic and financial experience." The Democratic *Berliner Tageblatt* called Sackett "a new year's present" because he was "an Ambassador who plays an important role in politics at home and has a sympathetic understanding of German problems." The Berlin newspaper recognized that the appointment involved the resolution of a domestic political problem, but did not see that as lessening its importance. Rather, it argued that by naming "a regular Republican Senator" to the Berlin post, President Hoover had elevated the German capital to "the same level as London and Paris. Only in the case of these three capitals have important politicians been chosen as American Ambassadors."[42]

The Sackett appointment was also applauded in the State Department. American diplomats were anxious to have a knowledgeable man of business in the Berlin post. Even though they recognized such a man would almost certainly be without diplomatic experience, they were prepared to undergo a period of transition in which the Berlin embassy would be under the actual control of a professional foreign service officer until the new ambassador "learned the ropes."

State Department officials were concerned about maintaining continuity of leadership in the embassy. Counselor of Embassy DeWitt C. Poole, was in the United States at the time and they thought he should return to Berlin for a while to help with the transition. Assistant Secretary of State Castle informed Poole that "it is important that when a new Ambassador is appointed to Germany, you should go there for a short time, say a month or six weeks, to get him started."[43] After interviewing Sackett, however, they were so pleased with him that they had full confidence he could take charge of the embassy from the start of his tenure with the help of the existing staff. Undersecretary of State Joseph P. Cotton informed Poole that there was no need for him to return to Berlin. "About all I can say about Sackett's appointment," he wrote, "is that it is less likely to require you there than we previously thought."[44]

Poole's temporary replacement was his friend John Cooper Wiley. After meeting Sackett, Poole informed Wiley that "Sackett is a peach. His wife is very nice. . . . What a delightful change it would be after the late regime. I am sure that you will find Sackett well disposed. I talked with him for several hours and gave him the low down on you all . . . am certain that you will get on grand with the new boss and win his support with the

42 *Providence Journal*, 30 December 1929, in Sackett Papers; Schurman to State, 7 January 1930, 123 Sackett, Frederic M./19; *Berliner Tageblatt*, 30 December 1929, p.m. edition.
43 Castle to Poole, 21 December 1929, Box 1, DeWitt C. Poole Papers; see Moffatt Diary, 18 January 1930.
44 Joseph P. Cotton to Poole, 3 January 1930, and Castle to Poole, 21 December 1929, Box 1, Poole Papers.

powers at home."[45] Walter de Haas, chief of the American Section of the German Foreign Ministry, was just as effusive. Wiley, he wrote, was "exceedingly happy . . . and so is everybody." Sackett's relations with De Haas were "very good indeed." The German diplomat was particularly impressed by the way Sackett "takes things on and tackles them straight away."[46]

For his part, Wiley was taken "rather aback" by some of the criticism of Sackett in the American press, which he thought was "unkind and unfair." He thought an article in *Time* magazine implied that Sackett left the United States "unwept and unsung." The *Time* article described the senator in uncharitable terms: "Short, sandy, round-stomached, he plodded through his term, rarely made a speech, much less an oration." In a spirited defense, Wiley contended:[47]

> As a matter of fact, he left on extremely short notice at the request of the President. Though deluged with invitations from every sort of institution or *Verein* interested in Germany, he refrained from uttering a single banquet platitude. He should be canonized not derided. . . . To find an Ambassador who does not wear his Embassy as a cloak to his own vanity and who is not centered on self-advertising is a refreshing innovation. . . . He has precisely the personality, the capacity and knowledge and the cool point of view that are needed for this post.

Wiley even defended the ambassador's physical appearance. He pointed out that Sackett's "figure stands comparison with those of the younger members of the staff and he plays sound and energetic golf." His appearance is "distinguished" with "kind eyes and a firm jaw." He summed up, echoing State Department assessments: "As a chief he is a peach."

There can be no doubt that Sackett was delighted with the solution to his political problems in Kentucky. He was not only surprised; he was exuberant. He confided to his sister that it was "all kind of a Xmas gift. Can you vision our feelings at so sudden a decision?" There is a touching and very human quality in Sackett's sense of pride in accomplishment. He confessed to his sister: "I can't help wondering what mother would think of it all. She was always so interested in everything that happened to us."[48]

The new ambassador embarked upon his new career with all the enthusiasm of a youth on an adventure. Upon his arrival in the German capital, in February 1930, Sackett scored an immediate public relations success. Before he made any official contacts, he sought out the German press

45 Poole to Wiley 23 January 1930, Box 1, John Cooper Wiley Papers, Franklin D. Roosevelt Library, Hyde Park, New York, hereafter cited FDRL.
46 De Haas to Poole, 3 March 1930, Box 1, Poole Papers.
47 Wiley to Laird S. Goldsborough of *Time*, 19 February 1930, Box 1, Wiley Papers, FDRL. The *Time* article appeared 3 February 1930.
48 Sackett to Mrs. Hazard, 31 December 1929, Sackett Papers.

corps and gave them a reception, which impressed the Berlin editors as an "amiable and impressive gesture." The *Berliner Tageblatt* observed that there was something "refreshing, unrestrained and sympathetic about this American business of diplomacy." The German newspaper further commented that Sackett was welcome to Berlin on the basis of his personal qualities alone.[49]

The handsome features and aristocratic bearing of the senator from Kentucky were impressive. Of medium height, with serious gray eyes and brown hair, which showed little silver despite his sixty-one years, Sackett imparted an air of decisiveness and authority. New England born, reared, and educated, the son of a Union cavalry officer, his soft voice, courtesy, and habit of saying "suh" captivated Berliners. Sackett expressed his determination to promote friendly relations with the Germans, but he also talked to the press about Kentucky, its beautiful women, racehorses, tobacco, and once-upon-a-time bourbon. His avoidance of any matter of substance suggested to the *New York Times* correspondent that the new ambassador was "equipped with something more than a correspondence course in diplomacy."[50]

The American embassy in Berlin reported that Sackett's reception was unprecedented for an incoming ambassador. While some Americans had been critical of Sackett's lack of credentials for a diplomatic post, German commentators were pleased that he represented President Hoover's policy of sending successful businessmen to look after American economic interests.[51] The Berlin newspapers especially stressed "his qualifications for his new post because of his familiarity with the economic and financial problems which extensively occupied him in the course of his Senatorial career and also in a private capacity."[52] The new ambassador ably fit the prescription outlined by the Germans who wanted "a businessman but one with political affiliations which would prove that he really represents the views of the administration."[53]

Sackett formally became United States ambassador to Germany on Abraham Lincoln's birthday anniversary. Foreign Minister Julius Curtius, who accompanied him, noted that Field Marshal President Paul von Hindenburg visibly impressed the new ambassador.[54] In his formal statement, Sackett enunciated a view that would color his analysis of German politics and lead him to draw some erroneous conclusions. He emphasized the "similarity of aims and ideals of the two republics."[55] What Sackett

49 *New York Times*, 7 February 1930; *Berliner Tageblatt*, 31 December 1929, a.m. edition.
50 *New York Times*, 6 and 7 February 1930.
51 Wiley to State, 7 February 1930, 123 Sackett, F. M./29; *Berliner Tageblatt*, 5 February 1930, a.m. edition.
52 *New York Times*, 6 February 1930.   53 Castle Diary, 12 July 1929.
54 Julius Curtius, *Sechs Jahre Minister der deutschen Republik*, 154.
55 *New York Times*, 13 February 1930.

failed to notice then, but more importantly what he failed to see later, was that there were significant differences in the goals of German and American politics, and that German diplomats were aware of the American misreading of German politics.[56]

But that was yet to come. The new ambassador had more exciting immediate prospects. He approached his mission with verve and enthusiasm. When he arrived in Berlin, the world he knew and loved still seemed intact, although severe disturbances in the stock market and in employment were going to require the attention of the world's leaders in government and business. Sackett's major concern was creating an establishment that would do honor to his country and properly display the wealth both he and his nation represented. The first consideration was proper quarters. Because the United States did not have a permanent embassy in Berlin, Sackett took up temporary residence in the Hotel Esplanade while the search for an embassy continued.[57]

Sackett was engrossed with the problems of creating an exemplary establishment. In April he opened his new home with all the amenities he conceived the world's leading nation should afford visitors to one of America's most important diplomatic posts. He effusively reported to his sister: "Having a French chef and a German butler and other servants will be an undertaking for Olive [Mrs. Sackett]. We are getting uniforms and liveries made now."[58]

The apprentice diplomat did not spare expense in emphasizing the social side of his mission. A Berlin diplomatic and social reporter, accustomed to luxury, noted that the Sacketts[59]

> are showing people here what "entertaining" means in the States. Even the international diplomats are stunned. The Sacketts serve lobster at tea, an unheard of luxury in Berlin! The Ambassador has rented a small but aristocratic palace in the most fashionable quarter of Berlin. A gigantic and aged butler commands a small army of footmen in discreet blue livery. Mrs. Olive Sackett-Speed is the astonishing possessor of a social secretary, an extravagant novelty here. She is the perfect hostess and gathers as many members of the prewar courtiers in her house as possible.

56 Friedrich von Prittwitz und Gaffron, German ambassador to the United States, to the German Foreign Ministry, 10 November 1932, *Akten zur deutschen auswärtigen Politik, 1918–1945*, 21: 315; hereafter cited ADAP. The German diplomat noted Schurman's frequent references to the United States and Germany as "sister republics."
57 See Sackett to Mrs. Hazard, 31 December 1929, Sackett Papers; *New York Times*, 6 February 1930. Sackett purchased for the United States the Blücher Palace close by the Brandenburg Gate on Unter den Linden, but before it could be occupied, it was destroyed by fire, Jesse H. Stiller, *George S. Messersmith, Diplomat of Democracy*, 29–30.
58 Sackett to Mrs. Hazard, 29 March 1930, Sackett Papers.
59 Bella Fromm, *Blood and Banquets*, 26. On Fromm, see Philip Metcalfe, *1933*, 61–68 and passim.

The splendor of Sackett's entertaining is indicated by the problem he encountered at the end of his mission. He was unsuccessful in pleading diplomatic immunity when he asked to take back to the United States, duty free, the remnants of embassy stocks of liquor amounting to four hundred bottles. Secretary of the Treasury Henry Morgenthau, a Democrat, simply refused to accommodate the wealthy Republican.[60] Sackett told his niece that his salary covered only his wine bill.[61]

Sackett made an impressive entrance into Berlin society, dazzling foreign diplomats and German officials with the opulence of his mission. He was able to befriend many of the most influential figures in German business, finance, and government. Conceiving his mission in the grand and aristocratic style of the past, Sackett was almost certain to be attracted to titled Germans. The Kentuckian must have seemed like a gift from heaven to that nationalist elite. He was not only a lavish host, he understood Germany's fall from glory and was sympathetic to German ambition to restore the nation's position among the world's great powers. The "old Potsdam set," who still refused to visit the French embassy, did not hesitate to drop their calling cards at the American embassy as soon as Sackett had presented his credentials to President Hindenburg.[62]

Sackett, who was impressed by the trappings, pomp, and protocol of the usually dull diplomatic receptions, was delighted to receive these men. Titled members of the German upper classes were frequent guests of the embassy, where they were able to influence the already well-disposed ambassador with their nationalistic views. They became important sources of information available to American diplomats in Berlin.[63] While Sackett was impressed by the German aristocrats, another diplomat, a seasoned British veteran, decried the "decaying state of the German aristocracy." Most remained on their estates, he wrote, but "those still to be met in Berlin included a sad proportion of spongers on the Diplomatic Corps."[64]

Sackett's attraction to the German elite among the aristocracy, politi-

---

60 Graham H. Stuart, *American Diplomatic and Consular Practice*, 293.

61 Marion H. McVitty, Sackett's niece, to Bernard V. Burke, *Re: Ambassador Frederick* [sic] *M. Sackett*, July 1966, hereafter cited McVitty memoir. A British diplomat's wife claimed that British ambassadors were paid three times the salary paid to Americans, whose salaries were about enough to pay the rent on a suitable embassy, Maude Parker Child, *The Social Side of Diplomatic Life*, 24.

62 Fromm, *Blood and Banquets*, 26.

63 Fromm, *Blood and Banquets*, 26, 32; Sackett to Mrs. Hazard, 24 January 1931, Sackett Papers. Titled Germans also were able to inform the German government about American policy after talking with Sackett. See, for example, Baron von Lersner-Nieder Erlenbach to State Secretary Bernhard von Bülow of the German Foreign Ministry, 17 December 1931, German Foreign Ministry Records, Microfilm Reel 1661, Frame D730140, hereafter cited GFMR with reel and frame numbers.

64 Sir David Kelly, *The Ruling Few*, 195; a British diplomat's wife claimed that entertaining impoverished aristocrats was especially the case in the British and American embassies, Child, *The Social Side of Diplomatic Life*, 37, 40.

cians, diplomats, the military, and men of business led him to become more sympathetic to Germany and its grievances than even Schurman had been. The former ambassador was reproached for his uncritical attitude not only by American diplomats, but by German officials as well. Sackett would prove to be just as pro-German as his predecessor and much more likely to take steps to help the Germans. He became an active and reliable supporter of the Weimar Republic, and of democracy in Germany, and he dreaded the implications of Hitler's rise to power.

Those implications involved a force that Sackett feared most of all – communism. Many observers, including Sackett, believed that a Hitler government would lead to chaos from which only communism could benefit. The new ambassador brought with him to Berlin an anticommunist outlook that was extreme for even those days so close to the Bolshevik revolution of 1917.[65] Although Sackett had no personal or direct knowledge of communism, his deep-seated fear was reenforced by events in his personal life. On a visit to the United States while on leave from his post in Berlin, he encountered one of the most notorious strikes in American labor history. Sackett's coal-mining interests were prominent participants in the violent Harlan County strike, and the deep involvement of communists in the strike served to reenforce Sackett's aversion for what he saw as the products of Bolshevism.

Trouble began in Harlan County, Kentucky, in February 1931 when coal miners were confronted with another wage cut. Sackett's Black Star Coal Company in Harlan County and his Pioneer Coal Company in adjacent Bell County were involved in the violence that spread through the coalfields. Located in the southeastern part of the state, the home ground of Governor Flem Sampson and Sackett's one-time opponent John Robsion, Sackett's mines employed nonunion workers, as was the custom in the region dominated in near feudal fashion by the mine owners. The United Mine Workers, the National Miners Union, and the American Communist party entered the field to organize the workers. The ensuing strike was characterized by violence, including the firing of workers suspected of union sympathy, as well as shootings and bombings blamed on "communists" by the police and on the owners by the labor organizers.

"Harlan County" became a symbol for violence among union activists, and Sackett's interests were directly involved. When hundreds of mine workers had a mass meeting in Pineville, the county seat, on March 1, 1931, the ambassador's Black Star Coal Company retaliated by firing thirty-five of them for attending. Although Sackett had resigned his presidencies in both coal companies when he was elected to the Senate in 1924,[66] he was still concerned about his interests.

65 See Edward W. Bennett, *Germany and the Diplomacy of the Financial Crisis, 1931*, 31.
66 *National Cyclopaedia of American Biography*, 37: 78–9; Sackett resumed the offices when he returned from his diplomatic mission in 1933.

The ambassador arrived in the United States just at the time Governor Flem Sampson sent four hundred National Guard troops into the strike-torn region to stem the violence. On May fifth the "Battle of Evarts" took place, with at least four killed. The violence continued unabated through the summer and fall until the strike ultimately failed. The mine workers were intimidated by the mine owners and their allies among the state's power structure. But the failure of the strike was probably just as attributable to the strikers' fundamentalist religious beliefs. The aggressive atheism of the Communist party agitators offended their patriotism and religion. It is clear that although they were willing to strike out against their feudal overlords, they were not ready for revolution.[67] From Sackett's point of view, the forces of righteousness won out against the forces of evil.

Sackett's aversion to communism would affect his judgment throughout his career as ambassador to Germany. As could be expected, he brought with him to Berlin a wide variety of attitudes aside from his views on communism. He could be unorthodox in his thinking, but always with a very practical turn of mind. Above all, his buoyant optimism helped him through some trying times. His familiarity with matters of business and finance made him a knowledgeable asset to the American embassy chancery in Berlin. With his new position the ebullient Kentuckian had reached a new, high level in an already successful career. Sackett was now at the center of some of the most important events of his time. His personal triumph enabled him to influence his government, but most importantly, his new position gave him the chance to observe how Adolf Hitler took advantage of his far more significant opportunity.

The years 1929–1930 proved to be pivotal in Sackett's career and were a period of greater importance for Adolf Hitler. The Nazi leader was able to take advantage of the Great Depression that was crippling the industrial world. There was much privation and suffering, but as usual in such troubled times, some were able to exploit people's problems to their own advantage. Such was the case in 1929 when Germany felt the first serious effects of what would become a long and miserable period of economic depression. At the time, Hitler was a minor figure in German politics. He rose to national prominence as a direct result of the serious dislocation that troubled Germany and much of the world. His rise to power depended on widespread discontent with the economic problems of the German people, but he also took advantage of the failures of the political parties, which could not resolve their differences in the interest of saving

67 George Brown Tindall, *The Emergence of the New South*, 383–386, 528–529; for contemporary versions of events see Theodore Dreiser et al., *Harlan Miners Speak: Report on Terrorism in the Kentucky Coal Fields, Prepared by Members of the National Committee for the Defense of Political Prisoners*, esp. 30, 35–36, 42–44, 56. Among the dozen authors, aside from Dreiser, were John Dos Passos and Sherwood Anderson.

the Weimar Republic. Hitler's opportunity came when Germany's governing parties were confronted with the first serious political crisis of the depression.

The German republic was governed originally by the Weimar Coalition, made up of the socialist Social Democrats, the Roman Catholic Center party, and the German Democrats. They were joined in 1928 by the German People's party to form the Great Coalition. In late 1929, a classic confrontation developed in the government between opposing points of view of how to cope with the incipient depression. At issue was the unemployment insurance fund, fast being depleted by rising unemployment and falling tax revenue. Labor union groups, staunch supporters of the Weimar Republic, were represented by the Center party and the Social Democrats, who wanted to meet the crisis by raising taxes on both employers and employees. The conservative, business-oriented People's party disagreed. Their leadership, and that of employer organizations, whose support of the republic ranged from ambivalent to hostile, called instead for a policy of retrenchment. Business leaders blamed the depression on the government's social policies.

The economic policy problem opened up a political standoff in which both sides refused to give way, maintaining their positions, and in so doing, undermined the coalition to the point that democratic government, and the Weimar Republic itself, were endangered. The political parties were demonstrating once again that their partisan concerns took priority over the wider interests of the nation. Many Germans thought the time had come to look for alternatives to parliamentary rule.[68]

Times of trouble for some are times of opportunity for others. In Germany, the political crisis of the Weimar Republic would bring down the Great Coalition and open the door to groups who would prey on the discontent of the voting public. As the depression worsened, a broader group of people had genuine complaints about the value of the political-economic system they had been asked to support. The defeat in the world war, the horrible inflation of 1923, and the widespread refusal to accept the Weimar Republic made Germany a perfect breeding ground for the nurturing of nostrums and panaceas that could be vended to a disenchanted public. Germans were ever more eager for an alternative to the system that developed out of the Armistice of November 1918. Right-wing opponents of the republic called it the "November System" of the "November Criminals." Hypernationalist and racist *völkische* groups abounded, and organizations aplenty pointed to new and better directions for Germany to take. Most notable on the political Left was the German Communist party.

68 Karl Dietrich Bracher, *Die Auflösung der Weimarer Republic*, 287–291; Gordon A. Craig, *Germany, 1866–1945*, 528–529; Erich Eyck, *A History of the Weimar Republic*, 2: 208–225; Helga Timm, *Die deutsche Sozialpolitik und der Bruch der Grossen Koalition im März 1930*, 97, 139.

Already a major opposition party, which refused to accept the republic because they saw it as the creation of bourgeois servants of capitalism, the Communists would exploit the situation to become even more troublesome for any governing combination. But they were not strong enough, acceptable enough, or willing enough to become a part of any national government, or even, by themselves, to threaten the existence of the Weimar Republic.

As economic and political discontent spread throughout Germany, the disgruntled found more reason to blame Germany's fate on the outcome of the world war. The Treaty of Versailles had been a rallying point for patriotic expressions of unhappiness with German defeat. As soon as it was signed, chauvinist groups sprang up in defiance of what they called the *Diktat* of the victor powers. The treaty was blamed for every imaginable problem confronting Germany. And then another reminder of the humiliation of defeat emerged in the New Plan for a final settlement of German reparations payments to be paid to the victorious European powers.

Reparations grew out of the defeat of the Central Powers: Germany, Austria-Hungary, Bulgaria, and Turkey, in World War I. It was compensation to the Entente Allies for the damage inflicted on them by Germany and her allies. The Germans were forced to accept the Treaty of Versailles in June 1919. Article 231, the "war guilt clause," assigned Germany full responsibility for the war, and as a consequence the Germans were charged to pay for all the damage they had done. Although President Woodrow Wilson was its most ardent advocate, the United States neither ratified the treaty nor joined the League of Nations it created. The United States ended the war with Germany in 1921 by unilaterally proclaiming the declaration of war at an end. It also reserved to itself all the privileges and benefits of the peace settlement, including the Treaty of Versailles, but without accepting any of the attendant responsibilities. In addition, the United States played no part in the reparations issue except to be certain that those payments were kept separate and distinct from the war debts owed to the U.S. government. In 1921 the U.S. Congress established the World War Foreign Debt Commission and forbade by law the cancellation of the war debts.

The Germans not only had to pay for damages done but had to surrender great portions of their territory. On their west, the Germans ceded Moresnet, Eupen, and Malmédy to Belgium. They yielded Alsace Lorraine to France, while the Saar was to be internationalized for fifteen years or more, during which time France was able to exploit its rich coal mines. The Rhineland was to be occupied for a minimum of fifteen years and a strip thirty miles wide on the Rhine's right bank was to be demilitarized. In the east, Memel was turned over to a newly created Lithuania; Posen and parts of Upper Silesia were lost to a re-created Poland, and Danzig became a free city tied to Poland by a customs union. The most humiliating loss was the Polish

Corridor; the cession of West Prussia opened a large strip of land on the Baltic Sea to Poland and isolated East Prussia from Germany proper. Being stripped of so much territory had a significant economic impact on Germany; it meant the loss of major markets, raw materials, and important manufacturing areas.

Although the Treaty of Versailles called for Germany to pay reparations to the victors, the final total owed and a schedule for its payment was left for the future. As the interests of the powers shifted with the passage of time, the reparations issue went through a series of changes. At the reparations conference at Spa in 1920 the percentages owed to the Entente Allies were determined, but the final total was postponed until later. France was to be awarded 52 percent of the final sum, while Great Britain was to receive 22 percent, Italy 10, Belgium 8, Japan and Portugal three-fourths of 1 percent, and the nations not represented at the conference, including Greece, Romania, and Yugoslavia, were to divide the remainder.[69]

While they negotiated with the Entente Allies over the total reparations bill, the Germans hoped for American intervention to moderate the demands placed on them, but the United States was unwilling to take the part of Germany against the Entente Allies, or to become involved in European politics. When the Germans proved to be uncooperative on reparations as well as other matters the Entente powers occupied the Ruhr cities of Düsseldorf, Duisburg, and Ruhrort.[70] While still reeling from that shock, the Germans learned the extent of the reparations bill.

In April 1921 the Reparations Commission fixed the total reparations liability of all the Central Powers at 132 billion gold marks or $33 billion. That figure would be modified in recognition of restitution already made and in the method of payment, so that the final figure of the Reparations Commission for all intents and purposes was 50 billion gold marks, or $12.5 billion, owed by the Germans. But that figure was based on the convertibility of the mark to the dollar at 4:1. Because by May 1921 the mark had fallen to 60:1 it would take 750 billion paper marks to pay the 50 billion gold mark assessment. But it got worse. The reparations bill included an ultimatum demanding that the commission's figure be accepted unconditionally and that the first payment be remitted within twenty-five days or the Entente Allies would occupy the Ruhr, the industrial heart of the Rhineland. To meet the obligation the Germans sold newly printed

69 Harold G. Moulton and Leo Pasvolsky, *World War Debt Settlements*, 8–13. Austria, Hungary, and Bulgaria were also assessed for reparations in the separate treaties they signed with the Entente Allies. Among the Central Powers only Turkey escaped the payment of reparations. The loss of territory the Ottoman Empire suffered as a result of the war was considered compensation enough by the victor powers. Moulton and Pasvolsky, *War Debts and World Prosperity*, 139 and n. 3.

70 The Entente Allies already had military occupation forces in the Rhineland. In keeping with the provisions of the Treaty of Versailles, the occupation was to last until 1935.

marks on the foreign exchange, which precipitated further depreciation of the mark until by November it had fallen from 60 to 310 to the dollar. The inflation that began with the war was now accelerated until the German government was bankrupt.

Because the United States did not ratify the Treaty of Versailles, it had no part in determining German reparations; as a consequence, France's position was dominant. The United States did signal its interest in the German position by sending an "unofficial observer" to the reparations conference. While the Germans struggled to fulfill their obligations and to win understanding of their plight, the British realized it was in their interest to modify reparations in German favor. Germany could legitimately pay its bills on a regular annual basis only through a surplus in government revenue over expenditures or by a foreign trade surplus of exports over imports. The British recognized that the German government was going bankrupt and that Germany needed to increase its foreign trade which would compete with their own. At that point, the war debts owed to the United States became a complicating factor.[71]

From the time the United States entered the war, in April 1917, until November 1920 the American government extended loans and credits to the Entente Allies amounting to about $10 billion. Great Britain received approximately $4.2 billion, France $2.97 billion, and Italy $1.6 billion. Others receiving lesser amounts included Belgium, $349 million; Russia $188 million; and all others a total of $135 million.[72] When the United States made it clear that it expected the debts to be paid in full, it undermined British efforts to modify German payments. In order to fulfill their commitment to the United States, the British were forced to insist that the $10 billion in debts owed to them by their allies also would need to be paid. The result was that the French, Belgian, and Italian governments demanded that the Germans pay the reparations payments due them so that they could meet their obligations to both Great Britain and the United States. The war debts owed to the United States became the starting point of a cycle in which the Entente Allies received reparations from the Germans in order to pay their war debts to the Americans.

By late May 1922 it was clear to the Reparations Commission that German payments were leading to the collapse of the mark and creating impossible transfer problems. When at the end of the year the Germans made an unimpressive offer to pay based on an international loan and with the proviso that Düsseldorf, Duisburg, and Ruhrort be evacuated by foreign troops, the Reparations Commission declared Germany in default. France then took advantage of a minor failure of the Germans to make a

---

71 Craig, *Germany, 1866–1945*, 436–443; an excellent survey of German-American relations is Manfred Jonas, *The United States and Germany: A Diplomatic History*, see 151–193 for the 1920s.
72 Moulton and Pasvolsky, *War Debts and World Prosperity*, 429.

delivery in kind and were joined by Belgium in the invasion and occupation of the Ruhr region. Neither Britain nor Italy participated in the military action, while at the same time the United States withdrew its occupation forces from the Rhineland. France dominated the invasion, which amounted to a continuation of the war.

The German government responded by organizing a program of passive resistance to the occupation. The German people accepted the policy, but the costs were staggering. When Germans in the Ruhr refused to cooperate, the French brought in their own workers. Chaos ruled. Germans were put out of work and strikers intimidated or imprisoned. When the French sequestered bank reserves and factory inventories the German government responded by offering aid to the victims of the occupation. With production curtailed and vital raw materials from the Ruhr denied to the rest of Germany, unemployment rose sharply. By August 1923 there were food riots and it was obvious that the German government simply did not have the resources to meet the claims of those who felt they were entitled to compensation for the consequences of Berlin's policy.

Although reparations were not paid to France and Belgium during the occupation, Germany continued to make payments to Britain and Italy. Depleting its meager revenues to pay the rising costs of supporting the passive resistance, and to meet reparations obligations, German expenditures began to far exceed government income. In an attempt to keep up, the Germans resorted to the printing press, which led to an inflation of hitherto unknown proportions.

The inflation of 1923 would imprint a lasting mark on the German psyche. German presses running around the clock produced marks that decreased in value at astronomical rates. In July 1922 the mark had fallen to 493.2 to the dollar. By January 1923 it had dropped to 17,972 to the dollar and the acceleration continued throughout the year, plummeting in July 1923 to 353,412, and finally, at the end of the year, to the unbelievable sum of 4.2 trillion marks to the dollar. Wage earners and middle-class families who had built some savings were impoverished by the inflation. But at the same time speculators were able to make a fortune through financial manipulations and the purchase of failing businesses.

When the impact of the inflation first spread beyond German borders many saw that the time had come to do something before the insanity infected the rest of the world. In Germany a new leader emerged in the person of Gustav Stresemann of the German People's party. A convinced monarchist, he became a devoted proponent of the republic as the only alternative to a dictatorship of the Right, or especially of the Left. It was Stresemann who decided to take the decisive step in bringing the policy of passive resistance to an end. Many Germans thought it to be a craven and unpatriotic capitulation to France, but Stresemann had the courage to make the move because he saw no alternative. He was driven from office before the year ended, but became foreign minister, a position he held until his death six years later. It was a period of serious danger to the very existence of the Weimar Republic, a time of potential revolution, especially from the Right, and featured Adolf Hitler's failed Beer Hall Putsch in Munich on November 9.[73]

In September 1923, when Stresemann put an end to the passive resistance he opened the door to American intervention. In President Warren Harding's administration both Charles Evans Hughes, the secretary of state, and Herbert Clark Hoover, the secretary of commerce, were convinced that only an economically strong and politically stable Germany could asssure peace and prosperity in Europe. They were equally certain that Germany would be willing to pay a reasonable amount of reparations.

Secretary Hughes was persuaded that worldwide depression threatened unless something was done. He believed that a committee of independent financial experts could deal with the problem and thus avoid any American political entanglements. First, the French had to be convinced of the need to act, and the surest way to get French approval and German compliance was through a study, by a committee of experts, of Germany's capacity to pay. The next step would be to get American financial experts to participate. The financier J. P. Morgan wrote frankly on the subject to Secretary Hughes: "If politicians, feeling themselves incompetent, request intervention of private parties," then the private sector "must be given complete freedom to arrive at their conclusions and report to the politicians, leaving the latter to act or not as they see fit upon such recommendations."[74]

In a December 1922 speech to the American Historical Association, Secretary Hughes tied German reparations to world prosperity. Enunciating a policy of "involvement without commitment," he denied any American responsibility but volunteered that the United States would act as an arbiter if requested by all the parties involved.[75] If the United States were to intervene, it would have to be with great caution so as to avoid any appearance of financial pressure on France or Germany. When Stresemann called off the passive resistance, he appealed to American Ambassador Alanson Houghton for the United States to take the initiative along the lines Secretary Hughes suggested in his speech.

The new president, Calvin Coolidge, was inclined to leave foreign policy in Hughes' hands, but like most American politicians at the time, he was extremely sensitive about potential reaction from Congress to any American involvement in Europe. Congressmen were adamant on the subject of war debts, which were considered a legitimate contractual obligation and therefore quite unlike reparations, which were an imposed political debt. The war debts had to be paid.

73 Craig, *Germany, 1866–1945*, 446–468.
74 Jonas, *The United States and Germany*, 170–171.
75 Jonas, *The United States and Germany*, 171–172.

When the British inquired whether or not the United States would participate in an inquiry concerning Germany's capacity to pay, Hughes was delighted. Arrangements were made immediately for American participation, but the U.S. government would not be directly involved. There is an indistinct border between international finance and foreign policy. In the postwar era the United States decided to rely on private citizens to manage matters of international finance in the belief that their actions would advance American foreign policy goals – a system now called "corporatism." Experts outside government were considered to be disinterested and in closer touch with the wishes of the people than government functionaries. Private citizens would take part in the investigation, but the United States would not incur any official responsibility. Nor would the government be party to any reciprocal debt agreements; above all, there should be no connection whatever between war debts owed to the United States and reparations due the Entente Allies.

In keeping with the policy of remaining aloof from European politics, an American delegation of private citizens was recommended to the Reparations Commission. They were all chosen by the State Department with careful attention that none was an advocate of canceling the war debts and that all could instill public confidence in their work. They were chosen with regional considerations in mind to insure wide acceptance. From the West Coast was Los Angeles banker Henry M. Robinson, a close friend of Hoover and later his personal adviser when he became president; from the East Coast, Owen D. Young of New York, chairman of the board of General Electric and a Wilsonian internationalist, and from the Midwest, Charles G. Dawes, a prominent Chicago banker and Republican.

Although the fiction was maintained that the American delegation represented private interests, Dawes and Young consulted with President Harding and Secretaries Hughes and Hoover in Washington and were accompanied by the State Department economic adviser and the chief of the European Division of the Bureau of Foreign and Domestic Commerce. In addition, Hoover instructed the commercial attachés in the London, Paris, and Berlin embassies to assist in the work of the delegation.[76]

The committee to address German problems was chaired by Dawes, and in spite of the fact that every delegate entered objections in one form or another, their plan was unanimously accepted in full, but only after strong British pressure in favor. Named after the American chairman, the Dawes Plan called for a total reorganization of German finances, major tax reforms, a large international loan to Germany, and the creation of an agent-general for reparations to oversee the complex plan. Another American banker, Undersecretary of the Treasury S. Parker Gilbert, was agent-general as a private citizen throughout the life of the Dawes Plan. The essence of the

76 Melvyn P. Leffler, *Elusive Quest*, 82–90; Michael J. Hogan, *Informal Entente*, 68–72.

plan was that Germany's reparations liability was reduced, but since there was no final payment, that left the total amount uncertain. According to its provisions Germany would pay by means of a complex schedule into an uncertain future.

Since the Dawes Plan called for a significant revision of the Treaty of Versailles, a conference of the Entente Allies met in London during July and August 1924. The Americans shared with the Germans an expressed desire to restore German territory and to revise the Treaty of Versailles further. Although not going that far, under new leadership France and Britain were eager for a settlement. Édouard Herriot of France and Ramsay MacDonald of Great Britain led the negotiations and presented the plan to Germany for its acceptance. After a pro forma protest, the Germans accepted the plan and opened the door to a period of relative stability.[77]

The Dawes Plan called for a major loan that would play an important role in American involvement with Germany. An agreement was signed at the Bank of England by American, Belgian, British, and French bankers with German financial delegates for a loan to Germany of 800 million gold marks, or $200 million. An American firm, J. P. Morgan and Company, organized the loan, which was fully subscribed to in a matter of a few days.[78] It was the first major loan of more than a hundred made to German governments at all levels and to private enterprises by American bankers from 1924 to 1931. The United States now became an important economic factor in European, and especially German, affairs, but without any political or military involvement. Any leverage the United States had was essentially economic, with the contribution of capital most important.[79]

American loans to Germany were the start of the economic revival of the defeated nation. They also became a third element in the cycle of war debt and reparation payments. American money eased German payment of reparations, which made it easier for Britain, France, and the other nations to pay their war debts to the United States. The key element, of course, was the American loans that supported the cycle. The Germans regularly met their reparations payments under the Dawes Plan thanks to the large amounts of American money loaned to the former enemy. Stresemann told the Reichstag that the United States was the "nation from which emanated the most important efforts directed toward the reconstruction of the [German] economy and, beyond that, the pacification of Europe."[80]

In the years immediately following, the "Period of Fulfillment" or the final settlement of the world war seemed to be achieved. In 1925, the Locarno treaties provided guarantees of borders between Germany, France, and Belgium. In a regional security compact of nonaggression, the three

77 Sally Marks, *The Illusion of Peace*, 52–54.   78 Leffler, *Elusive Quest*, 111.
79 Jonas, *The United States and Germany*, 182.
80 Jonas, *The United States and Germany*, 181.

powers agreed not to resort to war against each other. Great Britain and Italy served as guarantors, while behind the scenes, the United States' encouragement to the Germans helped make the settlement possible. Confrontation among the powers seemed to have ended, at least in the West, and a period of peace seemed to be assured. Locarno became the foundation for better relations between Germany and her former enemies in Western Europe.[81] As part of its provisions, Germany joined the League of Nations in the following year, and in 1928 was a signatory of the Pact of Paris. That agreement, proposed by American Secretary of State Frank B. Kellogg, grew out of Franco-American negotiatons in which Aristide Briand represented France. Also known as the Kellogg-Briand Pact, the agreement outlawed war as a means of achieving national goals. Because it called for the renunciation of war without providing any sanctions, twenty-three nations signed it, including the United States and Germany.

All was proceeding well, except that Germany wanted the Rhineland evacuated and France wanted a clearer policy on reparations than the open-ended Dawes Plan. That led to the call for a reexamination of the debt and, as it was commonly said at the time, "the final liquidation of the war." The Germans wanted American participation as a moderating influence, but this time the United States was not enthusiastic about becoming involved, even through the participation of private citizens. Finally, the United States agreed that Owen D. Young, the veteran of the Dawes Plan, could participate. Then, to insure that America's preeminent international financiers were represented, J. P. Morgan partners Thomas Lamont and J. P. Morgan, Jr., himself were named to the commission by President Coolidge. He admonished them to work only toward the completion of the Dawes Plan; to keep the war debts issue separate; to avoid political involvement or the establishment of precedents; and to strive for the political and economic stability of Europe by the use of American capital. In 1929 the final product of the committee was called the New Plan or, more commonly, the Young Plan.[82]

Named after Young, the principal American delegate and chairman of the committtee, the Young Plan revised the Dawes Plan in an attempt to place German reparations payments on a regular basis and to take reparations out of politics and make Germany directly responsible to meet its obligations as it would in a commercial matter. In the Dawes Plan there was no end to the German commitment. The Young Plan was meant to be the final settlement of German reparations to the Entente Allies, principally Great Britain and France, with payments to be made over a period of fifty-eight and a half years. It also provided for the further reduction of German reparations if the United States scaled down the war

81 Jon Jacobson, *Locarno Diplomacy*, 3–4.
82 Marks, *The Illusion of Peace*, 101–102; Leffler, *Elusive Quest*, 202–203.

debts Great Britain and France as well as other nations owed the American government. The plan also called for an early evacuation of the military forces occupying the Rhineland.

From the American point of view, it was an equitable economic settlement of a long-standing problem. From the German perspective, it was still a political obligation, but another step toward revising the Treaty of Versailles.[83] To extreme nationalists in Germany, however, the Young Plan was yet another affront to their patriotic sensibilities. It perpetuated what they believed to be the myth of German guilt for the world war and was a symbol of foreign dominance of what could, and should be, a powerful Germany. Reparations payments to Britain, France, and other powers were a central problem in German politics throughout the Weimar years. In 1929 the issue reached new heights as an instrument of opposition to the republic.

The New Plan was announced on June 7, 1929. Almost immediately Alfred Hugenberg, the head of the German Nationalist party, organized a broad group of opponents to the plan, all of whom not only opposed the new reparations settlement, but had a common aversion to the Weimar Republic. The Young Plan became the unifying symbol for the forces opposed to the republic. They included far Right organizations, such as the hypernationalist Pan-German League and the Stahlhelm, an organization of front-line veterans of the war. As their vociferous campaign developed, even the Communists joined them to take advantage of this new opportunity to attack the republic.

Hugenberg, with his abrasive style, had managed to alienate many of his Nationalist party followers, and was aware that he did not have the charismatic presence to sell his program of opposition. But he did have a large communications empire that could be used to spread the message of the malcontents. He enlisted the support of another party of the radical Right, the National Socialist German Workers' party, or Nazis, as they were called. Their leader, Adolf Hitler, a gifted orator and agitator, had a reputation as an outstanding propagandist. Hugenberg intended to use Hitler not just to defeat the Young Plan, but also to help bring down the Weimar Republic and restore Germany to her prewar glory. For Hitler this was a heaven-sent opportunity. The nationwide chain of newspapers, news agencies, and film interests under Hugenberg's control would be at his disposal. Hitler foresaw that he would become a figure of national importance, but there was a price to pay. Hugenberg, of course, would demand control of the campaign.

Among the Nazis there was a large contingent motivated by anticapitalist sentiment. This group, including Gregor Strasser as a notable leader, did not take kindly to an alliance with the Nationalist leader, who was

83 Jonas, *The United States and Germany*, 183–184, 191–193.

considered a bourgeois reactionary, one of those gentlemen in frock coats who were anathema to the Nazis. Faced with this dilemma, Hitler took a course of action that would be characteristic of him. He would work toward the defeat of the Young Plan and would continue to wage a vigorous propaganda war against the republic, but he must be allowed full independence in his campaign. Hugenberg gave in to Hitler's all-or-nothing stance, offering the Nazis full financial support from the committee formed to defeat the Young Plan.

Hitler now had what he needed to take advantage of the depression that was developing, and of the political crisis the depression had helped spawn. For the first time he had the money, the media attention, and the access to important people he had lacked for so long. Hugenberg was so dead set against the Weimar Republic and the Young Plan that he continued to support the Nazis even after Hitler publicly separated himself from the Nationalist leader and his party and openly attacked Hugenberg himself. With the advantage of national exposure through Hugenberg's press and film empire, Hitler was able to put his case before a national audience on a regular basis. The astute agitator would not turn back from the prominent position he had won for himself, for his party, and for the Nazi movement.[84] He took full advantage of his opportunity.

Events in Germany had very little impact on Americans, who focused their attention on domestic matters. Soon they were mired in the economic and financial anxieties brought on by the Great Depression. As the crisis in Germany developed, little was heard in the United States about Hitler and the Nazis. For example, in a brief story deep inside the *New York Times*, it was reported that Hitler, the "chief anti semite," was living in luxury with the material as well as moral support of German industrialists.[85] He was doing well with the opportunities Hugenberg opened up for him. Otherwise Americans paid scant attention to events in Germany. Neither Germany's political nor its economic problems appeared to be of major consequence. Americans had enormous amounts of money invested in Germany, but their confidence was not shaken by the mild tempest that was taking place.

The American ambassador to Germany, Jacob Gould Schurman, reinforced that perception of events. The former president of Cornell University and one-time minister to China had been head of the American diplomatic mission in Berlin since 1925. He was convinced that the innate conservatism of the German people made them immune to the blandishments of radical leadership and that Germany was irrevocably committed to democracy. Whereas some diplomats were critical of the multiplicity of political

84 Bullock, *Hitler*, 147–148; Fest, *Hitler*, 272–280.
85 *New York Times*, 3 November 1929.

parties in Germany, the American ambassador saw the score or more parties as a virtue that guaranteed democracy in government and moderation in policy. President Hindenburg gave further assurance that all was well in Germany, having used all his enormous influence to support constitutional government. Schurman felt that the president had shown himself to be the strongest bulwark of the republic. In 1928 the ambassador was convinced that the Weimar Republic was a stable fixture in Germany. He declared: "The Republic had in general commended itself to the people and grows every year with such strength and vitality that its permanence may now be taken for granted."[86]

What appeared to be a relatively minor German economic problem exploded into a major crisis with the stock market crash in the United States in October 1929. Americans were now unable or unwilling to invest money abroad. In Germany, unemployment grew at an even more rapid pace than before and with it came a spreading discontent. As the crisis in the German government worsened, the campaign to defeat the Young Plan reached new heights of abusiveness. Hitler, who was considered a local phenomenon, part of the lunatic fringe of Bavarian politics, had now become a political force of national dimensions, with stronger ties in the north than ever before. Hitler and Hugenberg opened a campaign in September 1929 for a referendum demanding an end to reparations and providing punishment for high treason to anyone in the government who agreed to continue further payments. Their bill would require the support of 10 percent of the electorate to place it before the Reichstag.

When the vote took place in October only 10.02 percent of the voters approved the act, a crushing defeat in light of the huge campaign mounted against the Young Plan. As the protest against reparations continued, the bill was resoundingly defeated in the Reichstag in November and then again in a national plebiscite in December. Hitler and Hugenberg needed more than 21 million votes in the December plebiscite, but they got less than 6 million. The defeat was a humiliation for Hugenberg, but the outcome of the voting was immaterial to Hitler. He had conducted a propaganda campaign of unprecedented proportions and had shown the German people the size and importance of the Nazi movement, even if his party had only twelve seats in a Reichstag of 491 deputies.[87]

Schurman's analysis of the campaign opposing the Young Plan focused on Hugenberg and his Nationalist party. American diplomats believed that the major potential threat to the Weimar Republic would be the restoration of the monarchy. "Prussian militarism" and the Hohenzollern dynasty constituted the principal dangers to democracy in Germany, and to peace

86 Schurman speech to the New York Chamber of Commerce, 1 November 1928, and speeches 17 March and 3 October 1930, Boxes 11 and 12, Jacob Gould Schurman Papers.

87 Bullock, *Hitler*, 148; Fest, *Hitler*, 274–277.

in Europe, in the American view. Hugenberg and his Nationalists were the most "actively monarchical" party in Germany, and were therefore keenly watched by the American diplomats. The Americans were delighted to report that they were now in trouble. Hugenberg's arrogant and bullying tactics alienated many of his party's leaders and several resigned rather than continue the bitter campaign that held out such minimal hope for success. Schurman reported he had heard one of the "most exalted personages of the old regime" discuss the tactics now being used by the Nationalists and was convinced that their cooperation with the "National Socialists or Fascists involved the greatest peril for the Nationalist party itself."[88]

American diplomats in Berlin paid meager attention to Hitler and the Nazis. They viewed the party as little more than a burden Hugenberg chose to bear. They were pleased to be able to report that the bitter campaign had seriously disrupted the Nationalists. The party was now divided into two factions, one of which gave its support to the republic, even if grudgingly, while the main body of the party remained "reactionary and irreconcilable." With this blow to the main monarchist party, the American diplomats assumed that one of Germany's most serious domestic political problems had been resolved. If Hugenberg continued his inept leadership, there would be no effective champion for the Hohenzollern dynasty in the Reichstag and the republic would be further assured. Moreover, the Americans were convinced that Hugenberg's intimidating style had not only discredited him within his own party but had given one-man party dictatorship a blow from which it could not recover.[89]

The Americans were, of course, patently wrong. They believed there was no longer any danger of one person dominating a political party in the future. We now know that the opportunity the depression, the political crisis, and Hugenberg's support had given the Nazis helped secure Hitler's position as party dictator. But the Nazis had not yet become a dominant force in Germany. More important matters commanded the attention of the Americans, concerns which were vital to relations with Germany. American investments were an integral part of the German economy, and the deepening depression forced Americans to pay closer attention to the fiscal crisis threatening the Weimar Republic. American interest was heightened because the German government wanted to borrow large sums of money to weather the crisis and American financial houses would become deeply involved.

88 Schurman to State, 5 December 1929, 862.00/2473.
89 Schurman to State, 9 December 1929, 862.00/2481; Schurman speech, 17 February 1930, Box 12, Schurman Papers.

2

American diplomacy, official and unofficial

WHEN AMBASSADOR SACKETT assumed his post in Berlin, in February 1930, the last majority cabinet in the history of the Weimar Republic was about to fall. What appeared to be the imminent collapse of the republic was fostered and welcomed on the political Right and Left. Observers at the time were uncertain about the direction Germany would take. Many feared that the Communist party was most likely to benefit from the turmoil. Sackett must therefore be credited with singling out Hitler and the Nazis as the major threat to the Weimar Republic soon after his arrival in Berlin. It is ironic that Sackett, appointed because of his qualifications in business and finance, would distinguish himself in political analysis. He had more time for that activity because he was kept out of the loop of decisions concerning the major American influence on the Weimar Republic – financial support. The ambassador was deliberately excluded from wielding this primary tool of foreign policy because American economic diplomacy left financial relations to the private sector.

Sackett, as a newcomer, was expected to learn the duties of a diplomat from his experienced staff of foreign service officers. He was fortunate to have John Cooper Wiley at his side while he acquainted himself with his day-to-day responsibilities, with the routine of the embassy chancery, with representing American interests to the Germans, and with the intricacies of reporting to the State Department. Sackett was a good student and an excellent administrator. He took to his tasks with aplomb and was quickly running the embassy and turning out impressive financial and political reports.

Not as readily expected were the lessons he was to learn from German mentors in the Reichschancellery, the Finance and Foreign ministries. Sackett took to those lessons as readily as he did to what he learned from the embassy staff. The Germans liked Sackett and he in turn liked them. They were favored by American policy that was meant to support Germany. Sackett agreed with his government's notion that by offering political support to Germany, the peace of Europe was assured; by extending financial backing, European and American prosperity were assured.

When Sackett made his first approaches to German officials, they looked upon him as a project to be worked on. They were at the same time convinced that he was worth working with and that he would soon come around to their point of view. His first contacts with German diplomats were not as auspicious as he had hoped. He approached the all-important reparations issue from an objective, disinterested position. In a word, Sackett told the Germans he thought they could very well pay reparations. Moreover, he instructed them in history. He pointed out that when Prussia defeated France in 1871, the Prussians assessed France a reparations bill thought to be beyond possible repayment for a hundred years. In spite of Prussia's blatant attempt to dominate the French with financial control, France paid its debt within a few years. The Germans were quick to react to Sackett's accurate rendering of history, insisting that the cases were quite different.

Although the Germans at first considered Sackett to be a hard-liner on the reparations issue, they came to see him as quite open and favorably disposed to the German view. In the Finance Ministry, his early position was regarded as extreme, but in the end the German officials agreed with their diplomatic counterparts that Sackett had only limited knowledge of the German problem. They assumed his position was based on the outlook he had assimilated in Washington, a problem that they could easily remedy to their satisfaction by introducing him to "the right people so he could gradually get a clearer picture of the German situation."[1] The Germans soon learned that Sackett not only understood but agreed with their views. On disarmament matters he was "thoroughly" versed on the German claims, and on reparations his position was close to their own and, moreover, his views were "not so far from reality as they first appeared to us."[2]

As already noted, American policy reserved foreign financial matters to the private sector, and in the area of Sackett's expertise, business and finance, the U.S. government did not fully employ his talents. The ambassador could have helped coordinate and oversee American financial activity. However, he played no role in the negotiation of several large loans to the German government, even though they were critical for Germany as well as for the United States. At no point was Sackett able to use foreign loan policy to gain concessions or as a means to reinforce diplomacy. He learned of the large loans being offered to the German government through rumors, and then cautioned the State Department about the danger they posed to

1 Memorandum by Karl Schubert, state secretary in the Foreign Ministry, 21 March 1930, ADAP, 14: 392–393.
2 Curtius Memorandum, 5 November 1930, Hans Schäffer, state secretary in the Finance Ministry, Memorandum, 21 March 1930, and Schäffer to Bülow, 10 March 1931, GFMR 2382/E197001–197002, 2375/E192122, and 2247/E111763.

German financial stability. When Sackett's knowledge and skill were brought to bear, the problems in finance had reached crisis proportions. Sackett had almost nothing to do with American loans to Germany, almost all of which were negotiated before he took up his post in Berlin. Those loans and American economic diplomacy were, however, critical to understanding American policy toward Germany and the problems Sackett inherited when he assumed his responsibilities.

Hundreds of millions of dollars in loans to Germany were organized by Americans and were transacted entirely in the private sector. The personnel involved were the unofficial diplomats of the United States government. The practice of conducting national economic diplomacy through private channels was part of a deliberate policy that had been adopted by the three Republican administrations following World War I. This blurring of the lines between the public and private sectors was not peculiar to the United States. The powers in Western Europe experienced a similar phenomenon.[3]

Since the end of the war, leading businessmen and bankers had played a significant role in the formulation and execution of public policy. The system of cooperation between the private and public sectors was meant to avoid the worst aspects of what were seen as the extremes of laissez-faire on the one hand and statism on the other. In Europe and the United States it was generally believed that expertise was the ingredient that would make this new formula work. In the United States, financial foreign policy became the special province of private sector experts who played decisive roles in formulating the Dawes and Young plans. These "public ministers without portfolio," men such as Charles G. Dawes, Thomas W. Lamont, and Owen D. Young, were perceived to be more in tune with the needs and aspirations of the general public, by which American leadership meant the investing public, and hence more likely to pursue democratic policy than government bureaucrats. Moreover, they were held to be better prepared to carry out public economic policy than any other group.

The Young Plan and the loan that accompanied it are an excellent example of private sector diplomacy at work. All the delegations, European and American, that made up the Young committee were private sector experts in finance. They were given the authority to act for their governments, and their final product was accepted by all the governments involved. It fulfilled public policy for each nation and was parallel with mutual goals of the public and private sectors. Private sector involvement for government purposes during the interwar years has come to be called "corporatism." It was a system in which organized private groups in business and labor, as well as consumers, were assigned public purposes defined by their governments.

---

3 Charles S. Maier, *Recasting Bourgeois Europe: Stabilization in France, Germany, and Italy in the Decade After World War I,* is a major study on corporatism in Europe.

The United States played a special role in Germany. Convinced that a stable Europe was in the nation's best interest, American leadership embarked on a program of lending money to Germany on the assumption that secure economic conditions there would lead to political stability, not only in Germany but throughout Europe as well. In the American view, Germany was the linchpin holding together a stable Europe. The United States therefore chose to see to it that Germany had all the money necessary to insure a stable economy. In the period 1925 to 1930 the American private sector loaned close to $3 billion to Germany – an amount more than twice the $1.3 billion the United States extended to the Germans under the post-World War II Marshall Plan.[4]

In the United States, the decision to invest great financial power in the private sector was motivated in part by the desire to stimulate profits to strengthen the domestic economy. But in a deeper sense the Americans, as well as the Europeans, were faced with the enormous costs of the world war. Leaders in government and business were moved by the desire to preserve and strengthen their own positions, which were threatened by the destabilized postwar conditions. To that end, the bourgeoisie in both the United States and Western Europe restructured their societies by granting more power than ever to the private sector. It was not a restoration of prewar society but, rather, a "displacement of power" in which elected officials and bureaucrats gave way to the "major organized forces" in the society and economy. This reorganization tended to blur the distinction between state and society, or between the government and the marketplace.[5]

In the United States economic diplomacy was an integral part of the corporatist scheme. In general, the policy was followed throughout the 1920s with the government actively assisting private investors. As secretary of commerce, Herbert Hoover had organized a vast foreign office within his department to alert American business to opportunities in foreign trade and finance. Investors responded with alacrity to the point where even Hoover was disturbed by the nature and extent of American loans to Germany.[6]

Secretary of the Treasury Andrew D. Mellon suggested that by granting

4 William C. McNeil, *American Money and the Weimar Republic*, 1-2; Jonas, *United States and Germany*, 161–196.
5 Maier, *Recasting Bourgeois Europe*, 8–10; Ellis W. Hawley, "Herbert Hoover and American Corporatism, 1929–1933," 101–119; a succinct definition can be found in Michael J. Hogan, "Corporatism," in Michael J. Hogan and Thomas G. Paterson, *Explaining the History of American Foreign Relations*, 226–236, and Michael J. Hogan, "Thomas W. Lamont and European Recovery: The Diplomacy of Privatism in a Corporatist Age," 5–7, 22. See also Herbert Feis, *Diplomacy of the Dollar*, Joseph Brandes, *Herbert Hoover and Economic Diplomacy*, and Richard Hemmig Meyer, *Banker's Diplomacy*.
6 Brandes, *Herbert Hoover and Economic Diplomacy*, 4–21, 184–185; Richard Hofstadter, *The American Political Tradition, and the Men Who Made It*, 290–292; Hoover, *Memoirs*, 2: 40–46, 79–91.

or denying private funds to the governments of Europe, American policy goals, such as payment of war debts, would be fulfilled. Secretary Hoover expressed the same interest, with the added proviso that investors should be guarded against poor loans. He hoped to provide this protection by disclosing information necessary to judge the soundness of investments and by public statements and private advice to bankers. In the State Department, Secretaries Hughes and then Kellogg were not eager to accept such broad responsibilities. Kellogg agreed that a "watch" was needed "in order that the Department of State may be in a position better to assist American undertakings abroad and may not be embarrassed in the application of its general policies."[7]

The policy worked too well. As American investments abroad reached record proportions, words of caution were expressed to dissuade American bankers from making unwise and unsound loans to Germany. S. Parker Gilbert, the American agent-general for reparations in Europe, had been sounding the warning for years that it would not be wise to lend large sums of money to an overborrowing Germany. In a letter to an American banker, he expressed his amazement at "the recklessness of American bankers" in offering the securities of German states to the public.[8] It was Gilbert's job to see to it that Germany remained fiscally solvent enough to be able to pay reparations.

Both Gilbert and the State Department objected to the excessive borrowing by German states and municipalities. As acting secretary of state, Wilbur J. Carr wrote Ambassador Schurman to warn that if the German government did not exercise some control over loans to the German states, the American government "might find itself obliged to consider seriously, both in its interest and in that of the general situation, measures designed to put a check on improvident borrowing."[9] It is important to note that the State Department warned the Germans against the folly of borrowing, but did not warn the American unofficial diplomats of the folly of lending.

The problem had become sensitive because of the dual role played by the government. On the one hand, the Commerce Department provided the "facts" to encourage investment: on the other, the State Department, acting as the official representative abroad, disavowed any involvement in the matter. It simply wished to be informed. Rather than act in concerted fashion to curb wild speculation, the various department heads circulated

---

7 Feis, *Diplomacy of the Dollar*, 8–9; see John Foster Dulles, "Our Foreign Loan Policy," *Foreign Affairs*, 5 (October 1926): 33–48.

8 U.S. Senate, Finance Committee, *Hearings*, 72 Cong. 1 Sess., "Sale of Foreign Bonds or Securities in the United States," 1581; Gilbert's letter is dated 3 November 1926.

9 Carr to Schurman, 26 September 1927, *Papers Relating to the Foreign Relations of the United States*, 1927, 2: 728–729, hereafter cited FRUS; see warnings by Gilbert to the State Department reproduced in Robert R. Kuczynski, *Bankers' Profits from German Loans*, 207–224.

warnings cautiously and quietly to bankers in the hope they might be heeded. No one in the government wanted to appear in the position of thwarting American initiative and enterprise. The hope was that, given enough information, bankers would voluntarily make the right choice. Not a single loan was ever denied under the corporatist system.[10]

Ambassador Sackett was a fledgling diplomat, but with considerable experience in business and banking. It was unfortunate, therefore, that he was not fully informed about the nature and extent of the loans made to Germany before he became ambassador. When he arrived in Berlin early in 1930, a major loan was being negotiated by the German government with American financiers. In keeping with corporatism, the American embassy in Berlin was kept in the dark as the Germans turned to the United States for money to ride out the short-term problems brought on by the depression. Financial problems had shaken the government and threatened the existence of the Great Coalition under Social Democratic Chancellor Hermann Müller. The Germans turned to the American banking firm of Dillon, Read and Company for a loan of $75 million to $100 million. The plan was stillborn after Hjalmar Schacht, president of the Reichsbank, opposed the transaction, insisting he could raise the necessary funds within Germany.[11] That was the position Sackett would take later when he learned of a subsequent loan.

Ambassador Schurman reported that failure to negotiate the American loan was the occasion for a cabinet crisis.[12] That did not deter Schacht, who was aware that aside from the aborted Dillon, Read loan there were two sources of foreign aid imminent. If approved, the Young Plan would include a substantial foreign loan. In addition, the Swedish "Match King," Ivar Kreuger, in the fall of 1929 proposed to loan the German government $125 million in return for a fifty-year monopoly of the nation's match industry and market.[13] Schacht privately contacted George Murnane, a partner in the venerable Boston firm of Lee, Higginson and Company,

10 Joan Hoff Wilson, *American Business and Foreign Policy*, 104–107; Brandes, *Herbert Hoover and Economic Diplomacy*, 185–186.
11 Gilbert to the Federal Reserve Bank of New York, 17, 19, 20, and 21 December 1929, enclosed with George L. Harrison, governor, Federal Reserve Bank of New York, to Joseph Cotton, undersecretary of state, 862.51/2819; Hans Luther, *Vor dem Abgrund*, 62; Hjalmar Schacht, *76 Jahre meines Lebens*, 323; Helga Timm, *Die deutsche Sozialpolitik und der Bruch der Grossen Koalition im März 1930*, 158; Schurman to State, 13 and 17 December 1929, 862.51/2811 and 462.00R296/3533; Gilbert to Federal Reserve Bank of New York, 10 and 12 January 1930, Serial Numbers 1792 and 1808, Binder 1, George L. Harrison Papers.
12 Schurman to State, 20 December 1929, 862.51/2812; Eyck, *Weimar Republic*, 2: 212–213; Luther, *Vor dem Abgrund*, 62; *New York Times*, 19, 20, 21 December 1929.
13 In many European nations the production and sale of matches was a government monopoly, a means of taxing wide segments of the population.

Kreuger's bankers, and learned that the Boston house would discount the Kreuger loan, making money immediately available to the German government.[14]

Murnane was one of America's unofficial diplomats. He negotiated hundreds of millions of dollars in loans to German governments, national and local. On this occasion, as on the others, his only motive for involvement was to realize a profit for Lee, Higginson and Company and its investors. He saw the loan as "a very high grade obligation" which would be quickly subscribed to by leading American and European banking houses because it was an "attractive short term" loan without political motivation on the part of the bankers.[15]

Ivar Kreuger was a skilled manipulator, a brilliant financier who would be exposed as a charlatan. A genius with timing and presence, he was considered a "European benefactor." What the admiring world did not know was that Kreuger was not in a financial position to make any kind of loan. Lee, Higginson, his American banker, had so much confidence in him that they never conducted an audit of his accounts. Kreuger shocked the world when, on March 12, 1932, he committed suicide. Only then were his financial manipulations revealed. The Lee, Higginson organization never recovered from the debacle. The firm's partners lost millions of dollars, while investors lost even more.[16] Ironically, at the same time, Samuel Insull, the utilities magnate who had the run-in with Sackett, fled the United States to avoid prosecution in another matter.

Before the world was aware that Kreuger was a swindler, he played the role of hero to the hilt while negotiating to extricate himself from his immediate financial problems. As just noted, the Lee, Higginson firm had always taken Kreuger at his word and thus had no way of knowing that the Swede had no money to loan. When he was exposed and the U.S. Senate began to investigate his activity, corporatism came in for severe condemnation. There was not only wide-ranging criticism but general

---

14 Eyck, *Weimar Republic*, 2: 230–231; *New York Times*, 29 September, 11, 13, 22 October 1929, 25 January 1930; George Murnane to Bernard V. Burke, 11 April 1966. On Kreuger, see Robert Shaplen, *Kreuger*, 129–130, 135–136, 163; Lewis L. Strauss, *Men and Decisions*, 96–97; Bernard V. Burke, "American Economic Diplomacy and the Weimar Republic," 213–217.

15 Murnane to Burke, 11 April 1966.

16 Edgar Racey to Edgar Racey, Jr., 3 May 1966; U.S. Senate, Subcommittee of the Committee on Banking and Currency, *Hearings*, 72 Cong. 2 Sess., "Stock Exchange Practises [*sic*]," Part 4, "Kreuger and Toll," 1146–1234, 1354; Samuel E. Morison, *Oxford History of the American People*, 939; C. E. Cotting, Lee Higginson Corporation, to Bernard V. Burke, 25 March 1966; *New York Times*, 15 August 1966. British Ambassador Ronald Lindsay reported that Lee, Higginson "is drawing in its horns tremendously," Lindsay to R. L. Craigie, 17 June 1932, British Foreign Office, United States Correspondence, 1932, Reel 6, Volume 15871, Frames 114–115, hereafter cited FO371 followed by year, reel, volume, and frame numbers.

disappointment with, and distrust of, the financiers in the private sector, who were held responsible for allowing the world's finances to deteriorate so badly.

Sackett, who already had expressed his displeasure with the operations of international financiers, was emboldened to launch an attack on them even before the Kreuger exposure. He was developing a growing distrust of the corporatist system and the financial "experts" who conducted all foreign loan activity. During the 1931 financial crisis, when Castle suggested that Sackett appeal to German patriotism to place foreign credits in the Reichsbank, the ambassador responded with a verbal explosion. Such an appeal to patriotism was "bound to fail" because it "would be addressed chiefly to a class of international money lenders notoriously not controlled by patriotism (you of course realize that the whole financial structure in Germany is in the hands of this class)."[17]

When Herbert Feis, the State Department economic adviser, read Sackett's protests, he was in full accord. He went further, stating: "But I do think that the Germans themselves are contributing to their difficulty by seeking even more resourcefully than the American bankers to get their funds out of the country." Sackett was harping on a theme he repeated often, that loans to Germany needed to be converted to long-term, or "at least a semi long-term character." Sackett had been conferring with bank officials "who have suddenly come over from America to look after their credits. . . . All are worried about the repayment of the money they have here on short loans." The ambassador was afraid that the losses from the loans would ultimately be transferred from "the books of the loaning banks to the United States Government. These loans to-day constitute the bulk of the working capital of German industry." Sackett was pointing to a major fault in the corporatist system. The private sector was concerned only with the profitability of its loans. Any failures, he feared, would become the responsibility of the federal government.[18]

There was some partisanship involved in the disillusionment of so many people. Felix Frankfurter, who would be appointed to the Supreme Court by Franklin Roosevelt, and Feis, who would stay on at the State Department in the Democratic administration, already had disparaging remarks to make about the expert financiers who had led the nation into so much financial trouble. Frankfurter fumed: "Nothing makes me sicker than that these incompetent leaders of finance should still swagger around as though they were entitled to respect." Feis seconded his friend's views, further adding that the Senate investigators "did not know how to cope with their smooth exposition and self-satisfied composure. . . . [The bankers] haven't

17 Sackett to Castle, 12 July 1931, 462.00R296/4437; the paraphrase in FRUS, 1931, 1: 251, softens the language to "international financiers."
18 Feis to Castle, 20 October 1931; Sackett to Stimson, 3 October 1931, Castle Papers–Germany, HHPL.

any conscience in the matter and little concern outside of the main chance."[19]

Despite the lack of confidence that would permeate American and European societies, there was still a somewhat hopeful mood right after the stock market crash. In one of his earliest financial reports Sackett noted that the German loan market "showed a surprising and unexpected improvement."[20] In that same month, March 1930, the Lee, Higginson discount of the Kreuger loan to the German government appeared to be the answer to meet their immediate needs. But not before there was considerable turmoil over the advisability of extending such a large loan.

It should be noted that the State Department was involved in foreign loan policy, but usually only at the end of negotiation, when pro forma approval of loans was requested of them. Official diplomats in the field were not informed at all by the government about loan requests or negotiations. British and German diplomats experienced the same handicap. Among British diplomats there was considerable unhappiness that all important economic matters were controlled by the Treasury. The Foreign Office initially ignored the issue and, until 1931, did not require an examination in economics for its foreign service applicants.[21] As a result of British policy their diplomats were not able to use economic concessions as a political weapon. The British even envied the State Department having an economic adviser and pleaded that they needed someone "who spoke the language of Treasurers." Robert Vansittart expressed the need for someone to address "the best financiers of the U.S.A. on level terms."[22]

Otto Kiep of the German embassy in Washington was unaware of the loan transactions taking place in the American private sector with his government. He complained to the Foreign Ministry that he was made ineffective because he was not informed about loan negotiations between Germany and the United States. Furthermore, he reported his embarrassment at being "fully uninformed" while talking with Murnane and other bankers in New York. Diplomats did not want to control loan policy, but they did want to use economic policy to reinforce diplomacy.[23]

Sackett was disturbed when he learned of the proposed Lee, Higginson loan. He only learned of the offer through rumors in Berlin and reported

---

19 Frankfurter to Feis, 19 December and Feis to Frankfurter, 22 December 1931, Box 54, Felix Frankfurter Papers.

20 Sackett to State, 3 March 1930, 862.51/2852.

21 Norman Rose, *Vansittart, Study of a Diplomat*, 99–100.

22 Lindsay to Vansittart, 21 January 1932, Vansittart to Warren Fisher, Treasury, 19 February 1932, and H. A. Caccia, Minute, 8 February 1932, FO371, 1932, 9, 15877: 327, 329, 323.

23 Norton Medlicott, "Britain and Germany: The Search for Agreement, 1930–1937," 1: 80–81; Kiep to Bülow, 30 September 1930, GFMR 2384/E198636–198638; other Germans complained of the same problem, see Ernst Eisenlohr to Paul Modenhauer, 15 March 1930, GFMR 2384/E198636–198638, 2247/E111843–111844.

to Washington as the original source of information about it. He explained that "a person of very high authority" confirmed that the loan was to be consummated. Of course, Sackett, an official representative of the U.S. government, was not privy to this important part of financial diplomacy; it was the concern of unofficial diplomats in the private sector. As Murnane later explained, loans to Germany "were initiated, negotiated and distributed among a limited number of bank participants without any involvement of 'American diplomats.'" The banker's relations with Sackett were never "more than pleasant visits."[24] The State Department was not yet aware of Murnane's negotiations with the Germans.

Sackett consulted with German officials and was convinced that the loan was inadvisable. His "person of high authority," he said, agreed that there was no immediate need for such a "huge loan." Sackett was perturbed that "there is evident secrecy on the part of both the government and bankers about the negotiations."[25] Another American, and unofficial diplomat, S. Parker Gilbert, as agent-general for reparations, intervened to stop the transaction. His responsibility was to see that the provisions of the Young Plan were fulfilled. Gilbert wanted to protect the market for the purchase of the $300 million worth of securities that were organized by the House of Morgan and would be issued to the public as part of the Young Plan. When Gilbert heard about the Lee, Higginson discount of the Kreuger loan, he voiced strong objections, mainly because the loan was to be offered to the public and therefore would compete with the general reparations settlement represented by the Young Plan loan.[26]

Sackett believed Gilbert was acting in the interest of France and J. P. Morgan and Company, with which Gilbert would soon be a senior partner. The House of Morgan had avoided lending to the former enemy, Germany, and their political sympathies were with Britain and France.[27] The French viewed the Lee, Higginson loan as political and joined Gilbert in the successful attempt to keep it out of the public marketplace. Finally, Schacht wired the Morgan firm to assure them that the loan would not threaten the market share of the Young Plan loan; it would be handled, he wrote, "as a merely credit operation."[28]

---

24 Murnane to Burke, 25 April 1966.
25 Sackett to State, 20 March 1930, 862.51/2846. For details of the Lee, Higginson discount of the Kreuger loan, see FRUS, 1930, 3: 96–102; Burke, "American Economic Diplomacy and the Weimar Republic," 213–223.
26 Gilbert to State, 21 March, 862.51/2847; Cotton to the embassies in Paris and Berlin, 22 March, 862.51/2849; Norman Armour to Cotton, Paris, 24 March, 862.51/2849; Sackett to Cotton, 26 March 1930, 862.51/2853.
27 Kathleen Burk, "Diplomacy and the Private Banker: The Case of the House of Morgan," 32, 38–39.
28 Schacht to J. P. Morgan and Co., 17 March 1930, GFMR 2247/E111956. German interest in the problem led to the creation of a separate file, "Fall Murnane" (the Murnane Case), in GFMR 2247/111832–112074.

Murnane shared Sackett's fear that Gilbert was working in the French interest. The banker expressed concern to the Germans that France and the State Department might "veto" the Lee, Higginson loan.[29] That is precisely what Gilbert hoped to accomplish, but without success. Sackett was required to struggle for information throughout the entire transaction. The principals to the negotiation simply did not let him know what was happening. His informants included Walter de Haas of the German Foreign Ministry, who insisted that the entire affair had been a great "psychological error." Not only had the Germans not consulted Gilbert, but those involved had behaved like "utter asses."[30] Sackett, De Haas, and their diplomatic colleagues agreed that the loan would provide the Germans with more time to avoid responsibility for their fiscal problems. Pierre Jay, the American assistant director of the Bank for International Settlements, expressed the same view. He wrote George Harrison, governor of the Federal Reserve Bank of New York, that Germany's financial difficulties stemmed "from an unwillingness during the past three years on the part of all the public authorities, and in the absence of any authoritative leader in Germany, to exercise economy and keep expenses within the available public funds."[31] In spite of Sackett's foreboding, shared by many, the transaction was brought to a successful conclusion. Murnane simply informed Gilbert that the contract would be signed.[32]

Just as the Lee, Higginson discount of the Kreuger loan was brought to a conclusion, the Young Plan loan emerged, in a more conventional fashion because Gilbert had played a part in its evolution. In keeping with the corporatist outlook, the American embassy in Berlin had been irrelevant to the entire process in both loans. As already noted it was characteristic of the time to believe that international finance could be kept clear and distinct from international politics; it was thought that "in the main the dollar should conduct its own diplomacy, select its own assignments, and make its own terms."[33]

When the Young Plan loan was announced, one American investors' service, in assessing prospects for its clients, was able to say that the Young Plan, "which is obviously a considerable improvement on the former reparations obligations, has taken them out of the political sphere, made the German debt a normal element of international finance, and relieved all controversial uncertainty; Germany will be enabled to raise the necessary foreign loans."[34] Although it must have been clear to any observer

29 German Ambassador Leopold von Hoesch in Paris to Foreign Ministry, 25 March 1930, ADAP, 14: 412–413.
30 Sackett to State, 2 April 1930, 862.51/2861.
31 Pierre Jay to George Harrison, 13 December 1929 – Jay, Pierre (April 1920–January 1943), Harrison Papers.
32 Gilbert to State, 21 and 22 March 1930, 862.51/2847; FRUS, 1930, 3: 96–102.
33 Feis, *Diplomacy of the Dollar*, 6.
34 *Moody's Investors Service*, "Foreign Letters Guide," No. 12, 8 July 1929, F40.

that the American government was cooperating with financiers to the best of its ability, the fiction that international money was taken out of politics was preserved because the government, though assisting, did not interfere.

The handling of the Young Plan loan in March 1930 epitomizes the close relationship of the State Department and unofficial diplomats and offers an excellent example of one form of the corporatist system. Thomas W. Lamont spoke for J. P. Morgan and Company, the managing bank for the loan. The personal relationship of the diplomats and financiers is clear from the letter to Acting Secretary of State Joseph Cotton, addressed "Dear Joe." Lamont set out the terms of the loan, which was to produce $300 million. Lamont commented that the "arrangement strikes us as excellent" because it engaged "the further good will and cooperation of Germany."

Lamont explained to Cotton that the loan had merit because it meant the fulfillment of American foreign policy, which the unofficial diplomat was carrying out. Asking for official affirmation that the loan met the standards of the State Department, Lamont argued that the loan conformed to those criteria because[35]

> this is the final liquidation of the War so far as the settlement of great economic questions is concerned, and obviously it is greatly to the interest of American trade to have this great Reparations question settled. Second, it was a cardinal principle of the American delegates at the Young Conference to urge that Germany be taken effecively out of receivership . . . and that she be put upon her honor to carry out her obligations. We feel that in this way the good will of her people could be best engaged. The present plan carries out that principle which is, if I may call it so, an American one and was well recognized and appreciated at the time by the German delegates.

Not only was Lamont saying that the loan would continue and further American policy with respect to Germany, he was also vouching for the soundness of the investment for the American public.

Since, unlike the Lee, Higginson transaction, the Young Plan issue would be offered to the American public, both the State Department and the financiers were more cautious. Members of Congress and the press were expressing vociferous opposition to the clandestine relationship between Washington and Wall Street. Corporatism was coming in for serious attacks. Lamont cautioned Cotton: "If you find by April 4th or 5th that there is serious difficulty at Washington, *then that fact should be privately communicated to me* through our firm here."[36] Obviously neither official government nor widespread public involvement in the loan process was acceptable to the bankers. They especially wanted to avoid interference by elected officials. Above all, the American leadership tended to think of the general public as being the same as the investing public.

35 Lamont to Cotton, 27 March 1930, FRUS, 1930, 3: 102–103.
36 Lamont to Cotton, 27 March 1930, FRUS, 1930, 32: 103, emphasis added.

The Young Plan went smoothly through the usual channels of American financial diplomacy – Wall Street, the State Department, and the president's office – all of it on the assumption that the government was not involved in any significant way. The private sector was executing American loan policy, and, as Lamont said, the plan was "an American one" and the State Department had no reason to object. The secretary of state informed J. P. Morgan, for public consumption, that his department "does not desire to interpose objection to the proposed financing."[37]

American policy was dependent on a financially solvent Germany. As long as the United States insisted that European nations pay their war debts to the American government, they would insist that Germany make its reparations payments to them. With the United States refusing to acknowledge publicly that there was any connection between the two problems, Germany was isolated, apparently with no alternative to paying reparations. The American financial community, however, with the full agreement of the U.S. government, provided an option for the Germans. The Americans agreed to loan money to the Germans in sufficient quantities to enable them to pay reparations, which in turn enabled America's debtors to pay on their war-related borrowing. The United States treated Europe as if it were a single entity, which made it difficult to sort out problems. There was considerable disagreement within the Hoover administration respecting this policy. The State Department, under Henry L. Stimson's leadership, was among the major opponents.[38] Nevertheless, the policy remained in place until the debts were effectively annulled.

Outside the administration, some saw the policy as potentially disastrous. One observer in the press commented: "The question is not whether cancellation of reparations and war debts must come. The question is whether it will take a Communist or Fascist dictatorship to bring it about or whether American statesmanship will forestall this or some other equally cataclysmic way of bringing to an end the present impossible situation."[39]

The American investing public was more sanguine. Not only did they not see the potential danger, they wholeheartedly agreed with the policy of loaning to Germany. In most prospectuses for investors, the tendency was to paint the best possible picture. The artistry appeared valid and true, for 135 loans to Germany were publicly offered in the United States during the years 1924–1931.[40] The investing public was informed; the fact is, they simply agreed with the policy. In outlining Germany's prospects as an investment market under the Young Plan loan, Moody's Investors Service

37 Stimson to J. P. Morgan and Co., 22 May 1930, FRUS, 3: 106.
38 Godfrey Hodgson, *The Colonel, The Life and Wars Of Henry Stimson, 1867–1950*, 195–212; Henry L. Stimson and McGeorge Bundy, *On Active Service in Peace and War*, 195, 212.
39 Lawrence Dennis, " 'Sold' On Foreign Bonds," *New Republic*, 3 December 1930, 65: 65.
40 Kuczynski, *Bankers' Profits From German Loans*, 150–155.

spelled out the policy and the problem clearly. It is quite evident, investors were informed, "that Germany can secure sufficient foreign currency only by continuing to borrow largely from abroad for some time to come ... the funds will be needed to provide new working capital and to replace the capital paid out for reparations." Drawing a historical analogy, the financial experts pointed out that "it is obvious that the problem of Germany's ability to pay is merely dependent on long-term borrowing for a period of time, following the example of the United States which was a debtor nation for over a century."

When the advice was published, in the summer of 1929, Hitler had not yet joined Hugenberg and the Nationalists in their campaign against the Young Plan. Therefore it was possible not to see any German political party as powerful enough to interfere with the loan. That enabled Moody's Investors Service to predict that "it is extremely unlikely that any party in the countries concerned would wish to shoulder the risk of its repudiation."[41] It would not be very long before American diplomats, official and unofficial, were very much concerned. Financiers were thought to be in closer touch with the public than bureaucrats. The moneymen conceived the policy of taking reparations out of the arena of politics as one way to engage the good will of Germany. They were incredibly wrong. They seriously misunderstood the temper of the German people. In a short time Hitler and the Nazis would emerge to tap the mood that would threaten the entire American scheme. Hitler, who did understand the Germans, called for the repudiation of reparations. In the minds of American diplomats and bankers, he was a perilous threat to the entire financial structure of Europe. They feared he represented the denial of all debts, public and private. A more serious threat to American interests was hard to imagine.

Sackett registered his objections to American foreign loan policy only in the case of the Lee, Higginson discount of the Kreuger loan. Otherwise, he remained outside the entire loaning system. He was, however, concerned that extremist groups in Germany might upset American financial diplomacy. That meant that the activities of the German Communist party had to be carefully watched. Sackett's concern for the dangers of communism were alleviated when, in his view, a new government emerged to nullify that threat and to carry out the policy that would save the republic and American interests in it. The man he believed could rescue the Weimar Republic was Heinrich Brüning.

A colorless figure who never won popular support, Brüning was a bachelor in his mid-forties. He was prominent in the Center party, and although associated with the Catholic trade unions, he was known as an economic conservative with a nationalist political outlook and monarchist

41 *Moody's Investors Service,* "Foreign Letters Guide," 8 July 1929, F-38–39.

tendencies that he rarely revealed in public. He appealed to President Hindenburg partly because he had won the Iron Cross as a front-line soldier in the world war.

Brüning and the Center party precipitated a crisis for the Great Coalition over the nation's weak financial condition. The major partners of the governing coalition divided over Brüning's call for a policy of retrenchment.[42] The Social Democrats were opposed, while the Center party joined in advocating the policy that the People's party had long advocated. In one of his first cables to the State Department, Sackett pointed out that the Social Democrats were concerned that their participation in the government might cause them to lose voter support to the Nazis and Communists. They had to contend with "dangerous competition for the labor vote from the extremes of both Right and Left." The Social Democrats were wary of being identified with a program designed to save capitalism in Germany. In addition, it was no secret that not only Hindenburg but the Center and People's parties wanted to oust Social Democratic leadership in the Reich. That meant the Socialists were less likely than ever to compromise. As Sackett put it, they would "not readily yield to 'bourgeois' demands."[43]

The Young Plan and disagreement over financial reform had split the Great Coalition wide open. At issue also was the fundamental question of whether industry or labor should bear the major burden in the economic crisis. Forces behind the scenes were maneuvering to settle the matter. Unaware of what was happening, Sackett, in Berlin less than two months, wrote his sister at the end of March 1930 that most diplomatic contacts were made socially and went on to explain: "Calls do not yield much opportunity. However I've met most of the leading Bankers in Germany as many were written to by banking friends of mine in New York who asked them to call. That has given me a very general and quick business acquaintance which has been valuable in getting me started." The ambassador had gravitated toward the familiar in the banking and business community, where there was relative stability in officeholders. The political situation was so confused, Sackett wrote, that although he was "getting quite well acquainted with the political people ... you never know who will be in office as ministers of the cabinet tomorrow."[44]

Faced with dissension in his government, and too tired and ill to cope with its internal problems, Socialist Chancellor Hermann Müller resigned with his entire cabinet on the evening of March 27. Confronted with the silent hostility of the president and the power brokers around him, the

42 Sackett to State, 3 and 5 March 1930, 862.51/2852, 2854; McNeil, *American Money and the Weimar Republic*, 238–240.
43 Sackett to State, 27 February and 5 March 1930, 862.51/2839 and 2854.
44 Sackett to Mrs. Hazard, 29 March 1930, Sackett Papers; George Harrison to Pierre Jay, deputy agent-general for reparations payments, 16 March 1930, Box 3, Harrison Papers.

Social Democrats had little chance of remaining in the cabinet. Hindenburg was tired of government by Socialists and welcomed the chance to get rid of Müller. For their part, the Socialists welcomed the greater freedom they would have outside the government. Sackett thought they would now be able "to cope better with the Communist competition for the labor vote. They will undoubtedly seek also to check the rapid growth of the National-Socialists whose demagogic slogans and tactics appeal to the working classes to whom the large labor party must look for support."[45]

Sackett was not privy to what was happening behind the scenes but was not surprised when Brüning was named chancellor on March 30, 1930. He did anticipate the authoritarian nature of the new cabinet. Appointed by the president, Brüning did not have majority support in the Reichstag, but he did have the full support of the president. Sackett explained that "President Hindenburg is committed to employ all constitutional means at his disposal to promulgate necessary financial measures in case budget failed of passage by April 1st." To his sister he complained that "the whole government resigned on Friday and today we have a new one and must make contacts all over again."[46]

While this political crisis worked to its conclusion Sackett and his staff turned their attention to the opposition parties. It was difficult to assess which of the extremist parties posed the greatest threat to the Weimar Republic. Sackett, under the influence of his chief professional aide, John Cooper Wiley, focused on the growing threat of Hitler and the Nazi party. At the same time he discounted the importance of the German Communist party. Wiley made an important impression on Sackett, especially since he was in effect his training officer. The professional diplomat had a low opinion of the effectiveness of the German Communist party and was not prone to follow an ideological approach to the Soviet Union. In his view, some Americans were always prepared to overemphasize "routine and unimportant Comintern activities."[47]

Still, with the Nazis as well as the Communists advocating anticapitalist solutions to German economic problems, it was difficult to point to the one party that was the greater threat to the troubled republic and to American interests.[48] Sackett began to move in the direction of discounting the immediate importance of the German Communist party as a danger to the republic. He reported a conversation he had with a prominent German

45 Sackett to State, 29 March 1930, 862.002/199.
46 Sackett to State, 28 March 1930, 862.00/2487; Sackett to Mrs. Hazard, 29 March 1930, Sackett Papers.
47 Frederic L. Propas, "Creating a Hard Line Toward Russia: The Training of State Department Soviet Experts, 1927–1937," 223–225.
48 Calvin Hoover, *Memoirs of Capitalism, Communism and Nazism*, 133; Alexander Gumberg to Senator William E. Borah, 14 July 1931, Box 5, Alexander Gumberg Papers.

newspaper editor. The newsman "described excessive fear of Bolshevism as part of the pessimism now prevalent in Germany with Moscow suspected of a hand in every event." Sackett explained that the German emphasized that after more than a decade of stressing the communist threat, nothing had happened. The ambassador went on to speculate that "in view of the sound common sense of the German laborers, it is hard to believe that Bolshevism could do serious damage in Germany today."[49]

Sackett, who had little direct experience with communism, learned of the nature of the Soviet impact on Germany from Wiley, who attributed Communist street fighting and other excesses to orders from Moscow. But they were merely a maneuver to divert attention from problems in the Soviet Union. The professional diplomat also saw the excesses as a tactic of the Communists to take advantage of growing unemployment, which provided fertile ground for militant propaganda. The Social Democrats, Wiley reported, saw the disorders as part of a strategy to deal the republic a fatal blow. The Socialists believed that the Communists, unable to achieve their own ends, were trying to force the government to institute a dictatorship.[50] The Communists perceived that any disruption of the capitalist republic was to their advantage.

Careful observers of the political scene tended to denigrate the dangers coming from the German Communist party. An American economist visiting Germany at the time observed: "I was astonished to find that neither Junkers nor industrialists had any great fear of Communism." The Communists had been put down easily in November 1918 and as a result were held in very low esteem by German conservatives. The observer went on: "The repeated defeats of Communist-led strikes and riots through the year and the incredibly inept Communist leadership had confirmed this feeling of contempt."[51]

The former American ambassador in Berlin, Jacob Gould Schurman, had paid almost no attention to the Nazis even though Hitler and his party played a prominent role in the campaign against the Young Plan. Sackett accorded them more attention, but placed them in the context of communist radicalism. By associating the Nazis with the Communist party in Germany, Sackett's reports lost much of the impact they might have had in Washington, where there was a tendency to ignore the Nazis. On the other hand, the German Communist party was considered one of the strongest and best organized in the world, outside the Soviet Union. Its activity was therefore a matter of major concern in Washington. In spite of State Department emphasis on the Communists, after Sackett arrived in Berlin the American embassy tended to disparage them and focus on the radical

49 Sackett to State, 25 March 1930, 862.00B/156. Sackett had talked with Georg Bernhard, editor of the Democratic *Vossische Zeitung*.
50 Wiley to State, 3 February 1930, 862.00B/145.
51 Calvin Hoover, *Memoirs of Capitalism, Communism and Nazism*, 131.

danger posed by the Nazis. Not until the Nazis' electoral success forced their attention on the world did diplomats in Washington begin to take them seriously.

It was under Sackett's leadership that the Nazis were introduced to the State Department. Just before Sackett arrived in Berlin, Wiley filed the first important report on the Hitler party. He recognized that very little was known outside Germany about "the role played by the National Socialists, or Hitlerites, who are usually known abroad as the German Fascists." This radical Right group, he wrote, served its interests by magnifying the danger of large scale Communist uprisings.[52] Not yet called "Nazis" by the Americans, the Hitler party was viewed as a growing phenomenon, especially since it had been successful in attracting Nationalist followers away from Hugenberg.[53] Sackett was quick to see the growing importance of Hitler and his party. They were growing, and not only at the expense of parties on the political Right. The danger he saw was that they were recruiting followers from the ranks of the Social Democrats, the most ardent supporters of the Weimar Republic. The Socialists, he wrote, had to be "zealous" to protect their position among labor voters against inroads from the Hitler party.[54]

Sackett agreed with Wiley in favoring the Social Democrats in almost all their reports. The Socialists were seen as the major bulwark for democracy and the republic, and the principal force to prevent the ascendancy of either the Right or the Left. Sackett complimented them for their "cooperation in Government with the bourgeois parties" and maintained that their posture had "served to stabilize the Republic." The ambassador pointed out that the Socialists were particularly strong in Prussia, "the former Junker stronghold and now the citadel of the Republic."[55] All the more reason to be concerned that they might be losing followers to the Nazis.

Sackett believed that the Social Democrats were strong enough to counter the extreme parties in a new election, even if, as expected, there was an increase in support for Nazis and Communists. The strength of the Socialists, he reported, should not be "underestimated," and with unemployment in their favor Sackett predicted that their role in a new Reichstag would be "decisive." In addition, in Sackett's analysis, there was slight danger of an authoritarian government as was happening in nations outside Germany because of the strength of the Social Democrats. In those "other countries" the "labor elements are not so well organized politically as in Germany."[56] The Communist party, on the other hand, was seen as an unrelieved potential menace, though its actions were often perceived as inefficient and

52 Wiley to State, 3 February 1930, 862.00B/145.
53 Wiley to State, 3 February 1930, 862.00PR/59.
54 Sackett to State, 5 March 1930, 862.51/2854.
55 Sackett to State, 22 March 1930, 862.00/2492.
56 Sackett to State, 6 and 14 April 1930, 862.00/2494 and 862.00PR/64.

incompetent. Whereas Socialist demonstrations were "impressive," Communist activity was "puerile," their hunger march "a fiasco."[57]

Sackett began to perceive the Nazis and Communists as two sides of the same coin, and without exception assessed the Nazis as the more dangerous of the two. He did not share the confusion of many observers as to which party posed the more serious threat to the Weimar Republic. Mid-March was the tenth anniversary of the Kapp Putsch, and Ambassador Sackett's staff took the occasion to write a report on the changes in political alignment in the decade since the abortive coup. After outlining the history of the putsch, an early attempt to overthrow the republic and reestablish the monarchy, Sackett pointed out that the Nazis were now the extreme Right party in German politics, replacing the Nationalists. Of the extreme Left, he reported:[58]

> The Communist following is much larger than that of their rivals on the extreme Right. Nevertheless their activities in Germany as the last May Day demonstrations in Berlin and the so-called "hunger marches" of this winter have shown, have been for the most part puerile and have caused only a temporary disturbance of the public order. They play no important part in the trade unions which are predominantly under the influence of the Social Democrats and the Center. Their following is recruited chiefly from the ranks of unorganized labor.

Sackett explained that Nazi methods and aims strongly resembled those of the Communist party; that Hitler stressed the party's revolutionary character and openly strove to overthrow the existing political order. Because the overthrow of capitalism and the establishment of socialism was the goal of the communists, Sackett assumed a similar aim for the Nazis.

Americans shared a fixation on communism with almost all the leadership of the Western European world. It was a contributing factor in their tendency to see all radicalism as a form of Bolshevism. That preoccupation led to the need to keep an eye on communism and communists everywhere. In the United States, Robert F. Kelley, chief of the Eastern European desk in the State Department, was quite an enthusiast for any information about communists. Just before Sackett's arrival in Berlin, he wrote Wiley to thank him for at least seven letters on communist activity that he thought were very "meaty." Kelley, somewhat tongue-in-cheek, wanted to hear more "about the present state of Bolshevik world revolutionary strivings. I hope that you will not conclude that you have been feeding us too well, for, as you know, we are very fond of rich food."[59]

The Berlin embassy continued its reporting on Communist party and

---

57 Wiley to State, 3 February 1930, 862.00B/145; Sackett to State, 22 March 1930, 862.00/2492.

58 Sackett to State, 22 and 31 March 1930, 862.00/2492 and 862.00PR/63.

59 Kelley to Wiley, 9 January 1930, Box 1, Wiley Papers.

Nazi activity throughout the spring. Most of the reports were about "the usual hostilities" between the two radical parties. In some places, such as Hamburg, they tolerated each other "on the basis of their mutual interest in overthrowing the state." Sackett saw their repeated clashes as leading to a "growing demand for prohibition against all semi-military organizations."[60]

Comparisons between Nazis and Communists continued apace, with particular attention to Nationalist fears that the Hitler party might make further inroads on their membership. Hugenberg's party was in agreement with Sackett's view that Nazi aims and tactics were the same as those of the Communists. The Nationalists even claimed that the Nazis regarded "Lenin as their ideal." Sackett bought the analogy, reporting that Julius Streicher, "ad latus of . . . Hitler," claimed that "only the Jewish question separates us from the Communists."[61]

Two strains ran through the American ambassador's despatches in the spring of 1930: the growing strength and danger of the Nazi party, and the reluctance of the Weimar parties to face new Reichstag elections. At no time did Sackett see the primary threat to the republic coming from the political Left. He certainly thought the German Communist party was potentially dangerous, and always disruptive, but he never saw the Communists as being as great a danger to the Weimar Republic as the political Right and particularly the National Socialists. Many contemporary observers, and certainly many others since that time, would have us believe that not only was the Communist party the major threat to all democracies, but that the Communists clearly constituted the major threat to the Weimar Republic. It served the purposes of German politicians from conservative to Right radical to perpetuate this fear. In fact, exploiting the "Communist Menace" was a Weimar tradition.[62]

Sackett never abandoned his fear and distaste for communism and particularly his misgivings about the Soviet Union. But that was his long-term fear. In reporting on Weimar Germany, in all his political despatches, he clearly recognized the Nazis as the chief danger to the republic. Sackett believed that the Brüning cabinet was a shift to the political Right designed to counter the Nazis. He cabled that the Right-leaning cabinet "doubtless reflects desire of moderate elements to combat growing influence of

60 Sackett to State, 21 and 28 May, 3 June 1930, 862.00B/171, 172, and 173. Specific reports on communism from the American embassy in Berlin were classified in a special State Department file under the title "Bolshevik Activities in Germany," Decimal File 862.00B. That made them readily accessible to anyone interested in communist activity. Early reporting on the Nazis usually contained material on the Communists as well and was placed in this file.

61 Sackett to State, 25 March 1930, 862.00B/156.

62 Edward Hallet Carr, *German-Soviet Relations Between the Two World Wars*, 9; John M. Thompson, *Russia, Bolshevism, and the Versailles Peace*, 20–21; even Stimson, *On Active Service*, 271, retrospectively wrote that Brüning's "equal enemies were the Nazis and the Communists, and on the whole it was the latter who were more powerful in 1931."

National Socialists." He also reported: "No chancellor has ever entered upon his task with such wide powers as the President is reported to have assured Dr. Brüning." At the same time, Sackett was convinced that the new government was committed to the Weimar Republic. The inclusion of Joseph Wirth, of the Center party, an outspoken advocate of the republic, had special significance for Sackett. The appointment was meant to "counter any contention that the Brüning Cabinet was subject to undue Right tendencies."[63]

The parties in support of the republic were committed to avoiding new elections. They knew that only the extremists could benefit. For that reason, Sackett was disturbed by Hugenberg's insistence on a resort to the polls. The ambassador claimed that Hugenberg knew a vote could only lead to large sections of Nationalist support moving to "the still more radical National Socialists." Because Hugenberg was devoted to destroying the Weimar Republic at almost any cost Sackett was moved to express the hope that Hugenberg's influence in the Nationalist party would "be weakened." What bothered Sackett was that Hugenberg's policy was playing into the hands of the National Socialists, whose strength needed to be "checked." Sackett was alarmed at the Hitler party's "ominous growth."[64]

Whereas Americans were developing their views on Hitler and the Nazis, Hitler's views of Americans and the United States remained constant. He never wavered in "his unshakable conviction that America was decadent and dominated by Jews." His opinion and knowledge of the United States can be summarized in one sentence: Americans live "like pigs, but in a luxurious stable." Hitler's scorn for Americans would persist throughout his life. He never learned nor did he ever alter his views.[65] Sackett's outlook was much different. His introduction to Hitler was as a threat to the Weimar Republic. In time he would come to appreciate and understand that the Nazi also posed a threat to American interests and European peace. Sackett never wavered in his attitude toward the Nazis, but it is important to remember that his fundamental fear was of the phenomenon of communism, a fear shared by the new German chancellor, Heinrich Brüning.

Almost as soon as Brüning became chancellor, Sackett began to report optimistically about him and the future of his government. The American was pleased. The new chancellor appeared to be just the champion needed to save the Weimar Republic. Brüning rejected the idea of a dictatorship and was committed to winning the "cooperation of a parliamentary majority." Sackett considered that to be "very significant as the strongest opposition" to Brüning "came first from those groups which are opposed to government by emergency decree on the basis of the much-discussed

63 Sackett to State, 31 March and 1 April 1930, 862.002/198 and 200.   64 Ibid.
65 Fritz T. Epstein, "Germany and the United States: Basic Patterns of Conflict and Under-
    standing," 307.

Article 48 of the Constitution." The Weimar constitution provided that legislation could be put into effect by edict from the president under prescribed conditions. When there had been talk earlier of Chancellor Müller's resorting to that device, Sackett considered it tantamount to a dictatorship. Now the ambassador began to see that it might be useful in the hands of Brüning. Sackett liked the way Brüning was handling the threat of using emergency decrees and new elections to keep the Reichstag parties in line.[66]

At this stage of his tenure in Berlin, Sackett was reporting on Brüning from the perspective of a distant observer. He did not know the chancellor personally but was impressed by what Brüning was able to accomplish. More than that, Sackett was optimistic that Brüning would succeed in maintaining democracy and preserving the republic. The new chancellor was in a "strategically more fortunate position than his predecessor" especially since he had the authority of President Hindenburg behind him. Sackett was convinced Brüning would be able to win passage of his budget by judicious use of threats, especially the warning that he could dissolve the Reichstag and call for new elections.

Sackett awaited the results of Brüning's strategy, after which, he wrote, "it will become clear whether Dr. Bruening actually possesses the extraordinary political talents which his friends claim for him. He will then have the opportunity to show whether he can obtain a majority in the Reichstag without threatening to dissolve it."[67] It would not be long until Sackett would join that group of friends who believed that Brüning did have that extraordinary political talent.

Sackett, however, made the mistake of equating the Center party leader and his aspirations with those of American political leadership. The ambassador assumed that Brüning was determined eventually to win a stable majority in the Reichstag. This attribution of American political pragmatism to German political parties would lead Sackett to faulty analysis of the prospects of success for the Brüning cabinet. His reports were shaded regularly toward faith in democracy and drew little distinction between American political experience and German realities. He persisted in the belief that the chancellor's principal goal was to save the Weimar Republic by building a Reichstag majority to support his government. He did not realize that for Brüning a Reichstag majority was only the means to a goal, not the goal itself, which was the restoration of the monarchy. Sackett was unaware both of how far Brüning was willing to go toward the political Right and of how far he was willing to depart from the usual methods of parliamentary government.[68] Although Sackett did not understand the

---

66 Sackett to State, 12 May and 17 June 1930, 862.00PR/66 and 862.00/2499.
67 Sackett to State, 12 May 1930, 862.00PR/66.
68 The misinterpretation of German politics was also characteristic of the American press. See George Bernard Hermann, "American Journalistic Perceptions of the Death of Weimar Germany: January 1932–March 1933;" Craig, *Germany, 1866–1945,* 531, 533, 539.

chancellor's ultimate purpose, he recognized that, for the present at least, Germany would be ruled by a minority government.[69]

Sackett knew that the Brüning government signaled the end of the Great Coalition, but neither he nor many others saw that it was the beginning of the process that would end the Weimar Republic. The "nonparty" cabinet was granted unprecedented powers by President Hindenburg, who gave the new chancellor "his unqualified support." Sackett was never truly cognizant that Brüning's final goal was the restoration of the Hohenzollern dynasty.

The ambassador did begin to place his full faith in the ability of the new chancellor to deal with danger coming from the extreme Right. The mandate Brüning received from President Hindenburg was to institute financial reforms but also to restore political order. He was to create a coalition of parties in the middle and as far Right as the Nationalists.[70] The Brüning cabinet, essentially authoritarian in structure, relied on the loyalty of civil servants, the support of the Reichswehr, and the authority of President Hindenburg. The government had not only moved to the political Right, it did not include one of the cornerstones of the Weimar Republic, the Social Democratic party. Neither the Socialists, the largest party in the Reichstag, nor the Nationalists, the second largest, were represented in the cabinet. With the Communists, the fourth largest party, clearly out of the picture, Brüning hoped to govern without the extreme Right – the Nationalists and Nazis – and maintain the support of the Socialists while excluding them from the government.

The cabinet had been formed swiftly, with much of the preparation carried on by General Kurt von Schleicher, Reichswehr Minister General Wilhelm Groener's "cardinal for political affairs."[71] Schleicher was one of several figures behind the scenes who were able to influence President Hindenburg. They wanted to return to the halcyon days of Imperial Germany when the chancellor had been responsible only to the head of state rather than to the political parties of the Reichstag. Although giving allegiance to the Weimar constitution, and varying widely in their commitment to representative government, the permanent sources of political power in Germany shared the same view. Stable and efficient rule were the goals of the Reichswehr and civil service. They arrogated to themselves the role as supreme arbiters of the national interest. Like President Hindenburg, they considered themselves above political parties. For them, the political problem was to ascertain those actions which would best serve the

69 Sackett to State, 28 March 1930, 862.00/2847.
70 Bracher, *Auflösung der Weimarer Republik*, 341–344; Eyck, *Weimar Republic*, 2: 255–257.
71 Gottfried Treviranus, a close personal friend of Brüning, told Calvin Hoover that Brüning's appointment as chancellor "had to be cleared formally with the Reichswehr." *Memoirs of Capitalism, Communism and Nazism*, 130.

national interest, after which the means and priorities would fall into place for any efficient, commonsensical German patriot.

With the political parties of the republic engaged in haggling over programs, and unable to come to any agreement, it was apparent to Schleicher and the professional civil servants that the only solution was to force through a nationalistic and conservative program by means of Article 48. Brüning could be trusted to pursue such a program with sympathy and vigor. That he would be unable to muster a majority in the Reichstag appeared irrelevant. His economic program would have the support of the power brokers in the nation, and if the Social Democrats and lesser parties objected, they had more to lose than the entrenched triumvirate of power – the military, the professional civil service, and the banking and industrial magnates.[72]

Sackett would come to accept the strategy adopted by Brüning as the best means to sustain the republic, but above all, the surest way to thwart Hitler's aspirations.

The authoritarian nature of the Brüning cabinet was made clear in the first pronouncement by the chancellor. On April 1, Brüning told the Reichstag it had been President Hindenburg's explicit request that the new cabinet "be identified with no party coalition." The Weimar constitution required that the chancellor and his ministers have the confidence of the Reichstag. The head of a minority government, Brüning threatened the Reichstag with dissolution if it denied him its support. He proclaimed ominously to the legislative body: "This cabinet had been formed for the purpose of solving as quickly as possible those problems which are generally comprehended to be vital to our nation's existence. This will be the last attempt to arrive at a solution with this Reichstag."[73]

While Brüning threatened the Reichstag with the possibility of new elections, he acted to assist industry and agriculture. A tax on beer mollified industry while an agricultural relief bill called for assistance to farmers to make up for their own deficiencies. Called "eastern aid," or Osthilfe, the program was one of Hindenburg's favorites, for it would help bail out his Junker cronies. Sackett mistakenly estimated that the legislation was inspired more by political than economic motivations. He was alarmed by the growing strength of the Nazi party in northern Germany, particularly in those areas where agriculture was hardest hit by the depression. In his view, the relief for farmers in Brüning's Osthilfe program was designed to head off growing support for the Nazis, which, he equivocated, "presumably" alarmed government circles. In fact, the Brüning government

---

72 Bracher, *Auflösung der Weimarer Republik*, 307–309; Wheeler-Bennett, *Wooden Titan*, 340, 342–344; Fritz Klein, "Zur Vorbereitung des faschistischen Diktatur durch die deutsche Grossbourgeoisie (1929–1932)," 887, 889–893.
73 Eyck, *Weimar Republic*, 2: 223, 256–258.

was less concerned with Nazi inroads in the north than with helping Hindenburg's East Elbian friends and cementing a closer relationship between president and chancellor.[74]

All agreed that the National Socialists were the group most likely to profit from elections. The consensus was that if they were to win, it posed a potential disaster because they were a party "incapable of active co-operation in government."[75] This characterization of the Nazis as spoilers without the potential to govern would persist in the minds of American diplomats; but it was a widely held view at the time.

In spite of their fears, the parties maneuvered for position in elections many predicted would take place in the summer months. Sackett discounted both Nazis and Communists and predicted the campaign would no longer be a contest between Right and Left, but rather "between Hugenberg extremists and the moderate Right, which has President Hindenburg's support." Sackett would betray his faith in the Social Democrats time and again, on this occasion revealing that leading Socialists had secretly admitted "that shortsighted trade union mentality was responsible for the political blunder which caused the fall of the Mueller Cabinet." Sackett unrealistically believed that the best solution to the problem was to restore the Great Coalition, without recourse to new elections. In his mind the Social Democrats were the strength of the Weimar Republic and could not be ignored.[76]

The Nazis continued to engage Sackett's attention. He had already expressed his concern that the Hitler party was making inroads into the agricultural regions of northern Germany. Now the Nazis were making themselves felt in the industrial north. Provincial elections were held in Saxony on June 22 in a campaign in which national issues, especially Brüning's financial program, overshadowed local concerns. What made the election of interest to Sackett was the "aggressive campaign waged by the National Socialists (Fascists) in this state which has long been a labor stronghold." The ambassador felt the Nazis had every reason to be "jubilant." Two years earlier they won 74,000 votes, the previous year 134,000, and now 377,000 with a gain of nine seats. The Communists gained only one seat and the Socialists lost a seat.[77]

From Berlin came a silver lining to the dark clouds gathering. Sackett saw the local election results as having "a distinctly potentially beneficial effect" because they demonstrated what all the parties should learn – "the

74 Sackett to State 2 April 1930, 862.00/2493; Wheeler-Bennett, *Wooden Titan*, 242–244; Eyck, *Weimar Republic*, 2: 258, 380–381; Hans Schlange-Schöningen, *Am Tage Danach*, 51.
75 Sackett to State, 10 March and 6 April 1930, 462.00R296/3694 and 862.00/2494.
76 Sackett to State, 6 April 1930, 862.00/2494.
77 Sackett to State, 24 June 1930, 862.00/2501.

very certain danger of holding new national elections at the present time."[78]
The Kentuckian hoped that the climate of extremism would keep the
moderate parties from risking any elections that might lure their supporters
to the radical parties.

Instead, the chancellor precipitated the very electoral crisis Sackett feared
would create a disaster for the Weimar Republic. Brüning's policy of retrenchment came before the Reichstag in the form of a budget bill in early
July. Strongly urging the adoption of the budget, the chancellor threatened
the Reichstag with the use of the president's emergency powers if it refused
to pass the bill. Confident of the correctness of his position, and in right-
eous disregard of the political consequences, Brüning threw down the
gauntlet.

In July 1930, the legislative body was given an ultimatum to accept his
policy of retrenchment or have it enacted without reference to their wishes.
The Social Democrats offered to compromise at the eleventh hour, but it
was too late. They entered the lists and defeated the second article of the
budget bill after abstaining from voting on the first. The chancellor responded immediately with the promulgation of the budget as decrees under
the president's emergency power. The Socialists countered with a motion
to nullify the decrees, which passed with a majority of fifteen votes. In an
act of questionable constitutionality, Brüning dissolved the Reichstag on
July 18 and put his budget into force in spite of the nullification.[79]

Brüning had gambled and lost. He hoped to govern with the support of
the president as defender of the Weimar Republic, and at the same time
to win the benevolent opposition of the Social Democrats. Following his
own and the president's inclination, he moved further to the Right, trying
to incorporate into his cabinet those elements on the conservative side of
the political spectrum who would nominally support democratic and
parliamentary government. In other words, he hoped to maintain a parliamentary form of government without reference to the composition of
the Reichstag or to the wishes of its majority.

If Brüning actually believed he could "secure a Reichstag with a
democratic majority through new elections,"[80] he had seriously misread
the signs of the times. Parties in vehement opposition to the Weimar
Republic already had command of more than 30 percent of the seats in the
Reichstag. With the nation in economic and political turmoil, most observers
saw the extremist opposition to the republic, and particularly the Nazis,
as the only possible groups to profit from new elections. The radical parties

---

78 Ibid.
79 Eyck, *Weimar Republic*, 2: 267–272. One German historian called the dissolution of the
   Reichstag "frivolous." Erich Matthias, "Social Democracy and the Power in the State,"
   in *The Road to Dictatorship*, 62.
80 Brüning, "Ein Brief," 12.

were certain to increase their numbers. If the Social Democrats joined the opposition, Brüning would face an overwhelming hostile majority of well over 60 percent. In spite of these ominous signs, the chancellor allowed the issues to be put to a vote of the people. He set the election for September 14, 1930, the latest date constitutionally possible.

Sackett displayed great anxiety over the unfortunate turn of events. He correctly predicted that the political extremes of the Right and Left would be the chief gainers in the elections, and reported that the "National Socialists in particular are expected to make considerable gains." The ambassador felt the Social Democrats would be able to hold their ground, but even so he saw little hope that the elections would enable Brüning to find a working Reichstag majority.[81]

His prognosis for the future of political democracy in Germany was bleak, but Sackett felt compelled to defend the Brüning government against charges that it was the beginning of a dictatorship. The German political Left and American newspapers were speculating that Brüning's use of emergency decrees meant the end of German democracy. Sackett, in an unsolicited protest to Washington, declared the charges to be unfounded. He protested that "most" of Brüning's cabinet were prorepublican in their outlook. The ambassador went on to defend the government's course, including the dissolution of the Reichstag.[82]

The summer of 1930 had been something of a trial, and the Kentuckian must have looked forward to returning home for a rest. When he accepted the assignment to go to Berlin, Sackett had notified the State Department that his business interests would require that he "come back for a month or two even after his first going there." He remained at his post almost five months before making plans to return to the United States. Ironically, although he began his arrangements to leave for home before the Reichstag was dissolved, his ocean liner was scheduled to sail on September 14, the day set for the Reichstag elections. He wrote that "the short time at my disposal will all be taken in Kentucky looking after my business affairs, which need considerable attention."[83]

In fact, the ambassador had an important election to work on in Kentucky. As part of the arrangement that sent him to Berlin he promised to campaign vigorously for Senator Robsion, who had taken his seat in the Senate and was now running as the incumbent. In spite of his apprehensions, Sackett was undoubtedly influenced by Brüning's optimism concerning

81 Sackett to State, 22 July 1930, 862.032/17.   82 Ibid.

83 Cotton to Poole, 3 January 1930, Box 1, Poole Papers; before he arrived in Berlin, Sackett declared that he would return to the United States as early as May, *Berliner Tageblatt*, 18 January 1930, p.m. edition. Sackett wrote to Nicholas Murray Butler that he planned to return in September; he engaged passage on the *Leviathan* by mid-July, Butler to Sackett 16 July, Sackett to Butler 29 September 1930, Nicholas Murray Butler Papers; Sackett to Mrs. Hazard, 23 July 1930, Sackett Papers.

the outcome of the German elections. The ambassador had faith that the forces supporting the republic were strong enough to withstand extremism. His growing respect for Brüning blinded him to the errors the Center leader was committing and led him to the belief that the austere chancellor could steer the nation out of the morass of partisan politics.

While the German people were going to the polls on that fateful Sunday morning in September, Sackett was embarking on the *Leviathan*, preoccupied with his business problems in the Kentucky coalfields and the maze of politics in his home state, from which he had so happily escaped only nine months before.

3

The landslide election

AFTER HE MADE his arrangements to leave for the United States, Sackett and his wife faced the hot, dull summer months ahead. While awaiting their departure date, and with the social season over, they decided to tour Eastern Germany. In April 1930, soon after Sackett arrived in Berlin, Julius Curtius, the German foreign minister, had urged the ambassador to make an information gathering trip to East Prussia as soon as possible. Walter de Haas, who like other Foreign Ministry officials found the American congenial, pressed the issue and reported that Sackett was prepared to make the trip when he had the available time. The Sacketts were unable to get free for the excursion until August, but when they made the trip to the Polish Corridor and East Prussia, they were delighted with the experience. More than that, Sackett became deeply ingrained with the German view of the inequities of the Treaty of Versailles.[1]

The Sacketts stayed at an ancient castle, Schloss Schönberg, and the East Elbian aristocracy went out of their way to impress the American diplomat with how unfair the granting of German land to the Polish nation had been. Nobility from forty miles around the castle drove in for a dinner in Sackett's honor on the night of his arrival. The ambassador found the aristocrats "delightful." He wrote his sister: "I am sure you would like all these people very much and they are charmingly hospitable."

All were enlisted in the effort to interest the Americans in the Polish Corridor issue. The governor of East Prussia and the president of the Free City of Danzig joined the aristocrats in entertaining the Sacketts. The two officials took the ambassador and his wife on a tour of the trouble spots of the area, and Foreign Minister Curtius's purpose in inviting them to East Prussia was fulfilled. Sackett wrote to his sister: "On yesterday we drove

---

1 Memorandum by Karl Schubert of the Foreign Ministry, 21 March 1930, ADAP, 14: 393; note of Curtius Memorandum, 1 April on 2 April, and De Haas handwritten note, 9 April 1930, GFMR 1492/D621011–621012.

all day being shown the Corridor of Poland and the Vistula river and all the difficulties that have come as a result of the Peace treaty as the Corridor question is the sore spot of Europe and a likely cause of war at some later time as it was very unfairly designed and is a constant irritation."[2]

Sackett was unfavorably impressed with what he saw in the Polish Corridor. The problem of the region was familiar to him in the abstract, and having been there "opened his eyes." He saw an area beset with neglect and, in his view, doomed to death. Terrible roads, decrepit bridges, and widespread uncleanliness were all in stark contrast to the well-cared-for adjacent German territory. Although he sympathized with the German desire to reacquire the land, Sackett was not satisfied simply to deplore conditions in the Corridor. He went beyond sympathy for German problems to press for pragmatic solutions.

He was so fascinated by the poor conditions in the region that he took a photograph of a boundary stone marked *Traité de Versailles*, and told the Prussian district president that Germany should do more to advertise its case. They should follow the French example, he advised, where in Paris every visitor to the Place de la Concorde was confronted with the grieving figure of Alsace-Lorraine. A similar dramatic symbol should confront every German and international visitor to the East. The Prussian official was pleased to report that his insistence on Sackett making an "on the spot" examination of the Corridor had paid off. The ambassador was convinced that the issue was not just a local matter, but a matter of international concern.

Sackett was persuaded that the Germans could not resolve the problem in their favor by themselves. In the interest of world peace, he suggested, they should first develop a unified determination to resolve the issue. Unless that were to happen the outside world would not act. Sackett, who had begun to offer the Germans advice on strategy to get their way almost as soon as he arrived in Berlin, told them that public opinion needed to be kindled to see the present situation as intolerable. But it was not enough that the German side of the issue be shown, he argued: international public opinion must also be aroused.[3]

The German cabinet was delighted with Curtius's success in winning Sackett's support. They believed that a majority of the French people sympathized with their position and realized that the Corridor issue was of fundamental importance to Germany and wanted an agreement with

---

2 Sackett to Mrs. Hazard, 14 August 1930, Sackett Papers.
3 Memorandum by Carl Budding, Prussian district president in Marienwerder and Budding, to Brüning, 14 August 1930, ADAP, 15: 454–455 and 454n; Memorandum by Schubert, 19 March 1930, and Minutes of Ministers Conference, 21 July 1931, where he advised the Germans on the favorable psychological opportunity for them to act in the London standstill negotiations; Karl Ritter to the German delegation in London, 23 July 1931, GFMR 1658/ D728464–728465, 1684/D787090, 1660/729628.

them. Foreign Minister Curtius reported to the cabinet that Sackett cautioned them to go slowly because he saw three dangers ahead. First, Sackett explained, was the danger of an early solution, a problem because it might enforce an incomplete resolution. The second danger was a negative outcome, and the third involved too much discussion of the matter. Sackett thought that excessive talk would raise the German people's hopes too far above realistic expectations.[4]

While it is clear that Sackett understood and was sympathetic with the German view of the Polish Corridor issue, the ambassador was only agreeing in this case with many contemporary Americans that the Versailles Treaty was unjust.[5] Within months of Sackett's trip to East Prussia, Secretary of State Stimson, partly influenced by Sackett's reports, embarked on a personal campaign to reshape the Polish-German border. Senator William E. Borah of Idaho, chairman of the Senate Foreign Relations Committee, was convinced that the best way to neutralize the Nazis was to restore the Corridor to Germany with assurances that the Polish minority would be treated well by the Germans.

Critics felt that, for Americans, "Poland figured less prominently as a country than as a problem." The Corridor was not perceived as a Polish-German question, but as a French-German problem, "a function of great power politics." To many Americans, giving the area back to Germany would mollify German opinion and open the way to a resolution of German problems with France. The Polish ambassador to the United States, Tytus Filipowicz, characterized the American attitude:[6]

> We do not know the facts of the matter, but we do know that [the Polish Corridor] stands as a barrier to disarmament and the stabilization of peace in Europe, and for that reason we think the problem should be settled in some fashion.

The Poles were, of course, more than reluctant to give up the territory.

Although Sackett sympathized with German national aspirations, he did not blindly accept German views. In fact, his trip to East Prussia was an excellent opportunity for a rest and vacation. In addition, soon after the ambassador arrived in Berlin, Consul General George S. Messersmith advised him to visit Germany outside Berlin, and Sackett was following that advice. Messersmith recalled that he told Sackett that "one of the great mistakes" diplomats made was to remain too much in the capital, to have

4 Minutes of the Minister's Conference of 20 August 1930, ADAP, 15: 471.
5 For example, see Gumberg to Borah, 14 July, and Borah to Gumberg, 18 July 1931, Box 5, Gumberg Papers; Stimson Diary, 12 and 21 October 1931; Stimson and Bundy, *On Active Service*, 274–275; Robert H. Ferrell, *American Diplomacy in the Great Depression*, 200–201.
6 Neal Pease, "The United States and the Polish Boundaries, 1931," 123, 131–133, 135.

most of their contacts only in Berlin. The consular official had suggested to Sackett that "it was very desirable for chiefs of mission to know the country thoroughly, and this they could do best by actually visiting the principal cities in the country and getting to know there, not only the heads of local government, but also the principal businessmen, bankers, and scholars. Sackett liked this idea and I arranged a visit to most of the principal cities in Germany."[7]

Sackett came to admire and respect Messersmith and, soon after the ambassador took up his post in Berlin, they formed a close relationship. The consular official represented the professional ranks of the foreign service held in contempt by traditional diplomats whose positions were based in part on their wealth. Messersmith had been advised to avoid entry into the political side of diplomacy because he did not have the income to afford it.[8] He was advising Sackett in political matters, an area of competence reserved for diplomats in the embassy chancery.

Messersmith's recommendation to the ambassador was just the sort of thing that set off the anger of the leading professional diplomat in the embassy in Berlin. George Anderson Gordon was the State Department's choice as Sackett's permanent counselor of embassy. A career diplomat, Gordon was a stickler for strict protocol and did not approve of the ambassador's making wide contacts outside official circles in Berlin.[9]

Able and punctilious, Gordon was an explosive personality. George Kennan described him as "an able man, intelligent, and highly experienced." Messersmith agreed with that assessment. He described him as "a particularly able man" with "a keen and penetrating mind . . . a man stooped in certain diplomatic traditions," which meant he did not like the idea of men with no connection with the diplomatic service or the State Department coming in as ambassadors.[10]

---

7 Messersmith, notes for memoirs; see Sackett to Mrs. Hazard, 23 July 1930, Sackett Papers, where the ambassador lists a number of cities just visited.

8 Jesse H. Stiller, *George S. Messersmith, Diplomat of Democracy*, 6–7.

9 Gordon was a man of patrician background, typical of the foreign service officers in his time. Born in Huntsville, Alabama, on November 19, 1885, he made New York his permanent home. He had the social and intellectual advantages of preparatory school education in both the United States and Switzerland. A graduate of Harvard College, he received a law degree from Columbia in 1912. He was an instructor in St. Paul's School, 1906–1909, but his only other civilian experience was in the practice of law in New York City in the years 1912–1917, broken by military service. Gordon served six months in the army in the 1916 intervention in Mexico, and then again in the war years, May 1917 through October 1919. The remainder of his life was spent in the foreign service. His first assignment was a temporary one, with the 1919 Peace Commission in Paris. In February 1920 he entered the diplomatic service permanently, serving in Washington, Budapest, and Paris, as well as at numerous conferences. He was named counselor of embassy in the American embassy in Berlin on March 26, 1930.

10 George F. Kennan to Bernard V. Burke, 23 February 1966; Messersmith, notes for memoirs.

Given his views and personality, Gordon got along with Sackett rather well. Described as "a gentleman of the most extreme protocol . . . school, with gray-white hair and mustache which looked curled, elegant dress, gloves, stick and proper hat, a complexion of flaming hue, clipped, polite, and definitely condescending accent," Gordon was a stickler for tradition and protocol, and had the appearance of an "Eighteenth Century courtier."[11]

Strong-willed and easy to anger, Gordon was a take-charge personality. He met little resistance from Sackett. The ambassador, according to Messersmith, "was a man of very good judgment. He was quiet, understanding, but a man of firm convictions." The consul general was impressed by Sackett's performance as a diplomat and later compared him favorably with William E. Dodd, Sackett's successor as ambassador. "Although one was a man of business and the other a scholar, Sackett was really a man in many ways much broader in his knowledge and in his understanding than Dodd." Unlike Dodd, Sackett was much impressed by the pomp and ceremony associated with diplomacy and fell right in with what was expected of an ambassador. He recognized that he would need to rely on the professionals, which he did without demeaning himself or relinquishing his position as the chief of mission. A man of considerable administrative ability, Sackett "knew how to use his staff," Messersmith later reported with satisfaction.[12]

Senior career officers became key personalities in the American diplomatic system, which used amateurs as diplomats, and ambassadors were often forced to turn to the experience of their counselors. If he were wise, a new ambassador took his cues from the second man in the embassy. Moreover, the counselor of embassy had considerable prerogative inherent in his position.[13]

Whatever their personal relationship, Sackett worked with and relied on Gordon even though the counselor was a difficult personality.[14] Messersmith later related an incident in which Gordon, while working with a distinguished German lawyer, became quite irritated and brushed all the legal papers they were examining onto the floor. The lawyer was forced to retrieve the papers while Gordon made no apology or excuse for his

---

11 Martha Dodd, *Through Embassy Eyes*, 20–31; see William E. Dodd, Jr., and Martha Dodd, eds., *Ambassador Dodd's Diary, 1933–1938*, 16, 43, hereafter cited *Ambassador Dodd's Diary*; Hugh R. Wilson to J. Pierrepont Moffat, 13 February 1933, bMS Am 1407(4) 1932, 0–2, J. Pierrepont Moffat Papers; Dodd to Roosevelt, 1 September 1933, Official File 523: Dodd, William E., FDRL.

12 Messersmith, notes for memoirs; Sackett to Mrs. Hazard, 24 January 1931, Sackett Papers. On Dodd, see Robert Dallek, *Democrat and Diplomat: The Life of William E. Dodd*.

13 *Ambassador Dodd's Diary*, 46; Dodd almost proudly notes that after preparing a speech Gordon, "had read it carefully and approved of every sentence."

14 Moffat Diary, 19 January 1931; William Schott of the Berlin Embassy staff to Castle, 9 April 1931, Castle Papers – Germany, HHPL.

behavior. Messersmith had to take up the matter with the lawyer the next day and was certain Gordon "had the usual remorse that he always did when he lost his temper this way. It was only one of a dozen incidents of a similar character." Gordon was famous in the State Department for his volatile temperament. In one instance Wiley wrote Kelley he would be terrified to send "any articles and translations from the press" in Germany to the State Department for fear that "George Gordon would bristle his moustaches and scalp the lot of us."[15]

Gordon's temperament had an important bearing on the sources of information that formed the basis for the embassy's reports. Most important of all was the fact that Gordon had almost nothing to do with Hitler and the Nazis. He never had a conversation with a highly placed Nazi. The counselor's lofty sense of protocol and of propriety severely restricted the circles he considered appropriate for diplomatic contact. Messersmith implies that Gordon knew few people in Germany beyond official government circles, and very few who were associated with business and finance.[16]

Attributions to "highly placed" persons in the embassy's despatches almost always referred to officials in the German government. Where sources from business and finance were cited, the despatches clearly originated with Sackett. The ambassador had a much wider circle of acquaintances than Gordon and was able to send reports to Washington from a broader base of information. Under Gordon's influence, aside from government officials and business circles, the American diplomats in Berlin appear to have had few contacts for reporting purposes. Parties out of power were ignored to a considerable degree. Nazis as well as Communists. The governing classes of Germany, and especially conservative businessmen, civil servants, military men, and aristocrats were the major sources of the embassy's information. Dodd ambiguously remarked to President Roosevelt that "Mr. Gordon's contacts here have not been the happiest, but this has been a trying post for a long time."[17] By the time Dodd arrived in Berlin in July 1933, Gordon was persona non grata in the German Foreign Ministry and did not get along with State Secretary Bernhard von Bülow.

To characterize Gordon as a snob understates the case. Ambassador Dodd's daughter Martha concluded that Gordon "had an almost psychopathic loathing of newspapermen." She attributed his attitude in part to his sense that they were socially inferior. Some insight into embassy contacts may be gathered from his attitude toward consular officers, that "they were outcasts as far as the American Embassy was concerned – they

---

15 Wiley to Kelley, 15 January 1931, Box 1, Wiley Papers; the private papers of diplomats are replete with Gordon stories.
16 Messersmith, notes for memoirs.
17 Dodd to Roosevelt, 1 September 1933, Official File 523: Dodd, William E., FDRL. See also Dallek, *Democrat and Diplomat*, 197–198.

and the journalists."[18] Despite his idiosyncracies, Gordon was well known and respected by diplomats. A careful, even brilliant political analyst, Gordon, like so many of his contemporaries, took great pride in the literary as well as the analytical quality of his despatches.

When Sackett sailed to the United States in mid-September, Gordon was in charge of the American embassy in Berlin. It was he who reported on the Reichstag elections. Sackett, forced to follow the German elections in the newspapers, was upset to be away from his post, but he had not expected the Nazis to have such exceptional success. The ambassador was convinced by Brüning that the elections would not be significant. The chancellor's explanation for dissolving the Reichstag was convincing enough for Sackett. Brüning believed that he could win a majority in the elections.[19]

American diplomats, including Sackett, had been misled by Brüning and the German embassy in Washington into believing that the elections would not hold any great significance. The Brüning government fostered the optimistic outlook picked up by the Americans in Berlin and Washington. Otto Kiep, the German chargé in Washington, explained the situation for the State Department's benefit. He assured Assistant Secretary Castle that "the election will not be very fiercely fought because all the different parties are hard up." The newly elected Reichstag, he said, would be constituted pretty much the same as the last, and Brüning would probably win a slight majority, at least enough to pass his budgetary plan. The National Socialists, he predicted, would likely become more radical, but the Communists would not change much.[20] With those assurances the Americans were complacent about the outcome of the election.

When Sackett learned the election results (see diagram, p. 75), he decided he should return to Berlin as soon as possible. Since leaving Washington he had tried to follow newspaper accounts of conditions in Berlin and was "rather disturbed." He was alarmed at the prospect that Brüning, "backed by the president" was moving toward "drastic financial reform" and if not accepted by the Reichstag, might "apply Article 48 for Dictatorship." The action would take place soon after the Reichstag convened on October 14 and he wanted to be there. He asked J. Theodore Marriner, chief of the Division of Western European Affairs, to inquire about an early return to his post. Above all, Sackett wanted to be informed in detail about "what we may expect."[21]

The ambassador was apprehensive about receiving uncoded messages

18 Martha Dodd, *Through Embassy Eyes*, 96–97; Jesse H. Stiller, *George S. Messersmith*, 29; Messersmith, notes for memoirs.
19 Heinrich Brüning, "Ein Brief," 12; Sackett to State, 22 July 1930, 862.032/17.
20 Castle, Memorandum of a conversation with Otto Kiep, 24 July 1930, 862.00/2504.
21 Sackett to Marriner, 1 October 1930, Box 2, J. Theodore Marriner Papers.

PEOPLE'S PARTY 45–30

CENTER PARTY 62–68	BAVARIAN PEOPLE'S 16–19
STATE (DEMOCRATIC) 25–30	ECONOMIC PARTY 23–23
SOCIAL DEMOCRATS 153–143	NATIONALISTS 73–41
COMMUNISTS 54–77	NATIONAL SOCIALISTS 12–107

Germany's major political parties arranged on a Left–Right spectrum based on their seating in the Reichstag: The first figure following the party name indicates the number of seats won in the election of May 1928; the second figure refers to the number of seats won in the September 1930 Reichstag elections. Under the system of proportional representation, seats were awarded relative to the number of votes cast. In 1928 there were 491 seats, in 1930, 577 seats. The data are based in part on *New York Times*, 9 November 1930.

from Gordon on conditions in Berlin but was placated when Marriner assured him that Gordon's despatches would be forwarded to him in Kentucky. Throughout the remainder of his leave in the United States, Sackett was able to read what Gordon was reporting to the State Department. He was satisfied that he could continue his political campaign on behalf of Senator Robsion confident that not much was going to happen in Germany in the immediate future. It was Otto Kiep again who assured the State Department that there would be considerable delay in any significant activity because the Reichstag would concern itself with other matters rather than risk an immediate dissolution. Sackett would try to make the most of the appalling election news, comparing the Nazi victory to Republican failure in the midterm elections as a protest vote, but still, he was anxious, confessing he was "getting rather nervous over the present situation in Germany" and would be "glad to be back there and on the job."[22]

Sackett was by no means the only one stunned by the magnitude of Hitler's success. So was everyone else. Even the Nazis were surprised at the extent of their electoral victory. They had vaulted from the fringes of German parliamentary politics, with 12 seats in the Reichstag, to a position as second largest party with 107 seats. The National Socialist German Workers' party was now the dominant factor in the formation of German governments. Twenty-eight months later, after much opposition maneuvering to counterbalance or control the Nazis, their leader, Adolf Hitler, was named chancellor of the German republic.

The elections of 1930 not only signaled the start of the Nazi surge to power; they marked the beginning of the end for the Weimar Republic. In

22 Curtius Memorandum, 5 November 1930, GFMR 2382/E197001; Marriner to Sackett, Confidential, 2 October 1930, 862.00/2594A; Sackett to Marriner, 4 October 1930, Box 2, Marriner Papers.

the few remaining years of the republic's life no chancellor was able to govern with a majority coalition. The political scene was characterized by bitterness and invective, which found expression in street brawls by organized groups and even flowed over into the halls of the Reichstag. The extremists, from the Communists on the Left to the Nationalists and Nazis on the Right, held the balance of power. They found common ground only in their opposition to the Weimar Republic. From 1930 until their victory in 1933 the Nazis dominated the extremist groups in numbers, making it clear that they were the one party with which any government must reckon.

The Nazi victory in the elections of 1930 was a landslide of unprecedented proportions in German political history.[23] Combined with the Communists on the Left and the Nationalists and Nazis on the Right, the parties in open and vehement opposition to the Republic controlled 39 percent of the seats in the Reichstag. When one counts the sizable minority of parties and leaders whose support of the republic was only lukewarm, it is plain the Weimar system was coming to an end.

The calling of elections was a serious political miscalculation by Chancellor Heinrich Brüning. The Nazis' total vote increased from 810,000 to 6,409,600. Although they captured many votes from the Nationalists, they also won voters from the more moderate parties. Perhaps most important, they won many new voters. Combined with the Communists and Nationalists, the Nazis represented a vote of protest against the republic of nearly 14 million Germans. In the 577-seat Reichstag the extremist opposition to Weimar controlled 225 seats. As the leader of the second largest party in Germany and the leading figure in opposition to the republic, Hitler could no longer be ridiculed and dismissed as a *quantité négligeable*. He had reached his first major goal – he led a mass party, and overnight "had become a politician of European importance."[24]

Although the extent of the upset election came as a surprise to everyone including the Nazis, its effect was lost on none. Under the German system of voting, the party submitted a list of candidates eligible for the Reichstag and to whom seats were alloted in turn, beginning at the top of the list and working down until the number of seats won was exhausted. The optimistic Nazis had not submitted a list of 107 candidates. Like most observers, they felt fifty or sixty seats would be a triumph.[25] Twelve years after the election Hitler recalled:[26]

> It was just before the elections on which everything depended. I was waiting at Munich for the results of the counting. Adolf Müller came in, very excited,

23 Eyck, *Weimar Republic*, 2: 280.   24 Bullock, *Hitler*, 161.
25 Rumbold to Henderson, 5 and 18 September 1930, in *Documents on British Foreign Policy, 1919–1939*, E. L. Woodward and Rohan Butler, eds., Second Series, 1: 505, 510, hereafter cited DBFP, all Second Series.
26 *Hitler's Secret Conversations*, 139.

and declared: "I think we've won. We may get sixty-six seats." I replied that if the German people could think correctly, it would give us more than that. Within myself I was saying: "If it could be a hundred!" Suddenly, we found ourselves with the certainty of a hundred seats. Müller offered to stand a round of drinks. It went up to a hundred and seven! How to express what I felt at that moment? We'd gone up from twelve seats to a hundred and seven.

Most observers thought the extremists would make some gains but the extent of their victory, particularly that of the Nazis, was a "tremendous surprise."[27] The Nazis had doubled most estimates.

Gordon's reaction to the election was typical of many Western observers. Although the Nazis were expected to make significant gains in the election, the extent of their victory was met with initial surprise and shock. There followed a period of disbelief in the barbarity of Nazi excesses, and then an attempt to explain away Nazism as a temporary aberration that would be modified and channeled by the responsibilities of participating in parliamentary government. This view that Hitler and the Nazis could be "tamed" was widely held by prominent German leaders as well as foreign observers.[28]

In his first cabled report Gordon stressed the popular interest in the election, with the largest voter turnout since the establishment of the republic. His initial impression was that the voters were disgusted and reckless. They were disgusted, he reported, with the failure of the moderate parties and the Social Democrats to run a smooth government and alleviate the economic depression. The parties had demonstrated a "prolonged failure" to operate the machinery of parliamentary government effectively. The voters, he wrote, feared that any changes proposed by the moderate parties to help resolve the nation's problems would come only "as a result of further sacrifices and hardships on their part." He felt the electorate was reckless in its willingness "to try anything else for a change even to supporting a party of irresponsible leaders and promises."[29]

According to Gordon, the failure of various governmental combinations to ameliorate their lot led many voters to feel "that any change meant everything to gain and nothing to lose, even though they could not see clearly how such gain could be brought about." Gordon guessed that this sense of disgust had led many otherwise sane voters to turn to the Nazis.

27 Gordon to State, 17 September 1930, 862.00/2518.
28 See DBFP, 1: 509, 512–513, 514, 519, 520.
29 Gordon to State, 15 September 1930, 862.00/2509, paraphrased in FRUS, 1930, 3: 76. One is struck by the similarity of language and analysis in the despatches of professional diplomats Horace Rumbold and George Gordon. For example, Rumbold to Henderson, 25 September 1930, DBFP, 1: 512. The British ambassador said of the election that "a large number of those persons who voted for the National Socialists were inspired by impatience, not to say disgust, with the ineffectiveness of the political parties in the Reichstag."

The situation was unfortunate, he maintained, because the intelligent citizens who voted for the Nazis were unable to see "that in thus voting they were taking the surest steps to increase the difficulties of government, to further impair foreign confidence – especially in financial circles – in the stability of German republican institutions, and in general, to intensify the economic and financial evils of which they complain."

Without discounting the serious implications of the election for the Weimar Republic, Gordon saw a ray of hope. He thought it most probable that a large part of the Nazi vote came from the very young, those who had just reached voting age. Anticipating war as part of the future with Hitler in power, he reasoned that this generation had "no personal knowledge of the horrors and hardships of war, but only the thought that the debt which it left behind will bear on them throughout their lifetime. To such a class repudiation pure and simple had an undeniably superficial attraction." This group of voters, along with others who had turned reck- lessly to the Nazis, might welcome a "return to safer and saner ground . . . if strong leaders with a strong program could be evolved from the present welter" of parties. The chargé also expressed the hope "that the young element . . . may become more balanced with increasing maturity."[30]

Since the Nazi party was now a significant force in German politics, Gordon decided to reiterate for the State Department's benefit "the extra- ordinarily confused, self-contradictory and opportunist character of their campaign." Outlining the Nazi position, the American diplomat explained:[31]

> Any constructive element in their so-called program is difficult to discern, even by inference; when seeking to win votes from the Communists the National Socialist orators declared that, as their social theories were similar, they appealed to them to vote for a Communist form of government directed by Germans rather than the same thing under the guidance of Moscow; when invading Nationalist territory, the party spokesmen emphasized their adherence to the principle of private ownership of property. Throughout the land their program consisted of asseverations that all the country's evils flowed from Semitism, international banks, the Young Plan, the Treaty of Versailles and all other international treaties with any provisions which might be considered objectionable from a chauvinistic point of view, the remedy being repudiation pure and simple of any written obligations, and a march on Berlin, for the purpose of establishing a reactionary dictatorship with however, not even a suggestion as to the alternative measures contemplated for remedying the conditions complained of.

30 Gordon to State, 17 September 1930, 862.00/2518, reproduced in part in FRUS, 1930, 3: 77–79.
31 Gordon to State, 19 September 1930, FRUS, 1930, 3: 79. The party's full name was NAtionalsoZIalistische Deutsche Arbeiterpartei (NSDAP) or National Socialist German Workers' party.

The National Socialists were becoming so important in the embassy's reports that Gordon began to use the local German acronym "Nazi" for the first time five days after the election.

Reemphasizing the opportunistic nature of the Nazi party's campaign, Gordon pointed out that with the more than 2 million additional voters in the election coming "all at the lower end of the age scale" the result was:[32]

> these immature citizens barely twenty years of age, afforded a ripe soil for the seed of empty and empiric – more plainly, charlatanic – catchwords and promises which characterized the National Socialist campaign. Finally, it must not be forgotten that it is pretty generally understood that the party had the secret support of at least a portion of heavy industry, which regarded it as a means of opposing the Social Democrats and Communists.

Gordon summed up his analysis by calling the elections a "body blow to the republican form of government" and a clear sign of the "dangerous mentality at present possessed by a large proportion of the population." Gordon temporized by pointing out that Germany had undergone similar political shocks in the past and managed to recover. Volunteering that the situation would be more serious if it were a new phenomenon in German politics, he went on to warn that the "body-blow is not necessarily a knock out blow, but the fact remains that some thirteen odd million Germans have by their votes declared their hostility to the present republican form of government."[33]

The Nazi triumph placed the existence of the Weimar Republic in jeopardy, but an additional threat to American interests was the possibility of German repudiation of both treaty and debt. Such denial of contractual obligations was looked upon as anathema by American diplomats everywhere. Sackett believed that the only barrier to such extreme measures was the Brüning government. His hope was that the chancellor could save the situation by unifying the support of all those factions which favored the republic. There was a danger, in Gordon's view, that repudiation would occur. It was that fear that kept Sackett in a state of uneasiness while campaigning in Kentucky. Gordon believed that the threat could not be explained away, as some government officials were prone to do. He thought that "a way remains open for all sincere supporters of the Republic to make common cause against this danger. If at such a juncture as this they fail to sink their personal and doctrinal differences, then indeed a serious situation will present itself."[34]

Germany was dependent on foreign, but especially American, loans to maintain a stable economy, and in the political crisis that was developing,

---

32 Gordon to State, 17 September 1930, 862.00/2519.
33 Gordon to State, 17 September 1930, FRUS, 1930, 3: 79.   34 Ibid.

it was likely that an infusion of more money would probably be required. American attitudes to the elections were therefore critical. Wolff's Telegraphisches Büro was devoting a "very large amount of its space to summaries of American press comment, both favorable and unfavorable," as well as a great deal of "fairly unadulterated propaganda" favorable to Germany. The German press bureau, for the benefit of Americans, was optimistic about the security of loans and pointed to the salutary effect of the elections in strengthening the middle parties. Gordon reported that official Germany shared the general interest in American attitudes. The Germans especially did not want Americans to become alarmed by rumors of a putsch. To counter American fears, Hindenburg, who, according to Gordon, broke his rule about not giving interviews, authorized Brüning to say that he fully shared the chancellor's view "that there was no danger of a Putsch in Germany, and that if one were to be attempted it would be immediately suppressed."[35] Rumors of an impending putsch had been reported by Gordon, who foresaw a period of disorder and bloodshed. But while fearful of "unfortunate developments," he saw "no immediate reason to apprehend any fundamentally adverse turn of affairs."[36]

Although most observers were unable to unravel the meaning of the elections, it is also apparent that the significance of the returns was not obvious even to the Nazis. They were not only surprised at their success, Gordon reported that they were also "considerably embarrassed as to how to use it." Gordon wrote that the Nazi's first reaction was to insist they be taken into the government, but after reflection the Nazi leaders evidently decided to move with caution and take a more temperate stance than they had taken in the campaign.[37]

After the election, Hitler refrained from inflammatory statements and insisted the party hoped to achieve power through legal and constitutional means. The Nazi leader abjured a putsch or a revolution, yet he insisted successes in elections were not ends in themselves, but rather means to an end. Gordon reported that Hitler maintained that his party was "a party of revolutionaries, but by that he meant 'revolutionaries of the spirit,' and what it aimed at capturing was the German consciousness and soul." Gordon pointed out to the State Department that the Nazi position was a far cry from what party orators were saying just before the elections. They had been advocating "a revolutionary dictatorship to be brought about by a march on Berlin." The American diplomat then proceeded to account for the new moderation of the Nazis.[38]

In analyzing the latest Nazi position, Gordon saw three important factors: Hitler's fear that a putsch would fail, hope that moderation would lead to

35 Gordon to State, 25 September 1930, 862.00/2529.
36 Gordon to State, 22 September 1930, 862.00/2512.
37 Gordon to State, 23 September 1930, FRUS, 1930, 3: 83–84.   38 Ibid.

Nazi inclusion in the government, and pressure from industrial interests who had given the Nazis financial support.[39] Without being explicit, the American diplomat had implied that the Hitler party disposed of sufficient force in its paramilitary army, the Sturmabteilungen, or Storm Troopers, to pose the threat of a putsch, but both the chancellor and the president were reported to be willing and able to suppress any uprising.[40]

Gordon assumed the government must be aware of the possibility of violence and was presumably prepared to prevent it. In his analysis, the diplomat saw little hope for Nazi success, placing his stress on Hitler's use of moderate language "to allay suspicion of a real purpose on his part to bring about physical and political upheaval." Gordon felt the crux of the matter was Hitler's "hesitation and uncertainty which might well be expected to befall a leader who, having based his whole political conduct upon avowed opportunism, suddenly finds himself in possession of unexpected power." Given the likelihood of failure in the use of force, Gordon saw a second Hitler motive in temporizing his position. The American guessed that if Hitler were to have a chance to enter the government, his party would "have to renounce its repudiation of parliamentary institutions."

Gordon stressed the influence of big business on Hitler. He had already suggested that leaders in heavy industry motivated, in part, by their opposition to the Socialists, the Communists, and the labor unions had given the Nazis money. The diplomat alluded to "very substantial financial support from certain large industrial interests" and guessed that "their influence at this juncture had been definitely a restraining one." Gordon went on to link that financial support to the efforts to bring the Nazis into the government.[41]

Nearly two decades after the events, in 1947, Brüning recalled two groups of advisers around Hindenburg who were divided in their counsels concerning the Nazis. Some sought to exclude the Nazis from a basically dictatorial government; the others wanted to include them. Among the latter were a number of German bankers who had given Hitler financial support. This group, according to the chancellor, had tried to persuade Sackett to support their pro-Nazi position against the Brüning government.[42] In fact, Gordon had reported that "important financial circles," not necessarily those who had given the Nazis financial support, "have been and are continuing to bring pressure on the Chancellor and other members of the government to try the experiment of letting the Nazis participate in the government."[43]

In the weeks following the Reichstag election rumors of all sorts were spread throughout Germany. There was general nervousness about the

39 Ibid.   40 Gordon to State, 25 September 1930, 862.00/2529.
41 Gordon to State, 23 September 1930, FRUS, 1930, 3: 83–84.
42 Brüning, "Ein Brief," 6–7.
43 Gordon to State, 23 September 1930, FRUS, 1930, 3: 84.

prospects of a Nazi putsch; and Americans feared the prospects of repudiation of debts. On the political Left there was apprehension that Brüning, with Sackett's help, was about to bring Hitler into the government. Brüning later implied that important people, especially bankers, had tried to influence Sackett to support Hitler. At the end of September 1930 the German Communist party charged that Sackett was involved in an attempt by Brüning to establish a dictatorship. A Marxist newspaper charged that the chancellor was given full powers by President Hindenburg to establish a dictatorship in which Article 48 would become the actual constitution of Germany. The paper further charged "that the financial program of the Government as well as its plans for the coup d'état were preconcerted" with Sackett. They claimed "quite positively that the American ambassador in Berlin was kept constantly informed by the Brüning Government. As early as yesterday he had the Government program in hand." Ignoring the fact that Sackett was in Kentucky at the time of the allegations, the Communist paper continued that "American capital informed both Brüning and Hitler" that it would be "expedient" to bring the Nazis into the cabinet. In support of Brüning's later charges, the newspaper asserted that "several big banks, above all the Deutsche Bank, would prefer an immediate government of the National Socialists."[44]

Gordon treated the German Communist party's allegations with considerable disdain. Confronted by an excited American newspaper correspondent, the diplomat dismissed the charges as absurd, suggesting the newsman consider the source. The diplomat did, however, check with the German Foreign Ministry to see if, "without keeping the subject alive by anything approaching a denial, it would not be possible for the author of this article to be personally and privately reprimanded for his gross impropriety in thus bringing the Ambassador's name into print." Gordon thought so little of the incident he did not deign to send his report on it by cable, but rather sent it off by regular pouch. When it arrived ten days later in the State Department, it caused no excitement and proved Gordon correct when he suggested "it would be inadvisable to take any further action in the matter."[45]

The entire incident was forgotten and there is no evidence to suggest American complicity in a conspiracy of any kind. However, the core of the Berlin newspaper's charges, and Brüning's later compulsion to reveal the pressures exerted on him as well as Ambassador Sackett, have the ring of truth. There were German and American bankers, among others, who out of opposition to the Marxist Left, out of sympathy for the Nazis' nationalist aspirations, and from a desire to see Germany's political crisis resolved,

44 *Die Welt am Abend*, 30 September 1930, enclosed with Gordon to State, 1 October 1930, 862.51/2933.
45 Gordon to State, 1 October 1930, 862.51/2933.

sought to see the Hitlerites included in the German cabinet. Such persons may even have sought to influence the German president, chancellor, and cabinet members as well as American diplomats. As already noted, more than a year later, in December 1931, Sackett did meet with a banker who very much wanted to excite the ambassador's interest in Hitler. It is clear, however, that Sackett was not impressed by Hitler as a prospective head of state, nor was he interested in seeing a dictatorship established. In fact, the reason Sackett was restive in the United States was the very fear that Article 48 might be used to create a dictatorial government.

In the end, the counsels advocating Nazi inclusion in the government were heeded, but there is no evidence to suggest that Ambassador Sackett, or any of his staff, ever looked with favor upon Hitler and his party. American diplomats clung to the contrary hope that somehow the middle parties would save the Weimar Republic and parliamentary democracy from the dangers posed by the Nazis. Although some Americans continued to fear the Communists most of all,[46] Gordon, and now Sackett, saw the Nazis as the chief threat to republican government in Germany. Sackett kept up with events in Germany by reading Gordon's despatches. It is clear from his position when he returned to Berlin that he agreed with Gordon's interpretations.

What alarmed American diplomats above all was the radicalization of the German electorate. An internal threat to the Weimar Republic's very existence had developed, but even more serious from the American perspective was the danger of the repudiation of debts and other contractual obligations. Some German business leaders were chauvinistic enough to justify nullifying reparations on the ground that they were an unjust political penalty. Gordon emphasized the seriousness of the financial situation, but he was optimistic in his prognosis. He believed that German politicians would come to their senses and rescue parliamentary institutions from their enemies.

Less predictable and more dangerous were the Nazis. They campaigned as an anticapitalist party and were not shy about advocating repudiation. Just four days before the election, they issued a manifesto that could have frightened anyone with investments in Germany. The Nazis promised to fight for "the German worker by getting him out of the hands of his swindlers and destroying the protectors of international bank and stock exchange capital."[47] In another official party manifesto, sounding very much like Communists, the Nazis complained of "debt-slavery to the international financiers" and declared that the "working classes" and the "rural

---

46 For example, Hearst's *American Weekly*, 28 September 1930. Lord Rothermere's London *Daily Mail* was more outspoken by directly praising the Nazis, much to Hitler's delight; see Gordon to State, 1 October 1930, 862,00/2541; Stimson and Bundy, *On Active Service*, 271.

47 J. Noakes and G. Pridham, *Nazism, 1919–1945*, 1: 72.

population" were of "predominant importance" to them. Jews were declared to be responsible for the German nation's problems and were charged with controlling the nation's finances.[48]

Hitler's campaign threw a scare into Americans who had invested in Germany, but obviously Jewish investors were most frightened of all. Sackett later reported that a "panic of fear" had seized the Jewish community after the elections, aroused by "the immediate incendiary statements that came from National Socialist leaders." The flight of gold reserves and foreign exchange amounted to one-third of foreign money held as cash balances in Germany. Of the remaining two-thirds, "approximately sixty per cent went out of accounts held in Jewish names. In view of the small number of Jewish accounts compared to the total number of accounts this made an extremely heavy percentage of the total, Jewish owned, and . . . foreign account withdrawals practically eliminated foreign deposits in Germany."[49]

Although George Gordon could do no more than write reports about the flight of capital, his counterpart in the private sector, George Murnane of Lee, Higginson, acted to help save the Weimar Republic. Both segments of the corporatist diplomatic community, public and private, had come to appreciate Brüning as the best hope for the salvation of republican institutions and even the capitalist system itself. The chancellor "seemed peaceful and constructive" in Murnane's estimation, and moreover he was "a cultured and intellectual personality, [who] gave evidence of leading Germany along constructive lines."[50]

As soon as the election results were in, Murnane had contacted the Federal Reserve Bank of New York with his analysis of the situation. The political problem was perceived to have originated in the economic depression. The increase in the Communist vote had been foreseen, but the Nazis had doubled even the highest estimates. Murnane continued, the election strengthened the "radical wings particularly of the right" as a direct result of Germany's economic crisis. With improved economic conditions, voters could return to the middle parties, which would be compelled to cooperate with each other to avoid domination by the extremist parties. The middle parties were expected to get together with relative ease since, in Murnane's view, they had so much in common.[51] The banker decided that he had to act.

Beleaguered by the Nazis, who were "actively promoting disorder," Brüning consulted leading German bankers, according to Murnane, who

---

48 Baynes, *The Speeches of Adolf Hitler*, 2: 767–769.
49 Sackett to State, 20 January 1931, 862.51/2992; see Stimson Diary, 24 February 1931.
50 Murnane to Burke, 11 April 1966.
51 Murnane to Lee, Higginson, 15 September 1930, handed to Jay Crane by Murnane, 16 September 1930, C261 – Germany, Federal Reserve Bank of New York, hereafter cited FRBNY.

advised him that if he wanted to keep Hitler out of power, he needed to borrow a substantial amount of money. Additional steps to thwart the Nazis included disciplined budgetary steps to rescue the economy from danger. As an expression of the faith of the American financial community and its "inherent belief in the economic and financial soundness of Germany," Murnane organized a short-term loan of $125 million to give the accompanying budgetary provisions time to take effect. "The loan in fact was designated the 'bridging over' loan."[52] It would allow Brüning to span the present political crisis by providing funds for unemployment benefits and postpone the day of reckoning when the budget deficit would be addressed.

Murnane found that it was not easy to raise the money for the loan. Bankers were reluctant to invest their cash in such a combustible situation, especially in the face of the flight of money out of Germany. The purpose of the loan proposed by Murnane was purely political and bankers recognized it as such. The French and British governments refused to participate directly and the Bank for International Settlements at the same time expressed serious misgivings, holding that "no immediate peril threatens, providing that the extremist elements in Germany are prevented access to control."[53] They missed the point. The loan was meant precisely to prevent extremists from gaining control.

John Foster Dulles wrote to Leon Fraser at the international bank that there would be no help from London and Paris and he expected little from New York. Fraser replied that the British position was that someone else should be "found to carry the burden" and for the French "it was pure politics." French leadership "was stand-offish, fearing that the ultimate beneficiary might be the Hitlerites."[54]

Murnane had to struggle to raise the money, and later admitted that it had been a "forced loan." The money was not successfully raised based on German credit, but had been "based on the prestige of the issuing houses in America."[55] After Hitler's success in the Reichstag elections there was widespread lack of faith in Germany. Murnane had argued that the loan was necessary. It was important to support Brüning against Hitler; the loan was made for political not financial reasons.

Influential Americans were expressing alarm at what might happen to the international financial community if Hitler were to come to power. Gates McGarrah, the American head of the Bank for International Settlements, wrote to George Harrison, governor of the Federal Reserve Bank

52 Murnane to Burke, 11 April 1966.
53 Norman Armour to State, 20 and 16 October 1930, 862.51/2949, 2937; Gordon to State, 14 October 1930, 862.51/2947.
54 John Foster Dulles to Leon Fraser, 10 October 1930, Fraser to Dulles, 14 October 1930, Box 137, John Foster Dulles Papers.
55 Sackett to State, 21 January 1931, 862.51/2991.

of New York, that it had been a mistake not to listen to the social classes that had suffered most in the terrible inflation of 1923. The people who lost their property, "those in the professions, teachers, etc. etc." were now voting for the Nazis. However, "Hitler and his lieutenants" had not "thought things through," and one happy consequence could result from this. If the Nazis did not come up with constructive proposals, their support "will drift away." There was a real danger, however, in their possible obstruction of needed economic legislation.[56] John Foster Dulles thought that Hitler's success was based on the German people's perception that they were disarmed while the French were armed. "It is easy," he wrote, "for demagogues to create the popular impression" that the disarmament provisions of the Treaty of Versailles were "a trick."[57]

The incipient optimism expressed by Gordon, and shared by Murnane, was shattered as Gordon observed political developments soon after the election. In an impassioned despatch on the activity of the Weimar parties, which revealed the American diplomat's devotion to German parliamentary democracy, he expressed his disbelief at the conduct of the parties that professed to support the Weimar Republic. What disturbed him the most, he said, was that the parties between the extremists of the Right and Left had "not yet learned their lesson." They constituted the groups with the most foreign connections and therefore could not be indifferent to foreign political opinion. In the recent elections they[58]

> received a sharp warning as to the results which follow upon their inability to agree on questions of fundamental importance to the maintenance of a republican and parliamentary form of government. One would think that an experience of so drastic a nature would awaken them to the necessity of amending their ways but, . . . there is no evidence to this effect. On the contrary, . . . the leaders of these parties are proceeding in the same manner as heretofore, and the jockeying, bickering and bargaining going on between them seems to be as pronounced and obstructive as ever.

The People's party, for example, refused to join in any grouping that included the Socialists, and made it their parliamentary goal to combine only with bourgeois parties. This aim mystified Gordon, who wondered how the party's leaders could "delude themselves" that they were "in any way facilitating the cause of good government." The chargé explicitly emphasized the importance of the situation by asking the State Department not to discount what he said on account of the "brevity" of the despatch.

As part of Hitler's tactical move to show a front of moderation, a representative of the Nazi party called on the American embassy seeking

---

56 Gates McGarrah to George Harrison, 10 October 1930, Box 11, Harrison Papers.
57 Dulles to Edward Alleyne Sumner, 25 November 1930, Box 137, Dulles Papers.
58 Gordon to State, 25 September 1930, FRUS, 1930, 3: 85–86.

an interview. The Nazis demonstrated the low esteem they had for the United States when, after Gordon agreed to receive a delegation, several days later only one obscure Berlin representative of the Nazi newspaper, the *Völkische Beobachter*, arrived to explain to the American diplomat how his party had been misrepresented and misunderstood, especially in the foreign press. In a lengthy despatch, Gordon summarized the Nazi's views for the State Department. Revealing that he had little personal knowledge of the Nazis, he reported that his visitor "by no means fitted the description of a hot-headed 'wild man' as the Nazis are often depicted in the local press." Gordon remarked that the Nazi was "noticeably well mannered and although the views he was attempting to explain were those of a partisan and a fanatic, his method of presentation had none of the latter quality and he expressed himself throughout in moderate and re-strained terms." More important, the diplomat observed, he presented the Nazi case as well as it could be done "but it obviously cannot stand up under the slightest analysis," and moreover "he made it evident that his party had no clear idea of just how it might be able eventually to accomplish its aims – in other words, on his own showing, its policy is one of sheer opportunism."[59] The pleasing manner of the Nazi must have put Gordon in a good humor. Having already called the Nazi program "empty and empiric" and "charlatanic," in a few days he was to characterize it with the very undiplomatic phrase "half-baked."[60]

The American diplomat was not taken in by the Nazi's demeanor. The major interest of the interview, he wrote, was that it provided further proof that the Nazis wanted "to dispel the impression that their course of conduct will be marked by violent and illegal measures."[61] Gordon was consistent in describing the Nazi program as opportunistic and negative. Although Hitler's original "half-baked program" was of only academic interest, he noted, "one may nevertheless gather from it something of the spirit which guides the party." Anything positive in their program was "equally vague and general. The clearest thing about their plans is the negative aspect – the idea of breaking down everything and then building it up differently – an attractive program for dissatisfied people."[62]

Far more significant interviews took place a few days later. Gordon had the opportunity to engage in prolonged dinner conversation with the newly appointed commanding general of the German army, Kurt Baron von Hammerstein-Equord, and Colonel Erich Kühlental, chief of the Intelligence Section of the General Staff. There had been considerable speculation about the Reichswehr's attitude in the political confusion surrounding the

59 Gordon to State, 19 September 1930, FRUS, 1930, 3: 79–83.
60 Gordon to State, 7 October 1930, 862.00/2549.
61 Gordon to State, 19 September 1930, FRUS, 1930, 3: 82–83.
62 Gordon to State, 7 October 1930, 862.00/2549.

recent election. Although he professed to discover nothing startlingly new, Gordon deemed it important to examine the role the Reichswehr would play "either behind the political scenes or overtly" if it came to putting down an uprising of the extremist groups.[63]

Hammerstein was known as an outspoken anti-Nazi and an ardent supporter of Hindenburg, if not of Brüning,[64] so his view that "a minority government of the middle parties would again have to be the order of the day" came as no surprise. The general exhibited considerable disdain for the Nazis, although he considered Hitler a "sincere fanatic" not motivated by self-seeking ends. Expressing his scorn for the Nazis and other parties that arrogated the word "national" to their party names, he gave voice to the deep-seated view of the German military. The "only real national element or group in Germany . . . was the army, which was animated by the uniform point of view of service to the Government and thus formed the backbone of the State." Dispelling any notion of a successful putsch, the general maintained "the army had no doubt of its ability to take care of any trouble which might arise from the present troubled political and economic conditions."[65]

Gordon found the views of Colonel Kühlental more startling. The general staff officer averred that he was "rather pleased than otherwise at the result of the recent election." He believed that among the 6 million who voted for the Nazis "were represented the 'best elements' in Germany, especially among the youth of the country." These voters represented the view, shared by army officers in general, that existing conditions needed to be changed. In a calculated understatement, Gordon found the colonel's views "somewhat paradoxical, to say the least." The American protested that many officers, such as Kühlental, "profess to be imbued with an unswerving devotion to the welfare of the Republic," but were pleased with the success of the Nazis, who were certainly hostile to the republican form of government.

The American chargé proffered several hypotheses to explain the otherwise inexplicable views of the intelligence officer. He guessed that the Nazis would indeed moderate their position and thus pose no dangers for the army or the police. At the same time they would "constitute a welcome counterbalance to the Marxist Social Democrats – who do not furnish the most fruitful field for recruiting." Gordon speculated that hostility to the Weimar Republic might not be unwelcome to the Reichswehr. The military was pleased by the energy and determination expressed in the demand for change. Such a dynamic force might be channeled to serve the Reichswehr's purposes, and at the same time sustain a more acceptable republican government.[66]

63 Gordon to State, 24 September 1930, 862.00/2534.
64 John W. Wheeler-Bennett, The Nemesis of Power, 224–225.
65 Gordon to State, 24 September 1930, 862.00/2534.　66 Ibid.

If Gordon was not clear about the Reichswehr's relations with the Nazis, neither were other contemporary observers. The military appeared to be divided on the issue. At the higher levels, General Groener, minister of defense in the Brüning cabinet, and the army's commanding general, Hammerstein, were clearly anti-Nazi. Others, such as Kühlental and many field-grade officers, looked for advancement in the expanded army that the Nazis promised. Some were committed Nazis. General Groener accused three such junior officers with treason. They were brought before the Supreme Court in Leipzig to face charges of disseminating Nazi propaganda in the army.

The high point of the trial came when Hitler was called by the defense. Gordon thought the Nazi leader had two motives in allowing the defense attorneys to call him. It was "an unparalleled opportunity for party propaganda" and "another occasion to tone down his pre-election utterances." Hitler insisted his party meant to come to power by legal, constitutional means and denied that his Storm Troopers were armed. Gordon observed parenthetically that "the conduct of the party organizations throughout the recent electoral campaign certainly does not lend verisimilitude to these latter statements."[67]

Hitler maintained he always took the position that tampering with the Reichswehr would be lunacy. After denying any secret, violent party aims, Hitler was then asked why prominent Nazis said it would be necessary to use violence. Gordon wrote that reports indicated that Hitler, perhaps carried away by his own grandiloquent oratory, dropped into his old spellbinding tone and asserted: "When our movement is victorious, it will establish a High Court before which the November criminals of 1918 will be tried, and this crime will be expiated. I freely admit that then heads will roll in the sand."

At the time of the trial, Gordon was attending a luncheon given at the Reichsbank by its president, Hans Luther. "Hitler's oratorical bombshell" appeared in the noon newspapers, just before lunch, and Gordon suggested its "unpleasant effect in the atmosphere can well be imagined." The American diplomat contended that Hitler did not in fact make the sensational statement. A cabinet minister attending the luncheon claimed his office had checked with officials in Leipzig and were told that Hitler did not say "heads will roll in the sand." At a subsequent meeting of Reich ministers the declaration by Hitler was reported as factual by the minister of justice. True or not, Gordon pointed out that "as this version was broadcast to the world and as Hitler has not seen fit to repudiate it, the result is the same."[68]

---

67 This account is based on Gordon to State, 1 October 1930, FRUS, 1930, 3: 86–88.
68 Minutes of the Ministers Conference of 25 September 1930, GFMR 1707/D784886.
More than two years later, British Ambassador Rumbold repeated the "heads will roll" cry as true. At one point he reported Hitler had said that "heads of the November criminals would begin to roll." Rumbold to Simon, 21 March 1933, DBFP, 4: 470.

In spite of the sensational coverage of Hitler's appearance at the trial, Gordon was convinced the Nazi leader not only intended to take advantage of a magnificent publicity opportunity, but to show a face of moderation. Most of Hitler's testimony was meant to do just that, according to Gordon. Alluding to the pressure being brought on Brüning to cooperate with the Nazis in the Reichstag, the American diplomat pointed out that the Economic party had recently rejected cooperation with the Social Democrats, leaving the Nazis as Brüning's only alternative. Hitler's "ill-advised exuberance" at the Leipzig trial had, however, cooled the ardor of many who had been urging cooperation with the Nazis.

The Nazi landslide victory in the September 1930 Reichstag elections had a profound effect on Sackett. Alarmed at the prospect of a Hitler government, he thought of Brüning as the potential savior of the Weimar Republic. Already inclined to agree with the chancellor on most subjects, he came to see the German's proposals as most likely to serve American interests. He became more than a supporter, he became an advocate. Brüning's main purpose was to put through financial reform, but without even the semblance of a Reichstag majority, and harassed by the parties on all sides, the most the chancellor could hope for was temporary agreement on his program. He adopted the tactic of organizing a periodic "adjournment majority" that would free the government to carry on without the Reichstag.

Both Sackett and Gordon adjusted their hopes as the chancellor's plight became clearer to them. In midsummer they had looked for a working majority as Brüning's best hope, even though they did not see the outlook as favorable. Sackett had denied the possibility of a Brüning dictatorship, asserting that there were too many pro-republicans in the cabinet.[69] By autumn, given the composition of the Reichstag, and the recalcitrance of even the middle parties, the two American diplomats shifted their position to accept "short formal sessions followed by successive adjournments" as the best chance Germany had to achieve some sort of constructive stability.[70] Sackett went so far as to see the Reichstag election results as "a blessing in disguise." He believed the results demonstrated the need for the political parties to support Brüning and that foreign distress over the election had a sobering effect on Germans.[71]

When Brüning published his economic program in early October, Gordon believed that, with modifications, it might pass the Reichstag and enable the chancellor to avoid the use of Article 48. The chargé, with renewed optimism, even held out hope that Brüning could put together a majority

69 Sackett to State, 22 July 1930, 862.032/17.
70 Gordon to State, 31 October 1930, 862.00/2563.
71 Sackett to State, 6 November 1930, 862.00/2564.

in the Reichstag. The Social Democrats had just passed a party resolution of cooperation with the government that made such an eventuality appear to be credible.[72] To facilitate such a possibility, the chancellor met with the leaders of all the parties, except the Communists.

Hitler attended in person, although the encounter was almost accidental in nature. Brüning asked the parties to send representatives, but did not invite them by name. Hitler, not yet a German citizen, was not eligible to serve in a high German political office. When Hitler appeared for the Nazis, according to British Ambassador Horace Rumbold, Brüning had no alternative but to receive the Austrian.[73] The meeting with Hitler ended without result; the Nazis and the Communists, according to Gordon, had rejected the Brüning program "a priori."[74] Neither Gordon, nor Rumbold, was aware that among Brüning's purposes in calling in party leaders was to get their agreement to extend President Hindenburg's term in office, which was about to expire. That goal was part of Brüning's continuing strategy.[75]

The situation in the Reichstag was complicated by the multiplication of small parties. The splinter groups were scrambling about in an effort to form blocs of the required 15 seats that would enable them to participate as recognized parliamentary groups. The only party that supported the Brüning program was the chancellor's own Center party. All the others ranged from outright rejection of the program to the demand for its modification. "In spite of this seemingly gloomy outlook," Gordon reported, Brüning "proceeds on his way with apparently undiminished equanimity."[76]

The attitude of the Social Democrats was encouraging to Gordon. That party's leaders had indicated in conversation that they recognized the imperative need for reform; they sought only to avoid public blame for measures they felt called for greater sacrifices on the part of their followers. Notwithstanding the problems, Gordon was optimistic. He was particularly pleased with the conciliatory attitude of the Social Democrats. He summed up by saying, "I feel that the situation has undergone an improvement during the past week, in the sense of holding out better prospects for getting through the winter."[77]

The Reichstag opened on October 14 and Gordon, who attended the proceeding, carried away the impression "of an astounding lack of dignity. The Hitlerites in their so-called uniforms of no coats, brown shirts with a swastika armlet and – in the majority of cases – with a single shoulder

---

72 Gordon to State, 6 October 1930, 862.00/2536.
73 Rumbold to Henderson, 10 October 1930, DBFP, 1: 517; Bullock, *Hitler*, 187, 820, places Brüning's first visit with Hitler in October 1931.
74 Gordon to State, 8 October 1930, 862.00/2547.
75 Heinrich Brüning, *Memoiren, 1918–1934*, 191–197.
76 Gordon to State, 14 October 1930, 862.00/2551.
77 Gordon to State, 9 October 1930, 862.00/2547.

strap worn in the guise of a suspender, and a simulacrum of golf trousers as a crowning touch, presented the appearance of an overgrown troop of boy scouts." The Nazis marched to their seats in the Reichstag to the taunts and derisive shouts of the Communists. Gordon felt he could detect among the Nazis "a certain amount of shamefaced embarrassment." Although the session was marked by noise and turbulence, there was no violence. The American chargé felt the activities of the Nazis in the Reichstag were important enough to warrant additional "descriptive despatches" from time to time.[78]

With the opening of the Reichstag, the optimism shown by Brüning, and shared by Gordon, was based on the general recognition that economic and financial reform were necessary.[79] Stringent cuts in wages, prices, and government expenses were to be facilitated by the Lee, Higginson loan of $125 million that George Murnane had initiated. Most observers saw the loan as strengthening the chancellor's position in the Reichstag, but major political and financial conditions were applied to it. The Brüning government had to give assurance that it would adhere to the Young Plan, that it would carry out the expenditure restrictions suggested by S. Parker Gilbert, and that debt liquidation legislation be passed by the Reichstag and not be put into effect under terms of Article 48 as an emergency decree.[80] Those provisions gave Brüning the leverage necessary to induce the Reichstag to support his program.

The board of the Bank for International Settlements now understood the political meaning of the loan Murnane had negotiated with so much difficulty, and they announced that it was intended to bolster Brüning's political position. Horace Rumbold, the British ambassador in Berlin, saw the loan as "a marked expression of foreign confidence in Germany." Press accounts matched the assessment of diplomats; the *New York Times* editorialized that the loan was an expression of faith in the Weimar Republic and its peaceful foreign policies.[81]

Gordon echoed Sackett's response to the first Lee, Higginson loan. The ambassador considered the loan huge and unnecessary. He believed it served no purpose other than to postpone serious German consideration of its budget problems. Sackett thought then and Gordon renewed the idea that Brüning would use the loan to meet current budget deficits and, as with earlier German-American financial relations, postpone the day of reckoning to an ambiguous future. Gordon thought that this second $125 million loan in less than a year might be an even greater mistake. He believed it to be a possible fatal illusion, as he reported, the loan "has

---

78 Gordon to State, 15 October 1930, 862.00/2552.
79 Gordon to State, 9 October 1930, 862.00/2547.
80 Werner Link, *Die amerikanische Stabilisierungspolitik in Deutschland, 1921–1932*, 491.
81 Rumbold to Henderson, 24 October 1930, DBFP, 1: 522; *New York Times*, 14 October 1930.

undoubtedly proven a most silver Fata Morgana."[82] In spite of the diplomat's foreboding, there can be no doubt that the loan made acceptance of Brüning's reforms easier and facilitated his plan to push through his economic program, adjourn the Reichstag, and take care of the future as it came.

The Reichstag elections of September 1930 had upset the calculations of American banking circles as well as those of Brüning. Americans had invested heavily in Germany and more money was in the offing. This fact alone can account for the inordinate American interest in the German elections. The banking syndicate headed by Lee, Higginson, as well as other investors in Germany, wanted to assure the American investing public of the stability of the Weimar Republic. A representative of Harris, Forbes and Company, after completing a political analysis of conditions in Germany, announced that American investors in that nation's securities had no reason to feel anxiety. Not only was republican government not endangered by the recent elections, the analyst claimed, but it was gratifying that the number of parties had been reduced and that there had been a "decided swing to the Nationalist parties, thus offsetting to some extent the large parties of the Left." The Harris, Forbes representative went on to assure American investors that German radical parties tended to moderate with power. "Therefore some of the comments that have appeared since the elections should not be taken too seriously."[83] For the American financial community the new multimillion-dollar loan was seen as "a concrete expression of their faith in Germany" and the announcement of the loan calculated to enable Brüning to open the Reichstag with good news.[84]

The Lee, Higginson loan, initiated after what amounted to Brüning's defeat in the Reichstag elections, was certainly calculated with political purpose. Nevertheless, the negotiation and closing of the loan took place without any direct participation by American official diplomats, even though it was expressly designed to assist the Brüning government to weather a political as well as an economic storm. Gordon was not privy to the negotiations but later saw the loan as quite unusual. Decreasing revenues from taxes and increasing unemployment costs, both aggravated by the flight of capital, were responsible for what he called "the extraordinary measures" represented by the loan. Assuming, correctly, that the State Department was not informed about the loan, he wrote his reports as if he were the major source of the Department's information about the transaction.[85]

82 Gordon to State, 6 and 13 October 1930, 862.00/2536 and 862.00/2545.
83 *New York Times*, 21 September 1930, an interview with Walter W. Ross, of the foreign department of Harris, Forbes and Company; see Link, *Die amerikanische Stabilisierungspolitik in Deutschland, 1921–1932*, 490n5.
84 *New York Times*, 13 October 1930; the newspaper editorialized that the United States was responsible for the republican government in Germany and had a great stake in that nation's financial recovery and political stability, 19 October 1930.
85 Gordon to State, 14 and 23 October 1930, 862.00/2947 and 2555.

While American private financial interests were carrying Brüning through another crisis and the State Department gave its tacit approval, an unimportant but poignant letter crossed President Hoover's desk in the White House. It was the first of what would later be a flood of wires, letters, and pleas asking the United States to intervene on behalf of the Jews in Germany. The telegram from Brooklyn implored Hoover "as champion of humanity" and as "President of the most humane and civilized country of the world . . . to do something, say something that will immediately check the flame that may take on greater proportions if left alone."[86] Gordon had been reporting instances of anti-Semitic violence by the Nazis,[87] but very little was heard of the problem on the American side of the Atlantic.

On the day it was received, President Hoover forwarded the telegram from Brooklyn to Stimson with a brief note stating: "I would be obliged if you would acknowledge it and make some reply to it."[88] The Secretary of State's reply was legalistic and typical of the responses that were to emanate from the department when the problem became acute. After acknowledging the wire, Stimson assured the writer that the State Department would give its attention to the rights of American citizens in Germany "to the extent to which they are affected by *the situation which you state* exists in Berlin." Stimson, unwilling to accept the fact of anti-Semitic violence in Germany, pointed out that the American government was "not in a position to intercede on behalf of persons other than American citizens, but the Embassy at Berlin will take all measures which are feasible and appropriate to safeguard the persons and property of any American citizens in Germany who may request its interposition."[89] The matter was thus disposed of and would not be raised again until after Hitler came to power.

86 Benjamin Ammerman to Hoover, 14 October 1930, filed with 862.00/2546.
87 For example, Gordon to State, 13 and 14 October 1930, 862.00/2545 and 2553.
88 Hoover to Stimson, 14 October 1930, 862.00/2546.
89 Stimson to Benjamin Ammerman, 15 October 1930, 862.00/2546, emphasis added.

4

Sackett takes the initiative

A DIPLOMAT'S ROLE can be frustrating. It is his task to report on events, to analyze the political and economic situation in the nation to which he is accredited, and to keep his national leaders informed about what to anticipate in the immediate future; at times a diplomat must speculate on long-term expectations. A diplomat may attempt to influence policy, but his essential purpose is to carry out the decisions made by foreign policy leadership at home, whether or not he feels the policy is wise or effective. Occasionally diplomats have gone out of their way to influence or even to extend their government's policy in new directions. They were aware that, if they went too far, they might be risking their careers.

Ambassador Sackett was not a career diplomat, but he was a personal, if formal, friend of President Hoover. As Sackett saw the problems of the Weimar Republic move toward a crisis, he was moved to act, to influence foreign policy, in the interest of saving democracy in Germany. He might not have been prone to do much had it not been for a remarkable political friendship he developed with Chancellor Heinrich Brüning. The two men grew to become close political allies; theirs was an alliance characterized by Sackett's commitment, almost devotion, to saving the Brüning government, while the chancellor for his part responded by suggesting new moves the American might make to achieve German goals. Sackett acted on Brüning's behalf beyond what one should expect from an ambassador.

The friendship had essentially one purpose: to help Brüning thwart Hitler and save Germany from chaos and communism. In return for American help, the chancellor promised nothing more than the preservation of his own government. This special arrangement started to blossom in the summer of 1930 when Sackett began to see Brüning on a personal as well as a professional level.[1] It grew into full flower when the chancellor was confronted with the Nazi electoral success in September 1930. In fact,

1 Brüning, "The Statesman", 112.

95

Sackett and his government made a commitment to the chancellor that was far out of proportion to what the United States could realistically derive from supporting him – unless the United States were willing to change its foreign policy to include direct political involvement in European affairs, a very remote possibility.

Ambassador Sackett learned of the election results while on the high seas en route to the United States and was disturbed by the news of the Nazi landslide victory. Like most informed observers, he anticipated considerable Nazi and Communist gains in the elections, but he was not prepared for the level of imminent political disruption. With partisan opposition to the Weimar Republic given such a strong voice in the Reichstag, the outcome could not be predicted. For Sackett and his fellow diplomats, American national interests in Germany were economic and the most dangerous threat to those interests lay in the possibility of repudiation of debt. Both the Nazis and the Communists freely advocated such renunciation and now were in a position to make their views felt.[2] Although together the two extemists parties did not control the Reichstag, they could, with their commanding position, conceivably accomplish their purpose by winning the support of patriotic-nationalist votes to repudiate reparations. Sackett had expected the Nazis and Communists to make gains in the Reichstag, but he had not been prepared for the very bad news he received while aboard the *Leviathan*.

While the embassy in Berlin was busy reporting on the Reichstag elections in Germany, Sackett debarked in the United States on September 20, 1930. He found the press eager to learn what was going on in Germany, and fended off questions about rumors of war in Europe with the terse response that "it required considerable money to start a war these days."[3] Then he declined to comment on foreign affairs at all, which was the usual response of diplomats to open-ended questions from the press. But in this case Sackett's reticence was fully warranted. The questions and reports he encountered revealed a woeful lack of information on the part of the fourth estate, some of whom had only a hazy notion of what was happening in Germany. One journalist, for example, in reporting on his interview with Sackett wrote of the "recent elections in which the socialists, or German Fascist party made notable gains."[4]

There was a general sense of foreboding wherever Sackett went. The threat of war and the potential for the end of democracy in Germany were reflected in the questions reporters asked the diplomat. In Washington, he tried to allay fears by emphasizing the common sense of the German people. In Germany, he said, business was slow and unemployment high, but that was the case nearly everywhere. Taking an optimistic tack, the

2 Sackett to State, 6 November 1930, 862.00/2564.
3 *New York Times*, 21 September 1930.   4 *Louisville Herald-Post*, 20 September 1930.

ambassador stressed the great strides made since the war and assured his questioners the Germans could overcome all their difficulties.[5] The *Louisville Herald-Post* agreed with Sackett. Anticipating the ambassador's speech at a dinner in his honor, the newspaper editorialized that "it will be instructive to hear from one who has been on the scene in days of ferment and, as some have hinted, of possible danger to the general equilibrium, a view the Herald-Post does not share."[6]

Sackett had anticipated the Berlin embassy's concern that Brüning might be leading his government toward dictatorship. American diplomats in Berlin began to recognize that the chancellor's failure to organize a majority in the Reichstag spelled the possible end of the Weimar Republic. Gordon described the government as a "veiled dictatorship," reporting General Schleicher's conviction that it was impossible to govern effectively with the Reichstag as it was composed. With apprehension, Gordon wrote that the general felt the need to "avoid the appearance of a dictatorship," but "however ineffective the parliamentary regime was under the present conditions, it could not be done away with – 'yet,' was what seemed to me to be the unexpressed thought in his mind at this point." Gordon quoted Schleicher as saying that times were difficult, but "all that is needed is determination and this '– referring to his clenched fist –' and we have them."[7]

The American diplomat and German general agreed that the only hope for saving the Weimar Republic was by frequent adjournment of the Reichstag. They further agreed that Brüning's handling of the legislative body had increased his prestige and tactical strength. He would be able to hold short formal sessions followed by successive adjournments, a "process which could be repeated *ad libitum.*" Concluding his report, Gordon emphasized two themes that were persistent in the analysis of American diplomats in Berlin. One was the belief that a resolution of the economic depression would solve Germany's political problems, restore order, and permit the return of party politics to the Reichstag. The other theme was fear of the danger the Nazis posed for the republic in the chaotic political situation.[8]

In Washington, Secretary of State Stimson strained to understand what was going on in Germany. In a conversation with the French ambassador, he was probably intent on allaying French fears and helping to halt withdrawal of French funds from Germany when he drew a naive analogy between American political conditions and the rioting and murders that were a regular part of German political life. When the French ambassador asserted the Germans had only themselves to blame for the fateful September

5 *New York Times*, 25 September 1930. 6 *Louisville Herald-Post*, 26 September 1930.
7 Gordon to State, 31 October 1930, 862.00/2563. 8 Ibid.

election, Stimson claimed it was easy to find disturbing groups in any nation. Although he too was troubled by what happened, he withheld judgment until he could see what followed on the heels of the election. Not disturbed by the Nazi victory itself, Stimson recorded: "I said that we had in this country communistic elements and violent elements which were as bad as those in any country, but that they did not represent the general sentiments of this country as he himself knew." The same was true in any country and Stimson was not going to judge Germany by "certain elements who probably did not represent the country as a whole."[9]

In the view of American diplomats in Berlin, one element of hope for the future of the Weimar Republic lay in the keystone state of Prussia. Comprising two-thirds of the German nation, Prussia was the stronghold of German republicanism and the particular target of the Nazis. Gordon's hopes for the republic were given a positive boost when the Socialist Karl Severing was named Prussian minister of the interior, a position that placed him in control of the Prussian state police. Gordon described Prussian Minister-President Otto Braun, also a Social Democrat, as "one of the most forceful personalities in German political life and a resolute defender of the Weimar republican regime." He portrayed Severing as similarly inclined, and added that his appointment was a clear sign that the constitutional parties were alive to the need for vigorous resistance to the extremist parties.[10]

Although they surely would never support socialist candidates at home, both Sackett and Gordon had unrelieved praise for German Social Democrats and their leaders. The American diplomats began to shift their views of foreign affairs to reflect the Socialist change in outlook. The Socialists were now willing to accept the Young Plan as simply "an inevitable evil" but only as a stopgap until revision was possible. They were approaching the view of the parties of the Right that the plan was "an unbearable burden and must be revised." The Socialists disagreed with their opponents only "on the method of procedure."[11]

When Sackett returned to Berlin on the evening of October 31, 1930, he began to see revisionism as inevitable, revision not only of the Young Plan but of the Treaty of Versailles. Many Germans felt, he said, that even if economic conditions were to improve, the resentment against the nation's international disadvantages would continue to feed the support for extremist groups. Still, there was some good to come out of the recent elections. If nothing else, they showed that better-informed groups, such as business interests, would support the government if only to avoid utter

9 Stimson, Memorandum of a Conversation with the French ambassador, 23 October 1930, FRUS, 1930, 3: 89.
10 Gordon to State, 29 October 1930, 862.00/2559.
11 Gordon to State, 28 October 1930, 462.00R296/3865.

confusion. The one great hope was the growing strength of the Brüning government.[12]

In his effort to help the German republic, Sackett drew closer to Chancellor Brüning and began to place greater emphasis on leadership to deal with the nation's problems. Earlier, Gordon had insisted on the need for "strong leaders with a strong program."[13] Brüning seemed to fit the bill with his sensible, conservative economic program, but the chancellor had serious limitations. Sackett described the chancellor:[14]

> Seen sitting at the end of the Government desk on the platform of the Reichstag . . . with his detached air, coolness, evident steadiness of purpose and attention to detail [he] seems the embodiment of certain of the qualities which contributed largely to the power of the Roman Catholic Church of which he is a son. However admirable and valuable in themselves, these more intellectual qualifications are less apt to catch the fancy of the masses and thus make him an idol of the people whose popularity could considerably lighten the difficult task of reform.

Although Brüning thus left something to be desired, Sackett could see no suitable alternative.

Looking about for leadership potential, the American ambassador could find none but Hitler. "Aside from President Hindenburg, whose appeal is more historic," he reported, "only Hitler can lay claim to broad, though by no means universal popularity." He went on further to explain that Hitler's ideas on foreign policy and domestic finance had not yet been firmly formed. Still, their lack of clarity did not detract from the "spectacular and sentimental appeal to the masses" of such popular slogans as "treaty revision" and "cessation of tribute payments." Because catchwords were so vague, they were "all the more elusive and difficult to combat."

While Hitler's ideas on most subjects lacked clear formulation, Sackett came directly to the heart of the Nazi leader's technique. Hitler's principles for propaganda, he wrote, had found lucid exposition in *Mein Kampf*, the Nazi's rambling statement of his views. In that semiautobiographical work, Sackett explained:

> Hitler aired his views on political propaganda, and his remarks are illuminating in this connection. Propaganda, he said in substance, with the many reiterations which he considers forceful, must not attempt to win over the educated and intelligent few but rather must be popular and adjust its level to that of the intellectually most limited. Its appeal should be to the feelings and not to the intellect, its methods repetition and bold assertion, denying even the shadow of rights to one's opponents.

12 Sackett to State, 6 November 1930, 862.00/2564.
13 Gordon to State, 17 September 1930, FRUS, 1930, 3: 90–91.
14 This account is based on Sackett to State, 17 December 1930, 862.00/2573.

The object was an "appeal to the masses, better suited than a budget debate to arouse nationalistic feeling." In spite of or, rather, because of the lack of clarity of Hitler's ideas, Sackett continued, Hitler "remains a factor to be reckoned with."

As the autumn moved toward winter, Sackett despaired of a resolution of the republic's political problems short of a Brüning dictatorship. He could not understand the reluctance of the parties that ostensibly supported the Weimar Republic to come to agreement, if only on the survival of the form of government. When the Reichstag convened in December, Sackett cabled that Brüning was able to repel motions of lack of confidence and the repeal of his emergency decrees, but that his support was wavering. The ambassador complained that the chancellor's position was even more delicate than it had been in the October session. What support he did have "is apparently becoming of such uncertain and reluctant character that it is questionable to what extent it will continue to be accorded."[15]

Although Sackett had trouble understanding the republic's political parties, he began to see more clearly into the nature of National Socialism. Sackett singled out the Nazis as the element most responsible for the endemic political riots, which had forced the authorities to place the Reichstag under police protection with all approaches to the building under guard.[16]

Sackett's earlier hopeful prognosis for the government had been shaken by the Nazis. He now predicted that new elections would result in further Communist but even greater Nazi gains. Recent local elections in various sections of Germany gave the Nazis a substantial increase in their votes. Sackett reported "the spread of Nazi doctrine is not confined to any one section and that the tide of Hitlerism not only has not yet spent itself but is still in full flow." He confessed that his earlier hopefulness "after the show of energy and vigor furnished by the Chancellor and his Cabinet" was now abandoned. The ambassador concluded: "Undoubtedly Hitler's lieutenants, who are constantly gaining greater experience in demagogism, have been able cleverly to exploit local causes of unrest and discontent. Nevertheless, these widespread local votes cannot be discounted on that basis alone, and they constitute an impressive warning of what, in spite of all the Chancellor's good work, is still to be expected should he be forced to dissolve the Reichstag and hold another general election."[17]

In the period immediately following the September Reichstag elections, Brüning's general strategy was to ignore Hitler, but by the end of the year, growing Nazi success in local elections and the uncertainty of the chancellor's parliamentary support led many to consider conciliation with the

15 Sackett to State, 8 December 1930, 862.00/2568.
16 Sackett to State, 9 December 1930, 862.00/2571.
17 Sackett to State, 3 December 1930, FRUS, 1930, 3: 90–91.

Nazis. Stronger talk of including them in the government was heard. The Reichswehr, always jealous of its prerogatives, was apprehensive about the prospect of sharing power with the leaders of a political army as large as the nation's military forces,[18] but Schleicher was willing to use the Nazis to the army's advantage. Sackett reported that the People's party, grown more openly nationalistic since the death of Gustav Stresemann, was advocating "the utilization of the live forces inherent in the National Socialist movement" and was now exerting pressure on Brüning to include Nazis in the government.[19]

Gordon had recounted the growth of a scheme to incorporate the chauvinistic notions of the Nazis, if not the Nazis themselves, into the Brüning program. General Hans von Seeckt, former commander of the Reichswehr, openly advocated Nazi participation in the government. Schacht and others made more qualified assertions that it should not be possible to govern without the second largest party in the Reichstag. Gordon, however, made it clear that there was no inclination anywhere to abdicate in favor of Hitler.[20]

The American explained that the People's party position was meant to broaden the base of the cabinet's support and was not a desertion of the party's program. In diagnosing the shift to the political Right, Gordon wrote:[21]

> That nothing succeeds like success may be a trite maxim, but it explains, to a certain extent, the gradual change which seems to be taking place – after the initial pained surprise at the Nazi success in the Reichstag elections – in the attitude of the parties to the right of the Social Democrats towards the Nazis. Furthermore, the Nazis are doubtless regarded by many as an effective possible ally for combating the Social Democrats, trade unions and Communism, as well as a means of exerting foreign political pressure.

Gordon pointed out that the advocates of fusion with the Right were drawing a fine distinction between the Nazi party and the Nazi movement, which amounted to a "rather naive attempt to steal Hitler's thunder without having anything to do with Hitler."

The diplomat went on to clarify the distinction between the Nazi movement and the Nazi party:

> The "Nazi Movement," based on faith in Germany and compounded of patriotism, idealism, youthful enthusiasm and fanaticism, is regarded as an eminently desirable instrument for bourgeois rejuvenation and unification, as well as for foreign political activity, while, on the other hand, the "Nazi Party" with its undigested political, financial, economic, social and racial

18 The Storm Troop membership had reached 100,000 by January 1931, Conan Fischer, *Stormtroopers: A Social, Economic and Ideological Analysis, 1929–1935*, 6.
19 Sackett to State, 17 December 1930, 862.00/2573.
20 Gordon to State, 30 December 1930, 862.00/2574.   21 Ibid.

dogmas, coupled with a deplorable absence of statesmanlike leaders, is still looked upon as a compromising associate whose contamination is to be carefully avoided, but whom it would at all events be well not to antagonize.

Co-opting the Nazi movement became the goal of politicians to the right of the Socialists, including Brüning himself. Sackett considered Hitler's views too extreme to be acceptable, but he did favor most of Brüning's nationalistic goals.

The chancellor had been brought into power to win the support of the Nationalists and form a Center-Right coalition to enable him to govern without the Social Democrats. Unable to come to agreement with Hugenberg, Brüning now faced a more formidable force in Hitler. His policy placed him in a position where he had to work with either the Nazis, implacable opponents of the republic, or the Socialists, who were the principal mainstay of the republic. Described as "a conservative and a monarchist at heart,"[22] a description that could aptly be applied to some Socialist leaders, Brüning could count on the support of Social Democrats at least to the extent that they worked together to sustain the Weimar Republic. Given the Rightist orientation of his cabinet, it can be no surprise that he attempted to win Hitler's support.

Sackett came slowly to understand the Brüning maneuver to conciliate Hitler. The pervasive nature of German extremism became clear to the ambassador during the widespread opposition to the American film *All Quiet on the Western Front*. The Nazis led the attack against the movie, which was condemned on all sides, except the Left, as un-German. In the view of many Germans it depicted their soldiers as defeatist, their leaders as brutal and uncaring. When the Brüning government suppressed the film, Sackett read the move as a stunning defeat for the chancellor. The foreign press, including Americans, interpreted the ban as a surrender to Hitler.[23] The ambassador attached the greatest importance to the incident, predicting that if the "irreconcilable Opposition" should succeed in forcing Brüning to resign, "it may well be found that the present event was a very decided contributive factor in such a result." In Sackett's view, Brüning had suffered a severe blow to his prestige, for Hitler had forced the chancellor to do his bidding, making him yield to "Nazi compulsion on a clean-cut political issue." The ambassador was adamant in describing the ban as a defeat for he maintained that the grounds on which the film was suppressed were not convincing, "and cannot be accepted by an impartial observer."[24]

22 John W. Wheeler-Bennett, *Wooden Titan*, 338.
23 Modris Eksteins, "War, Memory, and Politics: The Fate of the Film *All Quiet on the Western Front*," 79. For good brief accounts of American cultural influence in Europe, especially film, see Frank Costigliola, *Awkward Dominion*, 176–180, and Emily S. Rosenberg, *Spreading the American Dream*, passim, esp. 99–103.
24 Sackett to State, 17 December 1930, 862.00/2573, and FRUS, 1931, 2: 312, 314.

Less than two weeks later, reports from the American embassy related a quite different view of the film crisis. Sackett was away on vacation after having spoken with Brüning about the current state of German politics. Now, as a political intimate of the chancellor, Sackett was able to inform the embassy staff of the government's strategy and viewed the banning of the controversial film in an entirely different light.

Gordon now reported that it was Foreign Minister Julius Curtius who actually suppressed the film, but only after initially accepting it without objection. In a meeting with the Berlin censorship board, the Reichswehr ministry had strenuously objected to the film as damaging to the public image of Germany, but especially because it defamed the German army.[25] Gordon guessed that Brüning "may well have spoken a word sub rosa" that led to the government's giving in to the Nazis. Gordon further reported: "The way in which the Foreign Office, on second thought, gave in to the clamoring of the Nazi mob was so conspicuous that the suspicion arises that pressure was brought to bear from other quarters as well." The chargé now saw the move as "natural" particularly since the affair had reached the stage of a political crisis. He then revealed what he thought to be the chancellor's motives: "The Centrist Party, whose leaders are reputed to see life steadily and see it whole, has always been noted for its longsighted policy, and the prohibition of 'All Quiet on the Western Front' was perhaps the overture to an extension of the Government's front towards the Right," a strategy that would be in keeping with the People's party appeal to "utilize the live forces" of Nazism.[26]

Sackett's initial reaction to the banning of the film had been based on his perception of the problem from the point of view of the American film makers. His later position was based on his sympathy for and cooperation with Brüning in the chancellor's attempt to conciliate the Nazis, but at no time was he willing to have a good word for Hitler and his lieutenants. He now believed that showing the film "would have seriously unfortunate results." The Nazis would "welcome demonstrations involving physical violence as a means of keeping up the zeal of their followers."[27] Brüning probably opposed the film himself on patriotic grounds. After all, he had been a front-line soldier and was a nationalist in outlook.

In keeping with Brüning's position, the ambassador now wanted the State Department to intervene with Will Hays, president of the Motion Picture Producers and Distributors of America. He wanted to delay the American film industry's effort to show the film until a more favorable agreement with the German government could be negotiated. Sackett actually hoped to give Brüning time to mollify the Nazis. To show the film,

25 Eksteins, "War, Memory, and Politics: The Fate of the Film *All Quiet on the Western Front*," 63, 69–70.
26 Gordon to State, 30 December 1930, 862.00/2574.
27 Sackett to State, 11 March 1931, FRUS, 1931, 2: 315.

he observed, would be to invite "anti-American criticism" and "probable embarrassment" to the American government, which could result in the loss of an advantage in the negotiations concerning American film rights in Germany. Sackett uncharacteristically asked the State Department to inform him of their reaction to the suggestion, since he was "convinced that the matter is one of the greatest importance."[28]

The controversy was concluded when the State Department, at Sackett's suggestion, intervened with the Hays Office. The motion picture watchdog decided to delay any exhibition of the film until a satisfactory settlement of regulations covering the movie industry was drawn up. The department agreed with Sackett that any further showing of the film would only stir up further controversy and jeopardize American film interests in Germany.[29]

It was not until September 1931 that the film was re-released in an expurgated form for distribution throughout the world. A few scenes were deleted and the Nazis railed against the film again, denouncing "the pre-dominant Jewish influence in Germany." Sackett took a broad view of the event. By the time the film was being shown again, the Brüning govern-ment was no longer seeking to bring Hitler closer to, if not in, his gov-ernment. Sackett informed the State Department that the "chief present significance of the whole affair is that of a straw which shows which way the wind is blowing."[30]

The gusts had long since moved away from conciliating the Nazis. But when the film controversy first broke in December 1930, Brüning was in the midst of his campaign to create a Center-Nazi rapprochement. The chancellor had evolved a plan to rescue Germany, not just from the crisis of the depression, but from the restrictions of the Versailles Treaty. He assumed that if he were able to achieve the foreign policy goals that Hitler espoused, the Nazi party and its leader would fade from the German political scene.

Brüning's plan called for winning equality of armaments and ending reparations, a move that would help to erase the war guilt foundation of the Versailles Treaty and lead to further revisions. The second phase of the plan was to restore the monarchy. Brüning later claimed he hoped to achieve that goal by plebiscite before Hindenburg became too senile, but the field marshal, under the influence of his "unconstitutional advisers," refused.[31] An alternative open to the chancellor was to extend Hindenburg's term of office, which was about to expire. He needed Hitler's help to carry

28 Ibid.
29 Memorandum by P. T. Culbertson of the Division of Western European Affairs, 17 March 1931, FRUS, 1931, 2: 315–316.
30 Sackett to State, 12 September 1931, FRUS, 1931, 2: 316–317.
31 Brüning to Schurman, 7 December 1937, Box 17, Schurman Papers. Schurman had writ-ten to Brüning asking him to comment on Winston Churchill's *Great Contemporaries*.

out that scheme, because a two-thirds majority was necessary to amend the constitution to extend the president's term. It was important for Brüning to avoid a presidential election, something Hindenburg was extremely reluctant to face. With an extended term, the chancellor could prepare the way for a regency under Hindenburg and the ultimate restoration of the Hohenzollern monarchy. Hitler's support was therefore vital and thus Brüning made the first move toward conciliation of the Nazis.

On October 6, 1930, when Brüning first met with Hitler, Gordon was not aware of the chancellor's intention to ask the Nazi party for its support in extending Hindenburg's term. The American reported simply that the meeting was brief and inconsequential. Actually, Hitler was accompanied by Wilhelm Frick and Gregor Strasser, two of the Nazi party's ablest parliamentarians, to hear Brüning's offer. Hitler either failed or refused to understand what the chancellor proposed, and subjected him to more than an hour of violent oratory, making it clear, however, that he would not support Brüning on any significant aspect of his proposals.[32]

Undeterred by that setback, Brüning went ahead with the remainder of his plan. The United States was important to its success, but in order to sell the plan to the Americans, as a way to save the republic, phase two would have to be minimized or concealed from them, partly because Americans identified the Hohenzollern monarchy with Prussian militarism and war. It was in these circumstances that Brüning began a concerted, and successful, effort to win British backing for his policy, and to win the confidence and support of Ambassador Sackett.

After Hitler's success in September, Brüning escalated his strategy to win equality of armaments and to end reparations. To carry out his plan the chancellor enlisted the aid of the British and the American ambassadors in Berlin. At the end of October, Foreign Minister Julius Curtius opened up the campaign with British Ambassador Horace Rumbold. The disarmament issue was "a cardinal one in the eyes of the German Government," Curtius explained. The German people were very displeased that the victor powers had not disarmed as was provided for in the Versailles Treaty. The Americans, he said, wanted the disarmament conference to meet next year; the foreign minister was disappointed that Britain did not share that position.

Rumbold understood that the Brüning government wanted some foreign policy success. They needed relief not only in the disarmament issue, but in the reparations matter as well. Curtius said that the Germans needed "alleviations" in foreign policy. Rumbold believed that the Germans would not engage in a "foreign policy of adventure," but there were signs, he

---

32 Brüning, *Memoiren*, 191–197; see Gordon to State, 8 October 1930, 862.00/2547, as recounted above, Chapter 3.

wrote, that the Germans would "increase the *tempo*." The Young Plan came in for discussion between the two diplomats. Curtius maintained that circumstances had changed since the New Plan had been drawn up. Germany's capacity to pay reparations was dependent on the growth of its foreign trade, but the depression intervened to make the German position difficult if not impossible. Curtius then explained that Germany would need to examine the possibility of a moratorium in reparations payments for two years, as provided for in the Young Plan.[33]

The suggestions did not sit well with the British, who had become accustomed to German complaining about how desperate their situation was[34] and made it clear that a disarmament conference without adequate preparation could lead to abject failure. In addition, talk of a Young Plan moratorium could lead to financial disaster. The Germans would get no help from that quarter, but, still, the British were speaking in a "friendly tone."[35] Brüning kept the British in mind for further action, but meanwhile he turned to the Americans as a more likely avenue for immediate success. The chancellor had befriended Sackett, who was eager to help Brüning. But Sackett also had his own agenda.

The American ambassador was alarmed by Hitler's success in the Reichstag elections. In Sackett's view, American financial interests were exposed to the possibility of repudiation.[36] But, more likely, American foreign loan policy was responsible for a very dangerous imbalance in short-term loans to the Germans. Sackett was convinced that the Germans needed to convert their short-term obligations to long-term in order to avoid a financial debacle. He therefore sought out Brüning to discuss mutual German-American interests in a more solvent debt position.

Sackett was emboldened by his belief that Germany and the rest of the world looked to the United States for leadership out of the economic depression.[37] Moreover, Sackett's interests coincided with Brüning's. The chancellor now knew that a moratorium under the Young Plan would be difficult. He believed he could use the short-term-debt issue as an avenue toward reducing reparations payments without reference to the Young Plan. In the escalation of his plan to end reparations, Brüning now turned

33 Rumbold to Henderson, three despatches, 27 October 1930, DBFP, 1: 523–527.

34 J. S. Andrews of the British Treasury, 2 January 1931, Comments on Sir Arthur Balfour's Report on Conditions in Germany, 1930, British Treasury Reports, Reel 14, File Reference Number 1718.

35 David Carlton, *MacDonald versus Henderson*, 67–69.

36 Sackett to State, 6 November 1930, 862.00/2564.

37 Lindsay to Henderson, 25 September 1930, *British Documents on Foreign Affairs: Reports and Papers from the Foreign Office Confidential Print*, Kenneth Bourne and D. Cameron Watt, general editors, Series C, *North America, 1919–1939*, D. K. Adams, ed., vol. 2, *The Great Depression, July 1928–Feb. 1933*, hereafter cited BDFA, followed by series, volume, and page numbers, all from Part 2, *From the First to the Second World War*.

to the idea of an international meeting to deal with the reparations issue, but also to negotiate on disarmament, the debt situation, and the promotion of international trade and industry. What better way than to urge the United States to take the initiative to call a world economic conference.[38]

Sackett had already revealed a strong inclination to support the resolution of diplomatic problems through meetings of heads of state. He spoke to a German audience of a "vivid" American hope for "the substitution of the conference table for the gage of battle." Now Brüning was prepared to offer him just such an opportunity. The chancellor's wish was that an international meeting of the major heads of state could be convened to settle the world economic crisis. By this, he meant that Germany should be relieved of the burdens of reparations, debt, and disarmament. Diplomacy by conference was characteristic of the the interwar period and the idea of still another one was in the air. Calls for a world economic parley were being heard in Rome, Istanbul, and Paris, and Sackett had expressed his interest in "the conference table" as a means for settling international problems.[39] A conference also appealed to Brüning and it was Sackett who gave the chancellor the opportunity to exploit the idea.

In a discussion with Curtius, Sackett agreed that the Reichstag elections reflected a vote of protest against the way Germany was treated in the international arena. The American acknowledged that the Germans had a genuine grievance in the armaments issue. But he went beyond sympathy and asserted that his government was ready to act on the issue. Hoover, he maintained, was quite concerned about disarmament, an issue that was "close to his heart." Curtius was of course delighted, but Sackett was unable to give him any details.[40]

The American ambassador had opened a door through which the Germans were prepared to storm. Curtius met with former Secretary of State Frank B. Kellogg in the American embassy in Berlin on December 14. He pressed the idea that the United States should take the initiative to call an economic conference. The German foreign minister hoped that two matters could be discussed: the economic problems brought on by the depression and the extension of the Pact of Paris (the Kellogg-Briand Pact) to include consultation.[41]

---

38 Winfried Glashagen, "Die Reparationspolitik Heinrich Brünings, 1930–1931, Studien zum wirtschafts- und aussenpolitischen Entscheidungsprozess in der Auflösungsphase der Weimarer Republik," 1: 18–19, 266, 270–271, sees Brüning engaged in a deliberate, well-conceived strategy to end reparations in three escalating stages from his chancellorship to the Nazi Reichstag victory in 1930, thence to the meeting with the British at Chequers in 1931, and on to the Lausanne Conference in 1932.
39 See ADAP, 16, 318n4; *New York Times*, 16 March 1930.
40 Memorandum by Curtius, 5 November 1930, ADAP, 16: 104–105.
41 Memorandum by Hans Dieckhoff, 16 December 1930, ADAP, 16: 273; the Germans were interested in the Pact of Paris partly because it implied that going to war had been a legal means of carrying out policy before 1928. They also wanted to extend the pact

Especially cautious because Curtius was seeking an American initiative, Kellogg asked for a memorandum on the subject. The German pulled back immediately, claiming that he would need to talk to Brüning first. He maintained that the idea had come to him spontaneously and he was therefore unprepared to make any formal commitment. But Curtius got what he wanted. Kellogg, who said he would be returning to the United States soon, promised to relay the substance of the conversation to President Hoover.[42]

Five days later Brüning took advantage of a meeting with Sackett to press the matter even further. The American asked for the opportunity to speak with the chancellor "man to man." Right after Sackett returned to Berlin from the United States, following the September 1930 elections, he and Brüning had their first long, confidential conversation in the course of cementing a close political relationship. Brüning later confessed that "from the first I felt instinctive friendship and trust" for Sackett.[43] The ambassador, who was meeting Brüning with increasing frequency, had recently met with George Harrison of the Federal Reserve Bank of New York and with Reichsbank president Hans Luther. He now wanted to talk to Brüning about the general political situation in Germany and in Europe.

Brüning claims it was Sackett who brought up the idea of Hoover's calling an international conference. That is possible, even likely; moreover, it is quite clear from Sackett's earlier conversations with Curtius that he was eager to step in to help Brüning in some way. In any case, when the German chancellor and the American ambassador met on December 19, 1930, there was a harmony of ideas. The world economic situation was bleak enough that they agreed it called for special consideration. They wanted to avoid the mistakes of the past. In an interesting prelude to the decline of corporatism, Sackett especially wanted to avoid a meeting of experts. He was convinced that such a convocation would be doomed to failure.[44]

Another problem with past conferences, according to Brüning, was that they were far too narrow in scope. He wanted to include more than economics. In his view reparations, disarmament, the liquidation of debts, and other matters should come up for discussion. The chancellor painted a very gloomy picture of the world situation, but was especially concerned about the dismal and dangerous situation in Germany. He was convinced,

to include consultation as a means of clarifying public opinion in obscure cases relating to the use of war to settle disputes. The Germans hoped it would open the door to equality of armaments for them. See Memorandum by Stimson, 20 November 1930, FRUS, 1930, 3: 92–96.

42 Memorandum by Dieckhoff, 16 December 1930, ADAP, 16: 273.

43 Brüning, "The Statesman," 112; Gottfried Reinhold Treviranus, *Das Ende von Weimar*, 228.

44 Memorandum by Brüning, 19 December 1930, ADAP, 16: 288–289.

he said, that if Hoover could get the heads of state behind closed doors, without a staff of experts to hinder their discourse, the president with his special insight in economic and financial matters could lead them to a workable solution of the world's problems. Brüning was sure that the American people, under Hoover's leadership, had the natural talent to pull off the audacious scheme. Sackett took up the strategy with enthusiasm. He promised he would write a private letter to Hoover immediately and return to carry on the conversation further after the new year.[45]

In the course of their conversation, the specter of communism arose. Brüning characterized the proposed conference as a plan to save Europe and the world from economic and political chaos, and emphasized the danger of the spread of Bolshevism. Although both men were avid anticommunists, Brüning feared he had gone too far in raising the Red Scare. The chancellor later acknowledged for the record that the anti-communist shibboleth had been overused for the previous twelve years and had lost its impact. In this case he feared he had put Sackett off, for he detected the ambassador wincing skeptically when the matter was brought up. Convinced he had gone too far, the German was not confident that Sackett would forward the proposal to President Hoover.[46]

But he had not correctly measured his man. Not only did Sackett write to Hoover, but in an extraordinarily anticommunist letter, he denigrated the danger of Hitler and the Nazis and focused his full attention on the dangers of communism. The American diplomat shared with Brüning a strong aversion for communism but at the same time was aware that Hitler and the Nazis, not the German Communist party, constituted the major threat to the Weimar Republic; all the despatches he authored or signed after his arrival in Berlin attest to that. In the light of that knowledge, he was probably influenced by three factors: his personal belief that communism was the principal danger to peace and stability in Europe, in spite of the ineffectiveness of the German Communist party; his desire to be certain to gain the attention of Hoover, who was known to be concerned about communism but whose information about the Nazis was sketchy at best; and his susceptibility to Brüning's influence, as well as an almost total commitment to the chancellor as a virtual savior for Germany.

While on vacation in France, Sackett wrote a private, though formal, eight-page letter to Hoover on plain stationery. Three topics were covered: the call for an international conference; passing references to Hitler and the Nazis; and Sackett's almost obsessive discussion of the dangers of communism, which constituted the bulk of the letter. To emphasize the importance of the situation, Sackett informed Hoover that Kellogg had

---

45 Brüning, *Memoiren*, 222–223; Memorandum by Brüning, 19 December 1930, ADAP, 16: 288–290, copies of the memorandum were distributed throughout the German government.
46 Brüning, *Memoiren*, 223–224.

been in Berlin recently and met the major figures in German government and finance. Kellogg shared with Sackett the fear that internal problems, rather than war, constituted the "real menace to the peace of Europe." They agreed that communist revolution was the danger.[47]

Emphasizing the threatening nature of the situation, Sackett appealed to Hoover to act. He stressed that "the situation is so menacing, both to peace and the return of prosperity in all lands, that an international economic conference should be promptly initiated." Such a conference should be unlike previous conferences associated with the League of Nations and Geneva. Contrary to Brüning's suggestion, the ambassador wrote that the meeting should shun political matters, although heads of state should participate. In the letter, Sackett, probably convinced that Hoover would insist on private sector participation, modified his earlier view and suggested the meeting should include two of the best financial and business leaders from each nation to meet with the president in the United States.

In an appeal to Hoover's interests, Sackett pointed out that such a conference would be "quite effective in disarmament matters." The president was convinced that too many governments were wasting their limited finances on arming for war, a policy that severely drained their resources. Reparations, of course, would need to be dealt with; every German, the ambassador said, brought up the matter in almost every conversation. Above all, reparations needed to be studied, based on current revenue expectations, or Germany was doomed to a chaotic state. In other words, reparations should be adjusted downward to meet depression conditions. Neither Hoover nor Sackett thought that reparations should be canceled, so to mollify the president, the ambassador confidently claimed that "we can very well maintain ourselves in any such discussion." The ambassador was convinced that the American position on reparations was not well understood abroad, "even by responsible ministers, and we in America have soon got to meet reparations again in the open anyway."

To emphasize the danger confronting Germany and Europe, Sackett spoke of Brüning as representing his nation's "responsible thought," which expected a "very distressing and dangerous time" in the coming February and March. The situation was bad, but with growing unemployment it could become "much worse than even the pathetic present." The chancellor feared serious internal problems that he was not confident the government could handle, especially since "agitators against the established order" were being given more grist for their mills.

At this point Sackett dismissed Hitler and the Nazis as a serious problem. Brüning was alarmed, he maintained, but "his fear does not lie with the followers of Hitler, as he considers that party to be a mushroom

---

47 The following is from Sackett to Hoover, 27 December 1930, Foreign Affairs – Diplomats, Sackett, F. M., HHPL.

growth that has no cohesion among its members and is already showing signs of splitting into factions." It should be recalled that at this time Brüning hoped he could conciliate the Nazis and in the end remove them from the field by achieving their foreign policy goals. Sackett obviously went along with the view that the chancellor could steal Hitler's thunder and therefore render the Nazi leader expendable.

Remember that Sackett was not only expressing his personal beliefs; he was also attempting to get President Hoover's attention, and the Bolshevik specter was a better device than most. The American diplomat revealed that he "enjoyed a rather intimate acquaintance" with Brüning, and had "come to know him quite well." They met "occasionally in the late afternoon" and last week Sackett "was at his house for tea. As we were alone for an hour he discussed with me quite confidentially Germany's internal problems and international relations and developed some views which seemed to me might intrigue your interest."

His political intimacy with the chancellor established, Sackett proceeded to establish Brüning's credibility and stability; the ambassador considered him "the present strong character of Germany." Alluding to the parallel with Hoover's career, Sackett wrote that Brüning "is not in the ordinary sense a politician" although he had "wide experience in political life and understands it." As the head of a minority government, the chancellor was able to guide the nation through "severe political" problems with his "personal domination" and was able to restructure the nation's entire economic system, forcing reductions in government spending.

Having laid the groundwork for his own and the chancellor's credentials, Sackett reported that Brüning, in the course of their conversation, "continually spoke" not of Hitler and the Nazis but "of the menace of the Communistic group." The chancellor described for Sackett a combustible internal situation in which the German Communist party was quiescent, "under orders from Moscow to wait for the psychological moment." His fear was of "internal explosions" and "real industrial revolutions in capitalistic countries."

Sackett reenforced Hoover's resolve not to recognize the Soviet Union. "The world," he said, "is stupidly playing into Russia's hands in assisting her" with credits that enabled the Soviets to produce enough to undersell foreign nations and disrupt their economies. The liberal financial terms offered Russia should be eliminated and business done on the basis of cash or secured credit only. The public and private sectors should come to agreement to halt the long-term credits "which in turn serve to prolong the debacle in that strange land."

Hoover's response must have been gratifying to Sackett. The ambassador was able to get the president's attention and the promise of action. The president implied, in a short note, that he would act on Sackett's proposal, indicating that he was "very greatly interested" and that Kellogg had just been in to see him.[48] However, from Sackett's point of view, Kellogg's visit with the president was not successful. The former secretary of state emphasized "the necessity for European disarmament" and impressed on Hoover the need to use "all influence" to urge European nations "to accomplish this object." Sackett sent the letter to Brüning without comment; both Sackett and Brüning had to be disappointed that Kellogg stressed disarmament rather than an economic conference.[49]

Hoover did indeed act; Brüning later recalled that his reaction "was unexpectedly quick."[50] Sackett informed the Germans of Hoover's "lively interest," but a stroke of bad luck had intervened. Undersecretary of State Joseph P. Cotton prepared to make the requisite journey to Europe to sound out interest in an international economic conference. While making arrangements to depart for Europe, Cotton, who Sackett described as the "driving force" in American foreign affairs, was stricken with a minor ailment that was followed by complications and then his tragic and unexpected death.[51]

Meanwhile, in Washington, Ambassador Prittwitz was not optimistic about any action coming from the American president. He suggested that Hoover had all he could handle with domestic economic and political issues. No initiative in calling a conference was likely to come from Hoover unless he were to muster the "courage and expectation" that he could appeal to the American people over the heads of Congress and the Republican party, an implausible expectation.[52]

The shock of Cotton's death probably stunned Hoover into inaction. Moreover, Hoover was inclined to proceed with caution and began to have second thoughts about a wide-ranging conference. In any case, Sackett heard no more from the president. Beset by the domestic crisis, Hoover was preoccupied with the pressures to resolve the depression. Sackett, who now held out little hope for an immediate response from Hoover, began a barrage of warnings to the State Department intended to alarm the government into action over Germany's short-term loan situation, which had reached dangerous proportions.

48 Hoover to Sackett, 12 January 1931, Foreign Affairs – Diplomats, Sackett, F. M., HHPL.
49 Kellogg to Sackett, 24 January 1931, forwarded to Brüning; Sackett asked that the letter be returned to him, GFMR 1780/D811002–811003.
50 Brüning, "The Statesman," 113; but Hoover sought a conference only on silver and had approached the Canadians in February 1931. Hoover promised the United States would cooperate "to the utmost of its power and would send a representative delegation." The British showed little interest and Ambassador Mellon had "no use for such a conference." Lindsay, "Annual Report on the United States for 1931," 2 January 1932, FO371, 1932, 7, 15874: 13–14.
51 Bülow to Brüning, 2 February 1931, GFMR 1776/D808281; *New York Times*, esp. 16, 17, 18, 23 February, and 6, 10, 11, 12, 13, 14, 22 March 1931. Cotton died on March 10, 1931.
52 Prittwitz to Bülow, 19 January 1931, GFMR 2384/E199147–199149.

When he returned to the American embassy after the Christmas holidays, Sackett learned more of Germany's critical financial condition; but, more important, he discovered the deep and dangerous extent of American banking involvement in what could become a financial catastrophe. He spent more time than ever with Brüning, and also with Reichsbank President Luther and with private German and American bankers. The ambassador suggested that Luther compile a statistical profile of German short-term debts, but the information was not to be "circulated beyond official sources."[53]

Luther's response, aside from fresh information on German indebtedness, was a well-argued plea for treaty and reparations revision. The Reichsbank president estimated Germany's total foreign debt, exclusive of reparations, at 19.3 billion marks, or about $5 billion. Sackett argued that the major problem was the huge short-term debt. His solution was for Germany to convert those loans to long-term. Luther agreed with Sackett that such a solution would not only be helpful to the world economy, but was necessary for German domestic political and economic purposes. Luther concluded his long letter with another appeal for treaty and Young Plan revision, asking how long such a resolution "leading to real salvation" could be postponed.[54]

Sackett, unsettled by what appeared to be irresponsible American loans to Germany, undertook to study the problem and came up with a solution. He told Hans Schäffer of the Finance Ministry that he had discussed the matter with various government agencies and thought it possible to place "bond issues of German industry and governmental institutions amounting to billions" in the United States. In what Schäffer described as a "coherent exposition," Sackett explained that he was from the interior of the United States, far away from the "big stock exchanges" and was surprised to see that German securities had such a small share in the American heartland. Britain and France were doing a better marketing job than the Germans, who could improve their position by reducing the number and type of securities they offered. Sackett emphasized that "if it were possible to create great, consolidated German bond issues, then they would enjoy the same popularity and acceptability as the bond issues of the other great capitalist countries of Europe." German securities would prosper if Americans in the "smaller towns of the West and the Middle West" learned more about German issues, and could easily "get rid of them if one needed cash."[55]

Sackett was further alarmed at what he learned from George Murnane. He reported that the financier "gave me quite a shock in telling me the

53 Sackett to State, 25 March 1931, 862.51/3016.
54 Luther to Sackett, 27 February 1931, enclosed with Sackett to State, 25 March 1931, 862.51/3016, and GFMR 1776/D808223–808240.
55 Hans Schäffer, Memorandum, 9 March 1931, GFMR 2375/E192116–192121.

figures. He said that the Chase Bank had $190,000,000 here and the Guaranty Trust about $90,000,000 and remarked that it was the equivalent of nearly half the capital of the banks." Murnane revealed that short-term loans to Germany "now were in such volume from America that they could not be called or renewals refused without great danger to the financial situation in the United States." The banker also confided to Sackett that "the loaning business has actually been overdone to such an extent that the credits have become frozen and he is worried that his own advice to his American principals is largely responsible."[56]

The ambassador was able to get the full attention of the U.S. government. His warning of Germany's precarious financial condition was circulated throughout the State Department and to the highest echelons of the Hoover administration. Secretary of State Stimson forwarded the despatch to Andrew Mellon, secretary of the treasury, and to President Hoover with a covering letter. Sackett wanted to warn, even alarm, both his own and the German governments; but he also hoped to keep the whole mess within official government circles. Above all, he did not want to inform American private banking interests out of fear that they might withdraw their funds and bring down not only the Brüning cabinet but possibly even the Weimar Republic. Clearly, the corporatist system, as it was then organized, was breaking down. Official diplomats no longer had faith in their unofficial counterpart. Investment based solely on the return of profit was apparently not a solid basis for political stability. Sackett warned that "if even twenty-five per cent of these loans were not renewed there would be no way of Germany carrying on." The Germans simply did not have the means either to pay or to borrow elsewhere.[57]

As was the custom, American diplomats were unaware of significant loan negotiations being carried out in the private sector with the German government. But Sackett's position and influence were now so strong that George Murnane felt the need to confide in him. The financier told Sackett that the Germans wanted another loan "on quite a large scale" for the coming spring. The ambassador asked if Lee, Higginson could raise the money without difficulty and was told by Murnane that "he was not at all sure – that actually in the last loan, it was not successful as based on German credit, but as a forced loan based on the prestige of the issuing house in America." Murnane was concerned that he might have placed his principals in danger.[58]

The Lee, Higginson partner asked Hjalmar Schacht, the "financial wizard" and former president of the Reichsbank, to comment on the wisdom of the proposed loan. Schacht responded: "Murnane, you certainly will get

---

56 Sackett to State, Confidential to the Secretary and Undersecretary, 21 January 1931, enclosed with Stimson to Hoover, 14 February 1931, 862.51/2991.
57 Sackett to State, 21 January 1931, 862.51/2991; see also 25 March 1931, 862.51/3016.
58 Sackett to State, 21 January 1931, 862.51/2991.

your money back, though if it will be on the dates agreed upon may be in doubt. As to whether or not the loan is wise, I am unable to answer because of its political character."[59]

Sackett informed the State Department that the Reich was negotiating for a short-term "transitional loan."[60] The proposed loan was hedged with restrictions. The amount was $35 million, which was to be secured by the German State Railways and guaranteed by the German government. In addition Lee, Higginson requested that the Brüning government attempt to get French banks to participate in the loan, hoping that the implied improvement in Franco-German relations might be enough to get the full amount subscribed.[61] The ploy to win French participation in the loan caused a flurry of excitement in the State Department as well as in France. In Paris, American Ambassador Walter E. Edge telephoned Stimson to deny that the Germans were trying to negotiate a loan with the French. It was soon resolved when Edge reported that the French announced the magic formula – they offered no objection to the proposed Lee, Higginson loan.[62]

Sackett's influence in Washington and New York, as well as in Berlin, enabled him to persist in his attempt to help Brüning. Gottfried Treviranus, a close friend of the chancellor, claims that Sackett told Brüning not to take Hoover's inaction in calling a conference to be final. Sackett assured Brüning that prominent Americans in government and finance were in favor of a conference to deal with the reparations issue. Secretary of the Treasury Andrew Mellon and Albert H. Wiggin, president of the Chase Bank in New York, were convinced that resumption of reparations negotiations was essential. Owen Young, after whom the reparations plan was named, was certain that a reduction of 20 percent in reparations rates could be concluded. Treviranus claims that Brüning believed President Hoover needed to take the initiative with Congress to reduce or eliminate war debts, in spite of traditional opposition to such a consideration. But on February 2, Sackett acknowledged to Brüning that Hoover considered it unlikely that a majority could be found in Congress for such a move.[63] According to Treviranus, Sackett considered it important to notify Washington that Brüning would not take the initiative to call a conference.[64]

The next day, February 3, Sackett, certainly disappointed, opened up a new front in his effort to influence the president. He now turned to his

---

59 Schacht, *76 Jahre meines Lebens*, 344.
60 Sackett to State, 2 February 1931, 862.51/2999.
61 Murnane to Burke, 11 April 1966.
62 Edge to State, 29 January and 4 February 1931, 862.51/2989 and 862.51/2998.
63 British Ambassador Lindsay reported from Washington that "the outlook for revision of the debts by consent of Congress is about as black as it could be"; 17 December 1931, BDFA, C, 2: 182.
64 Treviranus, *Das Ende von Weimar*, 229–230.

boyhood friend Oswald Garrison Villard, editor of *The Nation*, to exert pressure on the British in the hope that they could get Hoover to take action on calling the conference. Sackett and his friend had been attempting to intervene in Germany's favor since Hitler's success in the September 1930 elections. Villard was spending a year in Germany and was privy to most important developments.[65]

The groundwork had been laid by the two friends. Villard was at the time visiting in London, where he found a receptive audience in several quarters, but ran into trouble with the British Foreign Office and attempted without success to see American Ambassador Charles G. Dawes. Sackett wrote Dawes that he was asking Villard to call on him, thus opening the way for the editor to sound out Dawes on the matter of an international conference. He introduced Villard as especially well informed on German affairs and as a person who had "the entrée with all circles" in Berlin.[66] But Villard, who had not made a favorable impression in the German Foreign Ministry,[67] now ran into more problems in London. Sackett's hopes were dashed for the time being. Dawes wrote Sackett: "Villard called on me the other day, and I had quite a talk with him. I was much interested in what he said, but not impressed with his suggestions as to America's initiative in the matter of a conference."[68]

Villard had even less impact at the British Foreign Office, where he was considered to be "an uncompromisingly unfriendly critic." Robert L. Craigie, who hoped "devotedly that we shall steer very clear of any scheme sponsored by" Villard, asked G. H. Thompson of the American Department to write a report on the American. Thompson's reply was that Villard "may perhaps be aptly described as in intellectual sentimentalist with a strong bias against" Great Britain. When Arthur Willert read the report, he concurred, adding that Villard was "extremely unsound" and that "his spiritual home was 75 percent in Berlin and 25 percent in Moscow."[69]

Villard ran into a stone wall at the Foreign Office but he did better

---

65 Sackett to Charles G. Dawes, 3 February 1931, Box 213, London Embassy/Routine Correspondence, Charles G. Dawes Papers; Sackett to Villard 11 January 1932, bMS Am 1323 (3374), Oswald Garrison Villard Papers. Villard's stay in Germany prepared *The Nation* editor to write *The German Phoenix, The Story of the Republic*, in which, among other things, he stoutly defended Brüning's position on ending reparations and revising the Treaty of Versailles, 43–92.

66 Sackett to Villard, bMS Am 1323 (3374), Villard Papers; Sackett to Dawes, both 3 February 1931, copy to Villard, Box 213, London Embassy/Routine Correspondence, Dawes Papers.

67 Bülow to Neurath, 30 January 1931, GFMR 2384/E199122–199124.

68 Dawes to Sackett, 14 February 1931, Box 213, London Embassy/Routine Correspondence, Dawes Papers; Dawes persisted in his opposition to a monetary conference, *Journal as Ambassador to Great Britain*, 344–345, 409.

69 G. H. Thompson, "*Mr. Oswald Garrison Villard*, Minute outlining his career and character," 30 January 1931, FO371, 1931, 7, 15134: 61–63.

among influential Britons. Meanwhile, a Hoover initiative in calling a conference was lost for the moment, but Sackett was persistent in his attempt to help Brüning and work toward resolving the German debt problem. In concert with Villard the ambassador did not give up hope that an international conference could be called. Villard had talked with Brüning at the end of January 1931 with a proposal to open reparations talks with the British. That opened another avenue for Brüning, who was eager for any discussions about the reparations issue.[70] Sackett, working through Villard, was able to accomplish a great deal more than appeared likely. Later he would share satisfaction that Villard had taken such a "momentous journey to England" and was instrumental in bringing the European heads of state together in many conferences.[71]

Brüning, whose memory was often flawed in recalling the events of his administration, later maintained that Hoover intended a full-blown conference. He seemed oblivious to the repeated American assertion that disarmament was essentially a European affair, that reparations were spoils of war, and hence subject to revision, but that war debts owed to the United States were borrowed money and therefore sacrosanct. Apparently Hoover did indeed want a conference, but according to Castle, he wanted to move one step at a time, convinced that too broad an agenda would lead nowhere. The president wanted to confine any such meeting to the consideration of one issue – silver – and moreover, he tried to shift the burden of calling a conference to Prime Minister Ramsay MacDonald of Great Britain. The Briton agreed on the advisability of a conference, but thought that Hoover should call it and that it would need to address more than silver; it would need to discuss the reparations and war debts issues.[72]

The Germans pressed in the meantime to find out what progress was being made toward calling a conference. They tried to distance themselves from the notion that they had originated the idea. In Paris, the German and British ambassadors discussed the matter. They agreed that the proposal for a new great international conference had come up in a variety of quarters and one could say that the idea was in the air. In an attempt to attribute the call for a conference to the British, German Foreign Minister Curtius asserted that he agreed with the British ambassador in Paris "that the official proposal can only come from the American government or from President Hoover himself." Curtius denied that there was any reason for him to join in a call for American intervention. Probably unaware of Brüning's talk with Sackett, he stated that it was unnecessary for him to act since the issue had already been brought up by "a person close to

70 Glashagen, "Die Reparationspolitik Heinrich Brünings 1930–1931," 1: 359.
71 Villard to Castle, 30 June 1931, and Sackett to Villard, 11 January 1932, bMS Am 1323 (529 and 3374), Villard Papers.
72 Castle Diary, 21 and 28 February, 8 March 1931; Dawes, *Journal as Ambassador to Great Britain*, 304, 344–345.

Hoover." He refused to discuss particulars until he heard Hoover's response to Kellogg.[73]

Brüning and Curtius were seeking to spread the idea that the French and the British wanted a conference so that everyone would come to believe that the idea was not German. Meanwhile they agreed to do nothing until they heard from Sackett, not Kellogg. In addition, they were under the impression that Sackett had written to Hoover on the day he met with Brüning, December 19, when in fact Sackett had delayed until eight days later. The timing was important because they expected to hear Hoover's response about January 13. They were prepared, in the event Hoover gave them a negative reply, to pursue the idea of a conference of heads of state on their own.[74] But that was an alternative they hoped they could avoid.

The issue confused officials in the Reichschancellery and in the Foreign Ministry. They believed that the idea did indeed originate elsewhere. German officials speculated about where it came from in the first place and were unable to find an answer. They could uncover no German source for the idea. In Washington, Prittwitz guessed that it was Sackett who had taken the initiative to ask Hoover to call a conference, and Bülow confirmed the truth of his guess. But Prittwitz surmised that nothing would come of it. He reported that he talked with prominent bankers and industrialists while in New York and none of them were aware of or expected a conference, and certainly not on the initiative of the United States. The Americans further asserted that the Germans should not count on Hoover taking action.[75]

It was the British who expressed the most interest, even though Villard made no headway with either Prime Minister MacDonald or Foreign Secretary Arthur Henderson.[76] However, Villard was making progress in some British quarters. He found support of many in and out of the British government for an attempt to cope with the problems beseting Germany. Many in Britain, especially in the financial world and in large industry, wanted to revise the international debt system so that the British trade situation could be improved. That made Britain a potential partner in the move for reparations revision.[77] The British Treasury was reporting alarming statistics which demonstrated that the British were being hurt by German payment of reparations. They tied the payments to foreign trade,

---

73 Curtius to Leopold von Hoesch, German ambassador in Paris, 29 December 1930, ADAP, 16: 316–318.

74 Memorandum by Planck, 30 December 1930, ADAP, 16: 324–325.

75 Prittwitz to Bülow, and Bülow to Prittwitz, 10 and 24 February 1931, GFMR 2384/E199152 and E199157; Hermann Pünder to Bernhard von Bülow, 3 January, and Prittwitz to the Foreign Ministry, 14 January 1931, ADAP, 16: 337, 404.

76 Bernstorff to Curtius, 6 February 1931, GFMR 1659/D728969.

77 Glashagen, "Die Reparationspolitik Heinrich Brünings 1930–1931, 1: 570, 2: 243–244n67; Craig, *Germany, 1866–1945*, 440.

the increase of which was the only practicable way for Germany to pay reparations. The report showed that during the years 1924–1929 German exports of manufactured goods increased from £281.7 million to £491.6 million. At the same time exports from the United Kingdom decreased from £618.6 million to £573.8 million.[78]

Under pressure, especially from "the City," the British decided to see what they could do to help Brüning. But they were also under constraints to help themselves. The British Treasury charged that gold was being heaped in France and the United States to the detriment of the entire world as a result of the reparations and war debts cycle. The system, they maintained, "has crippled our trade with Germany who is normally one of our best customers." The Young Plan, they contended, "recognized the inevitable connection between Reparations and the War Debts to America," and reparations revision would be impossible without "a revision of these War Debts." The Treasury position was that "Reparations and War Debts should be cancelled or reduced to a minimum."[79]

Given growing British interest, Foreign Secretary Henderson wanted Horace Rumbold, the British ambassador in Berlin, to explore ways in which the British could give Brüning "such support and encouragement" as was proper to "fortify" the chancellor's position, which was of course to achieve the cancellation of reparations. Henderson had discovered that it was the Germans who were maneuvering to induce the Americans to call a conference. He asked Rumbold to "ascertain discreetly what response, if any, the German Government has received at Washington in reply to its enquiries."[80]

Rumbold invited Sackett to dinner on the evening of March 3 and used the occasion to inquire about the possibility of a conference that might "devise a cure for the world economic crisis." Sackett admitted that he had suggested such a conference to Hoover, with a "view to helping the Brüning Government." He had done so, he said, at the German's request. The American ambassador then "spontaneously" remarked that such a conference would "naturally have to consider such questions as inter-allied debts, reparations and the movement of gold." Hoover, however, was preoccupied with domestic problems and had no time for such suggestions and had merely acknowledged the "several letters" Sackett had written to him.[81]

The seasoned British diplomat characterized Sackett as one of the "competent observers" who believed it to be "not only a German but a European interest that the Brüning government should remain in power and have their hands strengthened internationally." Sackett had suggested to Rumbold

78 British Treasury Report on Germany's Strong Export Position, n.d., 1931, Reel 16, 172/ 1747.
79 British Treasury Memorandum on German Reparations, n.d., 1931, 16: 1747.
80 Henderson to Rumbold, 19 February 1931, DBFP, 1: 561.
81 Rumbold to Henderson, 4 March 1931, DBFP, 1: 576–78.

that it would be of "great value" if the British could do something to "enhance the prestige of the chancellor. A gesture on the part of England would do more for the Brüning government than anything else." Rumbold agreed with Sackett that it was "not so much actual concessions that are needed as some tangible evidence, some indication of a readiness to consider the German point of view."[82]

In his determined effort to help his friend Brüning, Sackett overstepped the bounds of good diplomacy. He promised a great deal that he might not be able to deliver. Some he certainly could not deliver. In the proposed economic conference he virtually promised would come about, he advocated the discussion of issues contrary to American policy. The Germans wanted a broad discussion of many issues, whereas the Americans, if they were to participate, wanted a restricted agenda. Brüning, for example, wanted to bring up war debts, a subject that was forbidden ground for any discussion as far as the Hoover administration was concerned. It was important to the German because of its direct relationship to the reparations issue.

Sackett led the Germans to believe the United States would intervene in the disarmaments issue and would take the initiative for an international economic conference, and he even implied that American capital might be available to bail Germany out of its financial problems. The ambassador was behaving like a cheerleader, even a therapist salving German hurt feeling for the treatment they felt they were receiving in international affairs. Additionally, he had misled Hoover by stressing his own deeply held personal fears of communism and not explaining his official view of the danger Hitler and the Nazis posed for the Weimar Republic.

Meanwhile, Sackett was further emboldened in his efforts to help Brüning. Unable, as he thought, to influence his own government, he had turned to the British, who were well disposed to give the German chancellor all the help they could. And the British did help. Sackett took the initiative to get the British to invite Brüning to meet with MacDonald at Chequers, the official country home of the prime minister. Such a meeting was important to the German's international prestige. It would be the first visit of a former enemy statesman to England since the war. Sackett was credited by Stimson for being responsible for the meeting at Chequers.[83] But the Kentuckian did not work alone.

Villard took the lead in concert with Sackett. Villard's activity was responsible "to a considerable degree" (*im grösseren Masse*) for preparing the ground for the Chequers conference.[84] Sackett was playing an important

82 Rumbold to Henderson, 4 March 1931, DBFP, 1: 578–579; Curtius recalled that the Germans were invited to Chequers at the beginning of March, *Sechs Jahre Minister der deutschen Republik*, 213.
83 Stimson Diary, 4 May 1931.
84 Glashagen, "Die Reparationspolitik Heinrich Brünings 1930–1931," 1: 361.

role in influencing his own and the British government, but because of Hoover's caution, he was making better headway with the British, thanks to the intervention of his friend Villard.

Sackett's purpose was to enhance Brüning's stature and hence strengthen the German's position at home. The British agreed. Henderson instructed Rumbold to stress to the Germans that the primary purpose of Brüning's coming to Chequers was "to serve as a gesture of friendship and 'equality.'" It was not to be the occasion for detailed discussions of technical issues, but to reinforce the German government "*vis-à-vis* its own public opinion." Brüning understood and agreed. The meeting served its designated purpose. It helped "to distract public attention from the hardships of the situation in Germany," and, in Rumbold's view, continued to serve its purpose of aiding Brüning.[85]

Although the British played a major role in the move to cancel reparations, little was accomplished at Chequers aside from the public perception that good things were happening. Major public figures such as Chancellor of the Exchequer Neville Chamberlain were taking the lead in calling for the end of reparations. They agreed with the Germans that the war debts owed to the United States were essential to any resolution of their financial problems. They further agreed that nothing substantial could be accomplished until after the American presidential elections, more than a year away.[86]

Sackett was pleased with what he was able to accomplish for Brüning. The ambassador's influence in Washington was growing. Hoover agreed to the conference Sackett called for, but the unfortunate and unexpected death of Joseph Cotton delayed action while the deepening financial crisis intervened to reinforce President Hoover's proclivity for caution and delay.

Although Sackett's influence in financial affairs grew apace, his impact on political or military support for Brüning was reduced to insignificance. By emphasizing the danger of communism in Germany, Sackett may have inadvertently affected American policy in a negative way. Even though he was aware that Hitler and the Nazis constituted the most serious threat to the Weimar Republic and to the peace of Europe, Sackett chose to minimize that hazard in his personal and most influential communication with President Hoover. Communism was generally perceived as an internal problem, with leadership from an international organization dedicated to fomenting the subversive undermining of capitalist governments. There was little general concern that the Soviet Union was a military threat to Europe. Germany, however, was thought to be a potential military menace, and particularly so if Hitler were to come to power.

---

85 Henderson to Rumbold, 21 April and Rumbold to Henderson, 4 June 1931, DBFP, 2: 59–60, 67.
86 Robert Vansittart, *The Mist Procession: The Autobiography of Lord Vansittart*, 420, 429.

When Sackett denigrated the Hitler danger, he contributed to an already strong American reluctance to intervene in Europe. There was only a minimal possibility that the United States might assert its power more forcefully in Europe, but Sackett diverted Hoover's attention away from considering even the slightest need to participate more closely with Britain and France to stave off a Hitler government. Had Hoover been alerted to the immediate danger of an aggressive Germany, he might have been more inclined to act decisively in seeking the cancellation of war debts. That action alone would have gone a long way toward ameliorating the financial crisis and could have led to the end of reparations – which would have been a triumph for Brüning's policy. Hoover might also have been led to consider a stronger and more direct role in the disarmament question as a matter of vital American concern. Instead, Sackett chose to emphasize his personal bête noire – communism.

Sackett was now convinced that Hoover would not act. He had the assurance of Ambassador Dawes and others that no American initiative was possible.[87] Having accomplished all he felt he could to influence Hoover to act on behalf of Brüning, Sackett decided to return to the United States for a leave of absence. He would use the opportunity to explain further to Hoover and Stimson the importance of assisting the chancellor. There was no urgency in Sackett's plans; he applied for a leave of absence, with permission to return home, at the end of February and was scheduled to leave in late April 1931. It was fortuitous that one of the world's most serious financial crises struck just after he reached the United States. The gravity of the situation would afford him the opportunity to influence the United States government further to act decisively to assist Brüning and hold off Hitler.

87 Villard to Castle, 30 June 1931, Castle papers – Germany, HHPL.

5

Sackett and the financial crisis

THE FINANCIAL CRISIS of 1931 threatened to bring down the Brüning government. Ambassador Sackett was acutely aware of the danger for the Weimar Republic and of the opportunity the crisis presented to Hitler. More determined than ever to aid his friend Brüning and thwart Hitler, Sackett intervened to help preserve the Weimar Republic. He took advantage of his leave of absence in the United States to emphasize the depth of the impending crisis, and when it struck he used his influence with President Hoover to urge him to intervene to help Brüning. Sackett's reports to the State Department were a decisive part of the American deliberations leading to the announcement of the Hoover Moratorium, and in Washington he participated in the complex discussions that prompted the president to act. When Sackett returned to Berlin, he engaged in the trying negotiations with the Germans and again went beyond his instructions in the interest of helping Brüning.[1]

The crisis began in May 1931, when, first in Vienna and then in Berlin, major banks began to fail. The problem quickly spread throughout Europe, creating heavy new burdens for nations already beset by deepening economic depression. President Hoover decided that the United States would have to intervene. Faced with a financial crisis of international proportions, Hoover offered the European powers a one-year holiday in the payment of war debts owed to the United States in exchange for the Entente Allies

---

1 Sackett is remembered almost exclusively for his role in the financial crisis of 1931. The best and fullest account of his activity in the crisis is in Edward W. Bennett, *Germany and the Diplomacy of the Financial Crisis, 1931*. The historian searching for material on Sackett is disappointed to find that he is rarely mentioned in any study on the Weimar Republic in English or German. When he is mentioned, it is usually a brief notice that in 1931 he was in the United States to inform Hoover and Stimson of Germany's financial plight. One study, Sander A. Diamond, *Herr Hitler, Amerikas Diplomaten, Washington und der Untergang Weimars*, concerned with the collapse of the Weimar Republic, does not mention his name in a "Selected List of U.S. Diplomatic Representatives and Agents, 1919–1933," 143–145.

agreeing to forgo reparations payments from Germany during the same period.

It was a painful decision for the president because he maintained there was no connection between the bona fide war-related debts and reparations payments, the spoils of war owed by Germany to the victorious Entente Allies. Ambassador Sackett had already warned the U.S. government that Germany's financial condition was such that it could not go on paying reparations without some form of relief. But in February 1931, he was convinced that the Hoover administration was not yet ready to act.

Sackett was in Washington when the crisis broke in May, leading many to assume that he was there specifically to deal with the problem. In one account he is reported to have arrived "on an urgent mission camouflaged as a vacation leave."[2] A more contemporaneous version claimed he was in the United States to make his report in person.[3] Hoover's *Memoirs* lead one to believe that the president was learning of the significance of Germany's financial condition for the first time.[4] But Sackett had done about all he could to warn the Hoover administration about the seriousness of the situation. He had not hurried to the United States to warn Hoover. The ambassador thought there still was time before any action was necessary. In fact, neither he nor Brüning anticipated critical problems until the autumn.[5]

Despairing of precipitating any immediate action by the American government,[6] toward the end of February Sackett decided to return to the United States. At the end of the previous September he had revealed that he intended to return home "before very long."[7] In mid-February he confided to Ambassador Dawes that if the Reichstag were to adjourn he would "seize upon the opportunity" to return home for a six months' vacation.[8] When the Reichstag did adjourn for another long hiatus, Sackett's proposed vacation plans became public and caused considerable speculation in the press. The ambassador insisted to Rumbold, with whom he had established a relationship of mutual respect and confidence, that he was taking "leave in the ordinary course and without any ulterior object."[9]

2 Louis P. Lochner, *Herbert Hoover and Germany*, 82.
3 Mark Sullivan, "President Hoover and the World Depression, The Story of the Moratorium from Official Records," *Saturday Evening Post*, 205 (11 March 1933): 3.
4 Hoover, *Memoirs*, 3: 64–65; Lochner, *Hoover and Germany*, 83.
5 Atherton to State, London, 8 June 1931, FRUS, 1931, 1: 6–8; Herbert Hoover, "President's Moratorium Diary," Draft number 2, 6 May 1931, Foreign Affairs – Financial, Moratorium, HH Diary, HHPL, hereafter cited Hoover Moratorium Diary.
6 Villard to Castle, 30 June 1931, bMS Am 1323 (529), Villard Papers.
7 Sackett to Butler, 29 September 1930, Butler Papers.
8 Sackett to Dawes, 18 February 1931, Box 213, London Embassy/ Routine Correspondence, Dawes Papers.
9 Rumbold to Henderson, 1 May 1931, DBFP, 2: 61.

Sackett was scheduled to leave Berlin on April 23 and had not intended to visit Chancellor Brüning, who was away on vacation.[10] After reading press speculation about Sackett's trip, Brüning asked to see him. The chancellor returned to Berlin on the day of Sackett's departure and the two were able to get together that morning. Rumbold, who talked with Sackett after the meeting, reported that Brüning, "once again" described Germany's financial, economic, and political predicament. Rumbold wrote: "Expectation here is that Mr. Sackett, who is well disposed toward this country [Germany], will repeat what Dr. Brüning said to the president."[11] Sackett and the chancellor discussed current political problems and Brüning brought up the reparations issue. The meeting forced the German Foreign Ministry to deny reports that Sackett had a proposal from Brüning to the American government on the subject of reparations. Such accounts, they insisted, were "totally unfounded."[12]

After all his hard work, Sackett probably felt he merited a vacation at home. His last trip to the United States had been a working visit during which he had spent most of his time campaigning in Kentucky. This time he had the additional incentive of assessing the labor turmoil in his Kentucky coal mines. The ambassador certainly had his problems. Not only was there trouble at home in the Harlan County strike, but he had been discouraged enough to think that much of his good work for Brüning could have gone for naught.[13]

Meanwhile, Chancellor Brüning was finding reason to despair. The Americans had not come through as he had hoped and the Nazi party continued to grow and foment violence. Taking his cues from Chancellor Otto von Bismarck, who in the nineteenth century sought foreign policy victories to divert attention away from domestic problems, Brüning again searched about for a possible diplomatic victory. Very few options were available without foreign help.

In those circumstances Brüning turned to a plan that he had earlier rejected. Reparations relief and revision of the Young Plan were out of the question for the moment. Moreover, he believed that the idea of an international economic conference called on American initiative was apparently moribund, if not dead. The chancellor could think of no alternative and therefore turned to a proposal that, he claimed, arose out of the Foreign Ministry.[14]

The plan, which was announced on March 23, called for an economic union between Germany and Austria based on a customs agreement. Such

10 *New York Times*, 18 and 25 April 1931.
11 Rumbold to Henderson, 1 May 1931, DBFP, 2: 61.
12 Dieckhoff to Prittwitz, 30 April 1931, ADAP, 17: 271.
13 See Villard to Castle, 30 June 1931, bMS Am 1323 (529), Villard Papers.
14 Bennett, *Germany and the Diplomacy of the Financial Crisis, 1931*, 34–37.

a proposal was fraught with potential political danger because it would almost certainly be perceived as a preliminary step toward ultimate union of the two German-speaking nations, or *Anschluss.*

Brüning was willing to take such a drastic step in order to steal a march on Hitler. Gordon reported that the proposal did indeed take some of the wind out of Nazi sails.[15] By implying a strong position on the *Anschluss* issue, Brüning could wrest the leadership of the movement for a Greater Germany from Hitler and win additional support from the nationalistic Right. At the same time, Brüning would establish the basis for a quid pro quo, perhaps to drop the customs union proposal in exchange for reparations revision. Such a plan made sense, but the timing left much to be desired.

In addition to the customs union plan, and in spite of the claim that Germany was unable to meet its reparations payments without severe financial strain, the Brüning government supported one of President Hindenburg's pet projects. Legislation was proposed for the construction of fast and powerful pocket battleships to help reestablish Germany as a major naval power. The Reichstag voted the funds necessary to construct a second ship and made plans for a third while the first vessel was under construction. The vote came the day before the announcement of the proposed customs union with Austria.

Taken together, the suggestion of future political union with Austria, which was implicit in the customs union proposal, and the funding to construct a second pocket battleship caused alarm in some quarters. Although the naval vessels fell within the bounds of the Versailles Treaty, the suggestion of rearming in the face of financial problems seemed gratuitous to outsiders. It raised important questions about how serious Germany's financial plight could be.

Sackett's response to the customs union proposal was almost phlegmatic; his major concern was whether or not it might affect the American most-favored-nation agreement with Germany.[16] He professed not to know Brüning's motive in announcing the plan but reported that some foreign press comment suggested the move was part of a German plan to reopen the reparations question. Sackett and Rumbold "exchanged views" and agreed that the customs union was advanced for domestic reasons as well as the pressure of economic conditions. The two diplomats believed that Brüning was forced to take action because the European powers were unwilling or unable to do anything on his behalf.[17]

Whatever the Germans had in mind, Sackett contended that their "actions are viewed with suspicion abroad." Alluding to previous experience, he

15 Gordon to State, 4 May 1931, 462.00R296/3941.
16 Sackett to State, 23 March 1931, FRUS, 1931, 1: 566.
17 Rumbold to Henderson, 6 May 1931, DBFP, 2: 48.

reminded the State Department "that a customs barrier is the sole remaining reason for a frontier between the two counties and every tendency towards German unity in the past has begun with a customs union."[18] Later Sackett told Curtius and Brüning that Americans did not fear *Anschluss* and had received the customs union plan favorably as likely to be a good influence on the European economy in general.[19]

After Sackett arrived in New York on May 6, the issues of the customs union and the pocket battleships were fading into the background. Much more serious was the financial crisis in Central Europe, which became public just five days after the ambassador's arrival in the United States. The ambassador had taken vacation in the ordinary course, but he used the opportunity to spread the alarm about Brüning's financial problems. On the day he landed, he journeyed to Washington for conferences with President Hoover and Secretary Stimson. Sackett informed the president that although Germany's financial situation was critical, its breakdown was not imminent; but that by fall the weakened nation could collapse. Hoover recorded the ambassador as saying that the "political disturbances are so extreme, the misery of the people is so great" with unemployment continuing to grow, that the survival of the Weimar Republic was at stake. Sackett warned the president "that we must face the possibilities of a debacle or revolution unless something can be done."[20]

At dinner with Stimson that night, Sackett impressed the secretary with the urgency of the crisis and stressed Brüning's sensitivity to American interests. American leadership feared that the German chancellor might announce a moratorium on conditional payments under the provisions of the Young Plan. Such a step would alarm American creditors, who might call in the German short-term loans and set off a panic that would destroy German credit and bring down the Weimar Republic. Sackett therefore reassured Stimson on that score – Brüning would hold off any discussion of reparations at all "until it was absolutely imperative" and would in fact avoid the subject altogether.[21]

On May 11 the Austrian government announced that the Creditanstalt, the nation's principal bank, had virtually collapsed. However, it would not close its doors. The government felt the bank was simply too vital to the nation to be allowed to go bankrupt. More importantly, the Creditanstalt

18 Sackett to State, 24 March 1931, FRUS, 1931, 1: 566–570; Castle repeated the reference to history in his diary, 29 March 1931.
19 Curtius, Memorandum of a Conversation of Brüning with Curtius and Sackett, 10 June 1931, GFMR 1493/0621348; Anne Orde, "The Origins of the German-Austrian Customs Union Affair of 1931," *Central European History*, 13 (March 1980): 34, supports the view that the customs union was an economic move designed to help defeat the depression.
20 Hoover Moratorium Diary, 6 May 1931.
21 Stimson Diary, 4 May 1931. Stimson's diary, which was sometimes dictated after events, erroneously places the date of the dinner on May 4. Sackett did not arrive in the United States until May 6.

failure had set off the financial crisis that reverberated throughout Europe and the United States.[22]

The financial crisis was the delayed result of wartime problems that had not been adequately resolved by the European nations or the United States. The Hoover administration tended to place the center of the problem in Europe; but it was American policy that established the system of international exchange. The cycle of reparations and war debts payments was financially dependent on American loans. When the outflow of capital from the United States dried up, the system was bound to founder. Added to the dearth of money was the protectionist Smoot-Hawley tariff, passed in 1930, which shut off the American market from foreign goods, further worsening the situation.[23]

Although American policy played a role in the long-term creation of the crisis, decisions by the Germans, Austrians, and the French were responsible for the immediate precipitation of the crash. After the Austrian Creditanstalt revealed on May 11 that it had lost 140 million schillings, or all but 45 million of its capital, a series of moves was made to save the bank. Austria first turned to the League of Nations, which then turned to the Bank for International Settlements, which facilitated a series of loans from eleven nations giving Austria very short-term help. Further assistance was made nearly impossible when on June 14, France added political conditions for yet another loan – the French insisted that Austria abandon the customs union with Germany.[24] By that time the scene had shifted to Germany, which was heavily involved in Austrian finance and, furthermore, burdened with vast short-term debt to foreigners, especially the United States. The crisis culminated in the failures of a series of Germany's most important banks. On July 13 the Darmstädter und National Bank (Danat) and the Berlin Bourse closed their doors and the scene then shifted to London, the holder of the third largest amount of German short-term credit, after the United States and France.

The crisis was out of control and was even worse than the public was allowed to learn.[25] As it worked toward its peak, President Hoover wrestled with the problem of how to react. His critics have complained that he did too little and too late, and their complaints have some validity. However, he was not alone in his quandary about the right course to take. The entire international community moved with caution. They were all beset with domestic problems and political considerations, but paramount was their lack of comprehension of the problem's enormity. Further complicating matters was the delay occasioned by the long and complex negotiations

---

22 On the collapse of the Creditanstalt, see Bennett, *Germany and the Diplomacy of the Financial Crisis*, 100–104; James, *The German Slump*, 283–285.

23 Hawley, *The Great War and the Search for a Modern Order*, 196.

24 Charles P. Kindleberger, *Manias, Panics, and Crashes*, 197.

25 See, for example, Feis to Frankfurter, 30 November 1931, Box 54, Frankfurter Papers.

that accompanied every proposed action to check the crash. Bankers and politicians acted from a variety of motives. Financiers were involved in personal quarrels, fraud, excessive speculation, and a wide spectrum of the troubles that accompany classic financial crises. French politicians, working from a position of financial strength, attempted to wring political concessions from Germany, while the British tried to use the crisis to bring about far-reaching changes in the entire international economic system.[26]

From the time he met with Sackett on May 6 until the resolution of the moratorium, Hoover was in almost daily contact with Sackett, as well as American officials in the State and Treasury Departments, the Federal Reserve Board, congressmen (especially Senator Dwight W. Morrow, a former partner in the House of Morgan), and both foreign and American diplomats.[27] The president sought a course of action that would meet the approval of the American public, the Congress, and the conflicting views among members of his own administration. Stimson thought that the war debts should be canceled to help resolve the international crisis, while Andrew Mellon, secretary of the treasury, was adamantly opposed to cancellation.[28] Feis complained that since 1920 the Treasury Department had been a "firm force . . . against any really courageous action in the international economic field." The tendency was to believe that things "can be worked out no matter what happens elsewhere . . . until events again dispute it."[29]

On May 11, the day the Austrian Creditanstalt collapsed but before he heard that news, President Hoover decided the time had come to act. Sackett's analysis played a decisive role in Hoover's deliberations with Stimson. They agreed with the ambassador that both the war debt and reparations settlements had been based on the ability to pay in normal times. While denying to the end that there was any connection between the two issues, Hoover, strongly influenced by Sackett, came to the conclusion that "the whole fabric of intergovernmental debt [was] beyond the capacity to pay under depression conditions."[30] Before taking any action, however, the president decided to await the outcome of the intervention by the League of Nations and Bank for International Settlements. Although he

26 Kindleberger, *Manias, Panics, and Crashes*, 197; D. E. Moggridge, "Policy in the crises of 1920 and 1929," in Charles P. Kindleberger and Jean-Pierre Laffargue, eds., *Financial Crises, Theory, History, and Policy*, 180–181; for an excellent short summary of the Moratorium crisis, with emphasis on the French point of view, see Leffler, *The Elusive Quest*, 234–256.

27 Joan Hoff Wilson, "A Reevaluation of Herbert Hoover's Foreign Policy," 179. The British believed that it was Morrow and not Ambassador Dawes "who really carries weight with the Hoover Administration." Robert L. Craigie Minute, 28 April 1931, FO371, 1931, 3, 15119: 1, 3–5.

28 Joan Hoff Wilson, *Herbert Hoover, Forgotten Progressive*, 184–185.

29 Feis to Frankfurter, 12 August 1932, Box 54, Frankfurter Papers.

30 Hoover Moratorium Diary, 11 May 1931.

saw the need to do something, Hoover was still convinced that the financial crisis was essentially a European problem for which the European powers should assume greater responsibility.[31]

Sackett returned to Washington from his sojourn in Kentucky on June 2 and spent the day in discussion with Hoover and Stimson. The ambassador had suggested that reparations payments should be adjusted to the fall in commodity prices. But Hoover was persuaded by a simpler formula, which proposed that the entire debt complex should be adjusted to the capacity to pay under depression conditions. Sackett was asked to sail at once for Germany to assure Brüning that the Americans "would need to assist in the crisis" based on the formula of capacity to pay. Sackett was then to report back on German reaction to the idea. Meanwhile, Hoover conferred with Ambassadors Charles Dawes and Hugh R. Gibson, who agreed that such reduced payments should be limited to a two year period.[32]

The president, anticipating good news on the domestic front, was depressed by the failure of the stock market to recover by June. An ardent proponent of corporatism, Hoover hoped the market would respond for the common good. Instead, investors looked to their own interests. The continued slump was a "crushing" blow to him as he presided over a cabinet meeting on June 2 described by Stimson as "pure indigo." Events both at home and abroad were so disheartening that Hoover was further convinced he had to act. On June 5 he discussed with Stimson, Mellon, and Undersecretary of the Treasury Ogden Mills the possibility of a one-year moratorium on all war debts and reparations. The president wanted more time to study the situation but was prodded by a telephone call from the House of Morgan.

Morgan partners J. P. Morgan and Thomas W. Lamont urged the president to act to avert an even more serious crisis. It was imperative, they said, "that the United States take the initiative." They discounted the idea that it was politically impossible to act, offering the admonition: "May it not be politically impossible to do anything else?" The danger was "the breakdown in Central Europe" the consequences of which "are too unpleasant to visualize." Hoover asked the bankers to confer with his trusted friend Senator Dwight Morrow, also a former Morgan partner, which they did, and passed on a memorandum, clarifying their position, to the president.[33]

---

31 Stimson to Atherton, 15 June 1931, FRUS, 1931, 1: 18; Lindsay to Henderson, 4 December 1930, BDFA, C, 2: 141.
32 Hoover Moratorium Diary, 2–4 June 1931; Stimson Diary, 2 June 1931.
33 Lamont to Hoover, 5 June 1931, Foreign Affairs – Financial – Correspondence, HHPL; Leffler, *Elusive Quest*, 235–236. When Morrow died in October 1931, he was acknowledged to have played a large part "in the initiative of the moratorium proposal." The British considered his death an important problem for the United States: "When the poverty of the Administration in men with real knowledge and understanding of European

Convinced that he had to act because the situation had "degenerated much faster" than he had anticipated, especially after the Creditanstalt debacle, Hoover, alert to Sackett's admonition, feared it "might result in revolution and overthrow" if matters deteriorated further. Still, it seemed there was time before he would need to make his move. He checked with the British, who were engaged in talks with Brüning and Curtius at Chequers. Hoover learned that although the Germans would seek reparations relief, the situation would not "become acute" before September.

At dinner with Morrow and Mills on June 9, Hoover agreed with his guests that he should give the matter more time to develop before it could be presented to American political leaders and to European governments "with any hope of success."[34] Morrow emphasized the need to move slowly, and cautiously, but also stressed the importance of sounding out the French first as well as the need to avoid any dramatic unilateral announcements.[35]

As days passed, by mid-June, Hoover was less certain than ever that he needed to act at all. Stimson was exasperated with the chief executive, who, he said, always behaved that way after making tough decisions. The secretary thought Hoover would act when he learned of the fall of the Danat bank in Berlin, which caused a crisis in the German government. Brüning's resignation was a possibility that might be followed in a few days by a new government made up of the "discontented elements." Instead, Hoover saw new problems and was "steadily going backwards" from his position of June 5. Rather than acting, Hoover followed the advice of those who counseled caution and spent much of his time winning agreement among congressmen in the Republican party and consulting with Bernard Baruch and others about Democratic party support for his plan.[36]

The president was in frequent contact with financiers in the private sector who uniformly urged action. John Foster Dulles, at Hoover's invitation, discussed the situation "particularly as affected by conditions in Germany." Dulles was convinced "that *something* be done and, within reasonable limits, this is more important than *what* is done."[37] Whereas Dulles stressed that the problem was financial with political overtones, Bernard Baruch saw the issue as political, with "representative government" at stake in Central Europe.[38]

politics and the international financial situation is considered" the loss to the White House was "most immediately and deeply felt" because there was no adequate successor among Republicans. D. G. Osborne to Marquess of Reading, 8 October 1931, FO371, 1931, 10, 15142: 52, 54–55.

34 Hoover Moratorium Diary, 6, 8, 9 June 1931.   35 Stimson Diary, 10 June 1931.
36 Stimson Diary, 10, 12, 13, 14 June 1931.
37 Dulles to Mills, 15 and 18 June 1931, Boxes 115 and 134, Dulles Papers, emphasis in the original.
38 Baruch to Senator Thomas J. Walsh, 18 June 1931, Vol. 27, Bernard M. Baruch Papers.

Hoover returned from a trip to the Midwest on June 18 and found that the situation had reached the turning point. Secretary Mellon and the Treasury Department had reversed their earlier opposition to his plan for a moratorium, just as Feis had suggested they might. Hoover was already "half convinced, by events," but it was a long message from Mellon in London that was decisive.[39] MacDonald had informed Brüning and Curtius of his sympathy for their positions, but told them that "nothing could be done by the British Government alone." British support for definitive action regarding war debts and reparations was important, and it was their urging American action that gave Mellon the information and justification he needed to change his mind.[40] Given assurances that the Treasury Department had set its objections aside because of the seriousness of the crisis, Hoover now had the full backing of his administration.

Having already gathered more support from the Republican party, he again turned to Baruch, who assured him the Democratic party was behind him. Almost as if to confirm the close ties between the public and private sectors, Hoover opened the major American embassies in Europe to Baruch for information pertaining to the financial crisis, stipulating that he was to be "entirely trusted" in such matters.[41] With full support lined up, the president made his final decision when he heard from Sackett. From Berlin, the ambassador advised Hoover that the situation in Germany had become urgent and there was danger of "possible outbreaks of widespread disorder at any moment." When he decided to act, Hoover asked that Sackett get from Berlin "a clear cut statement signed by the highest German authority of the need for action."[42] Governor Eugene Meyer of the Federal Reserve Board persuaded Hoover that a declaration from President Hindenburg describing Germany's exigent circumstances was the only way to convince the American public of the seriousness of the situation.[43]

American officials worked feverishly to cover all bases before announcing a one-year moratorium. The single year's holiday in war debt and reparations payments was part of Hoover's cautious approach to the crisis as Morrow and Mills had advised. Then a leak to the press caused a precipitous response from Hoover, who decided that the displeasure of some governments was less risky than a garbled version of his plan's becoming the subject of public discussion. The president decided to make his announcement on June 20 even if he was convinced it was premature.[44]

39 Feis to Frankfurter, 26 June 1931, Box 54, Frankfurter Papers. Feis, who regularly wrote to the Harvard Law School professor and later Supreme Court Justice, outlined a chronology of events leading to the moratorium for the professor's benefit.

40 Glashagen, "Die Reparationspolitik Heinrich Brünings 1930–1931," 1: 515; the quotation is from F. L. Carsten, *Britain and the Weimar Republic*, 247.

41 Hoover to Stimson, 20 June 1931, 462.00 R296/4087.

42 Hoover Moratorium Diary, 18 June 1931.   43 Stimson Diary, 16 June 1931.

44 Hoover, *Memoirs*, 3: 69–70.

Hoover had Castle contact the German embassy to make sure that the announcement would not interfere with a statement by Hindenburg that would be "of very great use here."[45]

To cover the principal diplomatic base, Stimson quickly met with French Ambassador Paul Claudel to inform him of the proposed moratorium and was pleased at the favorable response he got. The French government had not yet been informed of the Hoover proposal, which meant that France would be denied reparations payments for a year. Stimson was careful to tell the French diplomat that he was the first to receive the announcement. The Frenchman declared the plan "was wonderful; that he had no idea that the President could go so far." Stimson was delighted that the response from the diplomats he briefed was not only favorable, it was "electric." All agreed that "it would have a tremendous effect in Europe and would save the situation."[46] Simultaneously Stimson cabled Urgent, Triple Priority messages to the embassies in London, Paris, and Berlin informing the diplomats that Hoover would announce the moratorium the next day because of the leak. For Sackett only, Stimson was "particularly anxious that this should not interfere with the making of a favorable statement by Hindenburg."[47]

After what had seemed like endless delay to those advocating action, the president now moved with considerable speed. Stimson called Sackett on the telephone asking for swifter action in getting a letter from President Hindenburg to appeal to the United States for assistance.[48] Brüning had no difficulty in cooperating fully and a letter was prepared, but was delayed because Hindenburg was in East Prussia at the time. The letter was hardly worth the effort in the end. Not only was it too dismal in describing Germany's condition, it was received too late to go out with Hoover's announcement of the moratorium, which it was designed to accompany. To make matters worse, the existence of Hindenburg's appeal was leaked to the press, and a scramble was on from both sides of the Atlantic to keep news of the statement quiet.[49]

When they saw Hindenburg's statement the Americans did not want it published. Hoover, Mills, and Harrison discussed it and decided to tell Stimson to withhold the letter. They were afraid the tone was so desperate sounding that it might "adversely affect the market and cause it to fall in Germany."[50] Sackett had to use his influence to keep the Hoover administration leadership behind the policy. The Americans were more than

---

45 Leitner to the Foreign Ministry, 20 June 1931, GFMR 1493/621373.
46 Stimson Diary, 19 June 1931; Stimson, Memorandum of a Conversation with the French Ambassador, 19 June 1931, FRUS, 1931, 1: 29.
47 Stimson to Sackett et al., 20 June 1931, 462.00 R296/4022A.
48 Stimson Diary, 20 June 1931.
49 Stimson to Sackett, 22 June 1931, FRUS, 1931, 1: 38; correspondence on the problem can be found in FRUS, 1931, 1: 33–42.
50 Stimson Diary, 21 June 1931; the statement is in GFMR 1776/D808188–808191.

annoyed with the unsuitability of Hindenburg's statement, but Sackett was able to temper their objections.[51] On the German side, the entire affair lacked the drama Brüning wanted to accompany what was, from his point of view, the first step in ending reparations once and for all. In addition, this was a Hoover coup, hardly what the chancellor had in mind. The German obviously wanted the success to be his for domestic political reasons, but the moratorium was a gift from the Americans, not a triumph of Brüning's diplomacy.[52]

German reluctance, even refusal, to cooperate with the United States when it was acting on their behalf would be illustrated time and again. On this occasion, after they sent it, the Germans did not want Hindenburg's statement used for publication. They also wanted a guarantee that Sackett would not reveal its contents. Those conditions, of course, were contrary to the very purpose of the statement. Since Hoover considered Hindenburg's declaration to be too dreary to use, he was grateful to agree not to make it public.[53]

In spite of the minor problem with the Germans the immediate response to the Hoover Moratorium was indeed "electric." It was greeted in all quarters, save one, as the solution to the world's financial problems.[54] The French government was the exception. It did not agree with Ambassador Claudel's favorable reaction. From the French point of view the plan amounted to an American ultimatum, providing debt relief to British and American investors as well as the German government but offering nothing to France but a loss in income and the threat of an end to reparations altogether. The result was feverish Franco-American discussions until a compromise solution was agreed to on July 6.[55]

Ambassador Sackett emerged again as a key figure in negotiations. He remained calm and solicitous throughout while he attempted to carry out American policy and at the same time maintain strong support for Brüning. Sackett always believed that Germany should pay some reparations, and he would now insist to the Germans that they had to compromise. The ambassador used his influence with the chancellor to convince him of the need to make some concessions. His intention was to mollify the French and get their support for the Moratorium. The Kentuckian's role began when, on his mission to Berlin to give Brüning the good news that President

51 Thilo Vogelsang, *Reichswehr, Staat und NSDAP*, 109.
52 Sally Marks, *The Illusion of Peace*, 118; Bennett, *Germany and the Diplomacy of the Financial Crisis*, 165.
53 Leitner to the Foreign Ministry, 21 June 1931, GFMR 1493/621375–621376.
54 Bennett, *Germany and the Diplomacy of the Financial Crisis*, 166–168.
55 Marks, *Illusion of Peace*, 118–19; correspondence on the negotiation is in FRUS, 1931, 1: 42–163; a summary of the French counterproposal and the negotiations is in Bennett, *Germany and the Diplomacy of the Financial Crisis*, 173–178.

Hoover had decided to act on his behalf, he altered his travel plans to meet Brüning and Curtius at Southampton. He told the two German statesmen that "something would happen."[56]

The Germans had just concluded their discussions with Prime Minister MacDonald and Foreign Secretary Henderson at Chequers. No specific agreements grew out of the Anglo-German talks, but Brüning emerged as a major figure among European heads of state. Not only was the former enemy greeted by the British as an equal, it became de rigueur to meet with the German chancellor after Chequers. Sackett had "quietly engineered" the meeting and was certainly pleased with what he had done for his friend.[57] The key to his activities was American and British determination not only to assist the German government but also, critically and especially, to help keep Brüning in office.

The Hoover Moratorium was, of course, the principal American intervention on Brüning's behalf. But that financial rescue effort would fail unless France agreed to accept the American proposal. The French were unwilling unless the Germans agreed to make political concessions, principally by abandoning the customs union plan and the construction of the second pocket battleship or, as it was called, Cruiser B. To make matters worse, Sackett reported that the Germans were responding negatively to every French suggestion for compromise on the moratorium issue.[58]

Both the American and British governments were in agreement there should be no political conditions attached to the moratorium proposal. They also agreed the Germans could not appear to be "taking everything and giving nothing." It was obvious that Germany had to make some concession to France if the moratorium was to be accepted. The American position was that the United States could not participate in any attempt of a political nature for fear that Congress would not agree to accept a moratorium with political conditions attached. Castle volunteered the British to do this bit of negotiating.

The Americans wanted to avoid any semblance of involvement in European politics. After speaking with Hoover, Sackett told the British it would be impossible for him to make any representations to the Germans. Sackett came forward with the idea, however, that if the British were to approach the Germans to abandon the customs union and the pocket battleship, as well as sustain their policy of retrenchment, Sackett could take the opportunity "of intimating informally" that the United States agreed with the British position. Accordingly, Henderson instructed the British chargé in Berlin, Basil Newton, to approach Curtius on the subject,

56 Memorandum by Curtius, 10 June 1931, ADAP, 17: 409–412; Curtius, *Sechs Jahre Minister der deutschen Republik*, 216.
57 Stimson Diary, 4 May 1931.
58 Sackett to State, 27 June 1931, FRUS, 1931, 1: 83.

but first to be certain that the United States had instructed Sackett to affirm that his government supported the British position.[59]

Sackett warned the State Department that the Germans would be stubborn in negotiations. He cabled that if the moratorium discussions were to break down, Brüning told him, "only in the strictest confidence, but quite frankly," that he would unilaterally declare a moratorium on conditional payments for July 14, the day before the Young Plan payment was due.[60] In other words, the Germans felt they could refuse to cooperate and still get what they wanted. From Brüning's perspective, a German-initiated moratorium had much greater domestic value than the Hoover plan.

Sackett had already suggested to the Germans that they should drop the customs union proposal, since he felt Brüning had won a major victory in the moratorium. He believed that the British representations would have the desired effect. But his judgment proved to be wrong. When the British approached the German government, Curtius had no comment to make to Newton, which the British diplomat took to mean that the answer was unfavorable. Sackett, aware that the American negotiations with France were breaking down, determined to make a decisive move. He would take the "responsibility of interpreting his authority" to make representations to Curtius because he felt they had to be "made promptly."[61]

After speaking with Curtius, Sackett told Newton that he felt further progress in the negotiation was "impossible" unless the "most extreme pressure were applied." The American was persuaded that the Germans would drop the customs union proposal only if the French approved President Hoover's moratorium without reservations, an unlikely prospect. Basil Newton thought Sackett was right. Sackett informed Newton that Curtius argued that Germany could not abandon construction of the battleship because their fleet was old and needed replacement and because the navy was cut down so far that further reductions would be impossible to accept. Most important was Curtius's contention that Hindenburg would resign over fleet reductions.[62]

The Germans were adamant that they were unable to make any concessions on the issue of the pocket battleship. Brüning could not agree with the American position that the Hoover Moratorium was a victory he could use for domestic purposes. As Sackett explained, Nazis, Communists, and Hugenberg Nationalists claimed it was inadequate and motivated by

59 Lindsay, "Annual Report on the United States for 1931," 2 January 1932, FO371, 1932, 7, 15874: 10; Henderson to Lindsay, Lindsay to Henderson, Henderson to Newton, 26, 27, and 29 June 1931, DBFP, 2: 104–105, 107, 109–110.
60 Sackett to State, 30 June 1931, FRUS, 1931, 1: 112.
61 Lindsay to Henderson, two from Newton to Henderson, all 30 June 1931, DBFP, 2: 111–112.
62 Newton to Henderson, 1 and 2 July 1931, DBFP, 2: 116, 119.

American, not German, interests.[63] The chancellor could not appear to be giving in on issues so dear to the heart of the political Right. The moratorium was hardly a major domestic victory from Brüning's perspective, and to abandon the battleship would only play into Hitler's hands.

President Hoover was unyielding on the subject of political interference, especially because the United States had shown strong disapproval of French attempts to use the moratorium to get political concessions from Germany. However, when the Germans refused to budge, he changed his mind and decided that the naval issue was a matter above "local political questions." He now took the position that Sackett could intervene on the battleship issue as a disarmament question, with the intention of ultimately serving the general interest. For the president, disarmament was a "paramount" issue and he wanted the Germans to recognize that primacy by a "spontaneous declaration" of their willingness to drop the battleship construction as a show of good faith.[64] In a strange twist of logic the Americans took the position that disarmament was not a political issue.

Sackett thus proposed to the Germans that curtailing construction of the warship, even if only temporarily, would go a long way toward resolving the impasse over the moratorium and increase the chances for a successful disarmament conference the next year. Acting Secretary of State Castle was becoming exasperated with the German reluctance to make any concessions at all. He was on the telephone with Sackett on a Sunday night and gave the ambassador "some very stiff instructions." He urged Sackett to get in touch with Brüning early Monday morning to put to him "strongly" that the American public would find it difficult to understand why the United States should make sacrifices for Germany, which was going right on with its military building program. Above all, there should be no intimation that the savings the Germans made on reparations were to be used for increased armaments.[65]

Castle was getting testy in response to apparent French and German reluctance to agree to anything the United States proposed. In an angry cable to Ambassador Edge in Paris, the acting secretary demanded: "You should make it quite clear that this Government does not propose to have its very generous proposal, made for the benefit of the whole world, used as a lever on the part of any nation to obtain political concessions [from] any other nation."[66]

Rudolf Leitner, the German chargé, dropped by Castle's office to inquire

63 Sackett to State, 24 June 1931, 462.00/4070.
64 Castle to Stimson, 29 June and Stimson to Castle, 30 June 1931, 462.00 R296/4176 and 4220.
65 Lindsay to Henderson, 1 July 1931, DBFP, 2: 117–118; Castle, Memoranda of Telephone Conversations with Sackett on 28 and 29 June 1931, FRUS, 1: 97–98.
66 Castle to Edge, 28 June 1931, FRUS, 1931, 1: 97.

about the progress of negotiations with France and was treated to a taste of the acting secretary's wrath. Castle complained that the United States was working hard for Germany and expected from them "some gesture which would assist us." Denying that he was involved in any political matter, the American diplomat again brought up the matter of the pocket battleship as a disarmament question. The whole effect of the moratorium would be lost, he complained, if the American people thought Germany was using money saved by the moratorium to build a warship. Castle noted that Leitner "seemed impressed and rather disturbed."[67]

Sackett worked closely with Brüning; he wanted to give the chancellor all the latitude he could, but he also wanted to get as much as possible for his own government to make the Hoover Moratorium a success. The ambassador disclosed to the State Department that his relationship with Brüning was strong enough that he could bring forward any issues and discuss them openly and frankly with the Germans. Sackett told Castle that "he was able to say anything to the Germans,"[68] which only confirmed what was now well known in the State Department – Sackett and Brüning were very close political friends. At Sackett's express request German ambassador to France Leopold von Hoesch placed himself at the disposal of Mellon and Edge during the negotiations in Paris. Sackett was making sure that the talks at that end were in consonance with what he was doing in Berlin and, of course, that he would be informed. He wanted the Americans to turn to Hoesch for help. Mellon and Edge were pleased with the assistance and asked Hoesch to return to confer with them after they met with the French and if "possible to give them new suggestions."[69]

With his special relationship, and very cognizant of the chancellor's domestic problems, the ambassador worked cautiously to get as much as he could without endangering Brüning's delicate control of the government. The American diplomat's careful maneuvering was then undermined by President Hoover, who was frustrated by French refusal to accept his moratorium proposal.

By the end of June, the negotiations between the United States and France over the provisions of the plan had reached a state of deadlock. Patience was running out because President Hoover had announced his moratorium to the world on June 20. American diplomats were aware that the psychological impact of the plan was far more important than any detail concerning its provisions; and Stimson was convinced that the talks with the French were "well within the zone of a successful solution provided

---

67 Castle, Memorandum of a Conversation with Leitner, 29 June 1931, FRUS, 1931, 1: 98.
68 Castle, Memorandum of a Telephone Conversation with Sackett, 29 June 1931, FRUS, 1931, 1: 98.
69 Curtius to Foreign Ministry and two Curtius memoranda, all 1 July 1931, GFMR 1493/ D621426–621428, 2382/E197336, E197339.

only wrong psychology is avoided."[70] Still, Hoover was becoming restive. Every report on negotiations brought further news of French and German intransigence. The president decided to act.

Hoover proposed that the negotiations with France be bypassed, and new discussions be undertaken with each nation separately. He wanted to get the moratorium under way with or without French cooperation. Stimson suggested this new demarche had little to do with the best financial solution and more with the political isolation of France. The secretary was still convinced that "patient firmness" with the French would lead to a successful settlement.[71] In spite of Stimson's objections, Castle told Sackett that the president was "considering" the alternative plan but first he wanted to find out what the German reaction would be.[72]

Sackett recognized that what Hoover was proposing meant the Germans would not need to make any concessions at all. They were already aware that they could simply declare a unilateral moratorium if the Franco-American negotiations were to break down. If the Kentuckian were to make this new suggestion, the Germans would know that all they had to do was either wait for the French to agree to Hoover's proposal, or, that failing, simply wait for Hoover's alternate proposal to go into effect. Sackett was astute enough to see that if he apprised the Germans of the new proposal, his own efforts to get concessions would be ended. Despite his commitment to Brüning, he was aware that it was important for the Germans to make some concessions, even if only an empty gesture. Sackett decided to ignore Castle's instruction. About four hours later he confessed to Castle what he had done or, rather, not done.[73]

But Sackett's efforts were undermined after all – the story of the alternative plan of offering a moratorium to individual nations separately was leaked to the press. Among others, Ogden Mills told the press about the new idea and the story appeared in print. Sackett was obviously upset that his attempts to win concessions were being thwarted by his own government. He now had almost no chance to get anything from the Germans.[74] Aware that he had little room to maneuver with Brüning, he pressed on to get whatever advantage he could for the United States.

Now with Hoover's approval, Sackett continued to intervene directly with the Germans. Stimson had cabled advising sterner involvement. The Germans were to be "warned" not to be "captious" or they, not France,

---

70 Stimson to Castle 1 July 1931, 462.00 R296/4234.
71 Stimson to Castle and Mills, 29 June 1931, 462.00 R296/4195.
72 Castle, Memorandum of a Telephone Conversation with Sackett, June 30, 11:15 a.m., 1 July 1931, FRUS, 1931, 1: 109.
73 Castle, Memorandum of a Telephone Conversation with Sackett, June 30, 3:10 p.m., 1 July 1931, FRUS, 1931, 1: 112.
74 Bennett, *Germany and the Diplomacy of the Financial Crisis*, 189 and n.37, 190.

would be held responsible for failure of the moratorium.[75] In order to wring some concession from the Germans, Sackett and British diplomats agreed to work in concert, Sackett on the pocket battleship and the British on the customs union.[76]

Sackett again brought up the pocket battleship issue with Brüning but ran into a dead end. The chancellor insisted that it was impossible to concede on the battleship issue because it was Hindenburg's "pet hobby."[77] Castle was furious when he learned of this latest stumbling block to diplomatic progress. He marveled that the German president could permit his personal interests to interfere with a matter of such diplomatic moment.[78] Sackett faced an impossible situation. The Germans were adamant that abandoning either the customs union or the pocket battleship was not only an unattainable goal [*unerfüllbar*], but in fact "inconceivable."[79]

Sackett was aware that Brüning would suffer a serious setback if he were to concede on the battleship issue. Hitler was certain to take advantage of this further caving in to foreign pressure. Notwithstanding the intractable position of Brüning and Curtius, Sackett pressed forward, again insisting they had to give up construction of the second pocket battleship, Cruiser B. In defending their position the two Germans decisively revealed how critical the military was to the Weimar Republic. They argued that it was impossible to halt the naval building program – not only was the warship a pet project of Hindenburg's, it was vital in retaining the support of the Reichswehr, upon which Brüning insisted his very government was dependent. It was part of German military enhancement and hence supported by the army.

In addition to that, the ship fell within the limits of the meager military allowable under the terms of the Versailles Treaty. The Germans further contended that they could not understand the request for reduction in arms coming before the disarmament conference. Partly convinced by the argument, partly stymied in the face of such unremitting obstinacy, Sackett finally agreed that if Brüning gave confidential assurances that plans for a third warship, Cruiser C, would be postponed, and that there would be further confidential commitment not to increase the military budget, the United States might be satisfied.[80]

British Foreign Secretary Henderson was convinced that the Germans were showing a "wilful misunderstanding of the situation." As frustrated

75 Stimson to Castle and Mills, 28 June 1931, 462.00 R296/4174.
76 Castle, Memorandum of a Telephone Conversation with Sackett, 29 June, and Boal, Memorandum of a Conversation with Lindsay, 30 June 1931, FRUS, 1931, 1: 97–98, 108.
77 Castle to Stimson, 1 July 1931, 462.00 R296/4220.
78 Castle Diary, 1 and 2 July 1931.
79 Bülow, Memorandum, 1 July 1931, ADAP, 18: 4.
80 Sackett for Hoover and Castle, 2 July 1931, FRUS, 1931, 1: 130–131; Bülow Memorandum, 2 July 1931, ADAP, 18: 14–16; Bennett, *Germany and the Diplomacy of the Financial Crisis*, 191–194.

as the Americans, he was unhappy with the German response to Sackett. He agreed that replacement or reduction of naval vessels was a matter for the disarmament conference. However, since Germany would be "living on the charity of other nations" during the "Hoover year," he argued that it was "only decent that during that period she should not be spending money on the construction of the new battleship." He thought it difficult to believe that Hindenburg might resign over the "satisfaction of his personal wishes."

Henderson did not want to act in any way contrary to what Sackett was doing. The British believed Sackett to be correct in assessing the situation. Sackett thought the Germans could abandon the customs union, and that they would issue a statement on the battleship issue. Henderson asked Newton if there was "any prospect of inducing" the Germans to parley with Sackett on the customs union as well as on the warship issue. The British believed Sackett could get Brüning to act when no one else could. But the Germans were hesitant to discuss the issue with Sackett. They were reluctant to continue saying no to the American ambassador. Sackett had "the impression that there will be careful abstention from consulting him."[81]

Sackett was not to be denied. Bülow complained that the American ambassador "has come again" concerning Cruiser B. Sackett pressed the issue when he met with Brüning and Bülow at the chancellor's residence while Newton simultaneously met with Curtius in the Foreign Ministry. Although Curtius told Newton that he was impressed by the "moderation" of the American position, Sackett later told Newton that Brüning was "most emphatic" that the government's position was "precarious." The chancellor insisted that any public reference to the battleship was impossible, especially since it might "impair the loyalty of the Reichswehr." Brüning again dredged up the danger that the military was "the last bulwark of the state against the threat of latent civil war."[82]

Determined to get all he could for the United States without damaging Brüning's position, Sackett pushed ahead. He now lodged a protest with Curtius concerning construction of Cruiser B. When Curtius began another chorus of the familiar reasons why Germany could not abandon the warship, Sackett interrupted. The American argued that any harm resulting from suspension of construction could be "very easily rectified if it served a higher political goal." But the German was impervious to argument. Curtius was convinced that his disclosures had made a "strong impression" on Sackett. Still the American asked that his view be presented "urgently" to the chancellor especially in the light of unanimous support of the proposal by the American and British governments.[83]

81 Henderson to Newton and Newton to Henderson, 2 and 3 July 1931, DBFP, 2: 119, 130.
82 Bülow to Foreign Ministry, 2 July, GFMR, 1493/621432; Newton to Henderson, 3 July 1931, DBFP, 2: 124.
83 Curtius to the Foreign Ministry and Curtius memorandum, both 3 July 1931, GFMR 1493/D621441–621443, 1660/D729420–729422.

After the rebuffs he received at the hands of the German on the pocket battleship issue, Sackett was persuaded that there was little to be gained in that direction. The ambassador was right in his conviction that the "most useful and likely concession" the Anglo-Americans could get was on the customs union issue. But Sackett believed that the Germans had to say something indicating they were not going ahead with battleship construction, and he finally got a statement from Brüning. The chancellor hoped it would not be used, but if it were it would be done "unobtrusively." Sackett was "very anxious" that it should be used, but Brüning was "very reluctant" that it should appear at all. When Sackett showed the declaration to Newton in confidence, the British diplomat remarked that it was "very meagre." All the chancellor stipulated was the promise that any money Germany obtained by reparations relief would not be, nor was it ever intended that it would be, used for military purposes during the moratorium year.[84]

The British were disappointed in Sackett's performance. They felt the negotiations on the pocket battleships were inconclusive because Sackett was "not determined enough." Had the American ambassador pressed further than he was willing to go, they believed that more might have been accomplished. Instead, he took Brüning at his word that money freed by the moratorium would not be used for military purposes. In the British Foreign Office, an irritated Robert Vansittart complained that "the Americans are poor and quite unreliable collaborators." He claimed that the British "acted alone at Berlin with only a little tentative tepid sympathy from the United States."[85] Vansittart and other British diplomats hoped there could be more and closer cooperation between themselves, the French, and the Americans.

Sackett was caught in the middle. The United States government was unwilling to participate in European politics, but had allowed the ambassador to proceed quite far beyond the usual diplomatic practice. On his own, Sackett had done more than his instructions called for in his effort to cooperate with the British. But he also had the handicap of attempting to balance Brüning's needs with those of his own and the British government's.

Criticism from Vansittart, the permanent undersecretary in the Foreign Office, seems strange. Especially since Vansittart understood the German wish for an economic union with Austria and thought Germany "entirely within her rights" in building the pocket battleship. Moreover, he thought the German case to be "on every ground of morality and equity exceedingly strong."[86]

---

84 Newton to Henderson, two on 3 July, 6 July, 1931, DBFP, 2: 126, 130, 141; Leitner to Foreign Ministry, 2 July 1931, GFMR 1493/D621434.

85 Vansittart to Ronald Campbell (Paris), 16 September 1931, FO371, 1931, 4, 15123: 29–30.

86 Klaus Jaitner, "Deutschland, Brüning und die Formulierung der britischen Aussenpolitik Mai 1930 bis Juni 1932," *Vierteljahrshefte für Zeitgeschichte*, 28 (1980): 464–465, hereafter cited VJZG. Vansittart's criticism is odd because he stressed that the German case

The American ambassador was unaware of British criticism, but had he known, he might ultimately have taken satisfaction in knowing that it was he who predicted that the Germans were most vulnerable on the customs union. In the end Brüning conceded on that issue by dropping the project and firing Julius Curtius, who was identified as its author.

By July 4, as negotiations with the French showed signs of improvement, Sackett decided not to make any further suggestions to the United States government, nor to make any more demands on the Germans. He thought it best "not to complicate the situation." The British and American governments wanted the Germans to give up the customs union to mollify the French. But even with Sackett's best efforts, the Anglo-American diplomats made no headway with the Germans, who felt they would win whether or not the French agreed to the Hoover Moratorium.

Further negotiations were necessary before France finally agreed to a slightly modified version of the moratorium. During the last hectic days the United States had moved from suggesting the Germans might postpone construction of Cruiser B to demanding that they abandon the warship, and finally to a vague statement that the Germans would postpone construction of Cruiser C. Incredibly, Brüning hesitated to make even this mild gesture, this time expressing fear that the French might take this concession to be the occasion for making further demands on the Germans.

To insure the chancellor's acceptance of this minor request, Sackett undoubtedly went far beyond his instructions again as he promised that President Hoover would support the Germans against any more political demands. He went even beyond that, assuring Hoover's support at the disarmament conference, and suggesting Stimson's coming visit to Berlin would be an opportunity to go further into that matter. To complete the surreal character of the talks, Sackett refused to admit that President Hoover was making any political demands of the Germans; he insisted the Germans would be offering a "voluntary gesture."[87]

No one could accuse Sackett of not doing his best for Brüning. But even Sackett had his limits. If the Hoover Moratorium were to be a success, France needed to accept it. The French had the most to lose and therefore it was essential that Germany make some concession, even if only as a signal that they appreciated what was being done for them. The Germans, however, persisted in their position that for every favor done for them a new request was readied for the asking. That led Sackett to join the gathering chorus of complaints. When he found Brüning unresponsive to his pleas for compromise, Sackett, who was becoming annoyed with the Germans, complained they were "willing to take everything and give nothing."[88]

was strong; he may have been influenced by his aversion for amateurs in diplomacy, Rose, *Vansittart*, 37, 92.

87 Bülow, Memorandum, 5 July 1931, ADAP, 18: 23–25; see also Brüning to Sackett, 5 July and Minutes of Ministers Conference, 6 July 1931, GFMR 1776/D808141, 1684/D786863.
88 Sackett to Hoover and Castle, 3 July 1931, 462.00R296/4264.

Along with the other diplomats in Berlin, Sackett was "disgusted beyond measure" at the attitude of the Germans, who did not bother to thank the Americans for all their hard work for the benefit of the Brüning administration.[89] After all the tension and irritation in the negotiations, Sackett "shouted with joy" in cathartic relief when France finally accepted Hoover's moratorium proposal. Ogden Mills, less euphoric than Sackett, commented that "the United States had now made the world safe for the Germans."[90]

All of these negotiations were conducted with the utmost secrecy out of fear that American congressmen would find out what was going on. The diplomats were all cognizant that the Hoover Moratorium would be in severe jeopardy if it were learned that the administration was trying to extract political concessions in the negotiations. Although the Hoover Moratorium had obvious political implications, the fiction was maintained that the United States was preserving its traditional policy of remaining aloof from European politics. In any case, the Americans clearly wanted as little to do with European politics as possible. To uphold this traditional stance, the Americans insisted that the issue of disarmament was not a political matter. It was on that ground that they pursued the quid pro quo and still maintained there was no political involvement. Castle insisted that Sackett get the Germans to abandon the pocket battleship; he hoped it would make it easy for the French to accept the Hoover Moratorium. Castle was at the same time reassuring Stimson that he was carrying out the policy of not allowing the plan to be used to win political concessions.[91]

The final acceptance of the Hoover Moratorium did not end the financial crisis. In fact, the worldwide depression worsened. Germany's internal financial situation was so bad that the United States agreed to a financial conference to resolve the matter, at least in the short term. President Hoover was convinced that the problem had become "solely a banking crisis and is solvable only by [German] banks." He soon was unhappy with the results of the initial conference in Paris. The president intervened again, after angrily noting that the conference was heading the United States "into an utterly impossible situation of political entanglements and at the same time would utterly wreck the situation in Germany."[92]

Hoover decided that the U.S. government needed to play a more direct role in the private sector and urged the British to call a conference in London. Stimson, who was already in Europe, participated in the conference of bankers that concluded in London on July 23. The bankers decided to renew a $100 million credit to Germany for three months, and agreed to

89 Messersmith, notes for memoirs.

90 Castle Diary, 7 July 1931; Ferrell, *American Diplomacy in the Great Depression*, 115.

91 Castle to Stimson, 1 July 462.00 R296/4220 and Rumbold to Vansittart, 16 July 1931, DBFP, 2: 207–208.

92 Hoover Moratorium Diary, 12 and 17 July 1931.

a "standstill" on private short-term credits, which would not be presented until after February 1932. They also set up a committee of their own members to carry out the standstill agreements and set up another committee to study Germany's requirements. After their study was completed, the bankers made it clear that neither Germany nor the other principal powers could resolve the financial crisis until war debts and reparations were reduced.[93]

Stimson was on his way to Berlin from London when another, minor, crisis arose. Press accounts claimed that he made the trip to discuss further financial aid for the Germans. Hoover and Castle were furious and wanted Stimson to deny the report emphatically. They believed the story originated with the Germans, who continued to emphasize their need for financial support as a means to insure that reparations would be canceled once and for all. Hoover and Castle feared that any evidence that the moratorium and standstill agreements had little impact on the German problem would further reduce confidence and cause an even greater run on investments.

Stimson, however, was reluctant to say anything that might appear critical of Brüning. Sackett's reports and conversations obviously had an impact on the secretary. In a three-way telephone conversation with Hoover and Castle, Stimson was convinced that he must not say anything that might in any way hurt the German chancellor. Things were bad enough for Brüning, he said, and he did "not want to smash him in the eye by making too strong a contradiction." As Castle pressed Stimson to deny the story, the secretary stood firm and revealed a powerful attachment to Brüning, and a clear policy of maintaining him in office. Resorting to hyperbole to make his point, Stimson said the German chancellor "is getting stoned every time he appears on the streets. He is really in the devil of a position. He needs very much to be buoyed up so that he can carry on."

Castle suggested that at least the secretary should persuade the Germans to "stop crying for money as this suggests bankruptcy." Hoover asked Stimson to authorize Castle to make a statement denying that the U.S. government was involved in any financial or banking negotiation with the Germans. Stimson was adamant; he refused to authorize anything that might even remotely harm Brüning. Just as stubborn, Hoover claimed the whole financial matter appeared to be settled but "it is all gone because the Germans have announced that they are still bankrupt and that they have still got to have financial help. Everybody is discouraged. If they had any appreciation of restoring confidence in themselves they would stop talking about being bankrupt and would begin to help themselves."[94]

93 Frank Costigliola, *Awkward Dominion*, 239–241; Bennett, *Germany and the Diplomacy of the Financial Crisis*, 204–312; Leffler, *Elusive Quest*, 246–256; Harris Gaylord Warren, *Herbert Hoover and the Great Depression*, 136.
94 Memorandum of a Telephone Conversation between Hoover, Stimson, and Castle, 24 July 1931, Castle Papers – Transatlantic Telephone Conversations, HHPL.

The matter was resolved with a vague statement from the State Department, but the conversation emphasized the extent to which the United States government was willing to go to support the Weimar Republic and, above all, how far Stimson was willing to go specifically to support Brüning. Hoover and Castle shared Stimson's views, but expressed their exasperation with the Germans who, with every concession made to them, came up with new demands.

The Germans refused to budge in spite of the fact that the United States virtually held a mortgage on the German economy. Contrary to popular belief that heavy investments in a nation bring with them control of that nation, the United States was unable to win concessions from the Germans on even a minor issue such as postponement of construction of a pocket battleship. The Germans in fact held the United States and its investments hostage to their policy goals. Repayment on loans and opportunity for new American investments were dependent on German goodwill, not on American initiatives. German refusal to cooperate in making more than an empty gesture of compromise rankled the Americans and even irritated Sackett, but the Americans were powerless to do anything but complain. In Germany the United States did have a great deal of influence, but it had no control.

No one worked harder than Ambassador Sackett to support the Weimar Republic. He gave it his all to help Brüning, and in that way thwart the Nazis. His influence on Stimson is quite clear. The secretary of state was impressed by what the ambassador had to report and praised his "good prophecy" on German affairs. Stimson considered Sackett "one of the best of our ambassadors. I have been receiving the best reports I have from any of the embassies through him."[95] Sackett played an active and significant role in the financial crisis from beginning to end and throughout went beyond his instructions, and invented new ways to help the embattled chancellor. More than any other American diplomat, Sackett knew how little room Brüning had to maneuver in domestic German politics. The German could grant very little without endangering his tenure in office, but he had the good fortune to have the Kentuckian laboring on his behalf.

When Curtius, the one German to do so, invited Sackett to see him so he could express his gratitude for what the American ambassador had done for Germany, Sackett was effusive. He was very pleased and "spoke proudly" about what he had been able to do. Sackett also expressed his satisfaction with what he had been able to accomplish the previous December and January when he had alerted Hoover to the dangerous situation confronting Germany. The two diplomats agreed that no further steps along those lines were possible until after the experts had been able to deal with the aftermath of the current crisis. It seemed to them that it

95 Stimson Diary, 4 May 1931, 11 October 1932.

was "inopportune" to expect any political settlement in the near future. They would need to be satisfied with what had been accomplished that summer.[96]

Hoover and the State Department were aware of most of Sackett's activity, but not all. The ambassador kept his own counsel on most matters in which he went beyond what was officially expected of him. On the whole he met with the approval of Hoover, Stimson, and fellow diplomats, but some felt he served German interests too well. It was common currency in the State Department to consider Sackett's predecessors in the Berlin embassy as too pro-German. Some felt Sackett had gone even beyond that. J. Pierrepont Moffat, a career diplomat in the Division of Western European Affairs, was highly critical of the Kentuckian, derisively claiming, for example, that in one instance Sackett agreed with everything Curtius said. The German foreign minister, Moffat said, assumed that Sackett "was agreeing on the basis of instructions received, etc." On another occasion, Moffat wrote, Sackett misled foreign diplomats based on his "yes – yes conversation with Curtius."[97] Eugene Meyer, governor of the Federal Reserve Board, added his name to the list of Sackett's critics, expressing resentment at Sackett's influence and activity during the financial crisis.[98]

In spite of some criticism, Sackett's performance was applauded widely. He certainly earned Brüning's gratitude. President Hoover expressed his appreciation directly and through Castle for the "splendid job" the ambassador was doing.[99] Curtius was equally complimentary, speaking of Sackett's "unobtrusive but statesmanlike manner" and calling him his "quiet wise man."[100] Messersmith was impressed that Sackett was "splendid," had "a very clear understanding of the situation," and had done "an excellent piece of work." Above all the professional diplomat appreciated Sackett's "sane counsel."[101] The press was just as kind. In Germany, the semiofficial *Deutsche Diplomatisch-Politische Korrespondenz* said of him that he was "an extraordinarily experienced and sharp-sighted observer of Germany and a warm advocate of the relief action initiated by President Hoover." In the United States, the Chicago *Tribune* called him the "good, silent Ambassador," the "right man, in the right place, at the right time."[102]

Although the British Foreign Office was critical of Sackett, his colleague in Berlin, Horace Rumbold, was more appreciative of what the American was facing in the negotiations with the Germans. Rumbold told Sackett's

96 Curtius to the Foreign Ministry, 9 July 1931, GFMR 1493/621469–621470.
97 Moffat Diary, 18 and 22 January and 26, 27, 28, and 29 November 1931.
98 Feis, Memorandum of a Conversation with Meyer, 13 July 1931, 462.00 R296/4626.
99 Castle to Sackett, 7 August 1931, Castle Papers – Germany, HHPL.
100 Associated Press, Berlin to New York, 21 June 1931, Box 19, Cables, Louis P. Lochner Papers.
101 Messersmith to Villard, 30 July 1931, bMS Am 1323 (2578), Villard papers.
102 Sackett to State, 30 July 1931, 033.1140 Stimson, Henry L./144.

harshest critic, Robert Vansittart, that "Brüning went as far as any German Chancellor or Government could" on the pocket battleship issue. The diplomats in Berlin might have said of the British Foreign Office what Raymond Atherton, the American chargé in London, said of his own government: "it really was impossible for people in Washington to 'get' the European atmosphere."[103]

All these encomiums were recognition for the fine job Sackett did for American foreign policy, for Germany, and above all for Brüning. But they do not conceal the fact that American intervention did not stave off depression. The U.S. government still refused to take the one step that might have lightened everyone's load – the Hoover administration refused to work toward canceling the war debts. Hoover's hope that he could rescue Germany from financial disaster with a temporary moratorium and that he could by that action defeat the worldwide depression proved to be first an illusion and then a failure. Moreover, Brüning was still in serious political trouble and Germany was reaching the bottom of the depression.

Brüning's government was saved in the short run because the crisis of 1931 was confined to the economic arena. There were few immediate political consequences. The concentration on financial matters made it less likely that anyone, especially Hitler, would volunteer to assume political leadership. One sign of the reluctance of party leaders to take on the onerous tasks Brüning faced was that there were no national elections in 1931. Sackett was led to believe that the financial crisis had helped to create a tamer Nazi movement, with Hitler more amenable to working within the parameters of the parliamentary process. In the new circumstances, Sackett saw Hitler as the moderate among Nazi leadership who would lead the party to a more conventional approach to coming to power.

The financial crisis worsened the depression and fueled the persistent attacks on Brüning by the Nazis and Communists. As the government relentlessly pursued a policy of retrenchment they characterized him as the "Hunger Chancellor." Unemployment increased, and so did the discontent. The ranks of bitter opposition to the Brüning regime grew in number, creating the fertile soil for the spread of simple solutions to complex problems. Leading the way for the discontented was Adolf Hitler, whose rough eloquence and vitriol found wider audiences as the depression worsened and as hope for better conditions under the Weimar Republic faded.

103 Rumbold to Vansittart, 15 September 1931, FO371, 1931, 4, 15123: 79–80; Thompson Minute on a Conversation with Atherton, 12 November 1930, FO371, 1930, 6, 14273: 195.

6

Perceptions of Nazism and communism, with an afterthought on fascism

CHANCELLOR BRÜNING'S strategies to win American support were fashioned to maintain his government in office. In 1931 he continued to hold his chancellorship in the face of unremitting opposition from both the Nazis and the Communists as well as a motley array of shifting opposition groups. In the face of that opposition, Brüning did little to alleviate the suffering of the German people. Instead, he pursued a policy of retrenchment, which he used to demonstrate to the foreign powers that Germany was confronted with bankruptcy. He wanted them to believe that the situation was so bad that it would be necessary to cancel reparations payments.[1]

American diplomats in Washington took exception to the course the chancellor was following. They felt that everything the United States could do for Germany had been done and that further demands were not possible to fulfill. Besides, German statements that the nation was near bankruptcy simply aggravated the situation and made the reestablishment of German credit a near impossibility. President Hoover was as upset with the Germans as he was with the French. As a consequence, Castle asked Stimson to refuse to discuss financial matters with Brüning to avoid any further misunderstanding.[2] For his part, Stimson lectured the Germans on militarism and told them that their case at the disarmament conference was being compromised by their insistence on building pocket battleships.[3]

---

1 In a continuing debate Knut Borchardt has maintained that Brüning had no alternative to a stringent policy of retrenchment. For an outline of the debate, see Jürgen Baron von Kruedener, *Economic Crisis and Political Collapse: The Weimar Republic 1924–1933*, ix–xxx; the remaining essays continue the argument and a response by Borchardt. Even the convinced anti-German Robert Vansittart agreed that Brüning had "no choice" to a policy of retrenchment, Vansittart, *The Mist Procession*, 418; Rose, *Vansittart*, 35–37 and passim.
2 Castle to Stimson, 24 July 1931, FRUS, 1931, 1: 551–552.
3 Stimson, Memorandum of a Conversation with Members of the German Government, 25 July 1931, FRUS, 1931, 1: 552; Stimson took the same line in discussing the German naval building program with the Italians, Stimson, Memorandum of Conversations with Dino Grandi and Mussolini, 9, 11, and 12 July 1931, FRUS, 1931, 1: 544.

The chancellor simply disregarded foreign opposition to his policy. He stubbornly refused to budge because he believed he had the issue that could help him bend the foreign powers to accept his policy. That issue was communism. Brüning wanted to use communism as a threat; he certainly did not want to be the instrument for its success in Germany. Many among the world's leaders began to express concern that his policies could indeed lead to that result. Especially because as the depression worsened, so did the scale of opposition not only to Brüning and to his government, but also to the Weimar Republic itself.

Much of the responsibility for the deteriorating economic and political conditions must be attributed to Brüning. Rather than focusing on solving the depression, the chancellor sought to exploit the nation's economic distress. By pleading financial failure he hoped to bring reparations payments to an end. Stringent domestic economic measures were meant to strengthen Germany's internal position so the nation would be free of foreign influence, emerge from the depression, and put an end to reparations. Simultaneously, the chancellor meant to achieve equality of armaments with a military force large enough to restore Germany's position as a decisive European power. With such foreign policy success he calculated he could achieve the revision of the Versailles Treaty without the need to discuss the matter with the powers.[4]

Brüning was determined to resolve the domestic political crisis, but his major concern was not communism. Above all he aspired to defuse the explosive Nazi party and its unpredictable leader, Adolf Hitler. His intention was to exploit the nationalist and antirepublican sentiment of the Hitler party to bring about a restoration of the monarchy.[5] In trying to carry out nationalistic purposes much like those the Nazis espoused, Brüning tended to be inattentive to the suffering of the German people. His failure to address their problems as a matter of first priority revealed a coldness in the chancellor, a commitment to retrenchment regardless of the consequences for the general populace, but most of all, a single-minded commitment to achieving his foreign policy goals.

Brüning faced a horrendous task. The financial crisis was both a cause and a symptom. The collapse of banks and credit worsened an already bad situation but was a sign of a deeper problem. Recent scholarship shows that one of Germany's fundamental problems was that it had not yet recovered from the 1914–1918 war. Not only was the war not paid for, but the Germans had evolved unproductive economic and financial habits, had made too many mistakes, and had suffered too many unremedied failures. Low growth plagued the nation throughout the period of apparent prosperity, 1924–1929, with the economy reaching a state of ossification. Desperately needing a restructured economy, the nation was faced

4 Brüning, *Memoiren*, 193–197.   5 Brüning, *Memoiren*, 194.

with a fiscal crisis in which all segments of the economy, as well as the government, sought to serve their own purposes even at the expense of the other segments.[6]

We should acknowledge that one scholar's concept of a German slump, Harold James, characterizes Brüning's position as nearly impossible. Another structural account, by David Abraham, perceives it as not only hopeless, but inevitable. Although similar in some respects, especially in discerning a structural base to explain the German political economy, the views differ in that the latter finds the basis of the problem to be class conflict and capitalism.[7]

Brüning was frustrated by his own policy and by the debilitating forces over which he had no control, and in one sense he was thwarted in his efforts by the American intervention. The Hoover Moratorium was of little help to the Germans. It provided relief for only a matter of days, but worse than that, it constituted a serious political problem for the chancellor. Not only did he fail to win much political credit for the moratorium, which after all was a gift from the Americans, but any further move in the direction of ending reparations was forestalled by the year-long holiday in intergovernmental debts. If he was to gain additional support for his government, it would be necessary to do something, and soon, to ward off attacks from his enemies and sustain the support of his friends. The chancellor consequently persisted in his struggle to achieve his immediate diplomatic goals.

He continued to push for an end to reparations in spite of all the help already extended to him. He also expected that the disarmament conference set for early 1932 would provide the opportunity to achieve equality of arms with the other European powers. The chancellor paid special attention to the United States. He intended to coordinate domestic problems with his foreign policy goals and do it all with careful regard for the American mind [*Psyche*] and timed to take advantage of psychological opportunities. For example, Brüning believed that President Hoover would act to cancel war debts once he had won a disarmament victory for the American people.[8]

Brüning persisted despite apparent American refusal to budge on the issues central to his strategy. From his point of view, his plans appeared to be viable because of the general fear of communism that infected all of

---

6 James, *German Slump*, 224–236, 418–419.
7 David Abraham, *The Collapse of the Weimar Republic*, xv–xli, 35, 269–270. Subject of an extended controversy, the book was revised to meet charges of careless scholarship and was issued in a new version, but without change in the fundamental argument; literature on the debate, xiiin1; all citations here are from the second edition. Abraham's work and also James, *German Slump*, are in consonance with the Borchardt thesis that Brüning's position was inevitable.
8 Brüning, *Memoiren*, 433.

Europe and was more virulent than ever during the financial crisis. He was emboldened by the widely held view, shared by American diplomats and businessmen, that Germany constituted the major obstacle to the spread of bolshevism in Europe. Almost all believed that communism would be the principal beneficiary of economic collapse and therefore German recovery was critical.[9]

Fear of the communist danger was endemic in the Western world from the time of the Bolshevik revolution in 1917. Americans were particularly susceptible to this fear. Even a casual reading of diplomatic correspondence reveals a persistent interest in the subject, sometimes bordering on the pathological.[10] The notion of a malignant movement of working classes whose ideas were infectious frightened the dominant forces in European and American society, who were constantly on the alert to stanch the flow. In 1922, then ambassador to Germany Alanson B. Houghton expressed that fear in a despatch to Secretary of State Charles Evans Hughes when he wrote: "Already the Bolshevist tide is beating against the barrier of European civilization. And if once those barriers go down . . . the time is past. That tide will sweep resistlessly to the Atlantic."[11]

Germany was of particular interest to American diplomats, partly because the German Communist party was large and active, but also because the German and Soviet governments had close diplomatic ties. As a consequence the American embassy in Berlin devoted much of its time to analyzing and reporting on communist activity. Two views emerge from Sackett's reports. On one hand, the German Communist party was large and active, but on the other, Sackett was convinced that the German party alone did not constitute a danger to the Weimar Republic. Sackett took a position similar to that of Warren Robbins, who in 1917 had experienced the Bolshevik revolution firsthand. In 1924, when Robbins was counselor of embassy in Berlin, he wrote to Castle that there "has been talk again of the dangers of Communism" but the only danger will come "if the bottom drops out of everything." The real threat was on the Right, Robbins maintained, and the republic was not in peril "unless some wild Nationalists sabotage the government."[12]

9 For example, Hogan, "Thomas W. Lamont and European Recovery," 8; Kenneth Paul Jones, "Alanson B. Houghton and the Ruhr Crisis: The Diplomacy of Power and Morality," 27; John M. Carroll, "Owen D. Young and German Reparations: The Diplomacy of an Enlightened Businessman," 43, 46, 47; Frank Costigliola, "John B. Stetson, Jr. and Poland: The Diplomcacy of a Prophet Scorned," 63, all in Kenneth Paul Jones, ed., *U.S. Diplomats in Europe.*
10 On the general fear of communism, see Peter H. Buckingham, *America Sees Red, Anti–Communism in America, 1870s to 1980s,* 31–43, 185–195; Thomas G. Paterson, *Meeting the Communist Threat, Truman to Reagan,* vii–xii.
11 Houghton to Hughes, 23 October 1922, FRUS, 1922, 2: 172.
12 Robbins to Castle, 2 April 1924, Castle Papers – Germany, HHPL.

In the State Department, communism was a major concern. Castle was particularly interested in any sign of Marxist-Leninist activity. At one point Schurman assured Castle that he would "continue from time to time to let you have pertinent information in relation to the doings of the Russians here." In fact, Schurman was putting Castle off for he had been asked, inappropriately, to request the German government to give him any information they could regarding communist activity.[13]

State Department interest in communism abroad was institutionalized with the creation of the Division of Eastern European Affairs. A selected group of young foreign service officers was trained in Russian language, history, and culture, under the leadership of Robert F. Kelley, and assigned to observe and analyze events in the Soviet Union. Because the United States did not recognize the Soviet state, it was not in a position to observe directly what was happening there. A partial remedy was found in the establishment of a listening post in Riga, Latvia.[14]

Although the Soviet-oriented division was planned to foster the study of Russia, it soon developed the wider mission of influencing American attitudes toward the Soviet Union. Given the task of "protecting the United States from the menace of bolshevism at home and abroad," the Eastern European Division found a natural leader in Kelley, who was convinced that Soviet control of Russia "posed an imminent danger to the United States and to world order."[15] With no diplomats in the Soviet Union, the United States was dependent on reports from Riga, but also from American embassies and legations, and anywhere information could be found. The Berlin embassy regularly reported on communist activity and kept the State Department abreast of developments concerning the German Communist party. Their reports were filed in the State Department under "Bolshevik Activities in Germany."[16]

General fear of communism was fed by the volatile financial crisis, and the Germans spared no effort to use the concern to their advantage. While at Chequers, in June 1931, Foreign Minister Julius Curtius made the point that if the Brüning government were to fail, the Communists would be the beneficiaries.[17] That theme was pressed upon the Americans by German diplomats in the United States and Europe, and was channeled to the White House. In a conversation with Pierre de L. Boal, chief of the Division of Western European Affairs, German Chargé Rudolf Leitner warned

13 Schurman to Castle, 7 September 1925, Castle to Schurman, 11 August 1925, Castle Papers – Germany, HHPL.
14 Frederic L. Propas, "Creating a Hard Line Toward Russia," 209–226.
15 Propas, "Creating a Hard Line Toward Russia," 209–210; see Douglas Little, "Antibolshevism and American Foreign Policy, 1919–1939, The Diplomacy of Self Delusion," 376–390.
16 Decimal File No. 862.00B.
17 Atherton to State, 8 June 1931, FRUS, 1931, 1: 6–8.

of the "underlying danger from communism in Germany," while the American minister in Stockholm was told by his German counterpart that his country "will be driven to 'bolshevism' " if Hoover's moratorium proposal was not accepted by German creditors.[18] Owen D. Young added his voice to the refrain, passing on to Stimson Schacht's view that the moratorium proposal "may save the world from Bolshevism."[19]

Benito Mussolini joined the chorus spreading the alarm being funneled to the White House. The noted newspaper columnist Walter Lippmann interviewed the Duce, but not for publication. The Italian leader was very pessimistic. He saw little hope for disarmament and declared that Germany was near bankruptcy and was "already suffering a very serious political social and moral degeneration and that an extreme crisis would come by next winter unless far reaching measures of assistance were given." The Duce feared that the German crisis would lead to a "species of Bolshevism either of the Left or the Right – he did not know which."[20]

Mussolini had hit upon another theme that worried many people at the time – the danger of a German civil war or a political uprising of both the Right and the Left. A simultaneous uprising of the Nazis and Communists in Germany was a persistent fear of Brüning and the Reichswehr. The chancellor often spoke of the danger with the emphasis on the role of communism and the specter of revolution.[21] Americans speculated as early as January 1931 that revolution would take place in Germany the following spring. Colonel Edward Carpenter, the American military attaché in Berlin, did not deny the possibility, but he did not think it could succeed. He assured the American government that the Reichswehr was overwhelmingly loyal to President Hindenburg and was large enough to put down any uprising.[22] During the crisis Brüning emphasized to Sackett that the political situation was critical enough to speak of "latent civil war."[23] Montagu Norman, governor of the Bank of England, warned American bankers of the dangers; in the State Department, officials spoke of the threat of imminent revolution and feared that once the "radical wave" set in "Germany may go Bolshevik . . . and Russia would not be slow to take steps to aid the situation – possibly moving her armies on Poland."[24]

18 Boal, Memorandum of a Conversation with Leitner, 12 June 1931, 462.00/R296/3983, copies of the memorandum were directed to Stimson, and to the White House; Morehead to State, Stockholm, 22 June 1931, 462.00R296/4029, a copy was sent to the White House.
19 Young to Stimson, 25 June 1931, enclosing his telegram to Schacht and the latter's reply of 22 June, 462.00R296/4247.
20 Garrett to State, 11 June 1931, 462.00R296/3963.   21 Brüning, "Ein Brief," 2, 4.
22 Moffat Diary, 9 and 15 January 1931.
23 Bülow Memorandum, 2 July 1931, ADAP, 18: 15.
24 Conversation with Norman, 20 June, 3 July 1931, FRBNY, 3115.2; Moffat Diary 21 and 22 May 1931; the quotation in Memorandum of a Conversation with Paul Scheffer, Washington correspondent of the *Berliner Tageblatt*, with Boal and Culbertson, 10 June 1931, 462.00R296/4875, also in the Stimson Papers.

Lord Robert Cecil was among the British diplomats who most feared the danger of communism. In his view, "thinking people" in Germany were "more afraid" of the Communists coming to power than of "a Hitlerite access to power." The British peer was convinced that the "Nazi movement" was on the decline and that any serious blow to national prestige would "turn a lot of the Hitlerites into communists."[25]

There certainly was widespread concern in diplomatic and financial circles about the danger of revolution or civil war in Germany. Brüning and Curtius repeatedly warned that a communist revolution could be imminent and almost certainly instructed German diplomats to emphasize that potential danger. The Nazis played only a minor role in all the speculation and then usually as an accompaniment to a communist lead. The general apprehension about communism became public and caused considerable consternation among seasoned observers of the German political scene.

Alexander Gumberg, a leading advocate of recognition of the Soviet Union, had been in Germany during the June crisis. A thoughtful observer of German politics, he reacted in disbelief when he read suggestions of the danger of a communist revolution in Germany. He wrote to his friend Frederick Kuh, the head of the United Press news service in Berlin: "Will you please tell me whether they are all cuckoo here [New York] talking about a revolution in Germany, or whether you and the rest of them in Berlin were revolution blind, and don't forget they are talking of a Communist Revolution and not of [a] Hitler putsch!"[26]

On a retainer with the Chase National Bank, Gumberg wrote his patrons not to be concerned about the problem. Informed people in New York and Moscow, he insisted, did not anticipate a communist revolution in Germany.[27] Gumberg was involved in American trade with the Soviet Union, and since he advocated American diplomatic recognition of the communist nation, he had a direct interest in the issue of whether or not communists were interfering in German domestic affairs. His friend Frederick Kuh, who had no such interest, agreed that there was no danger from communism in Germany.[28]

German leaders, above all Hitler, used the Red Scare for their own purposes. Some Americans were inclined to do the same. When members of the Hoover administration took up the theme of the communist danger in Europe, Gumberg speculated that it was another attempt to "yell about the Red menace and put a crimp in Russian-American trade."[29] From Moscow, Louis Fischer, a writer the State Department considered authoritative enough

25 Hugh Wilson, Memorandum of a Conversation with Lord Cecil, 11 September 1931, Box 41, Hugh Gibson Papers.
26 Gumberg to Frederick Kuh, 9 July 1931, Box 5, Gumberg Papers.
27 Gumberg to Walter T. Annett, 5 August 1931, Box 5, Gumberg Papers.
28 Kuh to Gumberg, 11 August 1931, Box 5, Gumberg Papers.
29 Gumberg to Walter Duranty, 9 July 1931, Box 5, Gumberg Papers.

about the Soviet Union to interview him for three days on the subject,[30] was even more emphatic. He argued that there was no substance to fears of revolution in Germany. It was his position that no one in Moscow expected or wanted one, and that the German Communist party would have been "the most surprised and disappointed people in the world" if events had forced one on them. Fischer also speculated that the issue was being used by the Hoover administration for domestic political purposes.[31] Without calling Hoover administration motives into question, Bernard Baruch recognized that there was a crisis of "representative government" in Germany, but was specific that there was no danger concerning the "Russian experiment."[32]

Sackett was not averse to using the Red Scare when it suited his purposes, as his private letter to Hoover in December 1930 certainly attests. He emphasized the communist danger when trying to get help for Brüning during the financial crisis. He continued along that line when Stimson was in Berlin, accentuating his agreement with Brüning's "fear of Communism in Germany."[33] When pressed by Brüning for help from Washington, Sackett reported the chancellor's claim that the situation was so critical that only the army could save Germany "from a radical debacle."[34] That view conformed with Colonel Carpenter's report to the War Department, and to Sackett, that the German army was in complete control of the situation, so much so that no one could govern with its active opposition.[35] Which added further affirmation of the predominant role of the military in the Weimar Republic.

Most objective observers in Berlin were unaware of a genuine threat of communist upheaval during the financial crisis. There certainly was turmoil, but there was no apparent movement on the part of any extremist group to seize political control in Germany. Although he stressed the possibility of civil war and revolution when he tried to get the attention of his government, Sackett did not believe there was a chance the government would be violently overthrown. In fact, when he had concluded the bulk of his negotiations with the Germans in the midst of the crisis, he reported to Hoover and Castle that "things have changed considerably in my absence, though I do not believe they are as desperate as perhaps they are pictured."[36]

Probably because of the influence of his staff, and because he found the

30 Kelley to Wiley, 9 January 1930, Box 1, Wiley Papers.
31 Fischer to Gumberg, 25 July 1931, Box 5, Gumberg Papers.
32 Baruch to Senator Thomas J. Walsh, 18 June 1931, Vol. 27, Bernard M. Baruch Papers.
33 Stimson Diary, 27 August 1931.
34 Sackett to Hoover and Castle, 2 July 1931, FRUS, 1931, 1: 130–131.
35 Carpenter to War Department, copy to Sackett, 18 July 1931, War/Mid Box 2082, 2657-B-735/5.
36 Sackett to Hoover and Castle, 3 July 1931, 462.00R296/4264.

Germans to be too rigid in the matter of concessions, Sackett could be found on both sides of the issue of whether or not the Communists constituted a serious threat to the Weimar Republic. The ambassador was more likely to talk about the dangers of communism if he was in the process of helping Brüning. The same was not true of the professional diplomats who advised him. They uniformly discounted the communist threat and regularly insisted that the Nazis were indeed the major danger for democracy and the republic. But there was a subtle difference in outlook. Whereas Sackett focused on communism as a general threat, the professional diplomats in Berlin concentrated on Nazism. Their views converged because Sackett and his staff were convinced that the Nazis were not capable of carrying out the tasks of governing and would in the end fail. The result would be the same. A Hitler government would lead to chaos and the Communists would come to power in the debris left behind.

Secretary Stimson was in Europe, partly for rest but also to find out firsthand what the chances for success were in the forthcoming disarmament conference. At the same time, he was "particularly anxious" to meet Brüning and assess the situation in Germany.[37] Allen T. Klots, his hand-picked assistant, accompanied the secretary and was assigned the task of finding out what diplomats in the field were thinking about the German situation. While Sackett was away on vacation, Klots spoke to Gordon and Messersmith as well as diplomats in the German foreign office. He found that the embassy and consulate staffs "have no fear of Communist ascendancy here in Germany." Klots expanded on that theme:[38]

> As to the danger of communism in Germany I have been very much re-assured on this question since my visit here. The people at the Embassy and Mr. Messersmith are very sanguine on this question. They feel that the German temperament is naturally unsympathetic to communism; that the German is naturally so orderly and used to a standard of living so superior to that in Russia that a thorough-going communistic Germany is difficult to conceive of. Mr. Messersmith took me all through the communist sections here in Berlin, and it is amazing to note how nothing whatever in the nature of slums exist.

There was nothing, he noted, like the slums of New York and London, and, in addition, the diplomats pointed out "the orderly character of most of the communist demonstrations and how submissive they are to the police."

37 Stimson to Elihu Root, 25 May 1931, Stimson Papers, 81: 376–377; Stimson Diary, 30 March 1931. The British were aware that Stimson's first interest was rest and then the disarmament conference. Craigie wrote that Stimson's "visit portends no American weak-ening in the debt question. The Germans are simply grasping at straws." Craigie note and Thompson Minute, 5 June 1931, FO371, 1931, 9, 15140: 82–83.
38 Klots to Castle, 18 August 1931, Castle Papers – Germany, HHPL.

Talks with members of the press further confirmed the view that neither the Soviets nor the German Communist party were a serious present problem for Germany. It is somewhat remarkable that, in his eleven-page report to Stimson, Klots mentioned neither Hitler nor the Nazis.[39] That omission perhaps makes it easier to believe that Stimson came away from his experiences in Berlin convinced that communism was a more serious danger to Germany than the Nazis.

The exclusion of any discussion of Hitler or the Nazis, the group perceived by most observers to be the greatest threat to the Weimar Republic, can be attributed in part to Stimson's conviction that communism was without doubt the most perilous movement facing Western civilization. It can also be ascribed to his demonstrated lack of knowledge of European affairs, a fact he admitted to in his memoirs. As late as 1947, Stimson maintained that the communists were the most powerful anti-Weimar force in 1931.[40] His single-minded concern about communism was reinforced by both Sackett and Brüning.

The German chancellor was preparing the Americans to see the need for a rearmed Germany. He succeeded. Brüning maintained that Hindenburg shared his view that the Soviets intended to take Bessarabia, which would lead to the spread of Bolshevism throughout Europe. Stimson recorded in his diary: "In this maelstrom Germany will be the buffer state and must be ready to defend itself and the rest of Europe against Bolshevism. For this purpose, purely defensively, it must be armed to meet the crisis." Brüning added to the sense of heightened danger when he told Sackett that there was a considerable increase in the movement toward communism in Germany as the result of propaganda broadcasts by radio from Moscow.

Sackett probably expressed his dual fears of both Nazism and communism in his remarks to Stimson. The ambassador's official view had always stressed the danger Hitler posed for Germany. But in his private correspondence with high-ranking American officials he frequently emphasized his personal fear of the dangers of communism. In any case, after speaking with him in Berlin, Stimson wrote that "Sackett rather sympathizes with Bruening's fear of Communism in Germany."[41]

Brüning persevered in his attempt to gain further concessions from the European powers with American help. His newest tack was to emphasize the precarious position of his government. The chancellor confided in Sackett that without a majority in the Reichstag his government was too vulnerable to the whims of the political forces beyond his control. He underscored the need to avoid elections for they almost certainly would lead to an increase in radicalism, and not just in the Reichstag. The cabinet

39 Klots to Stimson, 21 August 1931, Stimson Papers, 81: 822–833.
40 Stimson and Bundy, *On Active Service*, 157, 271.   41 Stimson Diary, 27 August 1931.

was also in danger of infiltration by radical elements. A radical government, he insisted, meant the repudiation of foreign debts and the destruction forever of German credit – a clear signal to the Americans that they could forget about war debts, and therefore reparations.

Brüning did not stop there. He complained to Sackett that Germany was overcrowded and the pressure of overpopulation worsened the problem of unemployment. The answer lay in a colony, to be given to Germany in a place where a surplus population could be accommodated and thus not only relieve Germany but be of great benefit to other nations. Of course, the Germans could not make such a suggestion, it would best come from a nation that had opposed Germany in the war.[42]

The none too subtle suggestion that the United States take further steps to assist Germany, not only in disarmament and reparations but also in colonial acquisition, probably went further than Sackett was willing to go to help his friend. There had been some serious talk in Great Britain about the possibility of restoring former colonies to the German republic. Tanganyika and Togoland in Africa had been mentioned.[43] Such a restoration could prove to be a triumph for Brüning, but would certainly meet with hostility in both Britain and the United States, not to mention France. The ambassador sent the information to Stimson in a personal letter, partly because what he learned was told in confidence, but also because it must have seemed like an excessive request to Sackett. Sensitive to the political turbulence that talk of colonies would evoke in both the United States and Europe, he forwarded the information without comment.[44]

Sackett was certainly sympathetic to Brüning's problems with disarmament, with reparations payments, with the dangers to German credit, and with unemployment, but almost surely he would avoid any support for the claim on colonies. Still, the fact remains, he put the German's intentions before the secretary of state, intentions that, when voiced by Hitler, would meet with outrage from Americans.

Political observers in Germany all agreed that elections would benefit only the radical parties; they disagreed as to who would benefit most. Although some Germans and Americans stressed the importance of communism as the principal danger facing the Weimar Republic, Sackett agreed with the staff of the American embassy in Berlin. In his official reports he emphasized the Nazis as the major problem and reported with apprehension on the party's phenomenal growth. His assessment of Nazi success in terms of numbers and their potential at the ballot box was accurate. However, because he feared the dire consequences of a Nazi government for the

42 Sackett to State, 3 October 1931, FRUS, 1931, 1: 327.
43 Martin Gilbert, *The Roots of Appeasement*, 129–130.
44 Sackett to Stimson, 3 October 1931, FRUS, 1931, 1: 331.

German republic, and for American financial interests, he was eager to see signs of Nazi problems and dissension. Sackett and his staff were influenced by wishful thinking; they hoped and believed that dissension would split the party and vitiate the gains the Nazis made in membership and in elections.

Sackett reported the rapid and frightening growth of Hitler's party. The "flash-in-the-pan" theories that had been used to explain Nazi success, he wrote, were generally being discounted. Most observers, he reported, conceded that in a new Reichstag election the Nazis would emerge with even more seats than they had won in the last contest.[45] For more than a year following the September 1930 Reichstag elections the party experienced steady growth. By the beginning of 1931 party membership had reached nearly 400,000; at the end of the same year it had doubled. Six million Germans had voted for the Nazis in September 1930 and later local elections indicated those numbers were increasing.

Hitler had also made alarming gains in paramilitary strength. At the end of 1930 he induced Ernst Röhm to return to Germany from Bolivia to assume command of the Storm Troopers. Röhm took over a ragged private army of 100,000 men, and developed it into the most efficient of party armies, numbering 300,000 early in 1932. This growth can be explained in part by Hitler's being unable to force any nationwide elections in 1931, which led him to concentrate on party problems and expansion.

American diplomats, cognizant of the Nazi growth, were fearful of its consequences for the Weimar Republic. They reported that Hitler was confident of success in the next Reichstag and Prussian elections, and was demanding that they be held soon. The Americans agreed, though unhappily, with Hitler's assessment, and thus George Gordon was enthusiastic about a chance to report that the Hitler party had experienced some significant setbacks. The Nazis lost an important cabinet position in one of the states, and a revolt among the Storm Troopers revealed a serious split in the Nazi party in the spring of 1931.

In Thuringia, Wilhelm Frick, the Nazi who had been minister of the interior for more than a year, lost his post when the provincial parliament voted lack of confidence in the coalition government. The opposition parties showed unusual fortitude and cohesion in throwing the Nazis out of the Thuringian government. Gordon reported that the Nazis had been "arrogantly confident" that they could hold the coalition together with the support of the People's party. When it became clear that the Social Democratic party's motion of no confidence would pass with People's party support, the Nazis panicked. They switched from their haughty posture of assuming People's party support to using "every means in their power," from offering major concessions to hasty eleventh-hour personal visits to

45 Sackett to State, 6 January 1931, 862.00/2576.

Weimar by Hitler and Goebbels "to ward off this calamity." Although the Nazis demonstrated an "unusually conciliatory attitude," their opponents were unyielding and the coalition was defeated. Aware that the Nazis had lost in a major political confrontation, Gordon could barely conceal his enthusiasm for what he called the "worst blow" Hitler had experienced since his success in the last Reichstag election.[46]

From Hitler's point of view, according to Gordon, "worse was still to come."[47] Sackett had reported that Brüning was cracking down on political violence. In an action demonstrating that communism was not Brüning's major concern, he aimed specifically at the Nazis. The chancellor issued a series of emergency decrees in late March. They provided severe penalties for incitement to political murder, and for trade in firearms; they gave the police the authority to suspend political meetings as well as to censor political pamphlets and advertisements, and made it illegal to bring religion into contempt.[48] Hitler, pursuing his policy of legality, ordered all Nazis to observe the decree and promised expulsion from the party of all violators.[49] As Gordon pointed out, Hitler's order "ran counter to the very nature of the storm detachments which were to serve as the vanguard of a Nazi *coup* against the Republic." At the time of Frick's "enforced retirement," Gordon reported there were strong signs that "a real storm was brewing." Then, following Hitler's order, an internal revolution erupted in the Nazi party, particularly among the Storm Troopers in Berlin.[50]

As the Nazi party grew, so did the bureaucracy that governed it. The Storm Troopers most resented this, the political branch of the party. They saw themselves as the front-line fighters against the "November Criminals," yet while they did the dirty work in the city streets, the political bureaucrats issued orders from their posh quarters in the Brown House in Munich.

Gordon perceived the Berlin Storm Trooper rebellion as a challenge to Hitler's leadership, but also as a showdown between the forces demanding a putsch, represented by Captain Walter Stennes, and the political bureaucrats, led by Hitler, who insisted on winning power at the polling place. Gordon's reaction to serious dissension among the Nazis was even stronger than his enthusiasm for their ill fortune in Thuringia. In his analysis of the "Stennes revolt" in April 1931, Gordon focused on three aspects of the crisis in the Nazi party: the meaning of Hitler's firing Storm Trooper Captain Stennes; Goebbels' role in the affair, and the consequences of this apparent blow to Nazism for the republic.

46 Gordon to State, 8 April 1931, 862.00/2588.
47 Ibid.
48 Sackett to State, 28 March 1931, 862.00/2586.
49 Gordon to State, 8 and 1 April 1931, 862.00/2588 and 2587.
50 The following account of the Stennes Revolt and its consequences is taken in its entirety from Gordon's despatch to the State Department, 8 April 1931, 862.00/2588.

Stennes, who was commander of Gruppe Ost, the Storm Troopers in Berlin as well as northern and eastern Germany, harbored "strong resentment" for Hitler's order to comply with Brüning's emergency decree banning political violence. Gordon characterized Stennes as the leader of a small but militant band of Nazi extremists. The Storm Troopers' commander launched an attack on Hitler's policy and tactics and then directed his criticism to Hitler himself. Stennes accused Hitler "with elasticity of conviction bordering on hypocrisy." In Stennes's words, Hitler had forsaken "the ideals for which thousands of the best men in the storm detachments had risked their lives." He went on to charge that the Storm Troopers' revolutionary ardor was being toned down by a "bourgeois and liberalistic tendency" growing among party leaders at their Munich headquarters. Moreover, these party leaders were driving the "best elements" of the party into the arms of Bolshevism.

Gordon's account stressed that "internal friction" was an almost certain development in a "movement attaining the mushroom growth of the Nazis." There had been signs of discontent in the party during the September election campaign, and on several subsequent occasions. The Storm Troopers were the most disaffected group, complaining that since they bore "the burden and heat of the day" they were "entitled to corresponding emoluments." Unhappiness led to violence and Stennes's followers attacked the Berlin party headquarters, taking possession of *Der Angriff*, the Nazi newspaper edited by Goebbels. Stennes read that he had been removed from his command in one of Hugenberg's publications and "resorted to a tactical move." Since he had not yet received an official notification of his removal from command, he declared that such a move would "constitute a breach of honor by Adolf Hitler," and refused to accept that such a step had been taken. His statement was published in *Der Angriff*, under temporary control by the insurgents, accompanied by an editorial proclaiming that Hitler had given Stennes assurance of his "everlasting confidence."

Hitler launched a counteroffensive, publishing one manifesto after another in the *Völkische Beobachter*, the principal Nazi newspaper. The Nazi leader threatened members with expulsion from the party if they obeyed any orders given by Stennes. Gordon then went on to say Hitler admonished the party

> that any man who attempted to incite an unarmed organization like the storm detachments to proceed against the Republic by physical force was a fool, a criminal or an *agent provocateur*. Referring to the ill-fated Hitler *putsch* at Munich in 1923, he said that he must now admit that any further attempt in this direction was sheer madness. He had declared under oath at Leipzig that his party pursued only legal means and he would not permit anyone, least of all Herr Stennes, to deter him from this course or it would be tantamount to perjury.

The Nazi leader was moving toward marshaling support of party "regulars" and reemphasizing his commitment to attain power by legal means.

The upshot of the Stennes revolt was that Hitler used the occasion to consolidate his own position as undisputed leader of the Nazi party. He entrusted Hermann Göring with "extraordinary powers" to collaborate with Goebbels in purging the party of "undesirable elements" and issued specific orders to Röhm that strengthened Hitler's personal control of the Storm Troops. All local Storm Troop commanders were given until April 12 to "submit a written statement pledging unconditional loyalty to Hitler." Failure to conform would lead to immediate expulsion from the party.

Hitler not only purged the party of dissident groups, he also tied his party army's leadership much closer to himself. Although he probably was not aware of it, he also drew Goebbels into a tighter relationship and greater loyalty to his personal position as party leader. According to Gordon's account, there was reason to believe that Goebbels, who was party leader in Berlin, "would not let the opportunity go by for doing as much harm as possible to Hitler, the only man above him in the party." Gordon speculated that Goebbels would take action only if he felt he had a "good safe chance" for success. If he held such views, Gordon wrote, he probably felt that the "opportune moment" had not "yet arrived to put them into practise."

Goebbels was in Weimar with Hitler trying to salvage Wilhelm Frick's position in the Thuringian cabinet when Stennes's supporters seized *Der Angriff*. As editor-in-chief of the Nazi newspaper, Goebbels was forced to take a stand on what Stennes's followers were publishing. Tying himself closely with Hitler, Goebbels issued a statement asserting his "solidarity" with the Nazi leader, and declared that the seizure of the newspaper and party headquarters were illegal and therefore he would institute proceedings to recover them by legal means. Gordon contended that by allying himself with Hitler, "Goebbels weakened the impelling force" of what everyone now saw was an open rebellion against the head of the party. Gordon believed that Goebbels had been sympathetic to Stennes's position in the past and was now charged by the Storm Troop commander with a "breach of faith." In order to avoid possible revenge by the insurgents, Goebbels left Weimar for Munich rather than Berlin. Upon his return to Berlin, with "extraordinary powers given him by Hitler to purge the party of all recalcitrant elements," he kept himself in hiding for several days before restoring control of the party newspaper and headquarters.

Gordon's account clearly established the American diplomats' view that Hitler had won tighter control over the party rank and file and the Storm Troop leadership, as well as the loyalty of Goebbels, deflecting any ambition of his to undermine the Nazi leader's authority. But that was not the import of the despatch. Gordon saw the events surrounding Frick's defeat in Thuringia and the Stennes revolt as especially significant because they constituted "an undeniably serious setback to the Nazi cause." The serious blow to the Nazi party was especially important because

> the Department is well aware what a danger the Nazi movement, based on practically unadulterated demagogism, has been to Germany in particular and to Europe in general since its extraordinary success in the September elections of last year. Accordingly, it has seemed during these past months as if what one wanted chiefly to be able to report were developments tending towards a weakening or decline of this movement.

But, Gordon warned, even though the moment had at last arrived when one could record "a definite check to the movement" one should not greet the good news "with undiluted pleasure."

Despite the heartening phenomenon of Nazi reverses, Gordon also saw a negative side to these developments. American diplomats had foreseen communist danger as a consequence of Nazi success. Now Gordon envisioned communist success resulting from Nazi failure. Ultimately he foresaw that the Stennes revolt could "lead to a certain increase in Communism." Stennes, he said, was an extremist, an advocate of "half-baked ideas" very close to "national Bolshevism." The danger lay in the fact that those ideas were but a step to the "doctrines of Communism." Many of the disaffected Nazis were expected to "go over to the Communist Party." However, there was even a positive side to that, for the Stennes followers would surely be "more localized and circumscribed" and hence should be considered "less dangerous than when forming more indefinitely part and parcel of the Nazi movement." What Gordon thought one should hope for was that "substantial portions of the population" did not follow them into the Communist party.

Always hopeful that parliamentary politics could be restored, Gordon found some solace in the fact that Hitler had strengthened his control of the Nazi party. The American diplomat surmised that the Nazi leader would now be more amenable to the regular political process. He explained:

> Now that the smoke is cleared away it is apparent that Hitler remains solidly in control of the party organization, and when the present process of cleansing it from these more extreme elements has been completed he will probably find himself able to dominate its policy more unrestrictedly than ever. As latterly he seems to have been developing an absolute passion for legality and constitutionality as the watchwords of his party policy, it may well be that the Government may henceforth find it easier to deal with the Nazis.

If Hitler's position was meant to reassure his critics, he certainly succeeded with American diplomats in Berlin.

Sackett and his staff were forming an essentially optimistic perception of the Nazi party's position in German politics. Gordon's report of the Stennes revolt reveals the hope American diplomats held out for the Nazis to become a traditional parliamentary party. That form of wishful thinking obviated the danger of both Nazism and communism. In their view, Hitler was a moderate leader surrounded by radicals such as Goebbels. Hitler's stress on legalism and avoiding a putsch was viewed by American diplomats in Berlin as proof that the Nazi leader was committed to becoming head of a party that could win a parliamentary majority and govern in the traditional manner. Such a move was only possible, in their view, if Hitler got full control of the Nazi party.

State Department diplomats in Washington, although aware of and encouraged by the Nazi setbacks, tended to discount the importance of the Hitler party. That position was encouraged in part by Sackett's ambivalent reporting. His official views stressed the dangers of Nazism, while his personal views accented communism. In addition, he and his staff advanced the idea that Nazi success ultimately meant communist victory. As a consequence, Stimson and others in Washington considered the Nazis little more than harbingers of communist chaos. Many believed that the Nazis served a purpose in the German domestic scene as a "political 'threat' party." Brüning was able to use the Nazis as a frightening alternative to his government if the powers failed to eliminate or reduce reparations. The current view in the State Department was that Hitler and his party were merely tools that could be used by Germans to get their way.[51]

The tendency to express concern about the Nazis while simultaneously minimizing their importance became common among many diplomats. Hugh Wilson, American minister to Switzerland, agreed with Lord Robert Cecil that "the Hitlerite movement" was in decline but that a "serious blow to [German] national prestige might turn a lot of the Hitlerites into communists."[52] French diplomat Pierre-Etienne Flandin and Wilson concurred in the view that perhaps Hitler's coming to power might be a necessary and desirable phase through which it was necessary to pass before a "real government" could be installed in Germany.[53]

When Lewis L. Strauss, a New York banker, raised an alarm about Nazi activity in the United States, further confusion about the Hitler party was revealed. Strauss, a friend of the president, was concerned that several Germans were establishing branches of the Nazi party in major American cities, where they were "disseminating propaganda of an inflammatory and dangerous character." The New Yorker wrote the president asking

51 See John Carter, Memorandum of a Conversation he and P. T. Culbertson, also of the Division of Western European Affairs, had with representatives of the Continental Illinois Company, 6 March 1931, 862.51/3007.
52 Hugh Wilson, Memorandum of a Conversation with Lord Cecil, 11 September 1931, Box 41, Gibson Papers.
53 Wilson, Memorandum of a Conversation with Flandin, 9 September 1931, Box 41, Gibson Papers.

whether or not the Nazis could be deported as undesirable aliens. The matter was investigated by the Immigration Service, which reported that the Nazis were a small group "but very vociferous and active." Their literature was definitely anti-Semitic, just as with the parent organization in Germany. There appeared to be little danger to public order, however, since the party seemed to be the "direct antithesis of the Communist party as the Hitlerites are not opposed to organized government but seem to be agitating for a strong centralized government of a socialist nature."[54]

The Americans tended to view the Nazis as an instrument of German government alarmism, as a stalking horse for some other group, or as a phase through which German government had to pass before a "real government" could be installed in Germany. These disparate views certainly presented a confused picture of the party and of Hitler's leadership. Above all, they relegated the party to insignificance and Hitler to the role of glorified spear bearer. Although they sometimes referred to the Nazis as Fascists, American diplomats simply did not force the issue and draw a parallel with fascism elsewhere. An occasional mention of Mussolini's "March on Rome" was used to illustrate the meaning of the Storm Trooper demand for a putsch but that was about as far as the comparison with Italian Fascism went.

Sackett and his colleagues spoke of Nazis as Fascists when they first reported on the party's growth. They used the analogy with Mussolini's Italian party principally because they knew so little about the Hitler party. They likened the Nazi call for a March on Berlin with the Italian counterpart, but there was little if any analysis of the two Right-oriented parties. Later, as they became more familiar with the Nazis, American diplomats no longer referred to them as Fascists. It was only after Hitler became chancellor that they again resorted to the analogy, and again because they did not understand the phenomenon they were witnessing. Comparisons with what happened in Italy was the closest experience they had available to them.

One reason Americans did not equate Nazism with Italian Fascism was that they deplored the Hitler party, but their attitude toward Mussolini ranged from ambiguity to appreciation, at least down to the Italian invasion of Ethiopia in 1935. Throughout the 1920s, American business publications expressed admiration for the Italian Fascist encouragement of hard work and thrift, for restoring efficiency and competence to government, and for returning the railroads and public utilities to private enterprise, but above

---

54 Lewis L. Strauss to Lawrence Richey, 14 November 1931, and William N. Doak, Secretary of Labor, to Richey, 19 March 1932, Foreign Affairs – Countries – Germany, HHPL; Kurt G. W. Ludecke, *I Knew Hitler*, is an account by one of the Nazis sent to the United States to organize Nazi party branches.

all for eschewing the dangerous ideas of communism in favor of the ideals of individualism.[55]

Fascism seemed an appropriate form of government for a people as unruly and disorderly as the Italians were perceived to be by many Americans. The prevailing image, reflected by the prominent journalist Edgar Ansel Mowrer, was one of an easygoing, indolent people, not capable of self-government. Moreover, Americans saw parallels in the Fascist corporate state and American corporatism. Producers and consumers in Italy organized cooperatives in both industry and labor, not unlike the formation of trade associations and cooperatives created in America, especially when Hoover had served as secretary of commerce. Americans appreciated the fact that the Italian Fascists promoted capitalism and business enterprise and were dead set against class war and state ownership. There were further parallels in the development of leadership by experts in all sectors and the fostering of strong cooperation between business and government. Not only was Italian Fascism admired in many quarters, Mussolini was honored as a man of action comparable to Theodore Roosevelt. Both men got things done, and in dramatic fashion, displaying exuberance, charisma, and showmanship.[56]

But whereas the unruly Italians needed a Mussolini, the orderly, stolid Germans did not need a Hitler. Examples of the perception of the German people as stable and obedient are replete in the papers of American diplomats, official and unofficial. The tendency was for some to see little danger of revolution in Germany, for, as one banker wrote, the Germans were the "best disciplined population in the world." Alan Klots, who toured the poorer, specifically the Communist, sections of Berlin, was "perfectly amazed." He saw no slums such as one could see on the East Side of New York, or in London. "The houses all seem to be neat – little clean white curtains at all the windows, etc. Even the Communist parades they say are usually very orderly and submissive – of course there have been these occasional shootings."[57]

Stimson reflected the American view of Germans as stolid and trustworthy. On a Sunday afternoon stroll through a Potsdam park with Brüning,

55 Lisa Walker, "Anti-Bolshevism and the Advent of Mussolini and Hitler," 46–71; Joan Hoff Wilson, *American Business and Foreign Policy*, xiv; "Why Mussolini Charms the American Business Man," *Literary Digest*, 9 June 1923, 73; James Warren Prothro, *The Dollar Decade*, 204–206; John P. Diggins, *Mussolini and Fascism: The View From America*, 146–148, 159–166, 297–299; Alexander DeConde, *Half Bitter, Half Sweet*, 14, 183–205, 307, 376–381; David F. Schmitz, *The United States and Fascist Italy, 1922–1940*, 6, 80–81, 134, 150, 168.

56 Walker, "Anti-Bolshevism and the Advent of Mussolini and Hitler," 51–55, 61–63.

57 F. F. Beer to George W. Davison, both of the Continental Hanover Bank and Trust Co. of New York, 4 August 1931, Harrison Papers; Klots to Castle, 18 August 1931, Castle Papers – Germany, HHPL.

the American secretary of state was impressed as people approached the chancellor. He told his companion that he "did not think there was any danger of revolution from such a crowd." Brüning was alarmed; the American was getting the wrong impression, he quickly retorted: "You have not seen the boys from northeast Berlin who are the communists." But Stimson was unmoved. He replied, "That may be so, but even if northeast Berlin started a revolution it wouldn't be recognized by the people I have seen, just as happened in the revolution right after the war." Defeated, Brüning conceded "that was probably true."[58]

It was no accident that the two men who called for closer attention to the Nazis were Jewish. As Jews, Lewis Strauss and Herbert Feis were more sensitive than most people to the anti-Semitic content of the Nazi program and agitation. Strauss was concerned with the spread of hatred in the United States, while Feis was more concerned with the success of the Nazis in Germany. Strauss wanted Nazi vitriol stopped in America and the perpetrators deported. It was Feis who called for a reassessment of Hitler and his party. Probably to counter the emphasis on communism that permeated the State Department, Feis, the department's economic adviser, predicted that the Nazis would come to power very soon. He wrote a brief memorandum to Stimson with his observations on what was happening in Germany. Hitler's strength, he wrote, was increasing "both on the basis of votes cast and psychologically." There was a general expectation that Hitler would either enter the Brüning cabinet or form a government of his own.[59]

In his desire to call attention to what could be expected if the Nazis came to power, Feis avoided any reference to anti-Semitism and focused on the parallel between Nazism and Fascism. An economist, Feis tacitly assumed knowledge of the development of the corporate state in Italy. He further assumed that Hitler would create a similar system in Germany because "his program and ideas seem to resemble those of Fascist Italy." The move to the Fascist style of government, with a close connection between government and industry, would be no problem for Hitler, he maintained, because Brüning decrees were already creating a relationship approaching "the Italian scheme and the step over to the Hitler program would not be very great." The only problem Feis saw was with the trade unions, which would need to shed their "international socialist character" and assume a "national Fascist complexion and be under the conrol of the central Government."

Feis characterized Hitler as playing up to international banking groups, assuring them of his "complete respect for their debts" not only to win

---

58 Stimson Diary, 26 July 1931; Schmitz, *The United States and Fascist Italy*, 121.
59 Feis to Stimson, 8 December 1931, 862.51/3292, the text is in FRUS, 1932, 2: 276–277, without attribution to Feis.

them to his side, but also to "rally them against France." He then compared Hitler to the Duce, asserting that "his patriotic utterances in general resemble those of Mussolini a very few years ago – national war cries without any defined objective."

Stimson passed on the Feis memorandum to Pierre Boal, chief of the Division of Western European Affairs, who in turn sent it on to Sackett for his assessment. Boal pointed out that the memo was based for the most part on newspaper reports and seemed accurate, but made no mention that it orignated with Feis, heading it as a memo prepared in the State Department. Boal thought the memo significant enough to mention that the Berlin embassy had not approached the problem of Hitler and the Nazis in quite the same way and asked Sackett to elaborate further on the issue.[60]

Sackett despatched a memorandum prepared by Alfred Klieforth, first secretary, which was a composite of embassy views including, of course, those of the ambassador. Sackett took exception to the staff's guess as to the probable outcome of a general election. Socialists and Communists, he predicted, would win more votes than his embassy staff estimated. The staff was correct. Sackett, who had just consulted with Brüning, was convinced, as was the chancellor, that the Social Democrats would remain the largest party in Germany.[61]

The staff predicted that the Nazis would become the largest single party in Germany. They attributed Hitler's "phenomenal gain in successive local elections" to the depression and unemployment. Party growth was made possible by winning votes away from the nonsocialist parties of the middle and Right. The Nazis were unable to make any inroads on the Catholic parties, the Center and Bavarian People's party; nor could they dent the parties of the Left, the Social Democrats and the Communists. Although Hitler was obviously doing well, the staff did not see unlimited growth by "geometric progression" in the Nazi future.[62]

On the basis of their analysis of elections to that time, they estimated that the Hitler party would win about 35 percent of the vote in a general election. The combined parties of the Left would win the same percentage, while the Catholic parties and the parties of the middle and Right would each win 15 percent. The staff predicated their estimate without calculating "further unexpected popular support" for the Nazis. As it turned out the staff prognosis was remarkably accurate. They had not guessed how much the Nazis would gain at the expense of the middle and Right parties, which won only 13 percent of the vote in the next Reichstag election in July 1932, whereas the Nazis emerged on top with 37 percent.

60 Boal to Sackett, 10 December 1931, FRUS, 1932, 2: 276–277.
61 Sackett to Boal, 12 January 1932, FRUS, 1932, 2: 277.
62 This account is based on the Memorandum by the American Embassy, 5 January 1932, enclosed with Sackett to Boal, 12 January 1932, FRUS, 1932, 2: 278–281.

Alluding to Feis's reference to Hitler's attempt to mollify the international banking community, the staff stressed that his talk about the sanctity of private foreign debts, and his emphasis on the capitalism of his program, had "cooled the ardor of many of the more radical elements" in the Nazi party. At the same time, while it allayed the fears of "certain business elements," it failed to attract to his cause any "outstanding individuals." They pointed out that the "prominent Germans who are avowed followers of Hitler may be counted on the fingers of two hands though several rich industrialists would be included." Hitler's recent speeches on economic matters, continued the embassy staff, while winning some business support, "have very much slowed up the intensity of his appeal to the particularly undigested youth in the country who were previously attracted to him as a crusader." Because there were far more of the young than of business votes, the staff concluded that most observers believed "that Nazi gains in voting strength will be considerably diminished in the immediate future."

Although merely qualifying what Feis had to say about Nazi strength, Sackett and his staff took strong exception to the economic adviser's comparison of Fascism and Nazism. They stressed two major differences: Nazi emphasis on anti-Semitism, which was "entirely lacking" in Fascism, and the importance of personality in the Italian system. There was very little the two programs had in common in spite of their certain similarities, such as the dependence on chauvinism and opposition to the "emigration of their peoples."

The "cooperative state" was the foundation of Fascism in Italy, they asserted, while "Hitlerism is based on the old Hohenzollern and Prussian idea of strong centralization, imperialism and expansion." Above all:

> The substance of Fascism is Mussolini's personality; the same applies in a much lesser degree to Hitlerism. Mussolini has the intellect and bearing of a martial hero; Hitler has the intellect of a crusading sectarian leader – oblivious of dangers which surround him – but with intense energy and relentless in the pursuit of his aims.

While the Berlin diplomats disagreed with Feis, finding Fascism and Nazism with little in common, they agreed that a transition from the Brüning government to a Hitler dictatorship would be easy. Under Brüning, there was already a "semi-dictatorial government," with banking, commerce, and industry already routinely functioning in the system. However, Hitler would have trouble trying to bring German unions "under a Nazi national dictatorship."

Sackett and his staff revealed again their conviction that the Socialists would in the end save the Weimar Republic from a Hitler dictatorship. The trade unions, they wrote, "make up the Social-Democratic party, oppose dictatorship and constitute the strongest opposition to Hitler, and the two movements are irreconcilable." The workers who support Hitler are from the "floating labor population," lack the discipline of those in the trade unions, and would back away from Hitler as soon as the depression came to an end. Hitler claimed that his Storm Troopers were formed only for the purpose of coping with "internal disorders" but should they attempt to gain power by force the Social Democrats had the weapon to defeat them – the general strike.

The Berlin embassy staff agreed with Feis that Hitler was trying to win over bankers, but they pointed out that although he promised payment of private debts in full, he would not pay "a cent of tribute," which meant he intended to cancel political debts, including, of course, reparations payments. Hitler and Mussolini both had territorial aspirations, and the Nazi leader aspired to the

> union of all German nations, that is Austria and Germany, and the return of all former German territory, as Memel, Danzig, Upper Silesia, and not excluding Alsace-Lorraine, under a strongly federalized German state, and a return of German colonies. While Hitler's war cries resembled those of Mussolini, following the past December he had become far more diplomatic so as not to offend Great Britain, Italy and the United States.

However, they pointed out, Hitler's real program, whether in economic reform or, especially, in foreign affairs, "has not been sufficiently revealed to enable careful examination."

Hitler and the Nazis had become a matter of central concern to the American embassy in Berlin and of increasing concern in the State Department. The interest had been almost entirely intellectual. American diplomats had had almost nothing to do with Nazis in person. That would change with the flood of elections in the spring and fall of 1932, and greater familiarity with the Nazis would develop as John Cooper Wiley replaced George Gordon from October 1931 to May 1932. Gordon left for Washington with his wife, who was pregnant and seriously ill. Wiley, who was almost flamboyant when compared to the stiff Gordon, would seek out the Nazis to learn more about the party and its aims. His analysis enabled the State Department to develop a more sophisticated perception of Hitler and the Nazis, a perception that made them more frightening than ever.

7

One end, two paths:
Brüning and Hitler in conflict

PERSONAL CONTACTS WITH Nazis, especially with Hermann Göring and Joseph Goebbels, enabled Ambassador Sackett to focus on the Nazi party with greater understanding. In 1932, as Hitler's position grew in strength and importance, Sackett had less to say about the dangers of communism except as a means of getting the attention of the American government. Faced with the real possibility of Hitler in power, he now stressed the significance of the Nazis and placed greater emphasis on Brüning as the one man to save republican Germany. Sackett believed not only that Brüning could save the Weimar Republic, but also that he was the single person who could deliver Germany from the danger of Hitlerism. One failing in Sackett's analysis was his inability to divine the close similarity between Brüning's nationalistic goals and those of Hitler. When he focused on the dangers of Hitler and the need to help Brüning as much as possible, Sackett saw the two men as worlds apart. One significant difference between them continued to escape Sackett, who failed to see that Hitler, rather than wanting to achieve specific goals, sought power as an end in itself.

Sackett's appraisal of the two German leaders was faulty because he worked so hard to help the one against the other. Hitler appeared to be far removed from Brüning because the Nazi did everything in his power to thwart the chancellor. That distance between the two men seemed greater than ever as Brüning sought to win Hitler over to surmount yet another formidable task. President Hindenburg's term in office was due to expire in April 1932, and Brüning hoped he could get Hitler's cooperation to support the reelection of the president. It appeared feasible to win the support of the major political parties, except for the Communists. Even the Social Democrats reluctantly expressed their approval for the Brüning scheme. Another option was to extend Hindenburg's term by constitutional amendment, which would require a two-thirds majority in the Reichstag. Either tactic required Hitler's cooperation.

Failing those alternatives, Brüning would be forced to postpone his plans in order to manage a distracting campaign to reelect the octogenarian field marshal. A chore made far more difficult because Hindenburg did not want to withstand another election, especially since he would have to rely on Socialists and Catholics in order to win. With the Young Plan signatories scheduled to meet in mid-January to discuss reparations and the major powers scheduled to meet in early February to negotiate a disarmament agreement, Brüning was compelled to act quickly to minimize his problems. First, he was able to maneuver a postponement of the reparations talks until June, and again turned his attention to winning Hitler over to the scheme to keep President Hindenburg in office. The chancellor counted on Hitler's cooperation to meet German nationalist goals on which they both agreed: certainly that reparations should be canceled and that German rearmament must come in the near future.

Hitler had refused on earlier occasions to cooperate either with the government or with the other parties in the Reichstag. He turned Brüning down in October 1930 when first asked to help extend Hindenburg's term as president. A year later, the Nazi refused again to cooperate with the chancellor. Instead, on October 11, Hitler joined the parties of the Right at Bad Harzburg in a mass demonstration of mutual and unequivocal opposition to the Weimar Republic. Thousands of paramilitary troops representing the Nationalist party, the Stahlhelm, and the Nazis paraded past the reviewing stand where Alfred Hugenberg, Hjalmar Schacht, and Hitler, among others, took their salute. Although he joined the "National Opposition" in this public display of contempt for the "November System," Hitler remained only long enough for his Storm Troopers to pass in review. Otherwise he made it abundantly clear that he did not want to appear to be cooperating with Alfred Hugenberg or any of the "gentlemen in frock coats" among his right-wing rivals.

The Harzburg Front was never an effective organized bloc. Its main object – to bring down the Brüning government – failed. It would remain as a mere symbol of the hatred the political Right harbored against the Weimar Republic. It would be revived when Hugenberg and Franz von Papen used it as the mounting block that gave Hitler a boost into the saddle of power.[1]

Hitler was willing to give the Harzburg Front only momentary attention. He wanted it known that he would act independently, free of the influence of Hugenberg, Schacht, and their ilk. That same posture was revealed earlier when Hitler joined Hugenberg in the referendum against the Young Plan. Hitler's instrument to win power was the Nazi party alone. He clearly shared many, if not most, of the same objectives as other members of the Harzburg Front. But rather than collaborate directly, Hitler insisted

1 Eyck, *Weimar Republic,* 2: 332–336.

on a separate identity, one that would allow him to concentrate on control of the Nazi party and would eventually lead to his leadership of an exclusively Nazi government.

It was easy for Sackett to assume a congruence of goals between the right-wing leaders Hitler and Hugenberg, but it was not as readily apparent to him that Hitler and Brüning shared many objectives. In fact, Hitler and Brüning were not very far apart on many issues, although they certainly did disagree on the means to achieve the same goals.[2] One contemporary noted that the only difference between Hitler and Brüning on reparations was that Hitler shouted his views "in forte or fortissimo from the housetops, while Brüning tries to do the same in piano."[3] In one respect Hitler and Brüning differed markedly, especially on the issue of their ultimate goal. Whereas Hitler intended to create a National Socialist state, Brüning and Hugenberg shared a different aspiration – the restoration of the Hohenzollern dynasty to the throne. On occasion Hitler seemed to agree, and although he sometimes appeared to waver on the issue, support for the monarchy was at least a potential area of agreement. Sackett noted that the Nazi program "has so far left the question of monarchy open for subsequent decision but has carefully refrained from repudiating restoration."[4] The ardent support of the Hohenzollern family for Hitler is evidence that they hoped and believed the Nazis supported the restoration.

Brüning's thought that extending Hindenburg's term in office was the best way to achieve at least two goals on which all three nationalist-oriented leaders found agreement – the end of reparations and the rearmament of Germany – was shared by many Germans, and not only on the political Right. It was on the issue of strengthening the Reichswehr that Brüning had his strongest card to play. If that end could be achieved, he believed that Hitler might be persuaded to support the effort to extend Hindenburg's presidential term. Like Sackett, he would continue to think that Hitler wanted to achieve nationalistic goals rather than power itself. To augment his position, the chancellor had General Groener invite Hitler to meet with him on January 6, 1932. The next day Brüning and General Schleicher joined the talks, at which Ernst Röhm was also present, probably in the hope that the Storm Troop chief could swing Hitler to the Reichswehr point of view. For a moment Hitler seemed to agree, but threw away any chance for a deal by insisting on the dissolution of the Reichstag and new elections. It became apparent that there was no hope for agreement with the Nazis.[5]

2 Sackett to State, 17 May 1932, 462.00R296/5664; this was the French view, Edge to State, Paris, 15 March 1932, 862.00/2702.

3 Max Winkler, "American Investors and German Bonds," American Council of Foreign Bondholders, 1 April 1932, Box 4, Jerome Frank papers.

4 Sackett to State, 8 March 1932, 862.00/2698.

5 Brüning's negotiations with Hitler and Hugenberg were a matter of public record, *New York Times*, 8–12 January 1932. See Elke Fröhlich, ed., *Die Tagebücher von Joseph Goebbels*, 1: 105–109, all citations from Part 1.

When talks with Hugenberg failed on January 9, Brüning was faced with the unhappy prospect of a presidential election campaign. The chancellor was persistent. He continued the conversations in private until the eve of the presidential election in the hope that the Rightist parties would change their minds and agree to extend the field marshal's term. To that end, on February 9, General Groener lifted the restriction on Nazis serving in the Reichswehr.[6] But it did no good. Brüning was frustrated at the refusal of the National Opposition to support Hindenburg, especially since he was convinced that "all parties, except the Communists" would help reelect the field marshal by popular vote.

Brüning preferred a popular referendum to extension of the president's term by the Reichstag and considered a contested election the worst of all alternatives. An electoral fight among German parties was the least desirable alternative, particularly because the president would be required to rely on the support of the Catholic Center party and the Socialists.[7] Desperate for a victory of some kind, Brüning turned to his friend Ambassador Sackett. The Kentuckian attempted to elicit closer American attention to Germany's problems by inviting Federal Reserve Board Governor Eugene Meyer to come to Berlin to get firsthand knowledge of the "critical economic situation" faced by the chancellor, but failed.[8] Sackett then tried to avoid intervening on behalf of American bondholders. To take additional pressure off the German government, he suggested they would act in a voluntary way to give relief to the Americans. But Stimson was insistent. The largest holders of the types of securities involved were clients of the prominent firm of Sullivan and Cromwell; it was clear the ambassador would have to intervene on their behalf.[9]

Although Sackett believed that the Germans should pay some reparations, he did what he could to help Brüning, who wanted them canceled. The French, of course, wanted the Germans to continue paying reparations in some form. Sackett thought that the French, who refused to budge in discussions on the subject, believed that delay in resolving the issue was working in their favor. What was worse, from Sackett's point of view, the French also assumed that delay would lead to a German collapse. Sackett was convinced that the French also assumed that German failure would bring down American banks and imperil the Federal Reserve system. The situation merited an urgent alert to Washington about the dangers inherent in the French strategy.

6 Wiley to State, 23 March 1932, 862.00/2710.
7 Sackett to State, No. 10, 12 January 1932, Foreign Affairs – Financial, HHPL; Eyck, *Weimar Republic*, 2: 352–353; Bracher, *Auflösung der Weimarer Republik*, 443–445; Walter H. Kaufmann, *Monarchism in the Weimar Republic*, 205–206.
8 Telegram, Sackett to State, 6 December 1931; triple priority telegram, Stimson to Sackett, and Feis to Meyer, 7 December 1931, 862.51/3283.
9 Sackett to State, 2 January 1932, and Stimson to Sackett, 862.51/3320; see also FRUS, 1932, 1: 666–668.

Sackett warned Hoover and Stimson that unless they did something Germany would not be able to meet its obligations by May or June 1932. To counter the French scheme, the ambassador suggested that if the American government were to issue a "strong statement" asserting that the United States was "no longer under a dangerous menace from Europe's economic difficulties," it could break the deadlock in the reparations issue between France and Germany. Sackett proposed that such a declaration should indicate that since the Hoover Moratorium, American credit had been restored and that it could assimilate any losses following any European problem. Sackett thought this would give the French pause and undermine their strategy.

In Washington, Gordon attached a memorandum of support for Sackett's recommendation. He justified his endorsement by explaining:

> For a long time, and even more concretely during the past year, it has been increasingly apparent that the principal European credit powers were becoming increasingly imbued with the idea that we were so deeply interested, as a result of our investments in Germany, in preventing the breakdown of the German financial and economic regime that we would feel compelled to go to any lengths to avoid it.

By issuing such a statement, Gordon thought that German complacency could be shaken and the French, "to a certain extent at least," made more reasonable.[10]

By prudent use of his influence, Sackett was able to get a hearing with both Hoover and Stimson whenever he thought it might be useful. The only problem was that they were less prone to take action than the ambassador hoped. Nothing came out of Sackett's appeal to his government. Still, he continued to extend himself to help Brüning in a variety of small ways. Hans Dieckhoff in the Foreign Ministry expressed the German view that the American ambassador was always "very open" and willing to cooperate. Sackett's ardent support for Brüning's position was revealed when he told the Germans that his only regret was that he was "not in Washington at the moment to intervene with help to set things right."[11]

If Sackett were to be helpful, he needed to do more. The German chancellor needed time to resolve his domestic political difficulties and prepare for the World Disarmament Conference at Geneva in early February. Brüning hoped that by winning postponement of the Lausanne Conference on reparations he would gain time to deal with Hindenburg's term in office and settle German strategy on disarmament. At the same time, he would position himself better to achieve the permanent cancellation of reparations. He calculated that a meeting in January could lead only to

10 Sackett for Hoover and Stimson, 8 February, and Memorandum by Gordon, 10 February 1932, FRUS, 1932, 1: 666–668.

11 Memorandum by Dieckhoff, 10 March 1932, ADAP, 20: 33–35.

a temporary postponement of reparations payments. The French were just feeling the effects of the international depression, and Brüning guessed that by June, when they had experienced more economic and financial hardship, they might be more amenable to a final settlement of the reparations matter.[12] In addition, Brüning felt he had already mollified the French when in October 1931 he dropped Julius Curtius as foreign minister over the customs union imbroglio. In a reorganized cabinet, Brüning had assumed the foreign ministry portfolio, which enabled him to concentrate more than ever on foreign affairs.

The German chancellor opened his campaign by telling Horace Rumbold, the British ambassador in Berlin, that Germany "could not and would not pay any more reparations."[13] The flat statement was leaked to the press, but Sackett was already aware of the chancellor's plan. Two days before the announcement, Brüning had spoken to both Walter Edge, the American ambssador to France, and Sackett at a stag dinner in the American embassy in Berlin.[14] Brüning understood that the Hoover administration was unable to do much until after the American elections in November and probably not until Congress convened in December. But he needed action right away. The chancellor complained that it was not possible to wait that long, but even worse, if a new president were elected, there could be no action until after the inauguration in March. But he had Anglo-American help waiting. The British were ready to see that reparations were settled finally and agreed to collaborate with American diplomats to that end.[15]

Sackett later reported that the leak of Brüning's statement on the end of reparations was "tapped" by the French ambassador in Berlin and forwarded to Warsaw. London, he said, had the news from the Polish capital twelve hours ahead of anywhere else, but the current rumor in Warsaw was that "one of the Hitler boys had let the cat loose."[16] Brüning's dramatic statement created a sensation in Paris and Washington and caused a flurry of activity among American diplomats. The French, who were entertaining the notion of extending the moratorium for another two to five years, were stunned to learn that Germany intended to cut them off from any further

---

12 Brüning, *Memoiren*, 497–500; Edward W. Bennett, *German Rearmament and the West*, 57–58.
13 Memorandum of conversation between Dieckhoff and Wiley, 9 January 1932, enclosed with Sackett to State, No. 1397, 12 January, Foreign Affairs – Financial, HHPL, the principal despatch is published in FRUS, 1932, 1: 643–646.
14 Sackett to State, 7 January 1932, FRUS, 1932, 1: 638–640.
15 Minutes of a conversation with Brüning, 5 and 7 January 1932, ADAP, 19: 347–353, 384; the British wanted all intergovernmental payments abolished, Lindsay, "Annual Report on the United States for 1931," 2 January 1932, FO371, 1932, 7, 15874: 12.
16 Sackett to State, 13 February 1932, 462.00R296/5525; Atherton reported from London that the British Foreign Office had been expecting the statement to be made to Rumbold in Berlin for some time, Atherton to State, 9 January 1932, Foreign Affairs – Financial, HHPL.

payments at all. In Washington, American leadership feared a disaster for international credit, even "international morality," if the Germans resorted to what they considered repudiation pure and simple.[17]

Sackett was certainly privy to what Brüning intended. He had already demonstrated considerable devotion to Brüning's government and now went further than previously in his attempt to serve his German friend's goals. His intent was to get the Hoover administration to accept not only that reparations were a dead issue, but that as a consequence, war debts owed to the United States must also come to an end. In a series of private letters and despatches he spread alarm throughout the U.S. government, hoping to win support for the chancellor's financial policy. He explained that both the British and Italians had approached the German government and everyone agreed on the need to end reparations once and for all.

To soften the blow, the Germans suggested temporary agreement on a "provisorium" rather than a "moratorium" because the former would imply an end to the Young Plan payments. Such a step was necessary to relieve domestic tensions in Germany "enabling Hindenburg to continue in office and keeping Hitler out." On the other hand, Sackett asserted, if the Germans agreed to another moratorium, Hitler would seize upon that fact to overthrow the Brüning government.[18]

The Kentuckian was expressing his own position when he explained that Brüning really was not intent on cancellation of reparations payments; he wanted only to postpone the Lausanne Conference for six months, until after the scheduled elections in Prussia and France. In what the chancellor anticipated would then be a more congenial atmosphere, Sackett suggested, Brüning hoped to negotiate in a way that would not be offensive to the French, and come to a final settlement of the reparations issue as a result of mutual agreement.

Sackett probably believed that Brüning was willing to negotiate for a minimal reparations payment, an unlikely prospect. The chancellor wanted payments ended. The ambassador revealed that repudiation was still in the picture. He was determined to get the full attention of his government. He explained that if Brüning was unable to achieve German goals by reasonable means, Hitler stood ready to let Europe know what was necessary to satisy German demands. Should the European nations refuse to meet German requirements, the chancellor seriously entertained the idea of turning the government over to the Nazis to show the recalcitrant nations what they could expect from the German National Opposition. In a personal letter to Castle, Sackett cautioned that[19]

17 Castle Diary, 20 November 1931 and 15 January 1932.
18 Sackett to State, Cable No. 7, 9 January 1932, Foreign Affairs – Financial, HHPL.
19 Sackett to Castle, personal and confidential, 11 January 1932, Castle Papers – Germany, HHPL.

the question of Hitler's taking office depends upon the success that Brüning may have in the negotiations on the reparations and for your own information it may be that Germany will find it necessary in order to carry its points in Europe to turn over the Government to Hitler for the effect, very much as you would give a drastic dose of medicine to a patient, in the belief that a short experience with that Government would bring about a chastened Europe.

Sackett pressed the theme of chastening Europe, meaning especially France, even further. In his despatch to the State Department regarding the possible cancelation of reparations, he warned that it must "be appreciated abroad that the advent of National-Socialism in the government would, with its irresponsible and radical Left wing, be fraught with grave dangers for the subsequent political trend in Germany."[20]

Sackett continued to press the idea that the danger for Europe came essentially from the Left; it was communism which was threatening stability in Germany and peace in general. This was his way of getting the attention of his own government. In one of the many resumés sent to Hoover and Stimson from the State Department's Western European desk, Hitler and the Nazis were characterized as a "threat" used by Brüning to exert pressure to the end that reparations be canceled. In other words, the president and secretary of state were being told that the Nazis themselves did not constitute the danger, but the "threat" was real, in the sense that no German government could last in office if it agreed to continue paying reparations.[21]

In another private letter, this time to Stimson, Sackett confided that he believed "Brüning was playing his cards in his controversy over reparations with considerable skill." If he were unable to get the creditor nations, especially France, to understand that Germany could no longer pay reparations, he might turn the government over to Hitler. As in the letter to Castle a few days earlier, Sackett wrote of the Nazis in power as a "drastic dose of medicine" for Europe to take. Brüning had explained to Sackett that such a potion was too much for a responsible leader to administer and the idea had to be rejected as too dangerous. Sackett went on to express a consistent theme espoused by the Berlin embassy – that is, that the Nazis were truly incapable of governing. But there was more. The incompetent Nazis could not carry on the serious business of government for very long. After the fiasco of their attempt to lead the nation, Germany

20 Sackett to State, No. 1397, 12 January 1932, FRUS, 1932, 1: 646.
21 Resumé of Sackett to Stimson, No. 1397, 12 January 1932, Foreign Affairs – Financial, HHPL and in FRUS, 1932, 1: 643–646; a stream of cables, despatches, paraphrases, and resumés, originating in London, Paris, Brussels, Basel, and Berlin, concerning cancellation of reparations by Germany, especially from January 8 to 12, were sent by the Western European desk to Stimson and to the White House, for example, Pierre de L. Boal, chief, Division of Western European Affairs, to Walter H. Newton, secretary to the president, 12 January 1932, with enclosures, Foreign Affairs – Financial, HHPL.

and Europe would be delighted to welcome the return of the man who was competent to lead – Heinrich Brüning.

Although it had to be ackowledged that Hitler might eventually come to power, Brüning told Sackett that he, of course, would not help with such an outcome. So that Stimson would understand the full import of the danger, Sackett explained what Brüning had in mind. The chancellor asserted that the Nazi party was not a unified whole but was, rather, divided into two wings. One, including Hitler and his followers, "was more or less of a conservative type," while the other wing, led by Goebbels and Gregor Strasser, "was much more violent and radical." Sackett wrote that the chancellor feared if the Nazis were to come to power, they would certainly fail, in which case the "radical wing would immediately group itself with the Communists and would become numerically strong enough to plunge the country into a national Communism of a disastrous type." Sackett alluded to his earlier report of December 27, 1930, in which he explained that Brüning thought the greatest danger faced by Germany was "the rise of the Communistic power."

Since he knew that even Brüning feared that the "cry of wolf" had undermined the effectiveness of the Red Menace threat, Sackett insisted to Stimson that the threat was real. The danger of communism had been raised so often, he wrote, "that people have come to think of it only as an empty threat and not a real danger and yet here is the responsible leader of the country who sincerely fears it as the greatest menace that faces his country in the future."[22]

Sackett believed that yet another factor made Hitler an even more dangerous potential head of government: he was not interested in coming to power until after the reparations issue was settled.[23] In other words, Hitler was reluctant to face the real issues of governing, matters of economics and finance. British Prime Minister Ramsay MacDonald suggested that Hitler was frightened by the "Frankenstein" he had brought into being and was proceeding in a cautious way.[24] Among statesmen and diplomats who saw the difficult task of dealing with financial matters as central to governing, Hitler represented an incompetent and menacing force that could turn the world of finance upside down. As it was, Germany's finances were in the hands of the conservative economist, Brüning, who was fast becoming one of the most favored of Europe's leaders, at least among fellow statesmen from abroad. Among Germans he was less esteemed and had earned the sobriquet "the Hunger Chancellor."

---

22 Sackett to Stimson, personal and confidential, 12 January 1932, 462.00R296 A 1/150.
23 Sackett to State, No. 1397, 12 January 1932, FRUS, 1932, 1: 644–645, and the enclosed Memorandum of a Conversation with Ministerialdirektor Ritter and Wiley, 8 January 1932, Foreign Affairs – Financial, HHPL.
24 MacDonald to Stimson, 8 January 1932, Stimson Papers, 82: 324.

With Sackett's help, Brüning was able to cause a furor over the reparations issue without any loss of respect or effectiveness abroad. President
Hoover was now aware that the Germans were not going to pay any more
reparations and that they would attend a conference dealing with reparations only if such a conference was "empowered to negotiate terms of
cancellation."[25] While he was winning support from abroad, Brüning was
at the same time gaining some breathing space at home. His initial position
leading to the end of reparations payments had been established. It remained
for Brüning to weather the spring season by coping with the presidential
election campaign. After that he need only maintain his position until the
conference at Lausanne was expected to meet in June. It was there he
hoped to win his major coup in the final chapter of the reparations issue.

As it turned out, Brüning had to use all the time and energy he could
muster to deal with an unexpectedly difficult presidential election. Rather
than the walk-through Brüning hoped for, the venerable field marshal was
confronted with a bitter contest. Hindenburg faced a roster of opponents
of the Weimar Republic and was put in the onerous position of trying to
win against members of the political Right, the very people his monarchist
sentiments favored. Even worse, he was burdened with the unhappy prospect of engaging in the political battle with the support of the Catholic
Center and the Social Democrats on the Left, not among his favorite
people.

The reelection of Hindenburg became an essential initial step in Brüning's
plans. It was important to his ultimate purpose, the restoration of the
monarchy. With Hindenburg in office, Brüning could establish a regency
until agreement was reached on an appropriate Hohenzollern to ascend
the throne. With the reparations issue out of the way until the Lausanne
Conference convened in June, Brüning could play down the disarmament
conference, which had already opened in February, just as the election
campaign was about to get under way. There was so little time and so
much to do, and the public assertion of German intention to rearm could
await a later, more propitious time, while in the meantime secret rearmament
went on apace.

It was hard for Brüning to convince Hindenburg to enter the presidential
contest. Sackett reported that the field marshal agreed to run only if the
chancellor could get a statement of support from the Stahlhelm. Brüning
was not optimistic about his chances of wringing such backing from the
front-line veterans' organization.[26] Hugenberg and both Stahlhelm leaders,
Franz Seldte and Theodor Duesterberg, were committed to the Harzburg

25 Memorandum of the respective positions of Germany, Britain and France on the present
   negotiations respecting reparations and debts, 21 January 1932; a summary was drawn
   up by Stimson and Boal and sent to Hoover, see Stimson Diary, 21 January 1932.
26 Sackett to State, 12 February 1932, Foreign Affairs – Financial, HHPL.

Front and refused to support the president, the candidate of the republic. They instead put up Duesterberg as their candidate in opposition to the field marshal.

None of the parties of the Harzburg Front were willing to support Hindenburg. The National Opposition could not come to terms in backing the president, Sackett wrote, because they lacked unity and had made "unreasonable demands for control of the government."[27] One alternative remained if Hindenburg were to be spared the ordeal of a contested election. The parties of the Right could agree on one candidate all could support.

The Nazis believed that Hitler could be the mutually acceptable candidate. If all could agree on the Nazi leader, it "might preclude Hindenburg's candidacy."[28] However, neither Hitler nor Hugenberg would yield first place to the other. Sackett now was able to cite "an authoritative Nazi source" as saying that when they attempted to agree on a common candidate "the Nationalists and Stahlhelm leaders adopted an intransigent attitude that [the Nazis] found intolerable."[29]

Wiley declared that the Harzburg Front was a shambles. The National Opposition would probably nominate two or three separate candidates and "Herr Hitler, the Staatenloss, will eventually stand for election." Hitler lost his Austrian citizenship when he enlisted in the German army in 1914 and was not yet a German citizen. He was finally granted German citizenship on February 26, 1932, by having himself appointed a Regierungsrat in Brunswick.

Appalled by the lack of responsibility among the National Opposition, John Cooper Wiley wrote that the view expressed by Stahlhelm and Nazi leaders[30]

> reveals a remoteness from political reality that is alarming. The timely accomplishment of what is politically possible is not one of their tenets. Intransigence is justified in their eyes as indispensable for the "spiritual regeneration" of the German people; for the revival of the German power of resistance. It is to be hoped that German common sense will survive the demagogic leadership of the Right and will manage, once again, to triumph. The final issue though is unhappily not clear.

Wiley was expressing a continuing belief held by American diplomats concerning how a system of government does, or should, operate: Responsible leadership, competent and honest, seeks accurate information upon which to make sound judgments for which they are held responsible by the electorate.[31]

27 Sackett to State, 29 February 1932, 862.00/2692.
28 Sackett to State, 1 February 1932, cable no. 24, 462.00R296/ (no file number).
29 Sackett to State, 23 February 1932, 862.00/2690.
30 Wiley to Stimson, 27 February 1932, 862.00/2688.
31 See Robert D. Schulzinger, "Complaints, Self-justification, and Analysis: The Historiography of American Foreign Relations Since 1969," 247.

In early 1932, Sackett was filing despatches for the first time from "authoritative Nazi sources."[32] With George Gordon back in the State Department, Wiley had taken over as temporary counselor of embassy in Berlin, where he earlier thought he would be posted permanently.[33] He had acted as temporary senior foreign service officer when Sackett first arrived in Berlin and had undoubtedly drafted the new ambassador's first significant despatches. It was Wiley who warned of the dangers of Nazism and denigrated the effectiveness of the German Communist party.

Wiley's presence in the Berlin embassy made a difference. Embassy policy under Gordon's influence had been to restrict contacts to government and official circles almost exclusively. Gordon was motivated in part by his rigorous sense of propriety, but in the case of the Nazis, a distaste for Hitler and his rabble was decisive. Gordon's position was typically narrow and proper. It was correct to maintain personal contact only with representatives of the accredited government; any other relationship could be construed as an intervention in domestic matters. Consequently, he had almost no contact with persons not likely to be invited to embassy affairs.[34]

Horace Rumbold, the veteran British ambassador in Berlin, assumed a similar stance. He "deprecated" any idea of meeting Hitler "ever personally" and believed there was little to be gained from such an interview. Rumbold, who never met Hitler before he became chancellor, thought that the only advantage from such an encounter would be to find out something about Hitler's personality or plans, but that the risk of "possible misconstruction would be difficult to avoid and would far outweigh any possible benefit."[35]

Gordon asked to be reassigned to the State Department on a temporary basis, leaving Berlin at the end of October 1931 to be with his wife in what proved to be a difficult childbirth.[36] Sackett asked him to discuss with Undersecretary of State William R. Castle some personnel matters of importance to the embassy.[37] The Berlin post was plagued with a shortage of staff at all levels, partly as a result of depression-driven budget cuts, but also because of a lack of qualified personnel to fill the open positions. Moreover, many were young and inexperienced.[38] Gordon would, of course, not report that he was the source of much of the difficulty with staff. Often the butt of insider jokes among American diplomats because of his

32 Sackett to State, 1 February 1932, cable no. 24, 462.00R296/ (no file number).
33 Poole to Wiley, 23 January 1930, Box 1, Wiley Papers.
34 The French ambassador in Berlin, André François-Poncet, claims that he had no contact with Nazis before 1933, *The Fateful Years*, xi, nor did Horace Rumbold, the British ambassador, mention any personal contacts with Nazis.
35 R. Graham, British ambassador in Rome, to Simon, 30 November 1931, DBFP, 2: 353–355.
36 Robert H. Ferrell, *Frank B. Kellogg, Henry L. Stimson*, 323; *New York Times*, 2 January 1932.
37 Privately, Sackett to Castle, 3 December 1931, Castle Papers – Germany, HHPL.
38 McVitty memoir.

overbearing demeanor and his rigid approach to matters of protocol, his reputation spread even to the White House. In at least one instance, the former chairman of the Republican National Committee intervened on behalf of a foreign service officer who had met with Gordon's disapproval.[39]

Wiley was a refreshing contrast for embassy personnel. A "tall, heavy-set man" with an "irrepressible wit," he characteristically could approach serious matters in a lighthearted way.[40] Years later, in 1948, when he was ambassador to Iran, he created an imaginary spy he named Major Lincoln. Then, through the embassy grapevine, he set in motion fabulous stories of Lincoln's amazing exploits. The ruse succeeded so well that the Soviet embassy entered a formal protest "about the scandalous activities of Lincoln." It was the sort of thing that delighted the veteran diplomat. Blessed with "natural mirth" he had a "grave, booming voice" that friends said had the tone of a howitzer.

The son of a diplomatic officer, Wiley was born in France, where his father was a consular official. Educated by private tutors in France and the United States, he graduated from Union College and attended Columbia Law School. Wiley was fluent in German, French, Spanish, Portuguese, and Russian, all of which served him well for his thirty-eight years in the Foreign Service. One high point of his career was to serve as counselor of embassy when the United States opened its Soviet embassy in 1933. He helped establish the diplomatic post under Ambassador William C. Bullitt, and with the assistance of young George Kennan, who served under him.

Far more flexible and open than Gordon, Wiley shared many views with George Messersmith, the consul general in Berlin. In spite of the Rogers Act, which in 1924 united the consular and foreign services on an equal basis, Gordon treated Messersmith as an inferior and virtually shunned him. But the ambassador did not. Sackett formed an attachment for Messersmith and followed his advice to get out of Berlin to discover what the rest of Germany and the Germans were like. Messersmith was the only official American representative in Berlin who had early and frequent contacts with Nazi leaders.[41]

Wiley agreed with Messersmith, and together they influenced Sackett to see more Germans than Gordon would ever condone. All four agreed that the Nazis were the key to Germany's future. It was therefore incumbent on them to find out all they could about the Hitler party. Only Gordon avoided contact with the Nazis. According to Sackett's niece, fifteen years old when she visited the American embassy in Berlin, the ambassador had taken to surreptitious sorties to meet with Nazi leaders. His favorite was Hermann Göring. Sackett "would send some minion in the Embassy" to find where the Nazi was dining and would then "just 'happen by.'"[42]

39 Charles Dewey Hilles to Theodore G. Joslin, 13 January 1932, Individuals, HHPL.
40 This characterization of Wiley is taken from the *New York Times*, 4 February 1967.
41 Messersmith, notes for memoirs.   42 McVitty memoir.

Sackett first met Hitler in much the same clandestine fashion. Brüning wrote that German bankers tried to influence the American ambassador to support a Nazi government after the September 1930 Reichstag elections.[43] The Communist party made similar charges at the time. In the only direct contact Sackett had with Hitler, referred to in the opening of this study, it was indeed bankers who maneuvered the meeting between Sackett and the Nazi. The German bankers tried to influence the American to see the Nazis in a favorable light. Schacht was the moving force behind the meeting, which took place at the home of Emil Georg von Stauss, a director of the Deutsche Diskonto Bank, who had introduced Schacht to the Nazis. Sackett had met the two when he was first assigned to Berlin. Both prominent bankers were "fellow travellers" who supported Hitler.[44]

At the small Saturday afternoon gathering on December 5, 1931, Hitler's introduction to Sackett and Klieforth as Herr "Wolff" was an awkward attempt to avoid the appearance of impropriety. Sackett reported that there had been "several attempts to bring me to a meeting with Hitler." The ambassador confessed that he was "a little disturbed" by the efforts, but he thought nevertheless that although he "should not seek intimacy with the opposition party in Berlin," he did not want to avoid such a meeting if a "proper opportunity" were presented.[45]

What amounted to a monologue opened with the host, Stauss, calling attention to the "distressing" economic situation in Germany. That was the cue for Hitler to launch into a long tirade, "speaking as if he were addressing a large audience." The Nazi attributed Germany's economic plight to the loss of colonies and former territory that reduced the nation's natural markets. Germany, he said, needed to create a large export surplus in order to pay its debts. The Nazi leader made clear that Germany would not "under any circumstances pay the political 'tributes'" but was "willing and anxious" to pay the "enormous private debts." That was only possible if the Versailles Treaty were revised in a way to increase German foreign trade. Hitler then demanded the return of colonies and the territory, such as the Polish Corridor, lost in the Treaty of Versailles.

Hitler maintained that France was armed sixteen times more than was necessary for defense. That huge army was meant to make Germany pay reparations by force. The French would occupy the Rhineland to collect the "tribute," and not even the Storm Troops could offer resistance. In fact his private army was not intended for warfare but only "for the purpose of keeping order within Germany and suppressing Communism." If France were to invade, and Hitler stressed this point "with dramatic intensity," Germany would not be "able to pay a cent of her private obligations."

43 Brüning, "Ein Brief," 6–7.
44 Henry Ashby Turner, Jr., *German Big Business and the Rise of Hitler*, 142–144.
45 This account is from Sackett to State, 7 December, and personal, Sackett to Stimson, 9 December 1931, 862.50/721 and 723.

Sackett was aware that "the object of his oratorical talk was to impress me with the statement that if France collected reparations by force, Germany under a Nazi regime, could not pay her private debts, which she was willing to do under other circumstances." This was part of a Nazi campaign to win respectability by countering earlier demands for repudiation of debts. The Nazis wanted to win foreign approval as the key to being accepted domestically.

Hitler did not impress Sackett. The magical quality of his personality, which captured so many admirers, escaped the American ambassador. A barrier existed between the German and American because Klieforth's translation diminished any personal charm Hitler might have exuded. During the long harangue by Hitler, Sackett remarked that the Nazi "did not put any questions to me nor did he appear to expect me to comment on his statements. My remarks were naturally only of a perfunctory character." The American formed a clear perception of the Nazi. He wrote Stimson:

> The impression I gained of Hitler is that of a fanatical crusader. He has a certain forcefulness and intensity which gives him a power of leadership among those classes that do not weigh his outpourings. His methods are those of an opportunist. While he talked vigorously, he never looked me in the eye.

Sackett was less than captivated by Hitler's charisma; on the contrary, he could not understand the Nazi's personal appeal.

The ambassador explained that Hitler:

> could not make an intellectual appeal and I do not believe his followers, . . . and they are many, can have been influenced by any personal contact with him, but are turning to his party in despair that former political allegiances provide no relief from present intolerable conditions.

Sackett repeated the embassy position that a Hitler government could not succeed:

> I sensed the feeling during the interview that if this man comes into power he must very shortly find himself on the rocks, both of international and internal difficulties. He is certainly not the type from which statesmen evolve.

Like so many of his contemporaries, Sackett saw Hitler as a demagogue and rabble-rouser, but was unable to envision the Nazi in the position of seriously governing Germany.

To avoid any repercussions from the meeting, Sackett informed the German Foreign Ministry of his visit. He did not want the Brüning government to suspect that he "was conniving with the opposition." His report was appreciated and he believed that the encounter was "fully understood" and that "without causing criticism" he had "established a contact that may be valuable to us in the future."[46]

It was not just coincidence that the meeting at the Stauss residence took place while Gordon was gone. Sackett took advantage of the counselor's absence to take the initiative for the encounter with Hitler. Such meetings were more in conformity with Wiley's style. When Wiley returned to Berlin, he had made it his business to contact Nazi leadership, and the State Department noticed it immediately. Wiley and embassy staff were sometimes accompanied by journalists who were more familiar with the Nazis than were the diplomats. Goebbels complained at one point that he was "squeezed like a lemon" by a group of American reporters and diplomats.[47] Douglas Miller, the assistant commercial attaché in the American embassy, was among the minor British and American diplomats who met with Nazis. In November 1931, after Gordon's departure, Miller, a junior British diplomat, and a *Chicago Tribune* correspondent met with Hermann Göring, who was accompanied by a young Nazi journalist and a bodyguard from Nazi headquarters. Göring held forth for two and a half hours in a "torrent of words" most of it "superficial" and some of it "a little wild."[48]

Several meetings of embassy staff with Goebbels resulted in a thorough despatch describing the Nazi party and its program. In what was a slight, aimed at Gordon, Boal wrote Wiley that "Goebbels' comments and your remarks have given us a much better idea of the Nazis than we have had heretofore."[49] Wiley responded, in effect defending the work of American diplomats in Berlin. The embassy, he wrote, had "pretty much" reported "all that it could learn on the National-Socialist movement." Even the consulates "have done likewise." He said, further, that any attempt "to give any concise statement as to the vague aims and vaguer program of the Party" raised the possibility "that a report from the Embassy might be more misleading than helpful."

The vagueness of the party program was related to the wide spectrum of opinion tolerated within the organization, according to Wiley. The nebulous character of the Nazi approach to issues was a consequence of Nazi recruiting from one economic and political extreme through the middle to the other and advocating different policies to attract different constituencies. Nationalism tied the disparate elements together. Goebbels told Wiley that the Nazi goal was to create a synthesis of national elements, to

46 In his acknowledgment of the Sackett letter, Stimson stressed his thanks that the ambassador had explained the circumstances leading to the Hitler interview. Stimson to Sackett, 23 December 1931, 862.50/723.
47 Frölich, ed., *Tagebücher von Joseph Goebbels*, 11 March 1932, 1: 139.
48 Notes of a Conversation between Mr. Yencken and Göring, 24 November 1931, Rumbold revealed that some of his staff met some Nazi party leaders in Berlin, Rumbold to Simon, 24 March 1932, DBFP, 2: 347, 3: 108–109. Miller later wrote the widely read book *You Can't Do Business With Hitler* (Boston: Little, Brown, 1941).
49 Boal to Wiley, 24 March 1932, 862.00/2703.

"appeal to the racial instincts of the population – *das Nationalgefühl*." The Nazi party "represented no caste or class or precise political or economic policy." What the party did represent was German racial unity, and to guarantee that unity, its target was the Jewish population.

Goebbels explained to Wiley that Nazism differed from Italian Fascism on the issues of anti-Semitism and racial questions partly because those "problems do not exist in Italy." The American went on to explain that "the Nazi idea is not to harm a hair on any Jewish head, but to treat them as foreigners; to tax them, but not to subject them to military service; to deport eastward as many Polish and Russian Jews as possible." The Nazi purpose was to raise the level of "German culture and morals . . . by excluding everything foreign (Jewish)." Goebbels assured Wiley that the Nazis intended to unite the German people and would use the power of the state "to bring the recalcitrants to heel."[50]

Wiley and Boal were, perhaps appropriately, more interested in international problems than they were to such threats to the German people. Still, their emphasis on American interests and the expression of minimal concern for the German populace is a sign of the sort of insensitivity inherent in their position as diplomats. In any case, they perceived the Nazis as becoming "more and more moderate." Goebbels assured Wiley that the Nazis certainly did not have repudiation of debts in mind at all, in fact they recognized private debts, including the commercialized Dawes and Young Plan loans. That undeniably was a moderation of Nazi policy. The Nazis also took a moderate position with regard to Germany's neighbors. They wanted to cooperate with France and Poland. Wiley reported that in spite of denials from Ambassador François-Poncet, the Nazis were "doing their best to flirt with the French."[51] In concrete terms they were ready to come to agreement with France on both reparations and disarmament. German Foreign Ministry officials convinced Wiley that "Nationalist elements in France are very anxious to see the Hitler régime come into being as soon as possible." The theory, subscribed to by some Rightist circles in France, and by the Nazis, was that such an event would almost certainly assure a right-wing victory in the French elections. More than that, it would have a "salutary effect" on American "debt cancellation" as well.

While Goebbels insisted that Germans were united on the question of the eastern boundaries, namely those with Poland, he was not able to say whether or not the Nazis meant to rectify the borders by peaceful means. Göring was more explicit. The Poles were willing to cooperate with Germany against Russia, and without any reference to communism. The former

50 Wiley to Boal, 17 February, FRUS, 1932, 2: 281–284; Sackett to State, 2 March 1932, 862.00/2695.
51 François-Poncet "sharply" denied that he was interested in the Nazi movement in a positive sense, Memorandum by Bülow, 28 November 1931, ADAP, 19: 191–192.

flying ace claimed that the Nazis were "implacable in hostility to Russia irrespective of political structure there." Göring contended that many Poles were ready to join Germany in an attack on Russia for which they would be compensated by Soviet territory. A British diplomat who heard of the same Nazi solution for rectifying the eastern boundaries described it as "floating frontiers." Wiley remarked that the policy "sounds like a rather dangerous theory; one of pure conquest."

Although there were some signs that Hitler and the Nazis were moderating their stand in the face of the presidential elections, Wiley was convinced that they were following a dangerous course, and that the German people were poised, ready to follow them. He found the situation "somewhat disquieting. The constant playing of the political passions of the people is certainly not wholesome. The German mind, as the war demonstrated, is particularly susceptible to nationalist appeal."[52] That was especially perilous because of the charismatic nature of Nazi leadership.

Although he was not impressed by Hitler's personal charm, Sackett confessed that "Hitler's magnetic appeal to the German imagination cannot be denied." As Wiley reported, despite the wide variety of points of view within the Nazi party, Hitler stood out as party leader; "the final decision always rested with Hitler." One saving grace was that neither Hitler nor his lieutenants could stand close scrutiny. They proved to be "disappointing." The American diplomats meant that neither Hitler nor his associates could stand the test of responsible leadership. If they came to power, the Nazis would engage in "political experiments and economic innovations" that Sackett was convinced would have "disturbing effects."[53]

Wiley found Goebbels to be "more intelligent than any other Nazi." The German "obviously has first-rate ability and much personal magnetism," and in government circles he was regarded "as particularly radical."[54] American diplomats found the Nazi program essentially negative, ranging from their anti-Semitism to their anticapitalism. Goebbels provided Wiley with a stack of Nazi pamphlets he had written to explain the party position. One in particular, "Little A-B-C for National Socialists," Wiley found to lack the kind of "logic and scientific structure" that even hostile critics attributed to Marxist literature. The American conceded that the pamphlet had the merit of appearing definitive. Presented as a catechism, the publication disguised the vagueness of the program it developed by enabling Goebbels to answer questions with an air of finality. Sackett provided one example of ambiguity by explaining that although Nazis supported a form of socialism, they did not advocate "Jewish Marxism."[55]

52 Wiley to Boal, 17 February 1932, FRUS, 1932, 2: 286.
53 Sackett to State, 2 March, 862.00/2695, and Wiley to Boal, 17 February 1932, FRUS, 1932, 2: 282.
54 Wiley to Boal, 17 February, FRUS, 1932, 2: 282.
55 Sackett to State, 2 March 1932, 862.00/2695.

During the course of many conversations with Nazi leaders, Wiley found much that was disturbing, probably nothing more so than Goebbels' prediction that Hitler would win in the presidential election. The Nazi had studied voting statistics for the party since it had been formed. Goebbels found that in all the elections the party had won, their total vote exceeded party membership anywhere from 20 to 38 times. The party was better organized in small communities than in larger ones, but he saw that in every case the multiple of votes related to party membership never fell below 20. By using a multiple of only 15, the Nazi foresaw a Hitler victory. Wiley was impressed, but insisted that he was "not yet ready to bet on Hitler or against Hindenburg!"[56]

Sackett reacted optimistically to the presidential election campaign in spite of dire Nazi predictions and expectations. Hindenburg appeared assured of victory as the candidate of the republican parties. The Social Democrats, who had opposed him in 1925, supported him *faute de mieux*. They now considered him their "chief bulwark against Right radicalism." As the campaign progressed the American diplomats increased their enthusiasm for a Hindenburg victory. In the State Department, Pierre Boal ventured a "Forecast of German Elections" in which he expressed the confident expectation that reality was about to catch up to Hitler. He sent a memorandum to Stimson in which he predicted that[57]

> chances would seem to be that the Nazis in general, and Hitler in particular, will find that they have taken on more than they bargained for and that the result of the election will be conducive to a somewhat more reasonable frame of mind on their part, possibly even to the extent of inclining Hitler to enter a Government working with and under Brüning and Hindenburg.

Boal's opinion expressed another theme, that of the taming of Hitler by reality; a widely held view that holding office, or even the immediate promise of office, had a tempering affect on its aspirants.

According to Sackett, Hitler suffered a severe setback as the political campaign opened. The Nazi made a concerted effort to emphasize that he meant to come to power by legal means, but the Prussian State Court declared, in what Sackett called a "highly significant decision," that civil servants who were members of the Nazi party were not eligible to hold public office because their party "was striving to overthrow the present order by force." Hitler was incensed. In an open letter to the foreign press, he expressed his indignation that the court failed to acknowledge the legality of the Nazi party and demanded to know what steps Hindenburg intended to take "to restore the principle of chivalry" during the electoral campaign. Sackett commented that Hitler's resort to a foreign forum for

---

56 Wiley to Boal, 17 February 1932, FRUS, 1932, 2: 283–284.
57 Boal to Stimson, 24 February, and Sackett to State, 23 February 1932, 862.00/2689 and 2690.

Table 1. *Presidential election results*

Candidate	March 13	April 10
Hindenburg	18,650,730 (49.6%)	19,359,642 (53%)
Hitler	11,339,285 (30.1%)	13,417,460 (36.8%)
Thälmann (Communist)	4,983,197 (13.2%)	3,706,388 (10.2%)
Duesterberg (Stahlhelm)	2,557,500	(did not run)

Source: Sackett to State, 12 April 1932, 862.00/2722.

an airing of his grievances had placed him in an untenable position from a nationalist point of view. The ambassador was convinced that Hitler and the Nazis had maneuvered themselves into "political isolation," which could have far-reaching repercussions unless success in the election justified that stand. Sackett estimated that Hitler's task was formidable because he needed to increase his following of 30 to 35 percent up to more than 50 percent of the entire electorate. "This undoubtedly is a gigantic task even for the popular Nazi movement."[58]

Hitler's open letter to the foreign press was part of his campaign to appear moderate and reasonable, especially when it came to private foreign debt. The Nazi demand for repudiation of reparations payments was interpreted widely to mean that a Hitler government meant the disavowal of all foreign indebtedness. In an effort to counter what Hitler considered misrepresentations, he issued a public statement asserting that once in power the Nazis would not annul private debts. To make their position clearer, the Nazis supported the Brüning government in defeating a Communist motion in the Reichstag calling for just such a repudiation of foreign private debts.[59]

As the campaign progressed Sackett voiced continuing concern that Hitler would do well, a prospect that worried him. He searched for evidence to demonstrate that the Nazi could not succeed. Any reverse suffered by Hitler was pounced upon as a subject for comment.[60] The election took place on March 13, and when the results became available (see Table 1), Sackett bemoaned the fact that Hitler had won so many votes. Hindenburg did not win a majority of the vote as required, but he did outpoll Hitler with 18 million votes to 11 million for the Nazi leader. A runoff election would be required. Although assured that the president's reelection was

58 Sackett to State, 1 March 1932, 862.00/2693.
59 Sackett to State, 1 March 1932, 862.00/2694.
60 Sackett to State, 1 and 14 March 1932, 862.00/2691.

"taken for granted," Sackett noted that the Nazis had become the largest political party in Germany, a most disturbing fact, even if it had been anticipated.[61]

Sackett searched for some consolation to make up for his disappointment at Hitler's high vote total. He noted that the republican parties were assuming "that the Nazi wave has reached its crest and that their physical limits are now more clearly discernible." The bright side of the voting returns was the belief that Hitler had done better than his party could do in a Reichstag election. Using the results of the provincial Diet election in Mecklenburg, which took place on the same day as the presidential election, Sackett showed that although Hitler garnered 20,644 votes, the Nazi party candidates got only 14,233. In fact Hitler's vote was far below Nazi expectations. Still, Nazi "strength should not be underestimated." They had increased their vote by nearly 5 million since the September 1930 Reichstag elections.[62]

The already torrid political climate in Germany reached new heights of vehemence in the runoff election campaign. Aside from disrupting opponents' meetings and engaging in street brawls, the Nazi strategy was devoted to the "glorification of Hitler" and to disavowal of the charge that their coming to power would lead to chaos and civil war.[63] Veteran politicians knew there was more at stake than the reelection of Hindenburg. He was almost certain to be the winner. The campaign was conducted with an eye to the Prussian Diet elections, which would follow the presidential runoff by two weeks.

All the campaigners considered the Prussian elections to be "the final battle for political supremacy in Germany."[64] It was thus no surprise that Hindenburg won an absolute majority of more than 2 million votes in the runoff election on April 10. The ominous sign was that Hitler increased his total by the same number. Sackett feared that the Nazi leader's power of attracting voters "has not been impaired." The ambassador saw some hope because Hitler's gains consisted mainly of "borrowed" votes. Many, if not most, Nationalists and Communists voted for Hitler, but many would probably return to vote for their own party in a parliamentary election. Still, Sackett felt compelled to reverse his earlier position that the Nazi vote had reached full tide:[65]

> The conclusion to be drawn from the election is that the crest of the Nazi wave has not been reached. On the other hand, the sanguine expectations of the Nazis that they could accede to power alone, without the cooperation of other parties of the Right, are not likely to be fulfilled, at least in the near

61 Sackett to State, 14 March 1932, 862.00/2691.
62 Sackett to State, 14 March 1932, 862.00/2708.
63 Sackett to State, 6 April 1932, 862.00/2717.
64 Sackett to State, 7 April 1932, 862.00/2720.
65 Sackett to State, 12 April 1932, 862.00/2722.

Table 2. *Prussian diet elections*

Party	April 1932 (422 seats)	May 1928 (440 seats)
Nazi	162	7
Socialist	93	137
Center	67	71
Communist	57	48
Nationalist	31	71
People's	7	40
State (Democratic)	2	22
Others	3	44

Source: Sackett to State, 25 April 1932, 862.00/2725.

future. However, while the prospects of the much-heralded Third Reich are still remote, the Nazi movement has become so strong that, if he wished, Hitler could play a dominant part in a Right coalition in the Reich.

Sackett believed Hitler could probably look forward to further successes, but Alfred Hugenberg had suffered a dramatic, perhaps permanent, loss. The Nationalist party leader had hoped he would hold the balance of power in his hands. He believed he could gain concessions for himself and his party by giving his support to the higher bidder for the votes he controlled. But the election results made clear he had not won enough votes to be in a position to help Hitler, nor had he gained enough to interest Hindenburg. Sackett thought Hitler's failure to win on the first ballot had none of the "tragic element" of Hugenberg's position. Still, he shared the "malicious joy" of the inner circles of the government. Not disappointed by the runoff, they were delighted that Hitler was required to run a second time and suffer a second defeat. The Nazis were forced additionally to endure a further drain on the party's financial resources, "already reported to be at a low ebb."[66]

The Prussian Diet elections held even more significance than the American diplomats anticipated. Not only did the Nazis win big, as they expected, but the Weimar Republic received an additional crushing blow (see Table 2). Sackett was alarmed that the "liberal bourgeois parties" were practically eliminated.[67] Similar results came from Diet elections in Bavaria, Württemberg, Anhalt, and Hamburg. Of 23 parties that had candidates in the Prussian elections, only 9 won seats. The "bourgeois" parties of the

66 Sackett to State, 16 March, FRUS, 1932, 2: 287–288.
67 Sackett to State, 4 May 1932, 862.00/2744.

middle had made repeated attempts to form a broad liberal party, but they never got beyond inter- and intraparty bickering. The dilemma of the middle parties was aggravated by the system of proportional representation. For example, the State (formerly German Democratic) party popular vote had been halved, but under proportional representation, they were reduced from 22 to 2 seats.

According to Sackett, only 4 main political groups remained in the Reich, with the Nazi, Social Democratic, Center, and Communist parties forming their core. The Nazis were predominant; their representation in the Prussian Diet leaped from 7 to 162. The Hitler party was likely to "swallow or dominate the remainder of the kindred Nationalist factions" while the People's party more and more resembled "an appendage of the Nazis."[68]

Of the major parties, only the Social Democrats suffered significant defeat. Their representation in Prussia dropped from 137, the largest previous bloc in the Diet, to 93, now second to the Nazis. Sackett saw this considerable loss as the price they had to pay for tolerating the Brüning government. While Sackett characterized the Socialist losses as "severe," he cautioned that the apparent defeat should not be overemphasized. Still committed to the hope that the Socialists could save the Weimar Republic, he insisted that what was left of the party was "still a solid bloc, excellently disciplined in all its members."[69]

Another hopeful sign for Sackett was the staying power of the Center party, which lost only four seats in a Diet whose membership had been decreased by nearly twenty. More importantly, he was convinced that the Catholics had "the most astute leadership of any party." Brüning would throw the weight of his "considerable influence" into the problem of creating a government in Prussia. If the Center party joined with the Nazis in Prussia, they would command a majority. While the Weimar Coalition of the Socialists, State, and Center parties had a majority in the previous Diet, it fell far short with the new body. Their total vote now exactly equalled that of the Nazi delegation.

Brüning and his party had to decide on which direction to turn – toward the Socialists or the Nazis. Turning to Hitler was easy only in the sense that a Center-Nazi combination constituted a majority of the Diet. There was a problem, however, because Hitler was making "sweeping demands." Sackett wrote that the Nazis would accept nothing "less than the lion's share" in any government. Hitler made it even more difficult with his insistence that the Nazis were not eager to enter either the Prussian or the Reich government. The party's latest watchwords were: "We are in no hurry," and "We can wait." A further complication to a Nazi-Center

68 Sackett to State, 25, 26 April and 3 May 1932, 862.00/2725, 2736, and 2742.
69 Sackett to State, 26 April and 3 May 1932, 862.00/2736 and 2742.

rapprochement was Brüning's position that the Catholic party would not join with Hitlerites in Prussia unless he had "binding assurances" of their support in the Reich.[70]

Hitler's tactic of waiting was based on the fact that the Nazi parliamentary and political position improved with the passing of every day. Sackett reported that the youth or "green" vote of all classes was "the prey of Hitler's and Goebbels' oratory and fine sense of advertising values." Making heavy inroads into the youth vote and feeling sure of the "Nationalist and floating vote," the Nazis, "true to their principle – if such it can be termed – of being all things to all men" were now directing their appeal to those "more firmly entrenched behind political dogmas, whether Catholic, liberal, or Marxist." Sackett quoted Goebbels as writing that the Nazis "must approach with entirely new means of propaganda those groups of people who appear to be frozen in the fronts of the Center and the two Marxist parties."[71]

Sackett reported that the Nazis were broadening their appeal to extend to both ends of the political spectrum. Prince August Wilhelm was elected to the Prussian Diet as a Nazi, the first Hohenzollern elected to a legislative body by popular vote. On the other end of the spectrum Communists flocked to Hitler "because the rapid rise of the Nazis held out greater promise that 'things would soon be different.'" This reaching out with a broad appeal was reflected in the Nazi party press, whose "toning down" of its intransigence was noticeable. After the elections, invective had "almost entirely disappeared" from the Nazi party press.[72]

Hitler was gaining voters and improving his position, but the Communists were not faring well. Although they gained seats in the Diet elections, they suffered "unexpectedly heavy losses" in the presidential election. They won just over 13 percent of the vote in the first presidential election, but dropped to slightly above 10 percent in the second ballot. To repair the damage, Sackett reported, Moscow sent a special committee to Berlin to help the German Communist party reorganize and reshape its future policy. Sackett maintained that the tactics of treating the Socialists as a more "formidable" political enemy than the Nazis was an error made by the Communist International. The American diplomat now believed that the Communists would attempt to reverse their policy in the face of "Hitler's penetration into the ranks of the Communist party."

Assuming that a rational way to address the problem would be for the Communists to concentrate their efforts against the Nazis, Sackett predicted that the Communists would "make stronger efforts to combat Hitler without, however, letting the hated Social-Democrats out of sight."[73] The

70 Sackett to State, 26 April 1932, 862.00/2736.
71 Sackett to State, 26 April, 3 and 11 May 1932, 862.00/2736, 2742, 2751.
72 Ibid.
73 Sackett to State, 20 and 26 April, 3 May 1932, 862.00/2727, 2736 and 2742.

Communists, however, persisted in viewing the Socialists as their principal rival until long after Hitler came to power. Until 1934 the Communists rejected any cooperation with the Socialists. A telegram from Moscow in June 1932 reprimanded those in Berlin who overestimated the Nazis and neglected the fight against the Social Democrats.[74] Just like their capitalist counterparts, they considered the Nazis to be only a second-rank enemy.

The outlook for Hitler was bright, but not so clear for Brüning. Both men were making progress toward achieving their nationalist goals, but were unwilling to work together. The chancellor had failed to win Hitler's support for a cooperative effort to achieve their mutual goal of creating a more powerful Germany. The consequence was the contested election for the presidency. It took two elections for Hindenburg to win the necessary majority in a bitter campaign. The outcome was disappointing for the Nazis, but Hitler demonstrated growing power to attract voters. Although he failed to win, his total reached an impressive high of more than 13 million votes.

Perhaps even more impressive was the Nazi victory in the provincial Diet elections. As the largest party in Prussia, they were in a position to form a government and to influence events in the Reich. Hitler was making great strides toward his goal of governing Germany alone, but he fell short of the majority necessary to govern in either Prussia or the Reich. He needed help from other parties, which placed Brüning and the Center party in a pivotal role. The Nazis and Center together controlled a majority in the Prussian Diet. Given their agreement on goals for Germany, there appeared to be a possibility for a union of interest to create a functioning government.

However, Hitler insisted on governing alone. Although they agreed on ends, notably a powerful Germany able to make a difference in Europe, Hitler and Brüning were far apart as to means. Hitler meant to govern alone with the intention of forming a National Socialist state; Brüning's fondest hope was the restoration of the monarchy in a constitutional state. The two men, unable to come to agreement, continued the contest.

Hitler made great strides at the polling place and seemed on the verge of even more victories. Brüning helped elect Hindenburg and was expecting further triumphs. The Lausanne Conference was at hand, at which, Brüning hoped, the reparations issue could be finally settled in Germany's favor. The disarmament conference was meeting in Geneva while the German elections were held and great opportunities seemed to be available for Germany. Brüning was confident he could win equality of rights in the armaments question. If he could settle both the reparations and armaments issues, he would be in a position to divert support away from Hitler to himself as the man who could achieve what the Nazis only railed about.

---

74 Siegfried Bahn, "Die Kommunistische Partei Deutschlands," 657–658, 669–671, 674, 685.

The achievement would be made easier than usual because the chancellor had the full cooperation of Ambassador Sackett. Still, Brüning's position was tenuous. Even Sackett feared that his friend's time might soon come. The American held out only the promise, accurate in the event, that Brüning would "remain as chancellor at least until the Lausanne Conference."[75]

75 Sackett to State, 3 May 1932, 862.00/2742.

8

Efforts to sustain representative government
in Germany

AMBASSADOR SACKETT continued to be optimistic about Chancellor
Brüning's tenure in office in spite of ominous signs.[1] The only solid support Brüning could count on was President Hindenburg, since he did not
have enough backing in the Reichstag to form a majority government.
Hitler's electoral success and Hugenberg's humiliating defeat positioned
the Nazi as undisputed head of the political Right, placing Brüning in a
precarious position. President Hindenburg clearly preferred a cabinet of
the Right, a political alignment that could not be fashioned without Hitler's cooperation. The predicament was more problematic because Hitler
was unwilling to enter any government he could not control. That impasse
appeared to put Brüning on the brink of losing office.

Worse yet, his government was confronted with a demand from the
heads of all the major German states that something be done about the
Nazi Storm Troopers. General Wilhelm Groener, who as Reichswehr
minister had authority over the army and simultaneously as minister of the
interior was responsible for domestic police forces, was under strong pressure
from provincial governments to put a stop to the domestic warfare being
carried on by Nazi Storm Troopers. At stake was the only solid support,
outside his own Center party, the chancellor could count on.

The Social Democrats remained the mainstay of the Weimar Republic
and they had committed themselves to supporting Brüning. Still in control
of Prussia, the Socialists exerted great pressure on the Reich government
to outlaw the Storm Troopers. The Prussian prime minister and the head of

---

1 President Hoover, *Memoirs*, 2: 332, 379, recalled that among the "broad policies of cooperation with other nations in the moral field as distinguished from the force field, I made
specific proposals in many directions," among which he listed: "Efforts to sustain representative government in Germany." The only specific reference to a policy, presumably in
the "moral field" was the decision to postpone payment of some private debts, "the standstill agreement, which contributed to the sustaining of democratic government in Germany
for some time."

the Interior Ministry vowed that Prussia would outlaw the Storm Troopers if the Reich government refused to act. Regional forces moved to action. The Social Democrats joined with the Bavarian government in assuming the leadership of several states demanding that General Groener outlaw the Hitler army.

Their arguments were decisive in convincing the general and Brüning that it was necessary to proscribe Hitler's private army as a matter of national security, but also to satisfy the most ardent supporters of the republic, notably the Social Democrats, who were demanding that something be done about Nazi depredations.[2]

Eleven days before the Prussian elections, on April 13, the Reich government struck at the heart of Hitler's power. Brüning and Groener convinced President Hindenburg to sign an emergency decree outlawing Hitler's Storm Troopers. Hitler was about to lose one of the major weapons in the arsenal he used against the Weimar Republic. With his massive private army of 300,000 men and growing, Hitler was able to intimidate political opponents. The Nazis meant to control the streets of German cities and drive their political rivals into joining them in creating a National Socialist state. Now that source of Nazi strength was taken away, although in practice it simply meant that the Storm Troopers could not publicly appear in uniform or in formation.

Supporters of the Weimar Republic were impressed by the apparent audacity of Brüning's action. It seemed to demonstrate the powerful support the chancellor could command from the president and the army. With such champions in his corner it seemed he could, after all, cope with Hitler and the Nazis. Without his political army, Hitler might be reduced to competing with the other parties on a basis closer to parity. Moreover, the decisiveness and strength of the chancellor's action might well win him the support of those voters on the political Right who cherished order above all.

There were additional benefits for Brüning. Among supporters of the Weimar Republic, Sackett wrote, the prohibition of the Storm Troopers was "hailed" as a move that would "strengthen the Government's authority both at home and abroad." Germany's position at the Geneva Disarmament Conference would also be strengthened by removing an argument the French might use against them.[3] Ambassador Edge reported from Paris that the French government felt that with persistent "threats of Hitler uprisings," it would be easy at Geneva to defend their position that it was necessary to maintain their present military strength.[4] Now, with the

2 On the dissolution of the Storm Troopers, see Gordon A. Craig, *The Politics of the Prussian Army, 1640–1945*, 445–450; F. L. Carsten, *The Reichswehr and Politics, 1918–1933*, 338–344; Bracher, *Auflösung der Weimarer Republik*, 481–490.
3 Sackett to State, 19 April 1932, FRUS, 1932, 2: 293.
4 Edge to State, 19 December 1931, 500.A15A 4/647.

disbanding of Hitler's private army, the French would not be able to claim either that 300,000 Nazis in uniform constituted a huge reserve force for the Reichswehr, or that Storm Trooper violence required a large French defensive force.

The initial action against the Storm Troopers took place after the first presidential election. On orders of Socialist Prussian Minister of the Interior Carl Severing, Prussian police conducted raids on the homes and offices of Nazi leaders. Goebbels complained that the police searched his home for three hours.[5] Unimpressed by the police raids, Wiley at first reported they were probably little more than a Socialist "election trick." The action was in response to the mobilization of Storm Troopers in preparation for a siege of Berlin on election day, March 13. The Nazis claimed they were preparing to counter a general strike by the Socialists; but as Wiley pointed out, Hitler had taken steps to make certain that any Storm Trooper assembly was acceptable to the Reichswehr. The Nazis maintained that Ernst Röhm and two other of Hitler's "trusted lieutenants" had cleared the action with General Groener. Wiley suggested that similar sensational disclosures by the Prussian police about Nazi activities "invariably turned out to be comparatively harmless affairs." Most such reports he said, were "at least exaggerated."[6]

When Hitler sought an injunction against Prussia in the Supreme Court in Leipzig, American diplomats took the raids more seriously. As a result of the proceedings, Wiley reported that "the outstanding development" was the revelation that General Groener had called the "feverish activities" of the Storm Troopers to the attention of Prussian authorities. The American explained that the disclosure caused a "political sensation" because the public widely believed that Groener opposed the action by the Prussian police. Moreover, many political observers thought that the Prussian Socialists were only engaged in a political maneuver in the hope that they could discredit the Nazis before the Prussian Diet elections.[7]

General Groener disclosed that the order to raid Nazi homes and offices was given after the election because of the fear that "disappointed subordinate leaders" of the Storm Troopers "might resort to acts of violence." Wiley was now convinced that the police raids were not a political gambit. The general claimed that there was evidence the Storm Troopers were preparing for an armed uprising "in the event Hitler received more votes than Hindenburg but not enough to be elected on the first ballot."[8]

American diplomats were reassured that the Reich government could handle Hitler and the Storm Troopers. Sackett, British Ambassador Horace Rumbold, and State Secretary Hermann Pünder, had dinner with Generals

5 Fröhlich, ed., *Tagebücher von Joseph Goebbels*, 2 April 1932, 150.
6 Wiley to State, 23 March 1932, 862.00/2710.
7 Signature page missing, probably Wiley to State, 29 March 1932, 862.00/2711.
8 Wiley to State, 29 March and Sackett to State, 7 April 1932, 862.00/2711 and 2720.

Groener and Hammerstein. Groener boasted that, as Reich minister of the interior, he could take over the Prussian police under the emergency provisions of Article 48 of the Weimar constitution, and, he added, "if necessary Hitler too." Sackett was unsure of what the general meant, but found "the tone to be reassuring." The implication was that the Reichswehr would, and could, handle the "Führer." For the first time, in this despatch, drafted by Wiley, the German word for leader was used by Americans to identify Hitler.[9]

Referring to the Hitler party as Nazis, and now to their leader as the "Führer," was a reflection of an ever-widening public's familiarity with the National Socialists. It also indicated greater understanding of the party by Sackett. He pointed out that the government had banned the Storm Troopers because of their special relationship to Hitler. Sackett explained that the soldiers in this private army "had pledged unconditional obedience to the head of the political party." They were a "state within the state and their mere existence was a source of alarm and uneasiness for the population." Especially because they were a constant threat to engage in physical clashes "bordering on civil war."

Sackett wrote that the Storm Troopers were not paid but lived in barracks free of charge. Some held jobs, but most of them were unemployed; the ambassador estimated that 80 percent were without jobs. If they were jobless, the troopers were given their food and a small allowance, an attractive lure in time of depression. Many of the unemployed Storm Troopers had been members of the Communist Red Front Fighters, which had been proscribed by the Reich government in 1929 according to Sackett.[10] It was an easy transition from one authoritarian camp to another. Ideology seemed to count for less than comradeship, plus free room and board.

Hitler's response to the banning of the Storm Troopers took Sackett by surprise. In spite of bringing suit before the Reich courts, Hitler did not seriously resist the dissolution, and in fact he appeared to welcome the action. It was not easy to understand such an unexpected attitude, especially concerning a militant paramilitary organization, which had been "taught to believe that the Third Reich was within easy reach." In explaining Hitler's motives, Sackett pointed out that a private army was very costly, a special problem in a period of expensive election campaigning. More importantly, they stood in the way of Hitler's participation in the Reich government.

Sackett again revealed his hope and expectation that Hitler would enter a coalition cabinet and get involved in the serious business of governing. From his perspective, the Storm Troopers were not a means to power but,

9 Sackett to State, 13 April 1932, 862.00/2724. In 1932 American diplomats began the practice of appending the initials of the drafting officer to despatches.
10 Sackett to State, 19 April 1932, 862.00/2729.

rather, a stumbling block to Nazis entering the government. As Sackett pointed out, the private army was "trained for service in a Third Reich dominated by the Nazis alone," and as a result they "constituted a serious obstacle to Hitler's participation in government on a coalition basis with its attendant compromises and concessions to other political parties." Although Sackett did not expect to see Hitler and the Nazi party coming into power alone, he did anticipate further growth of the political Right. The diplomat was able to distinguish between the Nazi party, with its many suborganizations and bureaucracy, and the Hitler movement, which included a wide spectrum of like-minded supporters of nationalist sentiment. It was the "movement" that Brüning and the Reichswehr hoped they could exploit to their own ends. Sackett was uncertain about the future of the Nazi party, but was confident that the "movement is still in the ascendant."[11]

Brüning had more good news: within days of his decree outlawing the Storm Troopers, he was led to believe that the British and American governments agreed to support the German position at the Geneva Disarmament Conference. To win that support, the chancellor had to convince the Reichswehr leadership that, as a diplomatic tactic, they should ask for far less than the actual German goal.[12] Brüning and the military were in accord that Germany needed to rearm sometime in the near future. Rearmament was contrary to the policy of the United States and Great Britain, however, both of which favored disarmament. Therefore the Germans agreed to seek only recognition in principle of German equality of rights in matters of armaments.

The Americans thought in terms of the disarmament of the European powers. Armaments were perceived as the cause of war, and their reduction as a critical initial step in the resolution of European political problems. Moreover, expenditure of public money on materiel of war was unproductive, not capable of creating additional assets, and a constant source of budgetary deficits. The British hoped to see armaments reduced in such a way that their own military weakness would not be revealed. Above all, the British were interested in disarmament; they were not interested in stabilizing military forces at their current levels of strength, they wanted them reduced. Both Britain and the United States interpreted disarmament to mean the reduction of French forces and the subsequent reduction of tensions in Europe. But, above all, the American, British, and French wanted to prevent German rearmament.[13]

As the disarmament conference opened, the positions of the powers were clear enough to the American delegation. The Soviets called for

11 Sackett to State, 21 April 1932, 862.00/2728.
12 Bennett, *German Rearmament and the West*, 55–59.
13 Bennett, *German Rearmament and the West*, 140–141; Carsten, *Britain and the Weimar Republic*, 243.

universal, immediate, and total disarmament. They were met with silence, probably in part because it was well known that the Soviets were in fact rearming. It was also widely known that the Germans were rearming "secretly" and cooperating with the Soviets. The German goal was equality of all nations in any system adopted. They placed disarmament before security.[14] Perhaps the clearest position of all was that of France.

French diplomatic and military interest in Europe seemed to Americans to focus on an obsessive concern with security. France favored an international military force and security before disarmament.[15] Invaded twice from the east, by Prussia in 1870 and by the German Empire in 1914, the French insisted on a military establishment large enough to hold off any German threat. They also concluded a series of alliances with Eastern European states, creating for the Germans a sense of encirclement. Beginning especially in 1932, and continuing throughout the 1930s, French military thinking focused on the potential threat of Hitler. An ocean away, Americans did not experience the same sense of urgency.[16] From the French perspective it was immaterial which German led the nation; either Brüning or Hitler meant the same nationalist goals would be sought.

While the French fixed their attention on security, the Germans insisted on equality of armaments. The two positions were incompatible in the French view. A further standoff was created by the French desire for naval disarmament, whereas the British, with a commanding navy, stood in opposition to large land forces.[17]

An already complex set of circumstances was made even more complicated by the position of the Americans, which reflected their optimistic, even naive, outlook. It may be a peculiarly American trait to believe that others see them as a disinterested party and that any suggestion they make should be recognized as offered in an objective and helpful way, without ulterior motives. It was just such a posture that the Americans brought to the World Disarmament Conference in Geneva.

The disingenuous American delegation expressed a certain amount of[18]

> impatience with the assumption that America must supply the leadership and even the ideas which are to lead to agreement in Europe but however unjustifiable this assumption may be the fact remains that unless we, from our somewhat detached position, lay down some obviously fair and simple plan

---

14 General George Simonds to Major General George Van Horn Moseley, 7 March 1932, Box 42, General George Simonds Papers.

15 Gen. Simonds to Gen. Moseley, 7 March 1932, Box 42, Simonds Papers.

16 See Jean-Baptiste Duroselle, *France and the United States*, 136; on the Geneva Disarmament Conference, see the thorough and admirable work by Edward W. Bennett, *German Rearmament and the West*.

17 Marks, *The Illusion of Peace*, 90–91, 114, 142.

18 Gibson to State, 26 March 1932, 500.A15A 4/941.

it is doubtful whether any other nation will have the moral courage and the prestige to do so.

The plan the Americans proposed involved solving the French demand for security in an imaginative way. It was obvious to the Americans that "the whole demand for security arises from fear of invasion." The answer was to prohibit offensive weapons. Without the means for aggression there would be no invasions and the problem would be resolved.

Secretary of State Henry L. Stimson came to the Swiss city specifically to play the role of disinterested statesman. Aware that there was little prospect for a successful disarmament program in Europe, the American placed his hopes in the resolution of political problems before tackling the more technical and difficult problem of disarmament. Purporting to be an "honest broker," he brought the British, French, Italians, and Germans together and offered solutions he assumed would help them resolve even the knottiest of their disagreements. He did not offer specific suggestions but, rather, offered them his views on how their positions appeared to an outsider.[19] Impressed with his own activity, Stimson took credit for injecting meaning into the disarmament conference.

Stimson invited Prime Minister Ramsay MacDonald of Great Britain, Premier André Tardieu of France, Foreign Minister Dino Grandi of Italy, and Brüning to meet with him at Bessinge, the villa where he stayed while in Geneva. They all came, but Tardieu did not meet with the entire ensemble. He did meet with Stimson and separately with Brüning. The talks were essentially between Stimson, MacDonald, and Brüning, and separate conversations with Tardieu, who was deeply involved in the French elections. Stimson succeeded in getting all of them to believe that they were to get what they wanted in the disarmament talks. The American secretary informed them that he and President Hoover regarded the disarmament conference as a "European peace conference" and affirmed that the United States had no "direct responsibility."[20]

The Bessinge gatherings amounted to what a recent study calls a "loosely structured summit meeting" after which the participants left in confusion. Stimson concluded from the talks that "Brüning was so conciliatory in temperament and so modest in his demands for concessions that a Franco-German agreement was imminent." Meanwhile, Tardieu left, concerned that the German chancellor refused to bind himself at all. Later, Brüning maintained that MacDonald had agreed to support his claim for the treatment of Germany as an equal in armaments, whereas the British prime minister did not think that he had agreed to anything of the kind.[21]

---

19 Stimson, *On Active Service*, 267.
20 Ferrell, *American Diplomacy in the Great Depression*, 200–201.
21 Gordon A. Craig and Alexander L. George, *Force and Statecraft*, 69; see also Bennett, *German Rearmament and the West*, 148–149, 154–156.

There was considerable disagreement about what was conceded to Brüning at Bessinge. The Germans were convinced that the Anglo-Americans agreed to "our demands for equality of rights in the sense of relief from Article V [of the Versailles Treaty] by a new disarmament convention and that our point of view was reasonable and legitimate [*berechtigt*]." Article V called for the disarmament of all signatories of the treaty. Brüning assured Stimson and MacDonald that Germany sought disarmament and had no intention of provoking an arms race. In Bülow's record, MacDonald asserted that by the end of the disarmament conference, Germany would have full freedom of armament and the French would get their security in fact because Germany would not initiate an arms race. Brüning reassured the Anglo-Americans that such freedom for Germany would give him the opportunity to use it as a lever to force the reduction in armaments everyone wanted. Both the Americans and the British voiced their dissatisfaction with the French attitude and expressed their satisfaction with the German approach to the total problem.[22]

Brüning was persuaded that he had won Anglo-American agreement on "equality of rights" and told the French that it was a conditio sine qua non to any further talks. Repeated subsequent German references to the substance of Bülow's memorandum of the discussion at Bessinge was testimony that the Germans thought they achieved their disarmament goal. They deemed the talks to be "very significant" and even assumed Anglo-American agreement to further advances in armaments. Bülow wrote that Stimson and MacDonald have the "somewhat naive idea" that German achievement of equality of rights meant that heavy weapons, although not completely, would to a considerable degree be abolished.[23]

Stimson and MacDonald were obliged to deny the German interpretation of the Bessinge conversations. A year before the talks, the British anticipated that equality was the extreme German position and speculated that the Germans would be content with "very much less."[24] Stimson was "greatly disturbed" when the German claim to equality became known. Neither he nor MacDonald had an official record of the conversations. They subsequently based their position against the German claim on the recollection of a minor French diplomat who acted as an "impartial observer" at Bessinge. The Frenchman asserted that he was able to "state positively" that nothing was said that would lead the Germans to believe that their claim to equality of rights by way of rearmament "had been in any way encouraged or approved."[25]

22 Memorandum by Bülow in Geneva, 26 April 1932, ADAP, 20: 149–150.
23 Bülow to Neurath, 4 May 1932, ADAP, 20: 164–165.
24 Henderson to Rumbold, 23 April 1931, DBFP, 3: 459, 517n4.
25 Francis Osborne, British chargé in Washington, to Simon, 7 September 1932, and French ambassador in London A. de Fleuriau to Orme Sargent in London, 5 October 1932, DBFP, 4: 137 and 219.

Critics today see such frequent meetings of high-level ministers as a potential source of mischief, lacking in reflection and precision in deliberation. After World War II the French government authorized an investigation to determine what effect, if any, the "new diplomacy" by conference had in contributing to the French defeat in 1940. The ensuing report concluded:[26]

> The abuse of direct conversations opens the door to numerous dangers. Engagements are taken too easily. They are often improvised. It is better to define the course of a negotiation by a note which has matured in the silence of the ministry than by chance exchanges that are likely to be imprecise.

What Stimson conceived as his achievements at Geneva were precisely what later commentators found to be the cause of misunderstandings and disappointments.[27]

The secretary of state boasted to his diary that he "accomplished a great deal" in the two weeks in his Swiss villa. He pointed out that it was his presence that "brought all the leaders of the principal Powers back to Geneva." MacDonald came only because Stimson was there; Tardieu came only because the American had "visited him in Paris and brought him." Then Brüning and Grandi returned to Geneva because Stimson was there.[28] Stimson took credit for making Bessinge the center of the conference; for setting up MacDonald in a leadership role, "which he alone can perform"; for getting "on friendly terms with Tardieu and Aubert"; and, finally, for inducing Brüning to take a conciliatory position "if inequality of Versailles T[reaty] abandoned."[29]

Stimson assumed that negotiations should start with agreement that the Treaty of Versailles was to be revised in Germany's favor. Sackett was in full agreement with the secretary. He took some credit for the fact that since he had first recommended an international get-together of heads of state "many conferences have resulted," and it was at least "interesting to see how much closer together the statesmen of the different countries now are than they were when they scarcely knew each other."[30] Most of all, Sackett could take considerable credit for the fact that Brüning, head of the defeated enemy state, was welcomed, or almost so, in nearly all the European capitals.

The American secretary of state left Geneva with the sincere belief that he had created the climate for an amicable settlement of the issues dividing the European powers. He had completed his task as "honest broker" and

26 Craig and George, *Force and Statecraft*, 66.
27 For a full discussion of the Bessinge talks, see Bennett, *German Rearmament and the West*, 147–156.
28 Stimson Diary, 1 May 1932.
29 Stimson, handwritten notes, "High Spots" "Disarmament," Stimson Papers, 126: 369.
30 Sackett to Villard, 11 January 1932, bMS Am 1323 (3374), Villard Papers.

left the peace of Europe for Europeans to settle. Far less successful was his primary purpose in going to Europe.

Stimson went to Geneva to get British and French agreement to an intervention against Japan in East Asia. It is evident that his intention was to get European assent to some plan to deal with Japanese aggression in China. Above all, he wanted to meet MacDonald to "get a joint policy" worked out with the British "in regard to the Far East."[31] Stimson was so absorbed in East Asian matters that he seemed to many to have no time or interest for other concerns. This preoccupation dated from the initial Japanese attack in Manchuria in September 1931. Herbert Feis, the State Department economic adviser, complained that Stimson was "almost invisible these days behind his Far Eastern barrage." He was "giving himself to it heart and soul and seems to be enjoying it immensely."[32]

American generals at the disarmament conference complained that the secretary paid scant attention to their interests. The army chief of staff, General Douglas MacArthur, believed that Stimson's trip to Europe had "little bearing upon the disarmament problem."[33] General George Simonds, an American disarmament delegate, agreed with British press reports that the bombs and guns of the Japanese attack on Shanghai were drowning out the conference. Simonds felt that Stimson did little to speed things up in Geneva and that "the principal object of his conversation was along other lines."[34] By his own admission, from 1932 to the end of his tenure as secretary of state, Stimson dedicated himself to the "purpose of obtaining and maintaining a world judgment against Japan."[35] However, his plan for an intervention in Asia foundered on both American and British shoals. The British were unwilling to act without a commitment from the United States. But such a commitment was not forthcoming from President Hoover, who, Stimson complained, "is so absorbed with the domestic situation that he told me frankly that he can't think very much now of foreign affairs."[36]

With Hoover immersed in domestic matters, especially the depression, and Stimson focusing on Japanese aggression, Sackett had almost no opportunity to intervene on behalf of Brüning. The ambassador wanted to play a significant role in the disarmament talks at Geneva, but, although he attempted to confer with Stimson while the secretary was in the Swiss city, he was rebuffed.[37] Sackett persisted with another avenue for intervention

31 Stimson Diary, 29 March 1932.
32 Feis to Charles P. Howland, 23 February 1932, Box 19, Herbert Feis Papers; Feis to Frankfurter, 12 October 1931, Box 54, Frankfurter Papers.
33 Gen. MacArthur to Gen. Simonds, 7 April; Gen. Simonds to Gen. MacArthur, 25 April, and to Lt. G. K. Gailey, Simonds' aide, 2 May 1932, Box 42, Simonds Papers.
34 Gen. Simonds to Gen. Moseley, 7 March, Simonds to Lt. Gailey, 2 May 1932, Box 42, Simonds Papers.
35 Stimson, *On Active Service*, 258.   36 Stimson Diary, 17 May 1932.
37 Stimson to Sackett, 19 April 1932, Stimson Papers, 82: 831–832.

on Brüning's behalf. Most observers believed that major political questions needed to be resolved before there could be any general agreement on disarmament.[38] Among the issues was the French attempt to create a Danubian confederation. Sackett thought he could help the German chancellor by alerting Stimson to a developing problem in that region.

To reenforce French security, André Tardieu presented a plan for the economic reorganization of the Danubian states and tie them closely to France. From March to May 1932, the French premier discussed his plan between disarmament sessions at Geneva. Sackett's informant in the German Foreign Ministry told him that the Germans were not invited to participate in the talks.[39] Essentially economic in nature, the Tardieu plan would have thwarted Austro-German *Anschluss* and serve to strengthen the status quo in Eastern Europe. But the Germans had also developed a scheme for economic penetration into southeastern Europe, which would undermine the status quo and, they hoped, would lead to a revision of Germany's eastern frontier. Sackett knew that both Brüning and Tardieu had attempted to get Stimson to intervene on their behalf in the "Danubian situation."[40] Fearful that his government might support the French and thus thwart Brüning's plans, Sackett wrote to Castle in the hope that he could add his voice in support of the chancellor's position.[41]

Sackett wanted to assist in the German chancellor's attempt to frustrate French ambition in the Danubian region. The American diplomat wanted the United States and Great Britain to cooperate to achieve another Brüning goal. France was taken to be the stumbling block in achieving a just settlement of the issue of who would dominate southeastern Europe. Sackett's analysis of the problem was consistent with Brüning's ambition to break what the Germans were convinced was a French ring of control around their periphery.

While visiting Paris, Sackett and Edge had "an unususal conversation with Monsieurs Tardieu and Flandin." Sackett maintained that the French purpose in proposing a plan for southeastern Europe was to build her "security," whereas the German intention was "to escape eventually from the bondage of the Versailles Treaty."[42] The ambassador wrote that Tardieu was convinced that Germany would default on its next reparations payment

38 See Gen. Simonds to Gen. Moseley, 7 March 1932, Box 42, Simonds Papers.

39 Sackett to State, 8 March 1932, FRUS, 1932, 2: 338.

40 Gibson to State, 17 March 1932, FRUS, 1932, 1: 57–58; Klots, Memorandum of a Meeting between Stimson, Brüning, and Bülow, 17 April 1932, 500.A15A 4/1015 1/2. For a succinct review of the Danubian schemes, their relationship to the Austrian Customs Union, and economic penetration of southeastern Europe, see David E. Kaiser, *Economic Diplomacy and the Origins of the Second World War*, 13–56.

41 Sackett to Castle, 6 April 1932, Stimson Papers, 82: 813–817.

42 Sackett's analysis is from Sackett to Castle, 6 April 1932, Stimson Papers, 82: 813–817; see Marshall M. Lee and Wolfgang Michalka, *German Foreign Policy, 1917–1933*, 130; Marks, *The Illusion of Peace*, 138; Leffler, *Elusive Quest*, 275–276, 296, 298–299.

in mid-July and thus had no intention of coming to an agreement at Lausanne. In the Frenchman's analysis, according to Sackett, there were two consequences. The first was that Germany would suffer such "greatly weakened prestige" that other nations would avoid close attachment to her commercial fortunes." The other, that German default in reparations payments would lead the United States to a "voluntary" release of France from her war debts.

German plans for southeastern Europe had "lapsed into a period of 'innocuous desuetude,'" but now Sackett reported that they leaped back into life as soon as the Germans learned of the Tardieu plan. Sackett was impressed with the "recent rapid work by Germany" to sign agreements with Romania and Hungary, as a result of which, if successful, "a spoke would have been put into the French wheel."

One of the German chancellor's plans was to extend economic hegemony over the Danubian region in the hope that he could break French domination of the European continent. The French had taken up what was initially a British idea for the establishment of a Danubian customs union. Hoover, Stimson and Castle viewed this planned confederation as a workable means of restoring the faltering economies of the old Austro-Hungarian Empire. Tardieu saw the federation as a method of countering growing German influence in Central and Eastern Europe.

Sackett framed the issue in the context of the Hoover administration attitude toward the Versailles Treaty and the League of Nations. Many, if not most, Americans believed the Treaty of Versailles to be unjust and especially unfair to Germany. Nor did they adhere to the principle of collective security inherent in the League of Nations. John Foster Dulles expressed the American position well. Peace treaties, he argued, "tend to keep the world static, resist change. War is at present about the only machinery for bringing about a radical change in conditions as now fixed by treaties, etc." Dulles believed that mechanisms were needed for the reconsideration of treaties that had become inapplicable. The solution was to give "some vitality" to Article 19 of the League Covenant, which provided for reconsideration and change.[43]

Sackett was fully in accord with Dulles's analysis and had certainly acted to achieve the kind of change suggested. Like many Americans, Sackett was committed to the idea that the Treaty of Versailles was not only unjust, it was ineffective. For him reconsideration, change, and peaceful settlement of disputes were far more effective ways to cope with problems than the static arrangements of the treaty. He was also devoted to the idea that economics were central to the long-term solution of Europe's political troubles.

Sackett used just such reasoning in an effort to dissuade the Hoover administration from supporting the French Danubian scheme. He explained

43 John Foster Dulles to Lewis Fox, 4 February 1932, Box 137, Dulles Papers.

that "there is building up in Europe a new kind of balance of power; not on the old basis of 'ententes' based on treaties (public or secret) backed by ample armaments, but of a different type based on economic dependence." The contestants in this struggle for power were the old enemies, France and Germany. The French, with greater financial power, hoped to tie nations to them and their interests by means of loans to the various governments. In an interesting twist, designed to discredit the French method, Sackett characterized this tactic as similar to the "Kreuger plan" of granting loans to governments. The Swedish match king, Ivar Kreuger, had just committed suicide, thus, as already noted, revealing a financial scandal of magnificent proportions. Obviously the French idea was the less desirable of the two.

Sackett continued that the Germans for their part, with the larger population and industrial capacity, would use their greater consumer market to purchase goods, and thus tie themselves to nations by means of trade. This economic competition "forms part of this new balance of power or economic entente that is building up out of the struggle. My purpose in giving you this picture is to emphasize the viewpoint that the hoped-for 'entente cordial' [sic] between France and Germany is not to be anticipated but should be looked upon as the will-o'-the wisp of present day diplomacy." With this economic scenario, Sackett hoped to strengthen American resolve to work independently of the French to help Brüning win his goal at Geneva as well as in the Danube region. Sackett evidently thought the details of disarmament talks paled in the face of the new struggle under way; perhaps the Americans could convince the other powers to concede the simple request of the Germans for equality of rights in armaments.

Sackett pointed out with respect to reparations that British financial circles supported their government's position that the payments should be brought to an end. MacDonald was under "insistent" pressure from "the city" to wipe out reparations payments completely. It was French policy, he wrote, to subvert that support. Sackett's letter was considered important enough to be forwarded to Stimson at Bessinge in time for his meeting with Brüning on the afternoon of April 19.[44]

Sackett persisted in his attempts to get the U.S. government to support Brüning in southeastern Europe long after Stimson left Geneva. He emphasized the "great political significance" of the German attempts to sign preferential trade pacts with Romania and Hungary and to penetrate the Danubian area. Such agreements, Sackett explained, were the "keystone of German opposition to the Tardieu Plan for the Danubian states." They constituted one of the "foremost points in German foreign policy" and he hoped the United States would not intervene in any way that might "result

---

44 Sackett to Castle, confidential, 6 April 1932, forwarded by Klots to Stimson, 19 April 1932, Stimson Papers, 82: 812; Gibson to State, 14 June 1932, 500.A15A 4/1124.

in handing over 'the Danubian and Balkan states to the lure of French gold.' "[45]

The State Department was sympathetic to Sackett's position and informed the Romanian minister that because of its own interests the United States "did not very much like this Treaty," but since its purpose "was going to help in the economic reconstruction of Central Europe" the government would hesitate to act in a negative way. The United States did protest the arrangements in order to protect its interests, but the plan foundered, not because of American intervention but because the Germans did not have the economic strength to make its plan work.[46]

Stimson went to Geneva as part of the American delegation's strategy to instill some life into the disarmament conference. The American delegation was nominally headed by Secretary Stimson, but in fact Ambassador Hugh Gibson, minister to Belgium and acting head of the American delegation, was in charge, along with Norman Davis, "a leading Wilsonian Democrat and Wall Street lawyer." The two diplomats hoped to bring the conference to a successful conclusion as soon as possible. Unlike the delegations from other nations which were well supported, Congress did not appropriate the money necessary for a prolonged meeting and therefore they had a "particular interest in getting prompt, highly visible results." To get the conference into motion, Davis had returned to Washington with two suggestions for the United States to consider: a dramatic proposal to be presented at a plenary session, and a suggestion that the secretary go to the Swiss city to initiate direct talks with European leaders. Both suggestions were accepted and, as we have seen, Stimson went to Geneva.[47]

Gibson and Davis judged Brüning to be conciliatory and ready to compromise, but thought the French were the principal problem in reaching accord. Ferdinand Mayer, a delegate to the conference and Gibson's counselor of embassy in Brussels, expressed a widely held American view when he referred to France as a "spoiled child." Americans were critical of France for not granting concessions to Germany on the ground that not to do so would lead to war brought on by Germany to get what France refused to concede. Mayer, in a private letter, wrote that the British military attaché in Berlin agreed with the American legation staff in Brussels that "if French intransigeance continues the Germans will go to war again in

---

45 Sackett to State, 23 May 1932, FRUS, 1932, 2: 344–345.
46 Memorandum by Castle, 26 May, Stimson to Sackett, 27 May 1932, FRUS, 1932, 2: 345–347; Kaiser, *Economic Diplomacy and the Origins of the Second World War*, 52–56. The British favored a Danubian customs union only if it were a genuine one and "not merely a scheme of preferential tariffs." Simon to Rumbold, 14 January 1932, BDFA, F, 3: 139.
47 Bennett, *German Rearmament and the West*, 142–144.

Europe in ten or fifteen years at the latest, starting with the Polish Corridor question."[48]

The French saw things differently. In the view of many in France, the chances of Hitler's coming to power were increasing all the time. Should that happen, there was concern that France would find it necessary "to deal with a Germany more disquieting for Europe than the Germany of 1914." They believed that threats of "Hitler uprisings" made it relatively easy for them to defend the need to maintain the present level of French military strength. Hitler's constant assertion of his opposition to the Treaty of Versailles and the payment of reparations made it seem impractical to negotiate with the Brüning government.[49]

With the conviction that the Germans were "leaning more and more towards Hitler," it was widely believed in France that "it is like building on sand to negotiate with the ever weakening [Brüning] government." Some thought that "any exhibition of weakness before the Nazi element would be dangerous" and would only "encourage agitation for general treaty revision." The semiofficial *Temps* declared: "In return for all the concessions that have been made to Germany, she has given nothing in return but nationalist agitation and Hitlerism to which she has abandoned herself with a sort of frenzy and which so dangerously compromises the policy of reconciliation and peace."[50]

To counter French fears, something significant was needed. Gibson, who had been designated as American ambassador-at-large in Europe,[51] arranged to give the opening speech at the renewed conference, although Tardieu had planned to open the session. In a dramatic proposal, the United States called for a reduction of land forces and the limitation of "offensive weapons," thereby eliminating fear of invasion by any power. The proposal for "security through disarmament" meant that France would be expected to seek its security by abandoning its most potent weapons, such as tanks and heavy guns. Tardieu, already upset by failure of his proposals for a Danubian confederation, was distressed more than ever by this latest affront to the French struggle for security.[52]

The American delegates now needed to redouble their efforts if they were to achieve results at Geneva. Gibson and Davis were joined by Hugh Wilson in an effort to induce the French to see the reasonableness of the American position. But French elections made their task more difficult. They would need to negotiate with the current head of the government,

48 Mayer to Gibson, 25 April 1932, Box 42, Gibson Papers.
49 Williamson S. Howell, Jr., first secretary in Paris to State, 10 December 462.00 R296 A/85; Edge to State, 19 December 1931, 500.A15A 4/647.
50 Howell to State, 10 Decmber 1931, 462.00 R296 A/85; Edge to State, 3 May 1932, 862.00/2740.
51 Hoover, *Memoirs*, 2: 335.
52 Bennett, *German Rearmament and the West*, 143–144.

André Tardieu, and the putative premier, Édouard Herriot. In addition, several major factors played a role in French thinking. The Nazi success in the Prussian elections gave French leadership pause. They took the position that any agreement they negotiated with the Germans would have to be acceptable to Hitler as, in their view, the Nazi would soon be part of the German government, if not in complete control. Allen Dulles, on loan from Sullivan and Cromwell as legal adviser to the American delegation because of his knowledge of disarmament matters, agreed. He wrote to his brother: "Personally I hope that their [Nazi] participation will be worked out, as I feel that any Government in France would be very reluctant to enter into any far-reaching agreements with a German Government which was not in some way underwritten or approved by the Hitler element."[53]

In the midst of the discussions, which the Americans expected would lead to a more reasonable French position on granting concessions to Germany, a new and distressing disclosure threatened to undo any progress that might have been made. In Paris, during the disarmament conference, *L'Illustration* published a series of letters written by the late Gustav Stresemann, the German statesman most identified with the fulfillment of the provisions of the Treaty of Versailles. Stresemann had served as German chancellor in 1923 and foreign minister until his death in 1929. As the series of Stresemann papers was published, it became clear that the German statesman had meant to achieve German nationalist aims while appearing to work toward fulfillment of treaty obligations as a matter of strategy.

The contents of one letter were summarized by Americans in Geneva for the State Department's benefit. Writing to the German crown prince in 1925, Stresemann outlined the four cardinal points of German foreign policy:[54]

> (namely, (1) a satis-factory settlement of the Rhineland question; (2) the protection of from 10 to 12 million Germans living under foreign yoke; (3) the rectification of Germany's eastern frontiers including the return to the Reich of Danzig, the Polish Corridor, and Upper Silesia and (4) the union with Austria) and urges the entry of the Reich into the League of Nations so that the German Government may have a springboard from which it can launch its claims in the problems of war guilt, general disarmament, the Saar, etc.

This damaging revelation of real German intentions was a shock to many and made for good press. However, most statesmen knew, or should have known, Stresemann's goals, which he made quite public.[55]

53 Allen Dulles to John Foster Dulles, 13 May 1932, Box 137, Dulles Papers; Gibson to State, Gibson to Davis, 31 March 1932, 500.A15A 4 PERSONNEL/487.
54 R. T. Pell, from Geneva, 26 May 1932, "The Stresemann Papers," sent by Moffatt to Boal and Castle, 9 June 1932, 762.00/59.
55 Lee and Michalka, *German Foreign Policy*, 84–85; Gaines Post, Jr., *The Civil-Military Fabric of the Weimar Republic*, 59, 281.

Stresemann, who had outwardly appeared to be an internationalist and champion of European cooperation, showed himself through his letters to be an ardent Pan-German nationalist. In another place he asserted that in the League of Nations, "we shall be . . . the mouthpiece of Germans everywhere, for all Germany will see in our Government the champion of Germanism."[56] Premier Tardieu was offended by the letters, "which demonstrate that the one German who had won French confidence was completely false." Gibson thought the letters were such a "shock to French public opinion as to constitute a set back to any move for good understanding." The French were now concerned about the possibility of armed aggression in the Corridor, or the seizure of Danzig.[57]

Boal wrote that the French, who had considered Stresemann "a practical European idealist," now felt betrayed. The one person they thought they could deal with in good faith was revealed as a dissembler of significant proportions. The American was concerned that the French had "lost faith in German honesty."[58]

By now Brüning was assailed from all sides. Under constant attack at home from both political extremes, and now identified with the presumed dishonesty of Stresemann abroad, he came under further criticism from his own government. General Kurt von Schleicher had a change of heart over the banning of the Storm Troops. The Nazis for their part had never forgiven General Groener for the prohibition. A "whispering campaign" began against Groener, and in Munich the Bavarian People's party press published "revelations" about "an alleged 'camarilla' of Reichswehr Generals – foremost amongst these General Schleicher, the 'Eminence Grise' – intent on ousting Groener and forming a 'military cabinet' with the Nazis." Sackett speculated that Brüning might resort to drastic measures, including "the appointment of a Reich Commissioner for Prussia."[59]

As the crisis for the Brüning government grew, Sackett held fast in his support of the chancellor. He reported more intrigues against his friend and General Groener but insisted that Brüning had the "full confidence" of President Hindenburg. The American even found reason to support the presidential decree prohibiting "Godless" organizations on the ground that it was not intended to interfere with freedom of conscience, but was designed to prevent provocative and aggressive propaganda of a clearly political character.[60]

56 Pell, "The Stresemann Papers," 9 June 1932, 762.00/59.
57 Gibson to State, 14 May 1932, FRUS, 1932, 1: 127–128.
58 Pierre Boal, "The Hitherto Unpublished Stresemann Papers," 9 June 1932, 762.00/59; Edge to State, 27 May 1932, 500.A15A 4/1096; Edge sent a copy of "Les Papiers de Stresemann" in book form to the State Department just before it was released for sale to the public, Edge to State, 27 May 1932, 500.A15A 4/1096.
59 Sackett to State, 3 May 1932, 862.00/2742.
60 Sackett to State, 10 May 1932, 862.00/2753.

The latest crisis reached its climax in early May when the Nazis and their allies in the Reichstag opened an attack on General Groener, while General Schleicher paralleled the assault from behind the scenes. It was clear that Groener no longer had the support of the Reichswehr, and he was forced to resign as head of its ministry.[61] Brüning was steadfast in supporting his cabinet colleague by insisting that Groener continue his position as minister of the interior; but the chancellor made no attempt to defend the general publicly.

Instead, Brüning launched an offensive in a Reichstag speech, which concluded with the admonition that now, "100 yards from the goal, it was especially necessary to remain calm." The remark stirred considerable speculation in the press and caused some consternation among Sackett and the diplomats in the American embassy in Berlin, who were puzzled by what they called the chancellor's "somewhat mysterious remark." Sackett drew the conclusion that the chancellor had grown in stature and combativeness. He recalled Brüning's Reichstag speech in February, where he "had shown qualities of a fighter who skillfully and forcibly repelled the violent attacks of the extremists of the Right." In his latest speech, he "displayed a degree of self assurance and an air of superiority heretofore unknown in the German Chancellor." Sackett summarized his speech as a "dignified appeal to the opposition parties not to disturb the domestic political equilibrium before the Lausanne Conference." The meaning was clear: Brüning was looking forward to the resolution of the reparations issue at Lausanne.

To ward off criticism from the Right, Brüning sought to show that there was little difference between his own and the Nazi position. To clarify his policy, Sackett wrote, he referred to an earlier, conciliatory speech by Gregor Strasser, and "very carefully pointed out that on certain important phases of German foreign policy the attitude of the Right opposition was not at variance with his own." The chancellor came so close to the Nazi position that they later claimed he had borrowed about 80 percent of it from them. Even Hugenberg was pleased, though with a "touch of sarcasm." One of his newspapers wrote that on the reparations issue, "Brüning spoke as if he had been Hugenberg." Nazi delegates had listened attentively to the chancellor's speech, which elicited from Sackett the guess that secret negotiations toward creating a coalition government with the Nazis might be under way. He doubted, however, that such a compromise was in the offing.[62] The ambassador remained convinced that Hitler was not ready to enter any government, and certainly not before the reparations issue was settled at Lausanne.

The French had been put off by the Stresemann letters, and now Brüning's

---

61 Sackett to State. 12 May 1932, 862.00/2741.
62 Sackett to State, 17 May 1932, 462.00 R296/5664.

move farther to the Right seemed to be a determined effort to throw road-blocks in the way of any settlement. Tardieu took umbrage upon learning of the German chancellor's Reichstag speech. He told Gibson that it was in "striking contrast" to the tone Brüning had used at Bessinge. The French premier thought it a matter of "grave importance" that Groener had been dismissed by subordinates in the Reichswehr. It was, he said, evidence that "the Hitlerites dominate the army."[63]

Progress in the disarmament talks was at an impasse when Herriot contacted Davis to suggest they meet for lunch in Lyons, where the Frenchman was mayor. Herriot, who would form the next French government, wanted to discuss disarmament. Davis cleared the meeting with Tardieu, the current premier, and with the State Department. Ambassador Hugh Wilson, also on the disarmament staff, accompanied Davis to the luncheon, which was to take place without publicity.[64]

In a meeting on May 22, 1932, lasting three hours, Herriot, Davis, and Wilson covered a wide range of topics, including war debts, the Stresemann letters, the Far Eastern crisis, reparations, and the French perception of a hostile American press. The main focus, however, was on disarmament. Herriot was not sure that agreement with the Germans was possible, especially in the light of the revelations in the Stresemann letters. Although he believed Brüning to be "a good man," he wondered whether or not the German chancellor could bind Germany. He complained that every time France granted a concession "to appease Germany," the result was increased demands. Davis offered that the best method "to combat Hittlerism [sic] was to convince the German people of France's desire to be just and reasonable but also to uphold her rights."[65]

Herriot was persuaded that the United States, Great Britain, and France were the only nations who could "sit down and talk freely and frankly" and work together out of "mutual trust and respect." He suggested it was "essential" that the three nations "consult frequently and frankly" to resolve problems such as they faced at Geneva. Davis and Wilson were impressed. They believed that Herriot "seemed to seek merely a full understanding and voluntary collaboration."[66] They were not pleased that Herriot had excluded Brüning and the Germans from the triumvirate he envisioned.

In their report of the meeting, the Americans suggested Brüning also be invited to meet in Geneva and that Herriot was receptive.[67] Davis and Wilson were exuberant about the possibilty of breaking the logjam at Geneva. All that was required now was to reassemble the informal meetings, this time with the French present to talk directly with Brüning.[68] But they were

63 Gibson to State, 14 May 1932, FRUS, 1932, 1: 128.
64 Davis to State, 21 May 1932, FRUS, 1932, 1: 132.
65 Telegram, Davis to State, 23 May 1932, 500.A15A 4/1066.
66 Davis to State, 23 May 1932, 500.A15A 4/1066.   67 Ibid.
68 Bennett, *German Rearmament and the West*, 156.

concerned that Herriot was "deeply under the impression of the Stresemann letters, and is in the depth of disillusionment in regard to Germany."[69] Herriot was certainly willing to meet with the Americans and MacDonald, and he especially was interested in Anglo-French talks. His aim was to establish close cooperation with the British. He did not want to meet with the Germans. In his view, including Brüning in disarmament talks with the principal powers would be tantamount to the recognition of equality of rights. Moreover, Brüning's major interest was reparations, not disarmament.[70]

It was the Americans, Gibson and Davis, who wanted to include Brüning in four-power discussions, something they were unable to accomplish at Bessinge. Their purpose was to help the German chancellor. Gibson informed Stimson that he and Davis were trying to work out a way to tell Brüning that it was "imperative" for him to come to Geneva before the Lausanne Conference. They wanted him to come prepared "to do his utmost" to counteract the "unhappy effect" the Stresemann letters had on Herriot.[71]

It is important to keep in mind attitudes of the time. In spite of great strides in acceptance, Germans were still considered the defeated and hated enemy in many quarters, especially among the French. That attitude was reinforced by the Stresemann letters. Sackett considered it a triumph that he had been influential in arranging for Brüning to meet with the British prime minister at Chequers. It would be another important step toward equality if Brüning were to meet at Geneva with MacDonald and Herriot and come away with a resolution of the disarmament problem. The American delegation certainly considered it very important that Brüning come to Geneva and help dispel the damage done by the Stresemann letters.

Gibson and Davis fretted over the means for getting the message to Brüning. They discarded the idea that they go to Berlin. Although they had been to Paris and London, their missions were of a "general explorative character." To go now to Berlin might create a public stir and even require that they go to Rome so as not to offend the Italians. They suggested instead that Frederic Dolbeare, a member of the American delegation, be sent to see the chancellor. The difficulty with that plan was that Brüning might feel a slight unless the message were delivered by a person of higher rank. They resolved that dilemma by suggesting that Dolbeare deliver a letter to Sackett, who would read the letter to Brüning. Dolbeare, who was fluent in German, would be there to answer any questions.[72]

Gibson sent his suggestion to Stimson by telegram on Monday evening.

69 Davis, Memorandum of a Conversation with Herriot, 22 May 1932, FRUS, 1932, 1: 139.
70 Gibson to Stimson, 14 June 1932, 500. A 15 A 4/1124; Bennett, *German Rearmament and the West*, 159–160.
71 Gibson to State, 23 May 1932, FRUS, 1932, 1: 139–140.   72 Ibid.

He proposed to send Dolbeare to Berlin on Thursday, May 26, if there were no objections. The next day, Tuesday, Gibson had good news from French military representatives, who said they were willing to have the American formula on "effectives" brought up for discussion. Effectives included all trained military personnel, including inactive reservists. The American plan called for the reduction of inactive military units available for duty. The reserve forces were to be divided between those used for domestic security and those for defense against foreign attack. The next step was to get agreement in principle. Gibson's hope now was that he would hear in a day or two if Tardieu and Herriot had reached agreement. He also asked whether the president was willing to have attrituted to him authorship of the idea of dividing effectives into two separate groups. Hoover had worked out the idea for the reduction of effectives in the summer of 1931.[73]

The American disarmament delegation's heartening report on French willingness to compromise on disarmament issues had an important impact in Washington. The diplomats were eager for success. Such an accomplishment in foreign affairs could have an encouraging impact on morale in a United States beset by depression, but especially it was just the sort of achievement that might save the Brüning government.

The Americans wanted to inform Brüning that in their estimation the situation was ripe for settlement in Germany's favor on the issue of disarmament, but that reparations needed more time to resolve at Lausanne. It was therefore imperative that the German make the trip to Geneva to undertake discussions with Herriot. Stimson acted cautiously. He suggested that the Americans might await the British response to their call for continuation of the Bessinge talks, and that Sackett and Rumbold together visit the German chancellor. In that fashion they would move toward "carrying out the idea of staging Franco-German conversations on disarmament under the joint auspices" of the British and the Americans.[74]

The relevant telegrams from the disarmament delegation were brought before the president's cabinet. Stimson read aloud from the long report recounting the talk Davis and Wilson had with Herriot in Lyons. Moffat had a brief conversation with Stimson immediately after the cabinet meeting and recorded in his diary that Herriot's position was characterized as "noncommittal" on matters of disarmament, but he did provide "some definite and welcome" information on reparations.[75]

There is still a controversy about what the Americans communicated to

73 Gibson to State, 24 May 1932, FRUS, 1932, 1: 140: Bennett, *German Rearmament and the West*, 141.
74 Stimson to Gibson and Davis, 24 May 1932, FRUS, 1932, 1: 142.
75 Secondhand information on the American cabinet meeting is from Moffat Diary, 24 May 1932.

Brüning. The Hoover cabinet meeting helps to account for the discrepancy in several different versions. Some reports maintain that concessions on disarmament were the topic, whereas other versions specify reparations as the subject of the message.

Count Kuno Westarp, a candidate to succeed Brüning, dictated a memorandum on June 1, 1932, in which he claimed that Sackett carried a letter from President Hoover concerning "a favorable development in the reparations problem." Gottfried Treviranus, a Brüning intimate who might have had direct knowledge of the message, insisted that the information was verbal and concerned French willingness to abandon their opposition to German equality of treatment in armaments. Brüning maintained that it was a letter from Gibson to Sackett and concerned concessions from Herriot on both reparations and disarmament.[76]

Given the American decision to minimize the reparations issue and to accept the French plan for a prolonged moratorium, and, at the same time, influenced by Gibson's "wildly optimistic" belief that the European nations were ready "to disarm themselves,"[77] it is likely that the Hoover cabinet concerned itself with both issues. Hoover, however, focused on the disarmament conference and favored "some new and dramatic gesture to revivify the [disarmament] Conference." Stimson responded "vehemently" in opposition to the president's proposal. The secretary and State Department officials raised serious doubts concerning the Davis-Wilson talks with Herriot.

When the issue of informing Brüning of the latest development arose, the question of "why?" was raised. Doubts of its importance were brought up, and it was asked, "What was there so new and startling on the political or disarmament phases to warrant sending an emissary to Berlin?" Affirming that disarmament was the central issue, there was concern that sending Dolbeare to Berlin might confuse matters because of his "reparation and banking background."[78] That there was no significant new proposal offered is confirmed by a query from the American disarmament delegation sent to Stimson four days later, after it was decided to send Dolbeare to Berlin. They inquired concerning what American policy was. They needed instructions because they did not know where their government stood on the issues before the conference.[79]

Stimson raised the significant question as to whether or not Brüning would be reluctant to go to Geneva. The German had good reason to avoid further talks. His government was placed in a very difficult position

76 Westarp, "Zu Brünings Rücktritt," in Werner Conze, "Zum Sturz Brünings," 285; Treviranus, *Das Ende von Weimar*, 319–320; Brüning, *Memoiren*, 601; see Bennett, *German Disarmament and the West*, 161n57.
77 Bennett, *German Rearmament and the West*, 161.
78 Moffat Diary, 24 May 1932.
79 Gibson to State, 28 May 1932, FRUS, 1932, 1: 145–150.

by Nazi success in the Prussian elections. He was unable to compromise any further on armaments issues, especially since he believed he had achieved equality in the talks at Bessinge. Moreover, Brüning had already deferred the Germans' real intentions with respect to the military. They meant to rearm in due course, but meanwhile their delegation at Geneva could manage whatever was possible at that stage. Brüning's main concern was reparations, another issue on which he could not compromise.

The British believed that the United States was prepared to see Europe cancel reparations without American involvement. Hoover was committed to the "stern avoidance of entanglement" in European affairs. However, Ronald Lindsay, the British ambassador in Washington, surmised that by thus giving in on the issue of reparations, the Americans thought they should be able to win concessions in the disarmament conference.[80] That would strengthen the American desire to have Brüning come to Geneva. But Lindsay was off the mark.

In the United States it was considered premature to consider the cancellation of reparations. Thomas Lamont of J. P. Morgan contacted the State Department to caution against supporting such a position. He claimed that, minimally, the British wanted reparations reduced and hoped to see them eliminated "for all time."[81] That was a mistake in the view of the financier. Just as important, Lamont stressed that Brüning could "make no concessions or if [he] would make concessions, will immediately fall." Lamont considered it critical to contact the chancellor.[82] Going to Geneva might provide strong enough a buffer to soften the blow the Americans expected Brüning to receive at Lausanne.

The United States adopted a policy in line with Lamont's suggestion and decided to soft-pedal the reparations issue. Feis proposed that the United States come to a decision. The question, he wrote, was whether or not the government "wishes to give any indirect or devious indications of its judgment and interest on this point to the German Government. Such would be sure to have considerable weight with Bruening."[83]

Sackett had just cabled the essence of his conversation with French Ambassador François Poncet, in which the Frenchman foresaw "considerable progress" in resolving the disarmament question. He called the American proposal to limit offensive weapons "very clever" and anticipated

80 D. G. Osborne to the Marquess of Reading, 18 September 1931; Lindsay to Simon, 27 April 1932, DBFA, C, 2: 168, 226–227.
81 Telephone conversation between Stimson and George Harrison of the Federal Reserve Bank, 18 November 1931, Debts and Reparations – Memoranda of Conversations, 1929–1932, Castle Papers, HHPL.
82 Feis, Memorandum, Apropos Lamont's Correspondence in Regard to the Lausanne Conference, 27 May 1932, Stimson Papers, 82: 1054–1055.
83 Ibid.; Leffler, *Elusive Quest*, 288–290.

"something constructive" could come out of it. The French diplomat was, however, very pessimistic about the outcome of the reparations issue at Lausanne, although France was willing to accept a prolonged moratorium.[84]

Two matters stand out. The first is so simple it is easy to overlook: The letter for Sackett to deliver to Brüning was probably little more than an urgent request that the German chancellor get to Geneva before the meeting in Lausanne so that disarmament would not be lost in the discussion of reparations. That, after all, was the whole purport of the inquiry Gibson sent to Stimson regarding how to inform Brüning. The German chancellor was to be there to take advantage of Anglo-American support for Franco-German talks. That was particularly important because Brüning's emphasis was on reparations. In fact he initially wanted to come to Geneva to discuss reparations, not disarmament.[85]

The second element might have involved the president's plan to reduce the number of all forces in service or, "effectives." Gibson was impressed by French willingness to get past that problem and onto "qualitative disarmament."[86] Edge wrote Stimson that "assurances of good will from the French General Staff continue."[87] The message from Paris was an indication that there was some progress toward achievement of German aims. Sackett had informed the State Department that François Poncet was confident of success at Geneva and offered his opinion that Herriot could go further toward compromise than Tardieu. The French diplomat also made it plain that French public opinion had hardened against Germany after Brüning's Reichstag speech.[88]

Because the letter that Dolbeare brought to Sackett has never been found, one can only speculate as to its content. However, several facts seem clear enough. The Germans were working on the assumption that they had Anglo-American agreement; that they would get acknowledgment of their equality of rights in principle, and also a "certain measure" of rearmament. The only remaining problem was to get French consent to such an arrangement.[89] There also was considerable concern about whether Brüning would go to Geneva, and whether Herriot and Tardieu were willing to accept the British and Americans in the role of intermediary. Although Gibson professed that he did not anticipate any problem in Brüning going to Geneva, he did indicate that the chancellor would need to overcome some domestic problems before making the trip. He also would need to be made to realize "the seriousness of the work to be achieved here in removing

84 Sackett to State, 27 May 1932, 500. A 15 A 4/1081, the cable was sent to Hoover.
85 Simon to Rumbold, 5 February 1932, BDFA, J, 4: 1.
86 Nadolny to Bülow, 30 May 1932, ADAP 20: 221.
87 Edge to State, 30 May 1932, Box 42, Gibson Papers.
88 Sackett to State, 27 May 1932, 500.A15A 4/1081.
89 Bennett, *German Rearmament and the West*, 155–156.

French apprehensions" and of the importance of finding ways to continue the disarmament talks while the Lausanne Conference was going on.[90]

Gibson was convinced there could be no progress in disarmament until the French were able to overcome their "disillusionment." With the French in that state of mind, any agreement with the Germans would require "a great deal of Anglo-Saxon help."[91] It is easy to forget today that an agreement granting equality of status in armaments to Germany would have been an important victory for Brüning.[92] Although Brüning thought he had it, the Americans were still working on the assumption that they could get it for him.

The problem of the controversial communication to Brüning may never be resolved because the demarche by the Americans was unofficial and therefore not part of the diplomatic record. Gibson and Davis did not want Rumbold to join Sackett in presenting the message to Brüning because that would give the move the status of "a formal and official communication." Their intention was to help the German chancellor as part of the American policy of "unofficial helpfulness."[93] That would be a continuation of the American "policy of involvement without commitment."[94]

Brüning, who has written on the subject, is little help on the contents of the missing letter, partly because he offers three versions of what happened. In the first, a letter to the editor of the *Deutsche Rundschau* in 1947, he assumed that a disarmament formula had been agreed upon at Bessinge by the United States, Great Britain, and Italy, and that Gibson had been negotiating for Herriot's acceptance. He claimed he had waited from "hour to hour" to hear from Sackett that "Herriot had accepted the disarmament formula in principle." He went on to assert that the Polish government had consented to begin negotiations in June for a new solution of the Corridor issue. In addition, he wrote that agreement in principle had been achieved for a final settlement of the reparations question. With all that accomplished, he claimed, "Herriot's acceptance of the formula for German disarmament brought the last, still outstanding greater question of foreign relations into line for settlement."[95]

The claim that he brought all the great foreign policy issues to the threshold of resolution fits nicely into Brüning's contention that his dismissal was a great German tragedy. He contended that he achieved all the goals fellow nationalists aspired to, and that bringing Hitler to power was a fatal and unnecesary move. In 1951 Brüning gave his second account of

90 Gibson to State, 25 May 1932, FRUS, 1932, 1: 144.
91 Davis, Memorandum of Conversation with Herriot, 22 May 1932, FRUS, 1932, 1: 139.
92 Craig, *Germany, 1866–1945*, 678.
93 Gibson to State, 25 May 1932, FRUS, 1932, 1: 145.
94 Jonas, *The United States and Germany*, 154.
95 Brüning, "Ein Brief," 10; Bennett, *German Rearmament and the West*, 160–161, is an excellent discussion of the controversial letter, esp. 161n57.

what happened, but not for publication, in a witness's report for the Institut für Zeitgeschichte in Munich, where he made the amazing claim that the United States had "compelled" Herriot to accept Germany's recommendations for disarmament.[96]

The most recent account appeared in 1970 in his memoirs. There he describes events in a different light. Sackett, he writes, came to see him at ten-thirty Monday morning, May 30. The American had arranged to see the chancellor before he was scheduled to meet with Hindenburg at noon. Sackett wanted Brüning to read a letter from Gibson before he met with the president. The ambassador told Brüning that "on his own responsibility he was going to do something which went against all diplomatic norms and against every tradition of American policy." The letter was from Gibson to Sackett, and Brüning claims it explained that Gibson and Herriot had discussed the reparations and disarmament issues and had reached agreement "in the sense of my demands." Gibson and Herriot were convinced it was imperative to save the Brüning government. "Herriot," the letter went on, "perceived the absolute and urgent need for strengthening my position in the general European interest." It concluded, in Brüning's account, with the words "Let the chancellor come soon to Geneva."[97]

Brüning's memoirs offer the most compelling explanation of what might have been in the enigmatic letter. There could be very little new and startling. It is, however, clear that the Americans wanted to save the Brüning government, and it is likely that so did Herriot. The simple explanation seems to be that the Americans wanted the German to come to Geneva to complete the round of talks on disarmament while the reparations issue was brought to a settlement at Lausanne.

One thing is clear. After hearing good news from both London and Paris, Gibson wrote a letter to Sackett that was meant for Brüning and was intended to help the German chancellor retain his position. Sackett did bring a communication to Brüning, meant for him only. The American ambassador was "visibly shaken" when he discovered that Brüning was about to resign, and it was then that he refused to give the letter to Bülow, the official representative of the German Foreign Ministry.[98]

Gibson reported that Dolbeare had returned to Geneva, and thanked Sackett for his cooperation. There was, however, no more to be done. The letter had been for Brüning alone. Gibson wrote: "I feel that the present situation offers so many unkown factors that it might be well to withhold all further action for the moment."[99]

Hindenburg was anxious to be off to review the German fleet in its annual parade at Skaggerak on May 30, 1932. He reset his meeting with

96 Bennett, *German Rearmament and the West*, 161n57.   97 Brüning, *Memoiren*, 601.
98 Nadolny to Foreign Ministry, 30 May 1932, ADAP, 20: 220 and n.3; Brüning, *Memoiren*, 601; Westarp, "Zu Brünings Rücktritt," in Conze, "Zum Sturz Brünings," 285.
99 Gibson to Sackett, 2 June 1932, GDC–3, Gibson Papers.

the chancellor a little earlier in the day than scheduled, so that he could enjoy more of the naval activity. Brüning had already made his decision to resign when Sackett arrived with his message. In a brief meeting with Hindenburg, involving little more than an exchange of pleasantries, Brüning presented his resignation, and that of his entire cabinet to the president.[100]

100 Brüning, *Memoiren*, 601–602.

9

Sackett loses heart with Brüning's fall

BRÜNING'S RESIGNATION came as a great shock to Sackett and took the personal meaning out of his mission to Germany. The ambassador had done all he could for the chancellor, the one person he and his staff felt was destined to prevent Hitler's rise to power in Germany. But now there was nothing they could do. Sackett was thwarted by American foreign policy, which prohibited direct involvement in European affairs. However, even if the United States intervened, there was nothing that could be done to help the chancellor. Not even if France were willing to offer concessions was there any hope of saving his government. The fact is that Brüning was compelled to resign because he had lost the support of the most powerful forces in Germany – forces that wanted a complete break with the Socialists, on whom Brüning was dependent. As Sackett put it, those who brought about Brüning's downfall wanted a sharp division with the Left.[1]

Hindenburg deliberately ignored the parties of the political Right and the conservative interest groups when he appointed Franz von Papen to succeed Brüning. Instead, he turned to individual members of the conservative establishment – the officer corps, the civil service, and the aristocracy. Hindenburg also moved farther in the direction established by Brüning. Neutral experts, who could be relied on to insure that the government would be run efficiently, were favored over representatives of partisan interests. The hope was to restore authority and stability in the state by reviving the ideals of civic virtue and the political relationships of the Bismarckian compromise.[2] The effort was another naive attempt to capture Hitler's support and tame his Nazi movement by meeting the supposed aspirations of his followers. This task was to be carried out under the aegis of General Schleicher, who had lost confidence in Brüning and used his considerable influence to remove him from office.

1 Sackett to State, 14 June 1932, 862.00/2794.
2 John L. Heineman, *Hitler's First Foreign Minister*, 1.

Americans were at a loss as to what to do next in their relations with Germany when the Papen government was installed. All attempts to help Brüning were aborted. They were intended for the man, not the nation. Americans had placed too much hope in a Brüning government and not enough in a well-considered German policy. Some thought that the Berlin embassy had been too optimistic in its reports from Germany, that their "cheering forecasts" were unwarranted, especially since events in Germany were "moving at an ominous rate."[3] American diplomats had placed all their thought and energy into supporting Brüning, and when he fell from office they had no alternative to a policy of support for their political favorite. They disapproved of the successor government and were reduced to wishful thinking, turning to their forlorn hope that Brüning would be restored to office.

American diplomats saw no alternative to Brüning. They had placed inordinate faith in a man that many later observers saw as merely adequate, if not simply mediocre. But to Sackett, he was "the discovery of Europe, a really great man . . . under a mission to save his country."[4] Rumbold said of Brüning that he was a "statesman," the Germans "respect a leader and they have got one now." He was Germany's "greatest asset and best trump card."[5] Stimson called him a "very careful, sincere and strong man," a man who has "shown great foresight and wisdom and has made very few mistakes."[6]

Like most other American diplomats, Theodore Marriner was "much impressed" by Brüning, "an ascetic tired looking man with a gentle voice."[7] During the financial crisis the German chancellor convinced everyone "by his absolute integrity, honesty and high mindedness. He is more like a medieval saint than a modern politician."[8] As astute an observer as columnist Walter Lippmann saw the German as a man with the "face and bearing of a priest" with a "kind of imperturbable conviction of his own mission – not a man people would love, but something strong and erect to hold on to in a hurricane."[9] The French ambassador to the United States, Paul Claudel, was among the many who admired Brüning, calling him a "wonderful man." Stimson agreed with the Frenchman when he characterized the chancellor as a "great man who was trying to do his best in this situation."[10]

American diplomats were saddened by the chancellor's resignation. They

3 Frankfurter to Feis, 10 June 1932, Box 16, Frankfurter papers.
4 Stimson Diary, 4 May 1931.
5 Martin Gilbert, *Sir Horace Rumbold: Portrait of a Diplomat, 1869–1941*, 337, 360.
6 Stimson Diary, 18 July 1931.   7 Marriner Diary, 21 July 1931.
8 Marriner to Castle, 20 August 1931, Castle Papers – Germany, HHPL.
9 Ronald Steel, *Walter Lippmann and the American Century*, 279.
10 Stimson, Memoranda of Conversations with Claudel, 28 May and 18 June 1931, Stimson Papers, 162: 133, 142.

experienced a sense of loss so severe that it affected policy. Governor George Harrison of the Federal Reserve Bank was afraid there was now no one in Germany who could speak for the Germans at Lausanne.[11] At Geneva, it was clear that the American disarmament delegation was more than disappointed. They reported that neither the British nor the French were willing to concede to Papen what they had agreed to for Brüning.[12] There was, Gibson wrote, a general sense of regret "at the disappearance of the personality of Brüning." But one benefit was that it was no longer necessary to take into account the German government's need "for face-saving." Certainly not "to the same extent as was the case when the other powers had an interest in keeping [the] Brüning Government in power."[13]

Mary Woolley, an American disarmament delegate, was convinced that the "overthrow" of Brüning had intensified a crisis in the disarmament talks.[14] Norman Armour, the American chargé in Paris, reported that the French were persuaded that with the change of government in Germany nothing further could be done. Decisive in demonstrating the significance in the change of attitude and policy was the bureaucratic order to save money. As soon as Brüning was out of office, Stimson cabled the disarmament delegation in Geneva to send fewer cables and cut down on delegation expenses. They were to reduce their factual reporting "to an absolute minimum" and send instead brief analyses.[15]

Ambassador Sackett soon let the Germans know that there had been a change in American policy and attitudes. He expressed misgivings about German intention to rearm and told them that the entire issue of "equality of rights" in the matter of armaments was "strictly a European question." Clearly Sackett had shifted the position he held when Brüning was chancellor. The Germans now perceived Sackett, who had undeniably demonstrated his pro-German attitudes, as being influenced by the French point of view.[16] Obviously, Sackett was upset by the changes that had taken place in Berlin.

The ambassador was impressed by the historical importance of Brüning's fall from power and set down his interpretation of events for the record.[17] Rumors of a falling-out between Brüning and Hindenburg, he wrote, began to circulate about May 25. The New York office of the National City Company wired their Berlin representative to run down a rumor of an

---

11 Stimson, Memorandum of a Conversation with Harrison, 1 June 1932, Stimson Papers, 164: 211.
12 Gibson to State, 14 June 1932, 500.A15A 4/1124.
13 Gibson to State, 5 June 1932, FRUS, 1932, 2: 152–153.
14 Woolley to Gibson, 1 June 1932, Box 31, Gibson Papers.
15 Stimson to the American Delegation in Geneva, 1 June 1932, 500.A15A 4/1089.
16 Memoranda by Bülow, 21 and 24 September, and Prittwitz to Foreign Ministry, 12 October 1932, ADAP, 21: 145, 154–155, 223.
17 The principal despatch is Sackett to State, 8 June 1932, FRUS, 1932, 2: 300–302, from which much of the following is derived.

impending break between the chancellor and the president. He was unable to find confirmation of the rumor, and the embassy had private assurances from Erwin Planck, of the chancellor's office, that there was no foundation to the story. Although aware that Planck was a close associate and confidant of General Schleicher, Sackett considered him to be "a most reliable informant" in the past and therefore assumed that "his present denial can be safely accepted."[18]

At the time, Hindenburg was in Neudeck, his East Prussian estate, "beyond the Polish Corridor," visiting Junker friends with whom he had "close and intimate relations." But Sackett did not suspect that Brüning was in danger in spite of the fact that the president left Berlin in the midst of a "smoldering Cabinet crisis." He suspected there would be some changes in the government, but assumed that Brüning was safe, at least until after the Lausanne Conference.[19]

Sackett guessed that something unusual was happening when Otto Meissner, the president's secretary, departed suddenly for Neudeck two days before Hindenburg's announced return to Berlin. It was then that Sackett began to supect that there was "something going on in governmental circles that was *sub rosa*."

Sackett did not trust Meissner. He wrote that the president's secretary is "very clever" and some people, including Brüning, did not have "complete confidence in his sincerity." His "antecedents" were of "the Army and the old regime." He and Colonel Oskar von Hindenburg, the president's son, had a great deal of influence on the president. The younger Hindenburg, who was assigned as his father's adjutant and lived with the president, Sackett continued, was "accredited in the public mind as exercising great influence with his father and with being decidedly anti-Socialistic. In view of these two powers behind the scene, the sudden trip of Meissner to Neudeck just two days before von Hindenburg's announced return, raised some questions in my mind as to its purpose."

The embassy had already reported on the "camarilla" that surrounded the president and exercised extraordinary influence. The military men, headed by General Schleicher, the "Eminence Grise," objected to the manner in which Hitler's Storm Troopers had been disbanded. Above all, they did not want to be put in the position of intervening against the political Right. Many, if not most, high-ranking officers shared an antipathy for the Socialists, and with Hindenburg and his son, resented the need to count on them for support of the government. Their first move to change matters was revealed in their ouster of General Groener as Reichswehr minister. Sackett reported that they wanted to form a military cabinet with the Nazis.[20]

18 Sackett to State, 25 May 1932, 862.00/2754.
19 Sackett to State, 1 June 1932, 862.00/2781.
20 Sackett to State, 3 May 1932, 862.00/2742.

The problems of military influence had been the topic of several discussions Brüning had with Sackett. The chancellor also recalled that on several occasions he had discussed the danger of political generals with Stimson, who, the Germans knew, had a "horror" of military men meddling in political affairs.[21] On the morning he resigned, Brüning told Sackett that his continuance in office was dependent on Hindenburg's willingness to put a stop to the intrigues. Brüning maintained that the president's refusal to take action to end military intervention in politics "was the sole cause of the Cabinet's resignation." Public statements that disagreement over new economic proposals was the reason for bringing his government to an end was nothing more than "subterfuge."[22]

Brüning had attempted on several occasions to put a stop to intriguing by generals. He wanted their political support; after all, they were responsible for the formation of his cabinet in the first place. Most of all he wanted assurance that they would support him against the Nazis. In a significant arrangement, during a dinner at the home of Gottfried Treviranus, the chancellor's friend and political ally, the Germans present were segregated from the other guests. The occasion was a talk by the vice-chancellor and minister of finance, Hermann Dietrich. Probably to be certain that Sackett would be informed of the purport of the discussion, Alfred Klieforth of the embassy staff, fluent in German, was the only non-German guest invited to join the select group.

Speaking for the government, Dietrich attempted to enlist the aid of the generals who were there. He especially appealed to Schleicher and Hammerstein to help undo the work of the political generals. He asked for their patience and support, promising them that Germany would soon recover from the depression. He implored them to "keep from rocking the boat" and the nation would be restored to its rightful place "ahead of all countries in the world, including the United States." By following an "orderly political course" he assured them, Germany would be able to "get the lead of the world."[23]

Brüning was unable to persuade the generals to be patient with his government. He had already lost their confidence. Sackett tried to divine the significance of the events leading to Brüning's fall and came up with an intriguing interpretation. Looking back on what happened, he wrote that Groener's resignation as Reichswehr minister was evidence that there was "a definite plan among the military chiefs to force the overthrow of the Government and bring about a change in German internal politics." Sackett thought it might "be of chief interest to the Department" that underlying the ouster of Brüning was "a definite challenge" to trade union

21 Prittwitz to Dieckhoff, 5 April 1932, GFMR 2380/E195661.
22 Sackett to State, 1 June 1932, FRUS, 1932, 2: 294.
23 Sackett to State, 2 May 1932, transmitting a memorandum by Alfred Klieforth, dated 30 April, 862.00/2745.

influence in government. It was "the land owning class and the big industrialists" who were intent on reversing the paternalism which dominated
German politics. By law and government decree, the trade unions and
Socialists, with Brüning's help, had fixed wages and otherwise undermined
"private ownership's control of their own properties."[24]

The ambassador reminded the State Department that the embassy had
reported "certain big industrialists" were giving significant financial support to Hitler. Far from being deterred from this policy of "playing with
fire," the industrialists increased their support as the Nazi party experienced
"rapid growth." The "land owning class" was moved by the same incentives
and joined the industrialists in a "showdown" with the Brüning government. For two years "their efforts to prevail upon him to curb the power
of the trade unions had borne no fruit – and would not as long as he
remained in office dependent upon the support of the Socialist Party."
They were determined that the time had come for a confrontation with
Brüning. "The method pursued took advantage of the discontent" among
army officers who were also displeased with the support the chancellor
gave to labor unions and the Socialists. Having decided to act, they relied
on the "redoubtable leadership of von Schleicher, the political strong man
of the officer corps, [who] engineered the _coup d'état_ which was responsible for the Government's fall."

On Saturday night, May 28, Sackett attended a dinner at which Brüning
spoke. In a private conversation following the event, the chancellor told
the ambassador of "certain plans" he had for the Lausanne Conference
and his expectation that President Hindenburg would give "public assurance of his complete confidence." Sackett explained that Brüning "had
little doubt that the next day his position would be thoroughly assured."
The German emphasized that it was imperative for the president to put the
generals in their place, but he "expected his full cooperation and he had
no real suspicion of the extent of the intrigues which surrounded him."

In Sackett's account of what happened on Monday morning, May 30,
he made no mention of any letter or other communication he had for
Brüning. The American effort to help the chancellor was an unofficial
gesture and found no place in the public record of the State Department.
In fact, Sackett reported that the chancellor "called me to his office at
10:30 in the morning." The reality that Sackett did not take the initiative
for the meeting is a clear indication that it was already too late to intervene to help Brüning. As a last gesture indicative of their political friendship,
and of German reliance on the United States, Sackett was the only foreign
diplomat the chancellor summoned to hear the news. Brüning told Sackett
in the "strictest confidence" that his cabinet would resign at noon.[25] The

24 The following account is based on Sackett to State, 8 June 1932, FRUS, 1932, 2: 300–
302.
25 Sackett to State, 30 May 1932, 862.00/2757.

president had refused his request to put a stop to the intrigues of the political generals and there was no alternative but to submit his resignation immediately. Sackett noted that Brüning's "surprise and chagrin at the outcome of his conversation with the aged President was quite evident."

Sackett was convinced that while Hindenburg was away from Brüning he had come under the influence of the Prussian Junkers who were among the president's closest friends. His neighbor Elard von Oldenburg-Januschau, "the clever and cunning leader of the East Prussian landowners," had used his influence to link Hindenburg's personal interests with those of the eastern landowners with whom he spent his holiday time. A Nationalist Reichstag delegate, the aged Junker had convinced Hindenburg that Brüning meant to foment an agricultural revolution with his program to help East Elbian farmers, the Osthilfe. The plan was to allot unused land in the large Junker estates to the unemployed in a rural colonization program. Sackett reported that the president had been "belabored" by his friends of the Right to get rid of Brüning. The most influential were the "East Elbian agrarians" who were disturbed by the prospect of a distribution of land. Oldenburg-Januschau, who lived next door to Neudeck, found it convenient to ride over "to whisper in von Hindenburg's ear and further the interests of the clique which downed Brüning."[26]

Sackett saw an analogy to the days of Kaiser Wilhelm II. The chancellor fell from office, not as a result of a lost conflict in the Reichstag, but because the president wanted to change the course of government. The comparison to the Wilhelmine past, he wrote, was "enhanced by resurgent military interference in politics."[27] Erwin Planck told Sackett that Hindenburg did not want to continue shouldering the responsibility of government by emergency decree. Brüning had increasing difficulty in getting the president's signature on each succeeding order. Since Hindenburg's sympathies were with the political Right, he "wanted a parliamentary majority to accept the responsibility."[28] Sackett gave the president credit for "an objective loyalty to democratic principles." He was influenced by his "agrarian and military associates," but also, given the swing to the Right in recent elections, Hindenburg felt compelled to honor the "will of the people" by forming a new government to respect their wishes.[29]

But Brüning did not escape blame, in Sackett's eyes, for the fall of his cabinet. The chancellor created the system of governing by emergency decree, he wrote, "at least in its present extent." That method, which kept him in office so long, was "also his undoing." Sackett speculated that two principal factors contributed to the chancellor's fall. One was the system

26 Eyck, *Weimar Republic*, 2: 265, 293, 382; Sackett to State, 1 and 2 June 1932, 862.00/2781 and 2783.
27 Sackett to State, 1 June 1932, 862.00/2781.
28 Sackett to State, 31 May 1932, 862.00/2764.
29 Sackett to State, 1 June 1932, 862.00/2781.

itself, "which emphasized and developed the power of the President." The other was Brüning's "avoidance of urgent domestic political problems." His failure to deal with the unemployment problem, his neglect to reform his administration or the organization of the Reich, "prevented his remaining in power long enough to achieve the foreign political aims he had set himself." When he realized that he did not have "clear backing at home," he precipitated the decision that led to his resignation.[30]

Both the public and the private representatives of the United States in Germany were at a loss as to what to expect with the fall of their favorite. Sackett reported that the embassy was informed confidentially that there would be no change in German foreign policy in the new government to be formed. Sackett also learned that Brüning refused an offer to stay on in a new government in the position of foreign minister.[31] In other words, the Americans should expect no change from the German government.

American interest, however, was not so much in the German government. The Americans were almost obsessed with the need, first, to keep Brüning in office, and now to see to it that he was returned to the chancellorship. Sackett ventured a guess that it was "too early to discuss intelligently the chances of his 'coming back,' but it may be assumed that a failure of a Government of the extreme Right would again put him on the map in Germany."[32] An American banker reported to the Federal Reserve Bank of New York that Brüning's resignation was a genuine calamity, for there was only a minimal likelihood that he would be returned to office in the immediate future. The chancellor's departure opened up the possibility of a military dictatorship and, worst of all, of a new government pledged to cancellation of debts.[33] Even the German Communist party's presidential candidate Ernst Thälmann, as late as autumn 1932, "still considered Brüning an important personage among bourgeois politicians and a man still on the rise."[34]

The Germans were aware of American apprehensions about not only the new government but also the loss of Brüning as confidant. To remedy those concerns, the newly appointed foreign minister, Baron Konstantin von Neurath, hoped to initiate a relationship with Sackett just as the ambassador had with Brüning. He sought an association with the American diplomat that would be close and intimate, involving frequent and informal talks, all in confidence. The foreign minister's son, a close friend of Alfred Klieforth of the American embassy, attempted to win support for his father by relating details of a confidential talk with the president at which only the Neuraths were present. Hindenburg was an admirer of

30 Ibid.   31 Sackett to State, 30 May 1932, 862.00/2759.
32 Sackett to State, 1 June 1932, 862.00/2781.
33 Telegram from James H. Gannon, sent to the Federal Reserve Bank of New York by H. W. Auburn, attention A. H. Wiggin, 31 May 1932, FRBNY, C-261 German Government.
34 Siegfried Bahne, "Die Kommunistische Partei Deutschlands," 677.

Brüning, he said. The president maintained he had the best relationship with Brüning that he had with any politician. Moreover, they both agreed on policy. The president and chancellor looked for a change to the Right in German politics as soon as possible. Hindenburg deemed it "essential that the prestige of the Reichswehr should be utilized in bringing about the desired change." Brüning, however, disagreed, whereupon "the President continued, Brüning lost his nerve and I guess I did the same thing."[35]

This blatant attempt by the Neuraths, father and son, to ingratiate themselves with the Americans fell on deaf ears. Sackett and the embassy staff were too dedicated to Brüning to be persuaded by such blandishments. Undeterred, the younger Neurath sought to win Sackett's approval with the confidential assertion that the new chancellor was only a "straw man" and that General Schleicher was the real boss. Moreover, the German further confided that he did not trust the general.[36]

It was bad enough in Sackett's view that Brüning was gone, he could not and would not accept his successor with anything less than incredulity. He found it hard to believe that Hindenburg appointed Franz von Papen chancellor. Stimson told the British ambassador that had Papen been appointed as German ambassador to the United States, he "would unhesitatingly be refused."[37] Sackett commented that while one could understand why, "in the eyes of the 'awakening Germany' of the Right, Brüning had to go, it is more difficult to comprehend why von Papen had to come."[38]

Sackett could explain Papen's appointment only in terms of Hitler's success. Hindenburg expected the Nazis to fulfill their obligation to the Reich by supporting a new government of the Right. But Hitler was determined to avoid any participation in the government for the present.[39] Even though the Nazis refused office, they achieved two of their major tactical demands. They wanted Brüning's resignation, and now he was gone. They then wanted new Reichstag elections, which they were promised in return for tolerating the Papen government.[40]

It was not only Americans who were incredulous about Papen's appointment. Sackett reported that the new chancellor was an "unruly" and an extreme right-wing member of Brüning's Center party. The Center party bloc in the Reichstag voted a unanimous resolution "sharply condemning the 'frivolous intrigues of persons devoid of constitutional responsibility'" which led to the resignation of the Brüning cabinet.[41] They then voted to

---

35 Sackett to State, 7 June 1932, 862.002/223.   36 Ibid.
37 Lindsay to Simon, 1 June 1932, DBFP, 3: 148.
38 Sackett to State, 1 June 1932, 862.00/2781.
39 Sackett to State, 31 May 1932, 862.00/2764; Moffat Diary, 14 July 1932.
40 Sackett to State, 31 May, 2 and 15 June 1932, 862.00/2762, 2783, and 2795, 1 June 1932, FRUS, 1932, 2: 294.
41 Sackett to State, 2 June 1932, 862.00/2783.

toss the new chancellor out of their party.[42] At a dinner with the Japanese disarmament delegation in Geneva, Theodore Marriner noted that there was much talk about the fall of the German government, but more emphasis on the "extremely unfortunate" choice of Papen as chancellor.[43]

Stimson was fearful that the French were right, Hindenburg had reverted to type. He had thrown himself into "the laps of the most reactionary elements" in Germany. The secretary was certain that Papen's appointment would make a "tremendously bad impression" in the United States.[44] What especially bothered Americans was the possibility of the restoration of the monarchy in Germany. Although Brüning was a monarchist, he withheld those views from the Americans. Sackett saw the personnel of the Papen government as strongly suggesting a military dictatorship tied to nationalists "having monarchical sympathies."[45] He had reported a resurgence of monarchist support growing parallel with the movement toward the political Right.[46]

In the State Department, J. Pierrepont Moffat noted that at a French embassy Bastille Day dinner, there was talk of a strong man taking over in Germany to form a regency in anticipation of a restoration of the Hohenzollern dynasty.[47] After talking with consular officers stationed in Germany, and taking into account additional information at his disposal, Pierre Boal, chief of the Division of Western European Affairs, was convinced that Papen would be instrumental in the restoration of the monarchy within a year. His guess was that industrialists who supported Hitler did not see the Nazi as proper stuff of which presidents and chancellors were made. They wanted a more responsible person, preferably a Prussian, who could appeal to the traditions and attitudes of the German middle class. Hitler, an Austrian by origin, was too difficult to control. They would probably support a coup that would bring a member of the Hohenzollern family to the throne. Boal noted that there was general discouragement with the republican experiment in Germany. Moreover, when "a German looks backward the first happy period his memory reaches is in the reign of the last Kaiser."[48]

German diplomats, fully aware of American antipathy for the Prussian monarchy and its associated militarism, tended to deny any possible return of the Hohenzollerns.[49] Rudolf Nadolny was an exception. Chief German delegate at Geneva, he had returned to his post as ambassador to Turkey, where he admitted to the American ambassador in Istanbul that the trend was back to monarchy. The only delay, he asserted, was in finding a

42 Sackett to State, 1 June 1932, 862.00/2768 and 2781.
43 Marriner Diary, 1 June 1932.   44 Stimson Diary, 1 June 1932.
45 Sackett to State, 1 June 1932, FRUS, 1932, 2: 294.
46 Sackett to State, 8 March 1932, 862.00/2698.   47 Moffat Diary, 14 July 1932.
48 Boal to Stimson, 4 June 1932, FRUS, 1932, 2: 295–296.
49 Boal to Stimson, 4 June 1932, FRUS, 1932, 2: 296.

suitable candidate for the throne.[50] Undersecretary Castle, who was particularly averse to a restoration, wanted assurance that it would not happen. He virtually asked the German ambassador, Prittwitz, for proof that the monarchy was not part of Germany's future.[51]

While German diplomats denied stories of a restoration, the new minister of the interior, Wilhelm von Gayl, publicly admitted not only that he was a monarchist, but that all the rest of the Papen cabinet shared his view. Sackett remarked that such a position "is perhaps only conceivable in Germany where a considerable antithesis between theoretical considerations and practical action is not necessarily regarded as inconsistent."[52]

Americans were apprehensive about the possibility that the Papen government was a portent for a restored Kaiser. But there was a minor positive side to the new German government. After a talk with the Polish ambassador, Stimson informed the embassies in Berlin and Warsaw that the Poles took a hopeful view of the change. The Poles learned that Papen was a member of a secret society "aimed against Bolshevism." They therefore might regard Poland as a bulwark against communism, and in this respect "the appointment may have grounds for hopefulness."[53] Despite any possible benefits in the struggle against communism, Papen's appointment was a serious problem for the American government; he was subject to criminal prosecution in the United States. In 1915, Papen had been implicated in organizing and financing sabotage while serving as military attaché in the United States and was expelled from the country.[54] With that problem in mind, Sackett inquired if the State Department had any special instructions regarding the embassy's relations with the Papen government.[55]

Stimson, not knowing what to do, advised Sackett to "be guided somewhat by the British attitude with regard to von Papen. I presume that it may be best, for the present at least, to deal with him politely but somewhat distantly."[56] It turned out that one indictment against the new German chancellor was still pending, and the other, for the plot to destroy the Welland Canal, had been "nolle prossed" on March 8.[57] The Americans soon saw no alternative but to forget the entire matter.

50 Charles H. Sherrill, American ambassador in Turkey, to State, 3 August 1932, 500.A15A 4/1432.
51 Castle, Memorandum of a Conversation with Prittwitz, 6 June 1932, FRUS, 1932, 2: 298–300.
52 Sackett to State, 15 June 1932, 862.00/2795.
53 Stimson, Memorandum of a Conversation with Polish Ambassador Tytus Filipowicz, 2 June 1932, sent to Berlin and Warsaw, 6 June, 1932, 862.00/2772.
54 Eyck, *Weimar Republic*, 2: 394.
55 Sackett to State, 1 June 1932, FRUS, 1932, 2: 293–294.
56 Stimson to Sackett, 1 June 1932, FRUS, 1932, 2: 295, in the original draft of the despatch, Stimson had written that Sackett should "follow" the British attitude, 862.00/ 2766.
57 Stimson to Sackett, 2 June 1932, FRUS, 1932, 2: 295.

Meanwhile, Hitler was achieving all he wanted for the time being. He had no intention of becoming part of a government the Nazis did not control. Sackett estimated that the Nazi leader was "averse to taking over power for a considerable time." He found two reasons to explain Hitler's political tactics. In the first place, he could not yet win a majority of votes in the Reichstag and therefore was forced to wait. Sackett estimated that based on results in recent elections, Hitler could expect no more than 45 percent of the vote in forthcoming elections. He next explained Hitler's reluctance to govern in terms of inadequate Nazi leadership. The Nazi leader was averse to entering any government because "he recognizes that in his party there is no proper Cabinet material available."[58] That was part of a widely held view that the Nazis would have to enter a government to "win their spurs" or, as was more likely, "discredit themselves by a public exposure of their practical incompetence."[59]

Sackett believed that Hitler was willing to tolerate the Papen government because he saw it as merely transitional. Promised new elections, the Nazis anticipated that the will of the people would be manifested in a new wave of enthusiasm that would sweep them into office.[60] Although he gave at least tacit support to the Papen government, Sackett wrote that Hitler refused to conform to parliamentary norms.[61] He counted on an acute economic crisis, even a general collapse, after the Lausanne Conference.[62]

In keeping with Hitler's goal of taking over power after a catastrophe, the Nazis resorted more than ever to unruly and disruptive tactics. They engaged in a "pitched battle" with the Communists in the Prussian Diet. In what Sackett called the worst conflict that had ever occurred in a German legislative body, he recounted that inkwells, water bottles, and chairs were thrown about, resulting in numerous casualties. The party war between Nazis and Communists spread widely through German cities, making it increasingly difficult for the authorities to maintain order. Sackett was lamenting by the last days of June that he could "distinctly sense a growing apprehension that the Government may find it harder than it has reckoned to resist exaggerated Nazi demands."[63]

Sackett found it difficult to find the difference between the goals of the new government and those of Hitler. Papen complained that the German people were being worn down morally by "cultural bolshevism." Socialists had made a welfare institution of the state and had permeated all fields of

58 Sackett to State, 4 June 1932, FRUS, 1932, 2: 297.
59 Rumbold to Simon, 15 August 1932, DBFP, 4: 29–30.
60 Sackett to State, 1 June 1932, 862.00/2781.
61 Sackett to State, 4 June 1932, FRUS, 1932, 2: 297.
62 Wiley Memorandum of a Conversation with Planck, 9 May 1932, Box 41, Gibson Papers.
63 Sackett to State, 1 and 24 June 1932, 862.00/2782, 2790.

public life with Marxist ideas. The American ambassador commented that Papen's references to "a 'new Germany' smack of the Nazi's 'Third Reich.' "[64]

The close ties between Hitler and the Papen government were disturbing to American diplomats. Not only had Brüning been removed from office, the Reichstag was dissolved on June 4. Sackett speculated that a third Nazi tactical demand would almost certainly soon be achieved.[65] Ten days after the Reichstag was dissolved, Papen lifted the ban on the Storm Troops. The Nazis appeared to be riding a wave of success. Sackett, searching for signs of ebbing, struck at the "lack of sophistication of the Nazi leaders in most matters except in the field of demagogic politics."[66]

Political reports from the embassy in June were replete with pejorative analyses of Hitler and the Nazis. Diplomats described the mounting violence and frequency of Storm Trooper clashes with the police and Nazi opponents.[67] The Nazis were certainly not a group Sackett wanted to see in government. It was therefore heartening news to learn of the ambivalence of Nazi success in provincial elections. Although they won seats, Sackett pointed out that Nazis had trouble winning votes in the large cities. German farmers were "particularly susceptible to Nazi agitation," and the "Nazi wave has not spent itself," but, most importantly, the Nazis were not capable of winning a majority in the new Reichstag.[68]

George Gordon was back at his post in Berlin and had drafted the despatch. Stimson circulated a handwritten note through the department quoting Gordon's estimation that the Nazis would not get a majority. He evidently hoped to bolster the morale of diplomats who feared Hitler's rise to power.[69] Still, there was a growing sense among Americans that with Hitler or without him, Germany was becoming an unpredictable and dangerous problem. At Geneva, General Simonds, of the disarmament delegation, viewed the Germans as much more "cocky." The membership of the German delegation had not changed, but their attitude was pronouncedly different. They let it be known they would sign no agreement that did not include equality of treatment and removal of the objectionable military clauses in the Versailles Treaty. These demands made general agreement next to impossible.[70] In the State Department, Feis complained that "the Germans grow more and more hysterically conscious of their own grievances and less and less aware of the judgment of the rest

64 Sackett to State, 7 June 1932, 862.002/222.
65 Sackett to State, 1 and 2 June 1932, 862.00/2781–2783; see Thilo Vogelsang, "Zur Politik Schleichers Gegenüber der NSDAP 1932," VJZG, 86–118.
66 Sackett to State, 7 June 1932, 862.00/2785.
67 Sackett to State, 20 June 1932, 862.00/2797.
68 Sackett to Stimson, 7 June 1932, 862.00/2786.
69 The note is filed with Sackett to State, 7 June 1932, 862.00/2786.
70 Gen. Simonds to Lt. Gailey, 17 June 1932, Box 41, Simonds Papers.

of the world." He saw good reason for alarm at what might happen in Germany.[71]

The unfolding of events in Germany accelerated American dismay when Papen moved to establish Reich control over the powerful Prussian state. A conflict between the provincial and central governments had been a continuing matter in Weimar Germany, worsened by the controversy over the Nazi Storm Troopers. Provincial governments had been responsible for the ban of the Nazi private army. After the prohibition had been lifted by Papen, the already severe differences between the states and the Reich government had deteriorated badly. Baden and Bavaria decreed local laws against uniformed Storm Troopers and prohibited Nazi use of radio broadcasting stations. Papen was exasperated by this evasion of Reich authority and resolved to do something about provincial exploitation of states' rights.[72]

The problem was particularly acute in Prussia, where the Socialists controlled the government but the Nazis were the largest party in the Diet. The Social Democratic leaders in the largest German state were not inclined to continue in office in an "acting" capacity. But there seemed no option since they could not govern effectively without Nazi cooperation and the Hitler party refused to accept any political responsibility. Papen decided to resolve the impasse by appointing himself Reich commissioner for Prussia and removing the Socialist government. When the Socialists declared the decree unconstitutional, Papen issued a second decree in effect placing Berlin-Brandenburg under martial law and removing the Socialists by force on July 20.[73]

The Papen government was aware that this move would alarm Americans. To forestall such a reaction, they informed both Sackett and Stimson. Papen invited Sackett to lunch the day before the action was announced. The chancellor explained that the move was imperative in the interest of maintaining public order. Sackett saw it as another attempt to placate the Nazis and win Hitler's support or toleration of the Papen government.[74] In explaining the need to take over the Prussian government forcibly, Ambassador Prittwitz told Stimson that the situation was "not as bad as it looked." He went on to explain that it was necessary in order to deal effectively with the riots between Nazis and Communists.[75]

Earlier, when Brüning had suggested the possibility of appointing a Reich commissioner for Prussia, with Nazi agreement, Sackett perceived

71 Feis to Frankfurter, 15 June 1932, Box 54, Frankfurter Papers.
72 Sackett to State, 20, 21, and 24 June 1932, 862.00/2797, 2788, and 2790.
73 See Rudolf Morsey, "Zur Geschichte des 'Preussenschlags' am 20. Juli 1932," VJZG, 430–439.
74 Sackett to State, 19 July 1932, 862.00/2803.
75 Stimson, Memorandum of a Conversation with Prittwitz, 21 July 1932, Stimson Papers, 162: 536–537.

such an action as a reasonable resolution of the impasse in Prussia. Even more, the American saw it as an effective means of dealing with the Nazis. But now, when Papen made a similar, if more highhanded move, Sackett disapproved and viewed the action not only as a way of placating the Nazis, but also as part of a campaign by the political Right to destroy the Socialists and the trade unions.[76]

Sackett maintained that the action would further exasperate the South German states and bring the Catholic parties that controlled them closer to the Socialists. Together they controlled the largest and most powerful trade unions in Germany and now Papen would be faced "with the united opposition of the Catholic and Left republican parties," which Sackett estimated were still a formidable force in support of the Weimar Republic.[77] Gordon calculated that Papen was giving the Nazi Storm Troopers free rein to campaign in the Reichstag elections. It was part of a general program by Papen to make concessions to Hitler in return for his support.[78]

Reichstag elections were set for July 31, and as their political support grew the Nazis became more rowdy and intractable. Hitler's refusal to cooperate with any other party, and his continuing attacks on the Papen government in spite of its frequent attempts to mollify the Nazis, were causing a shift in political alignments. Gordon noted that the "arrogance with which the Nazis consistently pursue their tactics of ignoring all other parties of the Right is viewed with manifest and growing apprehension." Parties that had "openly sympathized with the Hitler movement are apparently alarmed by the prospects of a Nazi Government" after the elections. Rightist parties were now more amenable to joining forces with the Center party "in order to prevent a purely Nazi regime." Gordon saw evidence that General Schleicher was working "to prevent a purely Nazi" government in Prussia.[79]

At the same time, the danger of a Hitler regime was causing some on the Left to consider cooperation between the Socialists and Communists. The idea was to combine those groups with wide labor union support. But, Gordon noted, the appeals for unity among Left intellectuals would remain a "pious wish so long as the Communists continue to insist that they are entitled to the leadership of a united labor party." The Communists were unrealistic, for they were losing members to the Nazis and their growth had been checked by Hitler. Their appeals to unity were, according to Gordon, merely a tactical move to win further worker support. He anticipated that the labor parties would enter the election as bitter enemies and further predicted correctly that "an oppressive dictatorial regime" under

76 Sackett to State, 3 May and 19 July 1932, 862.00/2742 and 2803.
77 Sackett to State, 14 and 19 June 1932, 862.00/2794 and 2803.
78 Gordon to State, 25 July 1932, 862.00/2815.
79 Gordon to State, 28 June and 25 July 1932, 862.00/2799, 2815.

the Nazis would "do more to bring about a cooperation of the two rival parties than all attempts by their own sympathizers."[80]

It did not appear possible, but in the campaign preceding the July 31 Reichstag elections, the severity of political violence worsened. The prominent role of the Storm Troopers in the ferocity of the contest again raised the issue of how Hitler's private army, now 400,000 men, was being financially supported. The embassy's answer consistently was that antisocialist industrialists were largely responsible. Then Sackett was confronted by a specific attempt to raise money for Hitler.

An official of the Chemical National Bank of New York informed Sackett of an attempt by the former Kaiser's financial agent to get a loan of 2 million marks. The ostensible purpose was to improve five Hohenzollern estates. Sackett perceived the political significance of such a loan since the Kaiser's "family has been notoriously sympathetic to the Hitler movement." The diplomat and the banker agreed that the stated purpose of the loan was unconvincing and agreed that the matter should be pursued no further. Sackett asked the State Department to consult with the bank's president and "to sound a note of warning at home," particularly since the embassy staff had been hearing rumors of late indicating that the Hohenzollerns were attempting to raise a considerable amount of money. It was evident to Sackett that the funds were earmarked for Hitler.[81]

According to Sackett, the election campaign was conducted under conditions that Papen made extremely favorable to the Nazis.[82] American diplomats shared the fears of many in Germany that political violence had gone far beyond acceptable bounds. Fighting and bloodshed were part of the German political scene and in Gordon's view did not warrant extensive reporting because they were so commonplace. But two recent incidents of political murder, he felt, were matters of "deep significance." On both occasions the Reichswehr was called in to quell the clashes. The rioters were fired on by the army and many were arrested; in all cases they were members of the Socialist Reichsbanner or other Leftist groups.[83]

Calling in the Reichswehr in the bloody disorders was an escalation of political violence that Gordon found alarming. This was especially true of the current incidents, in which the Reichswehr role was covered up in police reports. The American had no doubt that the army would obey orders if the offenders were Communists, or even, perhaps, if they were Socialists. What he feared was whether the Reichswehr might be so "permeated with Nazi propaganda that it would refuse to obey orders to fire on Nazi disturbers of the peace." The new military attaché in the American embassy, Lieutenant Colonel Jacob W. S. Wuest, speculated that

80 Gordon to State, 28 June 1932, 862.00/2799.
81 Sackett to State, 13 July 1932, 862.00/001 W64/145.
82 Sackett to State, 2 August 1932, 862.00/2820.
83 Gordon to State, 18 July 1932, 862.00/2812.

"fully ninety percent of the officers in Berlin are sympathetic toward the Nazi movement." That is, they were impressed by the spirit and nationalism of the Nazi following. They were not as drawn to Hitler, but there was a "strong leaning" toward Hitlerism among army officers. They regarded the Nazi movement as a phenomenon that would "be absorbed by the thinking classes of Germany."[84] This information was not likely to placate American fears that the Nazis might take over by force. However, Gordon had been assured by the "highest authority" that the Reichswehr's loyalty to the government was unquestioned. The issue, he felt, was "one of the most disturbing elements in the present situation of this country."[85]

Although the Americans were apprehensive about the escalating violence during the Reichstag elections, they rejoiced at the final results. Not only did Hitler fail to win a majority, his prospects for forming a majority coalition of the Right were "remote." In spite of the very favorable conditions under which Papen allowed them to campaign, the Nazis were able to increase their vote only slightly, a "significant and interesting development," according to Sackett. The ambassador was pleased to report that Hitler's party won only 350,000 more votes than he personally got in the presidential election. In Sackett's view, "the crest of the Nazi wave has probably been reached." The ambassador's only disappointment was that the voter turnout had not been as heavy as he "hoped and expected." He believed that more voters would have helped the Social Democrats and the Center.[86]

Hitler, Sackett reported, had failed in his goal to destroy the political Left. He had, however, inadvertently succeeded in hurting the parties of the middle. The Economic, State, and People's parties were now practically "wiped out." Hugenberg, who helped put Hitler where he was, "now cuts a sorry figure." His party, if combined with the Nazis, fell short of a majority by 21 seats, and there appeared to be no possibility of a Rightist coalition. The Nazis, now the largest party in Germany, won 230 seats in a Reichstag of 607 members. The Socialists had 133, the combined Center and Bavarian People's parties had 98, the Communists 89, and Hugenberg's Nationalists 37. With the support of smaller parties, Hitler might be able to command 283 votes when 304 were needed for a majority. Sackett wrote that although the election was not a "decisive set-back for the Nazis . . . it does tend to indicate that the consistent level of strength which they have attained and been able to maintain is about the maximum that they can hope for."[87]

84 Lt. Col. Jacob W. S. Wuest, memorandum, 30 June 1932, War/MID Box 2082, 2657-B-735/8.
85 Gordon to State, 18 July 1932, 862.00/2812.
86 Sackett to State, 1 and 2 August 1932, FRUS, 1932, 2: 302, 305, 2 August 1932, 862.00/2820.
87 Sackett to State, 1 August, FRUS, 1932, 2: 303, 2 August 1932, 862.00/2820.

Papen could find little to be pleased about in the election. The Nazi position was strong, but there was still little hope for Reichstag support for his government. Sackett had almost no sympathy for the chancellor, at one point characterizing several of Papen's declarations as "threadbare."[88] He now reported that the Papen cabinet had considered outlawing the Communist party so that a Right majority could be created in a reduced Reichstag. This step, which Hitler was to take less than a year later, was shunned by the Papen government on the ground that Communist voters would then support the Social Democrats, who, with the Center, could command a majority.[89] The chancellor was in trouble with no apparent way out.

Searching for support, Papen appealed to the United States. Sackett reported that, in a radio address directed to the American public, he left "the impression that a civil war would probably have broken out in Germany if his Government had not taken the reins of power, and that the Nazis are a harmless or even rather estimable patriotic organization." Sackett explained that the Papen claims required "some checking and analysis." In the first place, Germany might have been in a state of latent civil war, but Brüning had kept the situation well in hand. Then, in a remarkable lack of self-analysis, Sackett assailed the use of the Red Scare as a tool to achieve political goals.[90]

Forgetting his own use of just such threats on occasion, and his friend Brüning's more frequent use of the tactic, Sackett complained:

> To further their own political ends, leaders of the so-called national parties in Germany have frequently been inclined to play up the Communist menace in order to be able to accuse the more moderate parties of laxity in dealing with this problem. The deep-rooted aversion of the American people to Communism has apparently encouraged Chancellor von Papen again to resort to these tactics, this time for foreign consumption.

The entire speech, according to Sackett, "portrayed the Nazis in an unduly favorable light" and cleared them of their share of blame for political violence. Sackett then made his major point against the use of the Red Scare. Papen's description of what was happening in Germany, he wrote, "to my mind" had "the aspect of yet another phase of the 13 year-old policy persisted in by the German Government of exaggerating the dangers of communism in order to secure approval for measures which this Government has taken or desires to take." Sackett was obviously moving farther away from the notion that the Communists were a significant danger to the Weimar Republic.

As was so often the case, the ambassador rallied to the defense of the

88 Sackett to State, 15 June 1932, 862.00/2795.
89 Sackett to State, 2 August 1932, 862.00/2820.
90 The following is from Sackett to State, 2 August 1932, FRUS, 1932, 2: 303–306.

Socialists. Sackett wrote that it was mistaken to believe that "effective resistance to Communism" came only from the political Right. He went on to praise the Social Democrats as being "in many respects a most effective bulwark against Communism." At the same time Sackett emphasized that he meant in no way to diminish the importance of the Communists "as an actively subversive element."

Going into considerable detail to counter almost every point Papen wished to make, Sackett agreed that Communist fighting units could not be ignored. They were, however, illegal and were hardly the sole cause of political violence. Papen, he wrote, failed to mention that the much stronger Nazi Storm Troopers were allowed to engage in open-air demonstrations and wear their uniforms as a consequence of his lifting the ban imposed by Brüning. After Papen countermanded the Brüning order, the "political casualty list began to take on formidable proportions." The Nazis were obviously the principal source of political violence. Unlike the Communists, however, the Storm Troopers were legal, "permitted to wear uniforms and are for the most part housed in barracks."

The entire tenor of Papen's radio address reflected "the benevolent attitude" of his government to the Nazis, Sackett continued. In the recent election, "the Nazis had everything in their favor. Their strategic position was perhaps never more favorable" than it was in the election campaign. Even though Papen made many important concessions to Hitler, the Nazis persisted in conducting their campaign in opposition to his government. Still, Papen characterized the Nazis as "a constructive force striving only for national regeneration, while the aims of the Communists are purely destructive."

Sackett was disturbed by more than Papen's radio address. He questioned the ability of the government to cope with growing Nazi terrorism. Political violence continued to escalate after the election. The Nazis were reported to have established "a veritable reign of terror" in East Prussia. Disorders were reported throughout Germany "and made clear that a premeditated plan of terrorism was being pursued." Nazi attacks on Communists, Socialists, and Jews were a daily occurrence and were so numerous it was impossible to keep an accurate tally. In the despatch entitled "Nazi Outrages," Sackett pointed out that the thugs almost always evaded arrest. Police and civil officers were being dismissed "simply because they were objectionable to the Nazis." The morale of the police was very low, and the ambassador expressed the fear that Hitler might "demand the policing of Prussia, if not the Reich, by his 'private army.' "[91]

Political violence was so widespread that Sackett expressed his anxiety that Hitler might be brought to power to bring the disorder to an end. He

---

91 Sackett to State, 9 August 1932, FRUS, 1932, 2: 306–308, more in the original, 862.00/2827.

cabled that "the last two days have been intensely active politically behind the scenes. As matters stand this evening the dismissal of Papen by President Hindenburg and his offering of the chancellorship to Hitler appear as distinct possibilities."[92]

The shock of the brief cable's import shot through the State Department like a bolt of lightning. President Hoover evidently wanted to know what was going to happen in Germany, and several days were spent trying to unravel the meaning of events. But there was no further word from Sackett. There is no greater evidence that the State Department was paying close attention to Sackett's despatches than its alarm when the ambassador failed to send one. After waiting for five days to hear from Berlin, Undersecretary Castle shot back a cable of his own to Sackett:[93]

> I hope you will find it possible to send more frequent and complete telegraphic reports on the situation in Germany during these critical days. What we want is not so much factual reporting as an analysis of the political situation and the general trend of its probable development.

Just as had happened a year before, the embassy staff must have been stunned by the accusation underlying the brief telegram. During the financial crisis in 1931, the State Department made a similar demand, to which Sackett responded that the information had already been sent in numerous despatches and consular reports. He agreed, however, to consolidate the material in a summary for the secretary.[94]

As in the earlier instance, the crux of the problem was in Washington, not in Berlin. In mid-July, Jay Pierrepont Moffat remarked that the Division of Western European Affairs was in disarray. Within days, much to his surprise, he was placed in charge.[95] A few weeks later, he wrote Gordon that the weakest area in the division was in German affairs. There was no one who had been stationed in Germany or who could work in the German language. He considered Germany to be central to the entire situation in Europe but confessed that it had been given less than its due in the department. To remedy the situation, he himself meant to give it as much time as possible. This was a necessity because he had been unable to find a single qualified person on the list of 530 foreign service officers.[96]

When George Gordon returned to his post in Berlin in June, he restored the embassy to its familiar ways. That meant there would be no contact

---

92 Sackett to State, 10 August 1932, 862.00/2817.
93 Castle to Sackett 15 August 1932, FRUS, 1932, 2: 309.
94 Stimson to American Embassy, Berlin, and Sackett to State, 18 June 1931, 862.51/3051A, and 3052.
95 Moffat Diary, 13 and 14 July 1932.
96 Moffat to Gordon, 9 August, and Moffat to Boal, 20 August 1932, bMS Am 1407 (3), 1933, Moffat Papers; Moffat Diary, 27 August 1932.

with either the Nazis or the other opposition parties. Because Wiley had been the principal connection with Nazis, there was no foreign service officer in the embassy to pursue the meaning of the latest events, and particularly the alarming possibility that Hitler might be named chancellor. Moffat hoped he might be able to move Castle to shake up the embassy in Berlin for more analysis. He revealed he had written Gordon that he intended to place greater stress on German matters, and asked Castle if he might write Sackett requesting analytical studies more frequently. At the same time, Moffat suggested the possibility that the undersecretary raise the question of the embassy's lack of contact with opposition groups.[97]

Five days later there was still no word from the American embassy on what Moffat deemed to be an acute political crisis. He then drafted a cable, which was sent over Castle's signature, rebuking the Berlin embassy for its lack of analytical reporting. Moffat complained to Boal, who was now assigned to Canada, that the Berlin embassy had not sent a word in the preceding two critical weeks. Why then did the embassy remain silent in this period deemed so important by Moffat?

The overarching reason was that the heart had been taken out of the embassy mission when Brüning was removed from office. Even a cursory reading of embassy despatches reveals a lack of élan, supplanted by a general sense of distaste and foreboding. Papen was unacceptable to the Americans, and the possibility that Hitler might be named chancellor was an event nearly intolerable to contemplate. The sense of loss that permeated the embassy is understandable in Sackett's case since he was not a professional diplomat. It is less forgivable in Gordon, who, given his stiff attention to protocol, should have been able to handle the embassy's government-to-government relationship to Germany better than the ambassador. Gordon later explained that he was loath to cable any information because it would involve mere speculation.[98]

Part of the answer lies in the fact that very little actually happened. Hitler did have an audience with Hindenburg, but it led to no change in the situation. In spite of that, according to Rumbold, the result of the interview was "awaited with an interest which amounted to real anxiety."[99] A reader of the *Berliner Tageblatt* would have been exposed to tense anticipation beginning on August 9 and culminating on August 15 with the headline "Hitler Exposed, Wanted to Exercise the Same Power as Mussolini." [*Hitlers Entlarvung, Er wollte herrschen wie Mussolini.*][100]

One possible explanation for the lack of an American response is that the embassy might have been nearly deserted. It was vacation time, and the

97 Moffat to Castle, 10 August 1932, bMS Am 1407 (2), Moffat Papers.
98 Gordon to Castle, 2 September 1932, Castle Papers – Germany, HHPL.
99 Rumbold to Simon, 15 August 1932, DBFP, 4: 31.
100 *Berliner Tageblatt*, 9–15 August 1932, a.m. and p.m. editions; a feature story on August 15 proclaimed August 13 a day of historical importance.

embassy was shorthanded and in greater turmoil than ever with Gordon back in charge.[101] Even if that were the case, the fact is that they were caught off guard. They did not anticipate any significant activity. Sackett had just written a despatch revealing his expectation that it was likely that no "final decision" would be reached on the fate of the Papen cabinet until the end of August, when the Reichstag was to convene.[102] Sackett's factual reporting was excellent, but he was crippled in his analysis by wishful thinking. A Hitler government was unthinkable, which left him with the dream of Brüning's return. In any case, Sackett cannot escape the responsibility for the embassy's failure to report in a timely fashion on Hitler's meeting with Hindenburg.

Moffat complained that he learned more from Norman Armour, the counselor of embassy in Paris, than he got from Sackett. But what he learned was not credible in Berlin. After speaking with Premier Herriot, Armour reported the real danger was that the Germans were ready to repudiate the Treaty of Versailles. Germany might simply "thumb her nose at the rest of the world and ask what are they going to do about it."[103] The Berlin embassy undoubtedly did not report on such a probability because there was no evidence that the Germans were ready to take such a drastic step at that time. Instead, Papen tried to win foreign and especially American support for his position as a moderate.

The Castle cable did stir the embassy to evaluate the current situation in what Moffat described in glowing terms as among the best analyses he had ever read.[104] Later, Castle was moved to write a letter of apology to Gordon, confessing that the department had been worked up over the "lurid stories" they had heard about events in Germany. He commiserated with the counselor about the lack of qualified staff and requested that Gordon make some recommendations regarding personnel. But most important, he gently nudged Gordon in the direction of making contact with the Nazis. He recognized that the diplomat could not devote his time to such activity, but appealed for "someone in the embassy" to get on friendly terms with opposition parties, meaning, of course, the Nazis. That, Castle suggested, was "the only way the Embassy can get a complete and well reasoned picture of the country as a whole."[105]

When Sackett did take pen in hand, he drew up an astute reply that accurately predicted the course of events for the next several months. As soon as it arrived, the cable was sent to President Hoover as a reliable

101 Ferrell, *Frank B. Kellogg; Henry L. Stimson*, 322–323n12; McVitty memoir.
102 Sackett to State, 6 August 1932, 862.00/2826.
103 Moffat Diary, 16 August 1932.
104 Moffat Diary, 16 August, and Moffat to Boal, 20 August 1932, bMS Am 1407 (2), Moffat Papers.
105 Castle to Gordon, personal and confidential, 17 August 1932, Castle Papers – Germany, HHPL.

forecast of things to come in Germany.[106] Sackett cabled that Hitler had met with Hindenburg, Schleicher, and Papen on August 13. The Nazi leader's demand that he be named chancellor with power to form a Nazi government was refused. That meant that the political situation had lost its "immediate acuteness." Sackett outlined several possible combinations of parties that might be able to govern. The possibility he thought "most likely," and which proved to be correct, was the dissolution of the Reichstag and the calling of new elections. The only certainty he saw in "this maze of uncertainties" was that Hindenburg and his advisers would "not hesitate to stretch the constitution to the uttermost limit." It was difficult to predict what the Nazis might do, he complained, because they "are stable only in their complete intransigence." He was less certain of the loyalty of the Reichswehr than he had been a year before, but he was inclined to believe that the army would obey Hindenburg's orders. The American diplomat's despatch accurately predicted elections within sixty days after the dissolution of the Reichstag. The Papen government, he foresaw, would "remain in office for at least three months more."[107]

Sackett amplified his cabled despatch with a brilliant analysis of events and future prospects:

> The keynote of the present political situation would seem to be Hitler's dogged intention to rule alone. The expectation frequently voiced here that failure of his policies would result in large and immediate losses of following for Hitler does not take into account the blindness of great sections of his adherents. Hitler, one of the biggest show-men since P. T. Barnum, and his silver-tongued lieutenant, Goebbels, are past adepts at twisting events to suit their fancies and purposes, and indefatigable spellbinders. Readers of the *Voelkischer Beobachter* and *Angriff*, the two chief Nazi press organs, have read, and will continue to read, of nothing but Nazi successes, and this policy could be pursued all the more brazenly if Hitler were in power, and could suppress the opposition journals at will.

The ambassador added that Hitler was conducting a farsighted policy of directing successful party propaganda at schoolchildren. He regretted that "time is working in Hitler's favor as successive classes graduate and come of voting age," and winced at the image of youngsters "issuing from the schools singing the 'Horst Wessel Song,' the lurid Nazi Marseillaise."

The events of the summer had been unpleasant for Sackett. The ambassador was almost inconsolable about the fall of the Brüning government, and longed for his return to office. He found solace in the thought that Hitler had "suffered some loss of prestige" when he was turned down by Hindenburg. Resorting to wishful thinking again, he wrote of the "distinct possibility" that the Nazis movement would split into "two or more

106 Castle to Lawrence Richey, 17 August 1932, 862.00/2822.
107 This account is from Sackett to State, 17 August 1932, FRUS, 1932, 2: 309–313.

factions." The militant Nazis might rebel against the policy of "tame parliamentary opposition." Led by the "demagogue Goebbels," who "was constantly inciting to violence," they might demand that "Hitler and the more moderate leaders" abandon the policy of legality. Again casting Hitler in the position of the patient conservative, Sackett feared that the militants might get out of control "and force Hitler to disavow them."

Ambassador Sackett was able to discern much about Hitler, but he was unable to plumb the depths to which the Nazi leader would go. Like almost all his peers he had a blind faith in progress, and in the Enlightenment-style ideas that drove Western civilization. That made it nearly impossible for his generation to comprehend Hitler. Sackett perceived him as moderate on the one hand, but unrelenting in his determination to rule Germany alone, under a Nazi dictatorship. One hope the ambassador held out was that Hitler would contain the savagery associated with Goebbels. Another was that the Nazi was almost certain to lose support in the next round of Reichstag elections, and, as so many observers were prone to do at the time, Sackett placed his hope in the conviction that the responsibilities of office brought moderation with them.

Prospects for the German future looked grim. All signs indicated that Hitler would soon come to power.[108] Ever conscious of the Communist threat, Sackett wrote like-minded Undersecretary Castle that strong central government was inevitable in Germany. It was necessary to counteract growing Communist party strength in the Reichstag.[109] But in spite of his fear of communism, and his personal experience in the Harlan County strike, the ambassador would place his personal hope for the future of the Weimar Republic in a Leftist-oriented solution of the nation's predicament. He considered the Socialists and trade unions as the most powerful forces that could save Germany from Hitler and the Nazis. In an odd twist of the political coils, General Kurt von Schleicher, the man who brought Brüning down, became Sackett's choice as an acceptable alternative to Hitler.

108 Gordon to State, 7 November 1932, 862.00/2863.
109 Castle Memorandum, 10 November 1932, FRUS, 1932, 2: 318.

10

The decline of Hitler and the Nazis

TWO NEW CONCERNS would occupy Ambassador Sackett, frequently taking him away from the embassy chancery in Berlin. He would return to the United States to campaign for the reelection of President Hoover and busy himself with the organization of the economic conference he and Brüning had worked to realize. Meanwhile, Hitler's fortunes seemed to deteriorate beyond redemption. Before Sackett left for home in early October 1932, the outlook appeared to be optimistic for Hoover, and the international economic community appeared prepared to remedy its problems. There even seemed to be a good chance that the politics of the Weimar Republic could be resolved in a satisfactory way. But what struck Sackett as encouraging for a time would dissolve into one misfortune after another. Events and forces beyond Sackett's control worked to undo his best efforts.

As a political appointee, Sackett was obliged to campaign on behalf of his benefactor, President Hoover. It was a task the ambassador undertook gladly, and with enthusiasm. After Brüning's fall he wanted to get back to the United States right away. He could use the distraction. Sackett wanted to return home even before Brüning's resignation, but Hoover felt it was too soon for the ambassador to leave his post.[1]

It was mid-August before the president informed the State Department that he was "anxious" for the ambassador to return to the United States in the fall.[2] Castle and others discussed the matter and came to the conclusion that there was no immediacy because Hoover had not yet decided on "a clear cut policy for Sackett to preach."[3] The ambassador was in Geneva engrossed in organizing the World Economic Conference and was reluctant to leave that important work. As the outlook for Hoover's

---

1 Sackett to Hoover, 29 April, and Hoover to Sackett, 13 May 1932, Foreign Affairs – Diplomats, Sackett, F. M., HHPL.
2 Walter H. Newton to Castle, 15 August 1932, Foreign Affairs – Diplomats, Sackett, F. M., HHPL.
3 Moffat Diary, 7 September 1932.

reelection grew bleak, the president was adamant that he wanted Sackett "to come back immediately."[4] Walter Newton, of the White House staff, telephoned Sackett and arrangements were made for the ambassador to leave about October 5.[5] Beginning on October 4 Sackett went on furlough without pay until the campaign was over, on November 12.[6]

His assignment was to campaign in Kentucky, especially among German-American voters. Louisville had a large German population, most of whom were Democrats.[7] Hoover was apprehensive about losing the German vote, and he was so worried about the ethnic vote in general that he tried to get Ambassador Garrett in Rome to assert that the Mussolini government supported him. The ambassador objected, on the ground that not only was it improper, but it meant trying to get the Italian vote thinking Italian rather than American. Garrett feared an anti-Fascist backlash.[8]

Sackett was active and visible enough to draw criticism for campaigning while serving the nation abroad.[9] Regardless of the criticism, he was confident of success. He wired Hoover with the optimistic report that he was "meeting good response from German groups and believe you are gaining rapidly."[10] But in spite of Sackett's optimistic prediction, Hoover lost Kentucky and the national election to Franklin D. Roosevelt.

Sackett was far from the mark in assessing the president's chances in Kentucky. In 1928, Hoover had been the first Republican presidential candidate to win a majority in the Blue Grass state, with 59 percent of the vote. In 1932 the same majority voted for Roosevelt. The one-time Republican stronghold in the coal-mining southeastern part of Kentucky was suffering intensely from the depression. Voters from the scene of the Harlan County strike and the Battle of Evarts were moving into the Democratic column.[11] Roosevelt won the very area that had threatened Sackett's Senate seat and was instrumental in his becoming ambassador to Germany.

After the disappointing results of the American elections, Sackett returned to Berlin, where he was confronted by two paramount matters: the organization of the World Economic Conference, and the impending fall of the Papen government. In August, Sackett and Norman Davis had been

4 Ferdinand Mayer, "Diary of Conversations and Events at Geneva," 500. A15A A4/1469–1/2.
5 Newton, White House notes, 30 September 1932, Foreign Affairs – Diplomats, Sackett, F. M., HHPL.
6 FRUS, 1932, 2: 317n42; 123 Sackett, F. M./89; *New York Times*, 5 October, 12 November 1932.
7 Fenton, *Politics in the Border States*, 6; Pearce, *Divide and Dissent*, 28.
8 Moffat Diary, 22 September, 2 November 1932.
9 File, 28 November 1932, 123 Sackett, F. M./154.
10 Sackett to Hoover, 26 October 1932, Foreign Affairs – Diplomats, Sackett, F. M., HHPL, and Sackett to Villard, 24 October 1932, bMS Am 1323 (3374), Villard Papers.
11 Malcolm E. Jewell and Everett W. Cunningham, *Kentucky Politics*, 6–7; Pearce, *Divide and Dissent*, 28.

appointed to make the arrangements for the International Monetary and Economic Conference,[12] and Sackett was eager to get started. At the height of the campaign for President Hoover's reelection, he wrote to his friend Oswald Garrison Villard that he was expected "at Geneva at the earliest possible moment for the Economic Conference work."[13]

The idea for the international conference originated in December 1930 when Sackett and Brüning talked about President Hoover taking the initiative to call such a meeting of heads of state. In spite of several fits and starts, including long delays after the tragic death of Undersecretary Joseph Cotton, Sackett continued to intervene with Hoover to call such a conference. The Germans were eager for him to succeed and kept the idea alive.[14] But Sackett, no longer as enthusiastic as he had been when Brüning was chancellor, assured the Germans in June 1932, just after Brüning's resignation, that the economic conference was in the preparatory stages and that Germany would be officially approached later. As a mark of his lack of zeal, Sackett informed Bülow "on instructions from his government," rather than with the personal sense of triumph he would have exhibited had he been able to give the same news to Brüning.[15]

Republican administrations in the interwar years had refused to participate in international economic conferences at Genoa and Geneva. The depression, however, had undermined their confidence in the ability of private sector experts to handle the intricacies of international economics and its relationship to domestic economic concerns. The system of corporatism was going through a period of transition until it was discredited.[16] Sackett had little faith that the world's economic problems could be solved by experts from the private sector. He insisted, and would continue to insist, that responsible officials in the governments involved should take the lead.[17] The failure of the private sector to accomplish the reconciliation of domestic and foreign goals was recognized when those responsibilities were increasingly placed under centralized control.[18] Henceforth, in the United States, the federal government would play a more prominent role in international finance.

The latest step toward the conference grew out of the meeting at Lausanne. It was there that Papen reaped the harvest planted by Brüning and Sackett. In a complex set of arrangements, German reparations were

12 *New York Times*, 25 August, and *Business Week*, 21 September 1932.
13 Sackett to Villard, 24 October 1932, bMS Am 1323 (3374), Villard Papers.
14 See, for example, Memoranda by Curtius, 30 September 1931, and Bülow, 30 November 1931, ADAP, 18: 485–486; 19; 198.
15 Bülow Memorandum, 3 June 1932, ADAP, 20: 234.
16 Ellis W. Hawley, "Herbert Hoover and American Corporatism, 1929–1933." 101.
17 Memorandum by Erwin Planck of the Reichschancellery, 30 December 1930, ADAP, 16: 325.
18 Leffler, *Elusive Quest*, 299–300; see Andrew P. N. Erdmann, "Mining the Corporatist Synthesis," 196–200.

to be delayed in a three- to five-year moratorium, after which a minimal payment would be made. The issue of war debts was evaded, but the settlement was made contingent on the parties, including the United States, settling the matter.[19] The entire issue of war debts and reparations was allowed to wither and die, and in the end was chalked up as another example of the arcane complexities of international finance.

Among the agreements at Lausanne was the provision for the World Economic Conference that would meet in London in 1933. The meeting would not produce significant results, but Sackett, of course, was not privy to that consequence. Preparations for the conference were to occupy much of his remaining time as ambassador. Meanwhile, he had confided to Castle that he wanted to return to Berlin because "there were likely to be rather important political changes shortly and that he ought to be there." Sackett anticipated that Papen would be removed from office and wanted to be in Berlin.[20] It is also apparent that the ambassador believed that Papen's fall might be the occasion for Brüning's comeback. He had anticipated that if a government of the extreme Right failed, Brüning would again be "on the map in Germany."[21]

American diplomats in Germany considered the Papen cabinet virtually "a military directorate." The characterization as a "military government" was soon widely adopted by diplomats.[22] The Berlin embassy had nothing good to report about the chancellor, or his government. Sackett complained that Papen treated the political parties with "contemptuous disdain," while Gordon wrote of the "rough shod autocracy of the Papen regime."[23] Having alienated everyone, except President Hindenburg, Papen could find almost no support in the Reichstag.

Hitler also had problems, as he himself was well aware. Hindenburg refused to accept the Nazi leader as proper material for the chancellorship. With the president and the Reichswehr standing behind the Papen government, Hitler's chances of governing alone were remote. Frustrated, Hitler assailed Papen with the same violence he had used in attacking Brüning. The vehemence of the assault was motivated in part by Hitler's desire to hang on to the support he had won in the July Reichstag elections. Sackett reported that the Nazis were complaining that the Papen-Schleicher regime "had stolen their thunder." They feared that some of their supporters might return to the Hugenberg Nationalists.[24] For his part, Papen insisted

19 Leffler, *Elusive Quest*, 291–292.
20 Castle, Memorandum, 10 November 1932, FRUS, 1932, 2: 317.
21 Sackett to State, 1 June 1932, 862.00/2781.
22 Atherton to State, 16 September 1932, 893.01 – Manchuria/474.
23 Sackett to State, 19 September FRUS, 1932, 2: 314–315, and Gordon to State, 18 November 1932, 862.00/2869.
24 Sackett to State, 19 September 1932, FRUS, 1932, 2: 314, 316.

that Hitler was correct. "I am the one," he said, "and not he, who is pursuing the aim" that Hitler and the Nazis long for, "against party rule," despotism and injustice.[25]

Hitler's anxiety about the loss of public support reached a climax in August 1932 when five Storm Troopers were sentenced to death. They were found guilty of a crime heinous even for Nazis, having beaten and stomped a Communist laborer to death in front of his mother, and then proceeding to injure severely the man's brother.[26] When the sentence was announced, Hitler issued a manifesto. Sackett reported that it was "so luridly hysterical and fanatic in tone that it was too strong even for Dr. Goebbels – himself usually not exactly squeamish – who expurgated some of its most violent passages" when it was published by the Nazis.[27]

Sackett judged that the attempt to regain extremist support had back-fired. Hitler's outrageous defense of the brutal murder turned Hindenburg against him once and for all. The president had "lost completely" any regard he had for Hitler and the Nazi movement. The administration was confident, under Schleicher's leadership, that they could control Hitler and the Nazis. Papen's press chief boasted that Schleicher was successful in "taming the wild men of Germany." The Hitler movement, Sackett insisted, was now on the defensive, as well as in decline. With further loss of support for the Nazis in the offing, the Papen government decided it would use the tactic of new Reichstag elections to hurt, even destroy, the Hitler movement.[28]

It had been Nazi policy to agitate for frequent elections. In that way, Sackett wrote, they could maintain the intensity of their attacks on the government. Hitler employed that tactic because he was confident that with each election the Nazis would increase their support. But now, with all signs indicating a loss of support, the Nazis changed their tune and became "the champions of parliament."[29] They wanted to keep the Reichstag in session and were intent on showing that they were capable of making the legislative body "workable."[30] They made every effort "in obedience to orders from headquarters to give a striking display of their capacity properly to live up to parliamentary responsibility." Sackett declared they evinced that new posture by listening "relaxed and unagitated" while the aged Communist deputy Clara Zetkin delivered an hour-long speech. The Schutz-Staffeln (SS) in their black uniforms and the Storm Troopers in brown were behaving in stark contrast to their conduct at the opening of the 1930 Reichstag, when they had acted like an overgrown, unruly troop of

25 Sackett to State, 2 September 1932, 862.00/2842.
26 Eyck, *Weimar Republic*, 2: 420; Bullock, *Hitler*, 218.
27 Sackett to State, 23 August 1932, 862.00/2832.
28 Sackett to State, 1 September 1932, 862.00/2840.
29 Sackett to State, 19 September 1932, FRUS, 1932, 2: 315.
30 Sackett to State, 31 August 1932, 862.00/2831.

Boy Scouts. To accent the party's new demeanor, they presented "a far more spruce appearance."[31]

Sackett noted the disparity in age between the Nazis and the Center and Socialist deputies. The bulk of the Nazis were under forty-five, with many of them in their early thirties. In contrast, among the supporters of the republic, "hardly a [Center] deputy seemed under the age of 45" with very few young people among the Socialists.[32] Papen and his cabinet were cognizant of the youth of Nazi supporters. They prepared a decree to undermine that support in the next election. It would raise the voting age from eighteen to twenty-five.[33] The Nazis wanted to keep the Reichstag in session, and avoid elections, because they were aware that such a law "would cost Hitler a large percentage of his votes."[34]

When his friend Heinrich Brüning revealed his strategy for a return to office, Sackett held out little hope that it would work. Anticipating that he could control Hitler and the Nazis, the former chancellor took an active role in making it difficult for Papen to dissolve the Reichstag.[35] One tactic was to form a "Black-Brown," or Catholic Center–Nazi, coalition. There appeared to be a good chance for such a combination in Prussia. The Nazis had shared power in provincial governments, but they were reluctant to cooperate with the Center party in the Reich. Sackett explained that Hitler did want to keep the alternative open "for tactical reasons."[36] To avoid new elections, and keep the option of a coalition open, the Nazis and Center party agreed to cooperate, if necessary, to repeal emergency decrees and to vote together should a vote of no confidence come up. But they faced a dilemma. Papen had the weapon of Reichstag dissolution, an eventuality both parties wished to avoid.[37] The Center and Nazis continued to work toward agreement, a combination which did not please Sackett. The Black-Brown bloc wanted Hindenburg to drop Papen, "who was the main obstacle to a coalition" of the two parties and the Bavarian People's party. Göring, who had been voted president of the Reichstag, met with Hindenburg claiming that the Nazis and Center had a working majority and requested that the Reichstag not be dissolved. Their immediate strategy was to gain time by voting for adjournments. Sackett felt that strategy would only postpone "the evil day for them." He concluded that Hindenburg and Papen were "determined to dissolve the Reichstag if and when it seeks to take any action contrary to the course which they have mapped out."[38]

Only Hugenberg's position had notably improved. His Nationalists were

---

31 Sackett to State, 2 September 1932, 862.00/2842.   32 Ibid.
33 Gordon to State, 31 October 1932, 862.00/2858.
34 Sackett to State, 31 August 1932, 862.00/2831.   35 Ibid.
36 Sackett to State, 23 August 1932, 862.00/2833.
37 Sackett to State, 2 September 1932, 862.00/2842.
38 Sackett to State, 9 and 19 September 1932, 862.00/2835, 2848.

the only party that wanted new elections, assuming that they could increase their support at Nazi expense.[39] The opportunity was close at hand, although very few were aware of it. The Reichstag had the votes to bring the Papen government down and decided to act on a motion of no confidence. When it came to a vote, Papen's farcical conduct led Sackett to report that on September 12 the government claimed "to have dissolved the Reichstag."[40]

While the Reichstag was voting its lack of confidence in Papen by the overwhelming majority of 513 to 32, the chancellor tried to get Göring's attention to present him with a decree dissolving the legislative body. When the Nazi, as Reichstag president, finally accepted the decree from the distraught chancellor, Göring declared it to be invalid. It was, he maintained, signed by a chancellor who had just been shown to have the confidence "of only a negligible minority in the Reichstag." Göring, in a defense of the constitutional rights of the Reichstag, adjourned the body for the day, but convened it for the next day. "At this point," Sackett explained, "the Social Democrats completed the paradoxical spectacle of the Nazis championing constitutional parliamentarism by shouting 'there is no Reichstag.'" It was finally agreed, however, that the Reichstag was in fact dissolved.[41] New Reichstag elections were scheduled for November.

Papen again reached out to the Americans for support. Sackett reported the chancellor "would welcome any face saving formula that would allow Germany" to return to the disarmament conference in Geneva. Papen had distanced himself from Hitler and the Nazis. In a radio address, his "delivery was embittered, not to say passionate, and betrayed the depth of his resentment against the Nazis." He assured Sackett that he would remain in office "for a long time" to carry out a mission "to transform the status of German democracy as it now existed." Sackett was not impressed, pointing out that Papen had mentioned nothing specific, except the intention of changing "the mental attitude of the German electorate."[42]

Papen's attempts to win over American support, most recently with professions of commitment to democratic change, were met with disbelief in the embassy. The chancellor's claims were not consistent with their analysis. They had already characterized the government as a military directorate, with strong inclinations to monarchy. Sackett noted a clearly antidemocratic tendency and wrote that "caste feeling seems to be stronger in Germany" than ever. The attitude was reflected in Papen's relationship with Hindenburg. According to Sackett, the president felt in closer harmony with Papen than he had with Brüning. Papen was "an officer to the manner [*sic*] born" whereas Brüning was merely "a war-time officer." Hindenburg

39 Sackett to State, 19 September 1932, 862.00/2848.
40 Sackett to State, 12 September 1932, 862.00/2827.
41 Sackett to State, 12 and 13 September 1932, 862.00/2838, 2839.
42 Sackett to State, 15 and 28 September, 862.00/2844, FRUS, 1932, 2: 448.

respected the Center party leader for his "ability and integrity" but clearly was not comfortable with a person from the people.[43]

The support Papen attracted was not consonant with his professions to democratic sentiment. Sackett noted that industrialists had "reason to be pleased with the present conservative regime in Germany." Many of them had supported Hitler and the Nazi movement in the belief that they would "help to break the influence of the trade unions and reduce the onerous burdens of social legislation." With Papen in office, they began to withdraw their support from the Nazis.[44] It was obvious that they had found their man and had no immediate use for Hitler. The military attaché reported that, with the "military caste," the industrialists could support the Papen government. They now had "no further need for the movement led by Herr Hitler except for its exploitation by themselves when the proper moment arrives."[45] As Gordon observed, the mentality of the prewar days prevailed. The aristocratic makeup of the cabinet reinforced Hindenburg's status as being "only responsible to himself."[46]

Many observers began to see the Papen government, and Germany in general, as more dangerous than ever to peace, with or without Hitler. Marriner wrote from Paris that fear of Germany had broken out anew.[47] Germany, he commented, had become prey to "military madness," which was all the more frightening because many of the ideas were shared by the Left.[48] General Douglas MacArthur, visiting Berlin, saw the situation in Germany darker and more "ominous in potentialities" than ever. The Germans fully intended to rearm. Former enemies and ex-allies alike were preoccupied with German intentions. Papen, he wrote, was a lightweight with delusions who would soon be dropped because he failed in the task assigned to him. He had not "brought the Nazis into the government in acceptable form." The general, correctly in the event, expected Schleicher to succeed Papen.[49]

43 Sackett to State, 23 August 1932, 862.00/2833.
44 Sackett to State, 19 September 1932, FRUS, 1932, 2: 315.
45 Lt. Col. Jacob W. S. Wuest to War Department, 1 October 1932, War/MID Box 2082, 2657-B-735/14; this, as most of the reports over the military attaché's signature, was written by Herbert John Burgman, an American who served with the army during World War I and remained in Germany. He joined the attaché office in 1919, earned a doctorate, and served as an economics expert, translator, and factotum. In World War II, he was involved in broadcasting German propaganda and was later tried in the United States, found guilty, and sentenced to a six- to twenty-year term. Charles B. Burdick, *An American Island in Hitler's Reich: The Bad Nauheim Internment*, 13, 16n21; Charles B. Burdick to Bernard V. Burke, 27 October 1986.
46 Gordon to Castle, 2 September 1932, Castle Papers – Germany, HHPL; Gordon to State, 26 October 1932, 862.00/2852.
47 Marriner to Castle, 17 October 1932, Castle Papers – France, HHPL.
48 Marriner to State, 19 October 1932, 862.00/2857.
49 Extracts from personal letter sent from Berlin dated 15 October 1932 "from General MacArthur," 12 November, McBride, 862.00/2855 1/2; Moffat Diary, 8 November 1932.

Stimson was so disturbed by developments in Germany that he felt compelled to set down his "intimate convictions about the situation in Europe." He was particularly concerned that Germany was preparing for war and that "their state of readiness for war is greater than the public knows." The only way to stop them would be with Anglo-French co-operation, which was not likely. Consequently, Germany will "be able to get away with murder. The air in Europe is heavy. I can smell blood. The issue this time is: Democracy against Militarism." Without mentioning American responsibility, he complained that it was the "duty of democrats of all nations to unite in a demand that German militarism shall be curbed before it is too late." He held out little hope for action. The British, he protested, would come to the side of democracy only when it was nearly too late.[50]

Sackett confirmed the secretary's fears. On his way to campaign for Hoover, the ambassador reported to Stimson. As might be expected, he stressed the reparations and revision issues. The situation in Europe was bad, but in Germany it was worse. Sackett was no longer worried that Hitler might be a problem. Germany under Papen would probably repudiate any further reparations payments, and, moreover, was ready to rearm, in spite of the restrictions of the Versailles Treaty.[51] There was greater fear of war from Papen in the American mind because they identified militarism with monarchy in Germany, and they saw growing evidence that Papen was determined to restore the throne.

While delivering a speech in Munich, Papen took the opportunity to visit ex-Crown Prince Rupprecht. The call on the former heir to the Bavarian throne sparked rumors that Papen would not hesitate to place Rupprecht at the head of the Bavarian government, "paving the way to a restoration in the Reich."[52] Since Papen had so little support in the Reichstag, rumors of a restoration were rampant. One had Hindenburg resigning and naming the Hohenzollern ex-crown prince regent. A major concern was Hindenburg's age. If the president were to die, it would raise a "fairly ticklish situation" and spur interest in a restoration. In any case, Gordon wrote, there was a "definite increase in monarchical activity" and the "personal attitude of supporters of a restoration is noticeably more confident."

The chargé saw the best hope for failure in the division among monarchists who could not decide on which Hohenzollern to support. Moreover, the Bavarians would accept no Hohenzollern: the Prussians, no Wittelsbach. The depressing aspect of the problem for Gordon was that the supporters of republicanism were "greatly disorganized and in sad disarray." The one hope was that they would "gain cohesion if threatened by monarchism."[53]

50 Confidential Memorandum, 27 September 1932, Stimson Papers, 83: 617–618.
51 Stimson Diary, 11 and 19 October 1932.
52 Gordon to State, 15 October 1932, 862.00/2854.
53 Gordon to State, 24 October 1932, 862.00/2862.

The military attaché saw a ray of hope. The question was no longer "Hitler or not Hitler; but Papen or not Papen." The latter, he reported, could be seen as a "snow-plow for Wilhelm." As recently as last summer, "the front row of the Hitler meetings were invariably decorated with former nobility. Now the friendship has cooled off." Hitler faced the dilemma of losing his following in even greater numbers if he made an appeal to win back the support of the aristocrats.[54]

John Carter, a veteran diplomat and former Morgan partner, returned to his post in the State Department from a visit to Germany in October 1932. He talked to Moffat about his findings, and revealed that, much to his surprise, "Hitler himself was the brains" of the Nazi party. The party was emphasizing socialism in its campaign and as a consequence expected to lose 100,000 to 150,000 "upper class votes," but expected to more than compensate for that by "an increase from the lower and middle classes." The diplomat reinforced what had become common currency in the State Department: "If the Hitler movement failed, probably the next political growth in Germany would be the Communist party."[55] Although most of the signals pointed to a restoration of the monarchy, Americans, like so many others, still clung to their fondest fear – the danger of a Communist victory.

Speculation about division in the Nazi party grew in direct proportion to American apprehension about Germany's future. There were frequent reports of conflict over tactics, especially the serious question of whether the Nazis should continue Hitler's policy of legality, or, as the Storm Troopers would have it, launch a march on Berlin. Emphasis on socialism was another bone of contention. Facing the prospect of losing votes, the strategy was changed to emphasize socialism in order to appeal to a broad voter base. The War Department attaché in the embassy reported that military "extremists" spoke of the "early disintegration of the Nazi party with the better classes aligning themselves with Hugenberg and the present government, and the more radical elements going to the communists."[56] Sackett reported that Hitler's "lieutenants" and many of his "more sober followers" were "disgusted with him on account of his failure to participate in the responsibilities of government." Others were put off by the "excesses committed by his more unruly followers, as well as his own intemperate reaction to their condemnation."[57]

Gordon disclosed a new center of Nazi controversy. A political trial in Munich, the chargé wrote, "throws some interesting light on the

54 Major John H. Hineman, Jr., for Lt. Col. Wuest, 24 October 1932, War/MID Box 21082, 2657-B-735/16.
55 Moffat Diary, 24 October 1932.
56 Lt. Col. Wuest, 1 October 1932, War/MID, Box 2082, 2657-B-735/14.
57 Sackett to State, 2 September and 23 August 1932, 862.00/2842 and 2833.

extraordinary character of some of Hitler's lieutenants, as well as on the doings at the Brown House, Hitler's headquarters in Munich." The trial made public the creation of a group of Nazis, modeled after the Soviet secret police, that was planning to put Röhm and "his intimate circle of friends" at the Brown House "out of the way." Gordon said of Röhm, who was a homosexual, that it had "long been common gossip that he is a sexual pervert." The alleged attempts on his life, Röhm confessed, were serious enough that he did not "feel safe among his own men at the Brown House." Hitler, however, protected the Storm Trooper chief of staff. He "firmly rejected" the many demands from his subordinates that Röhm be dismissed. Gordon wrote that the conjecture was that the Storm Trooper chief "knows too much" of what was going on in the Brown House "to be dismissed like an ordinary subordinate."[58] Hitler's protection of his trusted lieutenant lasted just over nineteen months. In June 1934, on the "Night of the Long Knives," Röhm would be murdered, with his lover, on Hitler's orders. The carnage extended to Schleicher, Gregor Strasser, and scores of others, although Papen and Brüning were spared.

Hitler had many reasons to be apprehensive as the Reichstag elections scheduled for November 6, 1932, approached. Not only were there party problems, the Nazis were almost certain to suffer losses at the polls. Gordon reported the general expectation, which Hitler shared, that the Nazis could lose 30 percent of their popular support. The chargé correctly predicted a "15 percent loss which would reduce their Reichstag representation to approximately 200 deputies."[59] The estimate was based on the extent of Nazi losses in local elections. Sackett reported that "the crest of the Nazi wave" had been reached in the July Reichstag elections. Gordon was pleased to assert that Sackett's view was now confirmed. In local elections the Hitler party suffered their first heavy losses in two years. Their tactics exposed their fear that they would lose votes in November. They completely ignored the elections in their press and acted to obstruct a resolution to dissolve the Diet in Hesse. They did not "want to face the electorate at this time."[60]

There was considerable interest abroad in the Reichstag elections. The Germans, however, demonstrated less interest than usual. It was the sixth major election since March. Not only was the public exhausted by the frequency of the campaigns, the parties and politicians were drained, both emotionally and financially. Hitler was hit particularly hard by the extraordinary costs of so many contests. One consequence was that the campaign was unusually quiet. The major event in the final days of the election was an unsuccessful general transportation strike in Berlin, sponsored jointly

58 Gordon to State, 6 October 1932, 862.00/2855.
59 Gordon to State, 26 October 1932, 862.00/2852.
60 Gordon to State, 5 October 1932, 862.00/2853.

by the Nazis and the Communists. American diplomats in Berlin were able to stay on top of events, reporting with accuracy and speculating with informed and reasoned conclusions. In contrast with his earlier complaints about the embassy, Moffat was now praising Gordon for his "admirable" reports. His assessment of the diverse issues he covered in his accounts were, wrote Moffat, "borne out uncannily by the facts."[61]

There was far less understanding at the highest level of the State Department. One factor was clear in German politics: The multiparty system made it difficult to form coaltions because more than a dozen parties represented in the Reichstag had to be taken into account when forming a government. Stimson revealed that he was not aware of the problem at all. He thought he had put his finger on the major issue in Germany when he complained that "it was a great pity that the two-party system seemed to be losing ground." Prittwitz humored the secretary by agreeing with him.[62]

On Sunday, November 6, while President Hoover was in the last two days of his struggle to retain office, the German voters went to the polls. As predicted, the Nazis lost considerable support. Gordon was proud to claim that Nazi losses were "exactly as forecast." The embassy had estimated 200 Nazi seats, which was remarkably close to the 196 the Hitlerites won. In contrast with the Reichstag of the previous July, when there were 608 seats, there were now 584 total seats. The Nazis had controlled 230. With 196, they had lost a total of 34 seats and 2 million votes. At the other extreme, the Communist party increased its strength from 89 to 100 seats and nearly 700,000 votes. For Gordon, the depressing fact was that, combined, the Nazis and Communists controlled a majority in the Reichstag. This would make Nazi participation in the government "more desirable than ever."[63]

The election was a significant defeat for Hitler. His ambition of winning a majority of votes was "badly shattered." Even his "most ardent" supporters had to know "that the much-heralded Third Reich has become a very remote possibility." Gordon, again using the metaphor of the cresting wave, estimated that since it had begun to recede in the depths of the depression, and even before Hitler could enter the government, the magic of his "irresistible appeal to millions" of voters might be broken. Of pivotal importance to the chargé was the fact that the Nazis had suffered losses in each of the thirty-five German electoral districts.[64]

For Gordon, the "deep significance" of the election was the "growing radical tendency of the German people." The voters gave the two extremist

61 Moffat to Gordon, 21 November 1932, bMS Am 1407 (3), 1933, Moffat Papers.
62 Stimson, Memorandum of a Conversation with Prittwitz, 3 November 1932, 862.00/ 2861.
63 Gordon to State, 7 November 1932, 862.00/2863.
64 Gordon to State, 11 November 1932, 862.00/2872.

opponents of the Weimar Republic a majority. At the same time, the strongest supporters of the republic lost seats. Gordon reported that votes shifted as parties stole support from each other. The Center lost 5 seats; the Socialists, 12. Brüning's Center party suffered for its attempts to form a coalition with Hitler, a major reason for losing "a large number of Jewish voters." But Gordon was most unhappy that the Social Democrats "who represent the more moderate labor elements and have thus far proved to be an effective bulwark against Bolshevisation and radicalization of the masses are steadily losing ground." In one sense, the result made the Hitler party more dangerous than ever. Nonsocialist Nazis voted for the Hugenberg Nationalists or other Right parties. Gordon saw the shift as the result of a "growing socialist tendency" of Nazi electoral campaigning. One repercussion was to make the Nazis even more radical and "even ripe for active cooperation with the Communists."[65]

Papen had every reason to be pleased with the result. Hugenberg's Nationalists, the only party to support his government, increased their representation by 15 seats, from 37 to 52, and more than half a million voters. Gordon thought they would have won more if they had a more popular leader. Still, the unpopular Hugenberg held a pivotal position. In any important anti-Communist coalition he held the balance of power. As a consequence, "he no longer cuts as sorry a figure as he did after the election in July." There were problems in the construction of any governing coalition. Hitler still insisted on the chancellorship for himself and Hindenburg was no more inclined to give it to him than he had been in August. The Nazis and the Center rejected any cooperation with Papen, and Hugenberg was not interested in a change of government. The situation was even further complicated by Hugenberg's opposition to a Hitler chancellorship.[66]

Sackett had long suspected that Hindenburg would need to drop Papen. The problem was finding an acceptable replacement. Hitler was out of the question for Hindenburg, who still preferred, if he could, to retain Papen. The ambassador told the State Department he felt he should return to Berlin right after the American election. He thought it especially important because of the danger that the Germans might "make the mistake" of naming Schleicher chancellor.[67] Sackett expressed concern that "the munitions manufacturers in Germany and France" took advantage of "every trouble."[68] The Germans, he claimed, were determined to get back everything they lost in the Treaty of Versailles. They were rearming piecemeal, taking steps, "none of which can seriously threaten active reprisals." Asked by Moffat if the Germans wanted a restored monarchy, he replied that he did not think there was a majority in favor. In his opinion the Hohenzollerns

65 Ibid. 66 Gordon to State, 7 and 11 November 1932, 862.00/2863 and 2872.
67 Moffat Diary, 9 November 1932. 68 Stimson Diary, 9 November 1932.

would never be forgiven for "having run away in the hour of need," and he suspected that if there were a restoration, it would have to be a candidate from South Germany.[69]

Chancellor Papen had managed to alienate everyone with whom he came into contact. That left the close group around Hindenburg with very few options. They were not essentially interested in a Reichstag majority; what they wanted was a government of the Right. After managing to estrange all the parties and their leadership, Papen was no longer a viable leader. He commanded neither support nor respect.

Hitler was still the head of the largest party in the nation, and hence held a special position; but it was clear that he and Papen could not come to agreement. Sackett speculated that Hitler might "be willing to cooperate with some other Nationalist leader." By now the only way to form a government of the Right, so important to Hindenburg, was a coalition of the Nazis, Nationalists, and the Center party. Hugenberg was still not willing to concede the leadership role to Hitler, but Sackett surmised that there was enough Nationalist backing for the Nazis that Hugenberg "would have to step down and out."[70]

Sackett, still concerned about communism above all, and talking with the like-minded William Castle, expressed fear about the extent of Communist party support. Sackett believed that the government would carry on without the Reichstag. The "number of communists" had increased to such a degree that he felt "it was obviously important at the moment to have a strongly centralized more or less military Government."[71] With that attitude in mind, Hitler appeared a less fearful prospect in the cabinet. The Nazi was making every effort to announce, in Germany and elsewhere, that he would not attempt to come to power "by forceful methods." Unlike Mussolini, who had found such means fruitful, legal methods were more effective for the Nazis. Hitler insisted that constitutional means were better suited to "the German temperament" and, more important, the foundation had been so well prepared that "strong-arm methods were superfluous."[72]

The issue of who was to govern reached a climax eleven days after the Reichstag elections. Papen met with Hindenburg in the morning, and then the afternoon of November 17. Gordon had good reason to believe that Papen was empowered by the cabinet to offer either his own or their resignation. Papen hoped to form a government of "national concentration." The Socialists refused; the Nazis delayed; the two Catholic parties agreed to such a government, but not under Papen. Since a coalition was not likely, Sackett said Hindenburg wanted a "presidential cabinet," one

69 Moffat Diary, 9 November 1932.
70 Castle, Memorandum, 10 November 1932, FRUS, 1932, 2: 317.
71 Castle, Memorandum, 10 November 1932, FRUS, 1932, 2: 317–318.
72 Alexander Kirk, Rome, 6 October 1932, 862.00/2851.72.

"possessing to an extreme degree his own personal confidence."[73] Gordon explained that "the dictatorial nature of the government would necessarily be greatly accentuated." A new government would be like "the veiled dictatorship of the Brüning Government in its latter stages." In any case, the decision was now "very definitely in the hands of the President and a small group of his advisers."[74]

Hindenburg persisted in favoring Papen. Schleicher was the only acceptable alternative, but there was considerable concern that a general might not be well received abroad. Aside from the president's favorites, Hitler was the only likely candidate, but Hindenburg's "personal antipathy" to the Nazi leader made it impossible for the field marshal to hand over the chancellorship to the former enlisted man. To resolve the issue Hindenburg accepted the collective resignation of the cabinet on November 17. He then invited the party leaders, from the Nazis to the Catholics, to meet with him. As usual, the Communists were not invited, but this time, in a more forthright gesture than was customary, the Socialists were also excluded. To foster cordial discussions among those invited, Papen was not to be present.[75]

Sackett believed the German Republic had "never been in so bad a muddle politically speaking" as it was then.[76] But foreign policy seemed stable. In the State Department, Assistant Secretary of State James Rogers learned from Ambassador Prittwitz that political confusion in Germany was terrible, but was not likely to affect the continuity of foreign policy.[77] Meanwhile, the alternatives began to narrow. When it was clear that Papen was out of the question because of the overwhelming opposition to him by every party except Hugenberg's Nationalists, Schleicher came in for serious consideration. The general was reluctant to take over under such onerous conditions. Sackett explained that aside from Schleicher's reservations, Hindenburg and his circle of advisers were "somewhat uncertain and apprehensive as to where the General's restless energies and abilities may lead him."[78] That left the door slightly ajar for Hitler. Neither the general nor the Nazi was acceptable to Sackett.

Hitler met with Hindenburg on November 19. Sackett wrote that the president commissioned the Nazi leader to ascertain "whether and under what conditions" a government formed by him could "find a secure and workable majority with an agreed upon program in the Reichstag." The

73 Sackett to State, 1 December 1932, FRUS, 1932, 2: 318.

74 Gordon to State, 17 and 18 November 1932, 862.00/2868, 2869.

75 Gordon to State, 18 November 862.00/2869, and Sackett to State, 1 December 1932, FRUS, 1932, 2: 318.

76 Sackett to State, 1 December 1932, FRUS, 1932, 2: 318.

77 Rogers, Memorandum of a Conversation with Prittwitz, 1 December 1932, 500.A15A 4/1660.

78 Sackett to State, 1 and 5 December 1932, FRUS, 1932, 2: 318–319.

terms made it very difficult for Hitler. Hugenberg refused to countenance the Nazi as chancellor. That meant Hitler would need the support of both Catholic parties, Center and Bavarian People's, plus the votes of the People's party to organize a bare majority. Sackett wrote that Monsignor Ludwig Kaas, the Center party leader in the Reichstag, went through the motions of trying to form a majority with the sole purpose of showing that it could not be done.[79]

After several days of correspondence, Sackett revealed that Hitler found the task impossible and declined to form a government under those conditions. Instead he asked Hindenburg to name him head of a presidential cabinet. "This the President refused on the ground that a presidial cabinet headed by Hitler might develop into a party dictatorship" that would only worsen the already tense political climate. Hindenburg and his advisers were aware of Hitler's ultimate goal of a purely Nazi government. In a second conference, lasting only ten minutes, Hitler was told to decide if he was willing to form a government under the stated conditions. His reply was to be confined to the question of whether or not he was willing to form such a cabinet.[80]

The Nazis wavered. They were expected to reply that afternoon, but the delay into the evening led Sackett to suspect that the Nazi leaders were having significant problems in deciding on a course of action. There were strong signs that the more experienced Nazis, those who served in the Reichstag and in public office, were very much inclined to form a conventional cabinet. Among their number Gregor Strasser and Wilhelm Frick were the leaders. Goebbels and Göring represented the hard-liners, who were willing to hold out for a clearly Nazi government.[81] The only hope of holding them all together was to insist that Hindenburg appoint Hitler as head of a presidential cabinet.

Sackett detailed several more days of debate, including the publication of correspondence, which led to a public consideration of just what was a presidential cabinet. Otto Meissner, state secretary to the president, and a member of the small circle of his advisers, conducted much of the written debate with Hitler. Hindenburg, Meissner wrote, refused to entrust the powers of a presidential cabinet to the "leader of a party which has repeatedly declared its intention to govern alone" and whose attitude toward the president and all the political and economic measures he supported had been nothing but a negative response. Meissner reiterated the fear that Hitler would create a "party dictatorship." In conversations with Schleicher, Hitler reaffirmed his position that he would not cooperate with any government, directly or indirectly, if he were not named chancellor. With

79 Sackett to State, 25 November 1932, 862.00/2876.   80 Ibid.
81 Gordon to State, 18 November, and Sackett to State, 5 December 1932, 862.00/2869 and 2877.

that, Hindenburg declared that any further "oral or written discussions would be useless."[82]

In a final statement for publication, Sackett said, Hitler denied all the charges levelled by Meissner. Hitler claimed that prospects for a parliamentary majority were good, except for the conditions laid down by Hindenburg. He denied that he demanded leadership in a presidential cabinet, or that he insisted on a dictatorship for his party.[83] A coalition was "futile," the Nazi wrote, "at this time" because the president's advisers refused to accept any government in which "they did not have a decisive influence." Having placed the onus for failure on Hindenburg and his circle, Hitler and his staff "demonstratively left Berlin" to show that they were no longer interested in negotiating.[84]

After many days of "barren wrangling," Sackett suggested that Schleicher was the only alternative. He commanded more support in the Reichstag than Papen, and from "practically every other serious point of view," a Schleicher government was more likely to fulfill Hindenburg's expectations than Papen. The Nazis would attack a Papen government with "greater vigor" than they would Schleicher's. Sackett concluded that naming Schleicher "cannot much longer be deferred."[85] For his part the political general threw out a wide net to insure that if he took the job he would have more support than could be provided by Reichstag delegates alone. He consulted with representatives from industry and the trade unions, as well as with the political parties.[86]

Sackett was pleased with the latest turn of events. He confided to Stimson that although matters were "confused at present," the political situation was "really working out for the best." Hitler had been given a chance to form a government with a Reichstag majority and failed. Sackett was patently right when he asserted that the Nazi leader's "failure will be a decisive blow to the growth of the Hitler movement." Still, he guessed, there was likely to be a government with "dictatorial powers" formed with Hindenburg's authority, but that was not as dread an eventuality as a Hitler government would be.[87]

Hindenburg, whose advisers had negotiated with party leaders for more than two weeks, finally came to a decision. On December 2, the president virtually forced General Kurt von Schleicher to form a cabinet. Sackett was convinced that Hindenburg still preferred Papen, a much more dependable ally than Schleicher. The general had a reputation for being unpredictable, and although he was a professional soldier, Sackett characterized him as

82 Sackett to State, 25 November 1932, 862.00/2876.   83 Ibid.
84 Sackett to State, 5 December 1932, 862.00/2877.
85 Sackett to State, 1 December 1932, FRUS, 1932, 2: 319.
86 Sackett to State, 5 December 1932, 862.00/2877.
87 Sackett to Stimson, 25 November 1932, 550. S 1/387 1/2.

"a man of a different stamp" from Papen. Sackett had been unable to see any merit in a Schleicher government but began to change his view.

Although Schleicher had been reluctant to serve and preferred to manipulate appointments from behind the scenes, he reluctantly decided the time to step forward had arrived. He was able to assume authority with considerable force at his command. Hindenburg kept him in his position as Reichswehr minister, and also appointed him Reich commissioner for Prussia. The general further secured his position by retaining most of the Papen cabinet.[88]

American diplomats, who earlier had very little positive to say about Schleicher, were impressed by the general's determined efforts to get broad backing for his government. Sackett was won over when the general solicited the support of the trade unions. Strangely, Sackett and his staff, who surely would not support union activity at home, found union leadership the most politically attractive group in Germany. With their political base in the Social Democratic and Center parties, they formed the basic support for the Weimar Republic. The Americans learned from French Premier Herriot that Schleicher was negotiating with the Socialists, who agreed not to oppose the general in return for "some additional unemployment doles."[89]

Sackett took heart as Schleicher succeeded in broadening his base of support. But nothing gladdened him more than the general's attempt to split the Nazi party. His strategy was to form a Reichstag majority stretching from the Socialists on the Left, through the Center, to the dissident Nazis on the Right. From Sackett's point of view, the bold stroke by Schleicher meant the dissipation of both the Nazi and the Communist threats. He was delighted with what appeared to be the very credible possibility that the general could pull off the maneuver. It was only possible if Gregor Strasser could break away from Hitler and bring with him those Nazis who agreed that the party was doomed to failure if it continued its current course of refusing to compromise.

Sackett was aware of the deep division among the Nazi leadership. Hitler insisted on a strategy of all or nothing. He demanded that he be appointed head of a government or he would not participate at all. On the other hand, Strasser represented Nazis who saw that their only hope of winning an ultimate victory was to take part in Reichstag politics. Hitler had brought them to the peak of their electoral capacity. With that base he was unable to form a government. Hindenburg simply would not give him the authority. The August debacle, in which he was humiliated by Hindenburg, was followed by the disastrous defeat in November. All signs seemed to point to continued decline and ultimate defeat.

88 Sackett to State, 5 December 1932, FRUS, 1932, 2: 319.
89 Marriner to State, 28 November 1932, FRUS, 1932, 1: 480, enclosing a Memorandum of Conversation between Herriot and Davis, 26 November 1932.

Earlier Nazi defections, such as the Stennes revolt, centered on the demand of Storm Troopers for a march on Berlin and a seizure of power. Although that militant sentiment persisted, the major split now was over how to enter the government. Sackett had reported on the new division among Nazi leaders as early as August.[90] The issue reached crisis proportions when Schleicher attempted to form a "political non-aggression pact" that depended on the Nazis. Nazi Reichstag leaders, Strasser and Frick, feared another election would destroy the anti-Weimar majority they enjoyed with the Communists. They were willing to meet with Schleicher to support an adjournment of the Reichstag, probably until the following spring. Sackett explained that the meeting was called off at the last minute on the ground that only Hitler could conduct such negotiations.[91]

Undeterred, Schleicher pursued the Nazis and got Hitler to agree to come to Berlin to meet him. Although Hitler left Munich to meet with the general, the conference never took place. In the early morning hours, en route to Berlin, the Nazi leader and his staff left the train at Jena and drove to Weimar, where Hitler met with his lieutenants. After a confrontation later in the day, the Nazis denied that Hitler ever had any intention of going to Berlin. They claimed he was headed for the local elections in Thuringia all along. Sackett suggested that the claim was merely a "plausible explanation for the sudden change in Hitler's plans."

Sackett offered "one version" of what actually happened. Although subsequent historians have been unable to find a satifactory account of events because hardly any credible documents have survived,[92] Sackett's account conforms with all available evidence and appears authoritative. Göring and Goebbels intercepted Hitler, he explained, and got "the 'Führer' off the train before it reached its destination." Hitler's "only reaction" to the Schleicher offer was to reassert his demand for the chancellorship and to point out that "under the circumstnces another trip to Berlin would be useless."[93] The Nazi triumvirate of Hitler, Göring, and Goebbels had asserted their leadership and undercut Schleicher's strategy.

In addition, Hugenberg was not pleased with the prospect of a Schleicher cabinet. Sackett contended that Hugenberg continued to work for a restoration of the Papen cabinet, which gave him a "strategical position." At the same time, Hugenberg did not share the general's views on "organized labor and social welfare measures." Despite the nation's being "solidly opposed to a resurrection of the Papen regime," the Nationalist party leader continued his "intgrigue and political machinations" designed to frustrate Schleicher and foster a return of Papen. In fact, Sackett reported, "such a cabinet would be extremely handicapped from the very beginning."

90 Sackett to State, 23 August 1932, 862.00/2833.
91 Sackett to State, 5 December 1932, 862.00/2877.　92 Fest, *Hitler*, 368.
93 Sackett to State 5 December 1932, 862.00/2877.

The Socialists "issued a sharp warning," asserting that a Papen government "would be tantamount to a declaration of war against an overwhelming majority of the German people." Even members of the Papen cabinet saw the need to avoid a confrontation, especially in the face of a Socialist threat of a general strike.[94]

Throughout this "political maelstrom," Schleicher remained in the background. Sackett predicted he would follow a conciliatory policy, expressly to undo the damage done by Papen. His negotiations with the trade unions were an indication that he intended to modify the provisions of Papen's economic decrees, which were "vigorously opposed" by organized labor. Sackett attributed the recent growth in Communist votes to Papen and welcomed the policy proposed by Schleicher, which was anti-Communist but also conceived to win the support of the Social Democrats, those mainstays of the republic.[95]

Sackett expressed pleasure that Schleicher, who was often called the "friend of the workingman," was going to address the problem of unemployment relief as a principal goal of his cabinet. At the time, Schleicher was called the "red general" and was fond of calling himself the "social general." He was considered to be Leftist in orientation because he attempted to bridge what seemed the impossible gap between the Socialists and the least intransigent Nazis.[96] Sackett approved of the general for the enemies he made. These included Hugenberg, who disliked Schleicher because of his apparent new liberal views on labor unions and social welfare. The ambassador also thought Schleicher had put the Nazis "in an awkward position." The general had been "widely regarded as a friend of the Nazis," and only a few weeks earlier they had declared him to be the only member of the Papen cabinet in whom they had confidence. As a consequence they would find it "very embarrassing" to campaign against him if they were faced with new elections.[97]

Gregor Strasser was the Nazi most concerned with the prospect of facing more elections. New defeats seemed to be the Nazis' fate unless they entered the government. Strasser was convinced that the only way to avoid another campaign, and to have an opportunity to govern, was to cooperate with Schleicher. That decision would cause a significant break with Hitler and would ultimately be resolved when Hitler had both men murdered in the "Night of the Long Knives," strong testimony that Hitler probably believed Schleicher's tactic might have worked.

When Strasser moved to split the Nazi party and form a regular Reichstag faction in support of Schleicher, Sackett was almost gleeful in his accounts. With the Nazis divided, Sackett claimed, Hitler and the "all or nothing" advocates would be defeated. Moreover, the Communists would be barred

94 Ibid.   95 Ibid.
96 Fromm, *Blood and Banquets*, 324; Wheeler–Bennett, *Nemesis of Power*, 255.
97 Sackett to State, 5 December 1932, 862.00/2877.

from the door, the republic would be saved, and the prospect for Brüning's return would be brightened. Many Nazis were ready to challenge Hitler's leadership because they were convinced he was taking them down to defeat. Sackett saw the confrontation as the only way to end "the *intransigent* course consistently advocated by Goebbels, which of necessity would appear to mean a further veering toward Communism, even though this might be sought to be disguised by the shibboleth, 'National Communism.' "[98] Sackett's fear of a Hitler government was reverting again to his fundamental dread of communism and further beclouded his analysis of the Nazi party.

It was Otto Meissner who confirmed Sackett's view that the Hitler-Strasser split "was of really serious proportions." Strasser and Frick were "ready and willing" to support the Schleicher government. Sackett recalled that the general judged that "elements of national regeneration" in the Nazi movement could be exploited by a non-Marxist government. Meissner was satisfied that the "country at large" was backing the Schleicher government and that the Reichstag was proving to be "malleable" and could probably be counted on to adjourn "until after Easter."[99] Prospects for at least a temporary peace in the tumultuous German political situation appeared to be good.

It was just what Sackett wanted to hear. He was pleased to report that the Reichstag voluntarily adjourned and that a "political truce" had been agreed on. Schleicher got a "breathing spell" at least until the middle of January. The political peace was made possible, according to Sackett, because almost all the parties, except the Communists, dreaded the prospect of elections. The Reichstag, which was dominated by "an overwhelming majority" of opposition parties, was more productive in its three-day session than it had previously been in months. Sackett betrayed his newfound admiration for the political general when he pointed out that the calm was made possible by "the tact and skill with which Chancellor von Schleicher dealt with the situation, in striking contrast to the provocative methods of his predecessor."[100]

The ambassador was satisfied that the Nazis were making constructive moves in the Reichstag when they proposed a law making the president of the Supreme Court acting president of the Reich in the event of the death, incapacity, or resignation of the president. The measure required a two-thirds majority, which the Nazis mangaged to organize, with only the Hugenberg Nationalists and the Communists opposed. Sackett reflected on Nazi motives. There was much speculation on why the Nazis sponsored the measure, because none of them came forward to speak in its support.

Sackett suggested three motives. Possibly an attempt to thwart Hugenberg, who, in such an eventuality, might try to establish a regency leading to

98 Sackett to State, 12 December 1932, FRUS, 1932, 2: 320.
99 Sackett to State, 12 December 1932, FRUS, 1932, 2: 320–321.
100 Sackett to State, 12 December 1932, 862.00/2880.

monarchy. Or it might be an attempt to stop Schleicher. But the third
motive Sackett saw as "more plausible." It was an attempt to remove a
serious obstacle to Hitler's eventual chancellorship. Hindenburg and the
political parties might be more willing to accept a Hitler cabinet "if they
felt that he could be kept from taking over the presidential powers even
though temporarily." Someone in the State Department emphasized Sackett's
prescient statement with stress marks in the margin of the despatch. Hitler
would eventually evade the Nazi-sponsored measure when he became
president as well as chancellor upon Hindenburg's death. But for the moment
Sackett was satisfied to report that politics were steady under Schleicher's
leadership. However, the ambassador reported, the "unexpectedly smooth
functioning of the Reichstag was somewhat marred by a fight between 40
or 50 Nazi and Communist deputies in the lobby of the Reichstag."[101]

It was during the brief Reichstag session that the Hitler-Strasser split
reached its climax. The issue was whether to support the motion to adjourn, or to face another election in two months. Sackett reported that
Strasser, "who no longer believes in the possibility of a purely Nazi dictatorship," had been attempting to "pave the way" for Nazi participation
in the Reich and Prussian governments. Strasser was to be named Prussian
minister-president. The "immediate cause of the conflict" came when Hitler
dropped Strasser and proposed Göring for the post. Strasser then wrote to
Hitler complaining of lack of support and gave up his party offices, but he
remained a Reichstag deputy and kept his party membership, which Sackett
considered significant.[102] It meant that Strasser could still use his position
in the party to take his followers with him into the Schleicher government.

Sackett described Strasser in favorable terms as a "seasoned politician."
A veteran Nazi, he took an active part in the Hitler putsch in 1923 and
was the leader who kept the party together while Hitler was in prison for
his part in the putsch. Strasser, wrote Sackett, was a leader of those "who
realize that if the Nazis should get into power they could not well ignore
the wishes and needs of the bulk of their following, namely, the former
middle-classes which have now become economically dislocated." Sackett
recognized, in consonance with recent scholarship, that although Strasser
was an anticapitalist, it was hard to describe him as a socialist. His "socialist philosophy," the ambassador recorded, was "not easily definable."
Since he certainly was not a Marxist, there was hope for the dissident
Nazi.

It was a time of "national regeneration," Sackett explained, a time that
could be "exploited by a government – especially one of a non-Marxist
complexion."[103] Sackett saw a significant role for Strasser because there

101 Ibid.   102 Sackett to State, 14 December 1932, FRUS, 1932, 2: 321–322.
103 Sackett to State, 12 December 1932, FRUS, 1932, 2: 320; Peter D. Stachura, *Gregor
     Strasser and the Rise of Nazism*, asserts that Strasser was not a socialist and denies that
     there was either a Nazi Left or a Strasser wing, 109–111, 40–66, 115–116.

"was still hope" that the Nazis might realize their Third Reich. Sackett believed that Strasser would be a major player in German politics, even in a Hitler government. Thinking of the Soviet Union before Stalin's monstrosities had been revealed, he reported "it was understood that Strasser was to become the German Stalin while Hitler was to play a decorative role something like that of Kalinin."[104]

When Strasser was granted a three-week leave of absence, Sackett reported that it caused a "political sensation." The Nazis had tried to hide "the tension between Hitler and Strasser" that now broke out into "an open conflict." It was a sign of deeper "discord among the Nazi leaders." Strasser was now separated from Hitler and, in the ambassador's view, all the more able to split the Nazi party. Sackett pointed out the significance of what was happening by maintaining that this was "a palace revolution rather than an open revolt by the rank and file." Sackett used the Stennes revolt as an example of what usually happened when German political parties suffered a breach. The instigators "usually ended in obscurity without being able to do serious damage to the parent party." Although the Nazi press tried to minimize the importance of the division in the party, it was clear to Sackett that Hitler and other party leaders took it seriously. That was attested to, according to Sackett, when, after the Reichstag adjourned, "Nazi deputies gave the 'Fuehrer' individually and collectively a declaration of loyalty." That was followed by affirmations of loyalty from subordinates from all over the Reich.

Sackett was intrigued by the prospect of Strasser's success. He clung to the hope that the dissident Nazi could split the party and strengthen the Schleicher government. Sackett's position was closer to reality as it was perceived at the time than that of historians later who were influenced by Hitler's success and Strasser's failure. Sackett was reinforced in his commitment to Strasser's success because, as he noted, the Nazi movement was "now on the decline" and the Nazi press and speakers took pains to explain it away. Strasser's activity, Sackett claimed, had "doubtless served to stress this unpleasant fact." The ambassador thought this to be the most serious threat Hitler faced for control of his party. But when it became clear to many that the Strasser revolt had never even gotten off the ground, Sackett admitted that it might be "premature" to anticipate "an open split in the Nazi party" over Strasser's rift with Hitler. However, he held out hope "that it may have more serious and far-reaching consequences than similar conflicts which took place during the Nazi boom."[105]

Sackett took the position not only that the Nazi party was in decline, but also that Hitler's position had been measurably weakened by Strasser's palace revolt. In a conversation with General Hammerstein, Sackett, and

104 The following is in Sackett to State, 14 December 1932, FRUS, 1932, 2: 322.
105 Sackett to State, 5 December 1932, FRUS, 1932, 2: 323.

the military attaché, Lieutenant Colonel Jacob Wuest, all agreed that Nazi decline in power was "now well under way." They concurred that Nazi strength had passed its peak "some time ago." The general believed that the Hitler-Strasser break, however, was not dangerous because it was proceeding gradually. That, he said, was what was wanted. A sudden break, he thought, "would bring a great confusion and lead to difficulties with radicals." The positive side of dwindling Nazi power was that the number of parties was certain to be reduced. The general thought there should be no more than two or three.[106]

Sackett was convinced that he was witnessing slow progress toward disintegration of the Nazi party. He so dreaded the prospect of a Hitler regime that he indulged in naive and illusory hopes for the future. As did so many others at the time, he clung to the prospect of the "socialist" Strasser assisting Schleicher to form a majority in the Reichstag with labor union, Social Democratic, and Center support, combined with the "Left wing" of the Nazi party. That combination would thwart not only Hitler, but the Communists as well.

It is true that Strasser made Hitler's position more uncomfortable than it need have been. Gordon said Hitler was faced with the prospect of tolerating the Schleicher government or facing new elections. The split with Strasser made new elections even more dangerous than they would be otherwise. It caused Hitler "considerable uneasiness" for if the Reichstag were dissolved, forcing another election, "a split in the [Nazi] party may be unavoidable."

Gordon pointed out that Strasser's alienation from Hitler appeared to be permanent. After his leave of absence from the party had expired there were no "visible signs of reconciliation with the 'Fuehrer.'" A meeting, scheduled before the Christmas holidays, between Hitler and Strasser never took place. On the other hand, Strasser did meet with both Schleicher and President Hindenburg. Gordon reported that political "wiseacres" said that if Hitler persisted in his opposition to Schleicher, the chancellor "would not hesitate to give Strasser a portfolio in his Cabinet, thus causing an open split in the Nazi party." Whether or not the appointment took place, Gordon wrote that "Hitler is anxious to prevent such a contingency." One measure of Hitler's discomfort was the rumor Gordon reported that the Nazi leader was contemplating dropping his demand for the chancellorship. He would settle for the portfolio as Reichswehr minister and Prussian minister-president. Such an eventuality was not likely, wrote Gordon, because Hindenburg would not be willing to turn over the army and the police of the largest state to "the leader of a party with dictatorial aspirations."[107]

106 Wuest, Memorandum of a Conversation with Sackett and Hammerstein, 21 December 1932, War/MID, Box 2082, 2657-B-735–17.
107 Gordon to State, 13 January 1933, 862.00/2886.

Sackett waited for events to spin out to their conclusion, clinging to the hope that the Schleicher-Strasser alliance could be realized. The presumption was that Hitler and the Nazi party were in for more trouble and that Schleicher would succeed in resolving the immediate political problems. Meanwhile, politics were very quiet in Germany. Hindenburg acknowledged that the Christmas holidays had been the most peaceful in years, and many agreed with that view.[108] The American embassy output of political reports was reduced to a trickle. Moffat mentioned that "matters have been reasonably quiet" in Berlin, which gave young, new staff the opportunity to learn the ropes.[109] Feis believed that Germany had returned to "stability and revival in general, which will improve the whole European situation."[110] Felix Frankfurter was delighted to hear of Feis's assurances that Germany was making progress. "Your hope that things can move forward," he wrote, "is the most solid expression of hope from you in some time and correspondingly significant." He then asked: "How do you account for German revival, and how solid is it?"[111] The answer remained to be seen.

In the meantime, Sackett, who had clearly demonstrated his approval of Schleicher's attempt to form a Left-leaning government, left for Geneva. He had important matters to conduct in the second meeting of the organizing committee for the World Economic Conference. The ambassador later recalled that it was a period when political tensions in Germany were finally "relaxed."[112] It was the holiday season and there was little to do, so Gordon took the opportunity to take a vacation. The first secretary, Alfred Klieforth, was left in charge of the embassy.

---

108 Eyck, *Weimar Republic*, 2: 460, Eyck writes that the Strasser revolt was quelled in a few days, 2: 451.
109 Moffat to Gordon, 12 January 1933, bMS Am 1407 (3), 1933, Moffat Papers.
110 Feis to Frankfurter, 9 January 1933, Box 54, Frankfurter Papers.
111 Frankfurter to Feis, 11 January 1933, Box 16, Feis Papers.
112 Sackett to State, 4 February 1933, 862.00/2895.

11

Through a glass darkly

AT THE END OF 1932, Ambassador Sackett was quite content that the problems presented by Hitler and the Nazi party were being worked out in satisfactory fashion. It might take time, but the danger was past. The Schleicher government appeared to have matters in hand, and all indications were that the general would continue in office at least until spring. The new period of quiet was ideal for Sackett. He was firmly committed to making a success of the proposed World Economic Conference. The calm of the holiday season would enable him to address the preparatory problems in Geneva with an uncluttered mind. He would need all his time and energy to insure that the meeting even took place. The idea for the international economic conference had emerged from his talks with Brüning. Hoover had taken up the idea from time to time and finally committed the United States to participate. But the idea did not sit well with President-elect Roosevelt. Careful attention to the issue therefore was imperative in Sackett's eyes.

Hoover was convinced that international cooperation was the best way to defeat the depression; but he feared that Europe was depending too much on the United States to come up with solutions. Pressure from the Congress and also from the British finally induced him to act.[1] He still believed that the American economy, if left to its own devices, could solve domestic problems. But he also presumed that the failure of American recovery could be attributed to the problems in Europe. Once he decided to act, he hoped he could move swiftly and, with a psychological stroke, help to restore economic balance to the international economy.[2] It would be especially useful if all that could come about before the presidential elections. Unfortunately for Hoover's sake, he acted too slowly and serious

1 Osborne to the Marquess of Reading, 18 September 1931; Lindsay to Simon, 20 May 1932, and 22 June 1932, BDFA, C, 2: 169, 241, 250.
2 Herbert Feis, *1933: Characters in Crisis*, 21–22; Hoover's Message to Congress, 6 December 1932, FRUS, 1932, 1: x; Hoover, *Memoirs*, 3: 63–67.

planning for the conference did not occur until well after his defeat in November.

Sackett was Hoover's choice to help with the planning because he had advanced the idea to Hoover in the first place. Moreover, Sackett persisted in bringing up the idea of an international economic conference.[3] He was kept on in the transition between presidencies, probably to maintain continuity. In any case he played a minor role, except for the early arrangements. His major task was to see that the conference was held at all.[4] The question now was whether President-elect Roosevelt would support the idea proposed by Hoover. With that in mind, Sackett hoped to convene the meeting as early as possible. Both he and Stimson wanted to be certain that Roosevelt was committed to the talks.[5]

Sackett's hopes for an early meeting were stymied. He was confronted by delays from several sources. Sir John Simon, the British Foreign Secretary, was called back to London, which postponed the preparatory meeting to January 25. At that meeting, Sackett, who arrived in Geneva on January 13, hoped to get the date and place for the conference established. He urged that the meeting take place between late April and early May. But Roosevelt balked at that proposal; he wanted the conference delayed as long as possible. Then Hoover intervened in an attempt to insure that the war debt issue would not be considered.[6]

In their attempt to negotiate a smooth transition of administrations, Roosevelt and Hoover were unable to reach agreement. As they drifted apart, immediate interest in the World Economic Conference faded into the background. Neither man was committed to such a meeting except on his own terms. During numerous attempts to set a date, Sackett met with delay after delay. Foiled, the American diplomat refused to give up. He traveled to London on January 25 in an attempt to settle the matter of time and place. Sir John Simon suggested it was not possible to fix a time, but finally London was agreed on as the site and June was accepted as the date.[7]

---

3 See, for example, Curtius Memorandum, 30 September 1931, GFMR 1555/D666904–666906.

4 Castle to Atherton, 15 August, Atherton to State, 20 August, Stimson to Hugh Wilson, 14 September 1932, FRUS, 1932, 1: 820–822. Sackett is not mentioned in any of the major works on the World Economic Conference.

5 Sackett to State, 20 January 1933, FRUS, 1933, 1: 454–455; Stimson had been working toward the conference since May 1932, Stimson to Mellon, 26 May 1932, FRUS, 1932, 1: 808–810; Feis, *1933: Characters in Crisis*, 21–24.

6 Sackett to State, 20 January 1933, FRUS, 1933, 1: 455; Memorandum of a telephone conversation between Stimson and Roosevelt, by James Rogers, 23 January 1933, FRUS, 1933, 1: 458; Raymond Moley, *After Seven Years*, 90–92.

7 Feis, *1933: Characters in Crisis*, 46, 66–86, 169–258; Moley, *After Seven Years*, 102; Sackett to State, 22 and 25 January 1933, FRUS, 1933, 1: 457, 461; *New York Times*, 31 January 1933; on the conference itself, see Frank Freidel, *Franklin D. Roosevelt: Launching the*

Sackett placed a great deal of faith in what the conference could accomplish. When it finally did meet, what was now called the London Economic Conference failed to accompish any material results. Sackett was, of course, not aware that his prized idea for settling the depression and, more specifically, German economic problems, would lead to nothing. His attention would soon be riveted on events in Germany, which caught him and the American embassy completely by surprise.

At one in the afternoon of Monday, January 30, Klieforth cabled that Hitler had been appointed chancellor.[8] Within days, Sackett was back in Berlin trying to fathom what had happened. American diplomats were so sure that Schleicher had German politics under control that this, the dreaded eventuality, seemed too remote, too unthinkable to contemplate. Sackett's first despatch reflected his perplexed reaction to the disturbing events of the past several days. He stressed that he had no idea what to expect.

Political tensions, he noted, which were relaxed under Schleicher, were "again visibly increasing." Anticipated measures against communists were not as "drastic as was generally expected." However, authoritative sources indicated that decrees would soon appear to establish control over antigovernment and "especially the Jewish newspapers." The embassy was unsure of its ability to predict what else might happen. Sackett, probably recalling Moffat's call-down of the previous August, notified the State Department that, "for the present," he expected to limit himself "to factual and analytic telegrams." The Reichstag had been dissolved and elections scheduled for March, so that the next several weeks were certain to be "fraught with varying political possibilities." Rumors were rampant, making careful analysis difficult. As the situation unfolded, he hoped "the outlook may become clearer but the make up of the present cabinet with its normally discordant elements furnishes a fertile field for trouble."[9]

In their attempt to fathom what happened, Sackett and his colleagues reviewed what had taken place during the preceding several weeks when the embassy staff was even further reduced than usual. The first hint of a new direction came in early January when Hitler met with Papen at the home of Baron Kurt von Schröder, a Cologne banker. Gordon did not consider the meeting to be especially significant. Reminiscent of his tardy report on Hitler's meeting with Hindenburg in August, he did not report on it until nine days after the event. Although it was supposed to be a secret, rumors and conjecture preceded the meeting with a chorus of charges,

New Deal, 31–41, 110–111, 369–389, 454–489; Feis, *1933: Characters in Crisis*, 169–258; Jeanette P. Nichols, "Roosevelt's Monetary Diplomacy in 1933," 295–317; Ferrell, *American Diplomacy in the Great Depression*, 255–277.

8 Klieforth to State, 30 January 1933, 862.00/2889; the telegram was forwarded to Hoover, Mills, and Secretary of Commerce Roy Chapin.

9 Sackett to State, 4 February 1933, 862.00/2895.

countercharges and denials that there was to be a meeting at all. It is clear that there was a meeting, although Hitler, who finally admitted it, denied its importance. The government issued a statement denying that Schleicher had anything to do with it, and the general claimed that he was in "no way alarmed by the alleged plot against him." After the meeting, Papen met with Schleicher to show that there was no plot, although they admitted that there were differences between them.[10]

Gordon accepted the "prevailing belief" about the meeting. The issue was Nazi finances. The Nazi leader and Papen met on the initiative of "Hitler and a group of industrialists who have been financing the Nazi movement." The chargé knew that Schröder was the conduit through which industrialists' money reached Hitler, and therefore assumed that was the purpose of the meeting. Some of Hitler's financial backers, such as Fritz Thyssen and Otto Wolf, were trying to get Hitler to modify his "all or nothing" position so that he could participate in the government. Gordon assumed the meeting was an attempt to reconstruct the Schleicher cabinet and that Papen was there so that he could use his influence with Hindenburg to make it possible. Gordon emphasized two major considerations: Nazi financial trouble, and Hitler's reluctance to face new elections.

Gordon stressed the critical state of Nazi indebtedness as the more immediate threat for Hitler. The debt was estimated to be more than 12 million marks and was "rapidly increasing." Gordon did not doubt that Schleicher would use his authority to exert pressure in "a practical sense" if the Nazis were unable to discharge their obligations.[11] The debt was becoming a burden that could destroy Hitler's chances of ever becoming chancellor. Industrialists were satisfied with Schleicher, and the military attaché reported that they wanted to avoid elections and the political unrest that accompanied them. The military diplomats guessed that the principal meaning of the Hitler-Papen meeting in Cologne was to get Hitler's agreement to "avoid a conflict with Schleicher."[12] Hitler, facing the loss of financial support from industrialists, wanted to avoid elections more than ever. The Nazi debt, however, still posed a serious problem for him. In fact it was so serious that Klieforth reported that a Göring aide had approached him about the possibility of "obtaining a loan for the Nazi party in the United States."[13]

The issue of new elections was directly related to the Hitler-Strasser breach. American diplomats persisted in their belief that Strasser and his followers were a serious threat to Nazi party unity. If the party were divided, new elections could be a disaster for Hitler. In the military attaché's review of the political situation, he estimated that in the Reichstag, forty

10 Gordon to State, 13 January 1933, 862.00/2886.   11 Ibid.
12 Wuest to War Department, 7 January 1933, War/MID, Box 2082, 2657-B-735/19.
13 Klieforth to State, 23 January 1933, 862.00/2892.

Nazis were willing to follow Strasser in the formation of a new party.[14] A leading authority on the history of the Hitler-Strasser crisis asserts that the Reichstag faction was Strasser's principal source of strength and that as many as one-third of the Nazi delegation, perhaps sixty to seventy deputies, were inclined to support his desire to form a coalition.[15] Gordon reported that the dissident Nazi had met with Hindenburg and Schleicher, and there were insistent rumors that Strasser would enter the cabinet, thus "causing an open split in the Nazi party."[16]

The issue of an "open split in the Nazi party" has not been treated as a real possibility by most historians. With the advantage of hindsight they can see that there was little or no chance for Strasser to divide the party, or that he ever intended to do such a thing.[17] At the time, however, seasoned observers concluded there was a strong probability, even likelihood, that Strasser would lead a significant number of Nazis into the Schleicher government. Strasser seemed to them to offer the best chance to avert a Hitler government and tame the Nazis by drawing them into the conventional political process in a Rightist government. Conservative Germans of a nationalist bent were apprehensive about Hitler, a demagogue and a former enlisted man, as head of a new government. In the Foreign Ministry, Bernhard von Bülow expressed a general sense of malaise about what was happening in Europe in general and Germany in particular. Like so many Germans, he was almost despondent about the revelations of Ivar Kreuger's scandalous duplicity. The League of Nations was discredited, he wrote, parliamentarism was dead in many nations, including Germany, alarming numbers of people had abandoned religion, and figures of authority, the greats in economics and finance, such as Kreuger, whom people had believed in earlier, were discredited and had lost the repect and confidence of the people.[18]

With the formation of the Schleicher cabinet, all that seemed to have changed. Sackett, who was distressed by the prospects of a Hitler government, shared the optimism of many who saw better days ahead. Bülow's attitude was almost euphoric compared to his earlier outlook. By January 1933, he shared with Sackett the view of many observers that things were looking better. Bülow wrote that the crisis in government was not over, but a "wave of guarded optimism" had spread throughout Germany. There were signs of improvement in little things everywhere. What made matters so much better was the imminent collapse of the Nazi party. The German

14 Wuest to War Department, 7 January 1933, War/MID, Box 2082, 2657-B-735/19.
15 Stachura, *Gregor Strasser and the Rise of Nazism*, 110–111.
16 Gordon to State, 13 January 1933, 862.00/2886.
17 Eyck, *Weimar Republic*, 2: 450–451; Fest, *Hitler*, 365–371; and Stachura, *Gregor Strasser and the Rise of Nazism*, 103–120, which lists the historians who believe Strasser could split the party, including Bullock, *Hitler: A Study in Tyranny*, 239.
18 Bülow to Constantin von Neurath, 4 May 1932, ADAP, 20: 165.

diplomat celebrated the fact that the "Nazi party structure has been rocked and their financial situation is bleak." Many people, he wrote, were led to ask whether or not the Nazi party would soon disintegrate in circumstances so rapid that their votes would be absorbed by other parties. Bülow hoped that Hugenberg would resign as party head and enable the Nationalists to reach out to former Nazi partisans and voters. Bülow was so pleased with political developments that he showed only slight concern that many Nazis would pass over to the Communists. At least, he wrote, "the Nazi-Communist logjam would be broken up."[19]

Rumbold shared the optimism expressed by Sackett and Bülow. The British diplomat characterized Strasser as "the ablest" of the Nazi leaders and a "strong man." Although it was apparent that Hitler had "thrust" Strasser "aside," Strasser was in constant contact with Chancellor Schleicher. Erwin Planck spoke of Strasser as a possible vice-chancellor under Schleicher. While Strasser was not on speaking terms with Hitler, he did engage in discussions with Hindenberg, Schleicher and Hugenberg which made it evident to contemporary observers that his political fortunes were not dead. One historian maintains that the meetings in which contemporaries placed so much hope "had an air of unreality about them, and must be seen as little more than a tawdry epilogue" to the Hitler-Strasser crisis.[20]

Americans persevered in what was perhaps little more than wishful thinking. They surely wanted Hitler to fail and Schleicher to succeed. In the United States, the Yiddish-language press was among those who held out hope that the Nazis could be divided with a Strasser faction participating in the Schleicher government.[21] At this stage, with Strasser unwilling to take any action at all, it appeared to many observers that what they perceived to be a palace revolution had ended. In spite of that expectation American diplomats were still persuaded that Strasser might enter the Schleicher cabinet.[22]

Unaware that Hitler's meeting with Papen was a major step in the negotiations that would give the chancellorship to the Nazi, American diplomats sensed no urgency. Now in charge of the embassy chancery, Klieforth reported that there was no perceptible change in the political situation. Matters were about the same as the previous November when the attempt to bring the Nazis into the government failed because of Hitler's insistence on the chancellorship.[23] Klieforth's reports emphasized that Schleicher was attempting to force Hitler to take a "clear-cut" position on his cabinet in the Reichstag.

19 Bülow to Prittwitz, 19 January 1933, ADAP, 21: 566–568.
20 Stachura, *Gregor Strasser and the Rise of Nazism*, 119.
21 Charles Cutter, "The American Yiddish Daily Press Reaction to the Rise of Nazism, 1930–1933," 30–31.
22 Gordon to State, 13 January 1933, 862.00/2886.
23 Klieforth to State, 21 January 1933, 862.00/2884.

The Nazis were evasive, posturing as if they did not fear another election, but hoping to postpone the next meeting of the Reichstag until spring. They wanted to delay as long as possible, in the belief that, given enough time, Schleicher's position would be weakened. The American guessed correctly that Papen was now acting as an intermediary between Hitler and Schleicher in an attempt to bring the Nazis into a coalition government with a Reichstag majority. While the parties maneuvered, the "sly fox" Hugenberg played "a double game." He negotiated with Schleicher, to form a new cabinet, and at the same time talked with Hitler with an eye to "a regeneration of the Harzburg Front in order to pave the way for a Chancellor acceptable to the Nazis."[24]

Events were rushing toward a climax. On January 27, Klieforth learned that Hugenberg had teamed with Papen to defeat Schleicher. Major Erich Marcks, the head of the government's press bureau, told the American that the chancellor would demand a renewed expression of confidence from President Hindenburg. Negotiations between the parties had reached a state of intensity mixed with intrigue that did not look good for Schleicher. His position, Klieforth wrote, was "greatly weakened."[25] The next day the American reported the resignation of the cabinet. Schleicher had asked for the authority to dissolve the Reichstag and was refused, at which point the entire cabinet resigned. Hindenburg then commissioned Papen to approach the Reichstag parties with a view "to clarify the politicial situation." Schleicher, fearing the appointment of Papen, cautioned the president not to appoint a presidential cabinet, but one based on the parties. Klieforth, correct on both counts, predicted that Papen's negotiations would result in a "firm dictatorial regime or a coalition government of the Right headed by Hitler."[26]

When Hitler was appointed chancellor, American diplomats were caught off guard. They did not, however, misunderstand the desperate situation into which the Nazis had fallen. Papen, believing he could handle Hitler, had stepped into the picture again, this time to rescue the Nazi leader. The meeting in early January had resurrected Hitler's chances. Klieforth pointed to Papen as the chief architect of Schleicher's downfall.[27] What probably misled the Americans was that Hitler played almost no role in Schleicher's failure. That work had been left to Papen, who lived next door to Hindenburg and was "a welcome and frequent visitor in his house."[28] Klieforth attributed the general's defeat to his inablity to "secure the cooperation of the Nazis, his conciliatory attitude toward organized labor, and his refusal to yield to unreasonable demands by the powerful agrarian interests." The general was a victim "of political intrigue by a small group

24 Klieforth to State, 23 January 1933, 862.00/2892.
25 Klieforth to State, 27 January 1933, 862.00/2887.
26 Klieforth to State, 28 January 1933, 862.00/2888.
27 Klieforth to State, 31 January 1933, FRUS, 1933, 2: 183.   28 Bullock, *Hitler*, 245.

of Nationalists," reactionaries who, "through personal contact" with "Hindenburg and his immediate advisers" were able to bring down the Schleicher cabinet. The first secretary said that Papen deliberately did not inform the Center party of his negotiations, which "were conducted with unusual secrecy, reminiscent of von Papen's activities during the war."[29]

Giving the chancellorship to Hitler was, Sackett reported, a "sudden and unexpected triumph" for the Nazis. The ambassador was not misled by the contention of many Germans that Hitler had seized power. Right-wing opponents of Schleicher, the "social general" who had the audacity to attempt a revival of government with Socialists, were able to convince Hindenburg to hand the chancellorship to the Nazi. It was the government of national concentration that Papen and Hugenberg had been striving for all along but that had met with one failure after another. Now the Harzburg Front was restored, but, as they thought, with a much restrained Hitler. The arrangement called for Papen, who was named vice-chancellor, to accompany Hitler in any audience with Hindenburg, who still could not abide the former enlisted man. In addition, Hugenberg was a member of the cabinet. The two authors of the Hitler chancellorship, Papen and Hugenberg, thought they had the Nazi leader ringed by their influence and control. Aside from Hitler, Göring and Frick were the only other Nazis in the new cabinet. The Nazis, the Stahlhelm, and the Hugenberg Nationalists were the base of the new government, which Klieforth characterized as predominantly "reactionary and monarchist," but that its actions would be moderate because it was dependent on the Catholic parties for a majority in the Reichstag. Without the Center and Bavarian People's parties, Hitler, Papen, and Hugenberg could muster only 270 votes when 293 constituted a majority.[30]

Hitler acted to remedy that problem. His initial reaction was to outlaw the Communist party. At the first session of the new cabinet Klieforth revealed that a plan to expel the Communist deputies from the Reichstag was considered. With their hundred seats eliminated, Hitler would not need the support of the Catholic parties to organize a majority. He did, however, need their votes if he were to get the two-thirds majority necessary to pass an enabling act. With such legislation, he would be authorized to govern without the Reichstag. Moreover, eliminating the Communists raised a whole series of problems the Nazis wanted to avoid, at least for the present. Klieforth learned the plan was abandoned when Foreign Minister Constantin von Neurath pointed out that the Soviets would resort to reprisals and Germany "could not afford to jeopardize her trade with Russia."[31]

29 Klieforth to State, 31 January 1933, FRUS, 1933, 2: 183–184.
30 Klieforth to State, 30 January 1933, 862.00/2890.
31 Klieforth to State, 30 and 31 January, 20 February 1933, 862.00/2890, and FRUS, 1933, 2: 183–185, 193.

The cabinet felt compelled to dispel the apprehensions that swept the world. The Hitler government frightened people in Germany, but also throughout Europe, the United States, and as far away as Japan. Wilhelm Frick, the new Nazi minister of the interior, announced to the German and the foreign press that the government "was not planning to change the Constitution or to suppress the Communist Party." His main purpose was to assure republicans and labor elements that they had nothing to fear.[32] As soon as the Hitler cabinet was appointed, State Secretary Bernhard von Bülow sent a Foreign Ministry circular to all diplomatic missions.

German diplomats were instructed to give assurances that there would be no change in foreign policy. They were to point out that Neurath, who had served in the two previous cabinets, had again been called on to serve because he had the confidence of President Hindenburg. Continuity would be assured by the presence of other familiar figures. But most of all, as for German domestic politics, Bülow asserted that Germany had avoided and would continue to avoid "making her attitude toward other countries dependent upon the tenets of whatever Government happened to be in office at the time. In this respect German necessities and conditions are the sole determining facts of the future government policies of the German Government."[33] This honest statement reflected the fact that there was continuity in German foreign policy throughout the Weimar years, and well into the Third Reich. It was the methods, not the goals, that differed.

The Germans made a special effort to reassure the Americans. Hjalmar Schacht, who was destined to become Reichsbank president again, invited Klieforth to dinner. He assured the diplomat that "the Nazis will make no attempt to carry out any of their well known demagogic reforms . . . and that American business in Germany had nothing to fear." The German banker claimed that "all big business viewed the regime with sympathy." But Klieforth would have none of it. The claim, he reported, was exaggerated. That morning, an executive of the Reichsverband der Deutschen Industrie told him that "the 4-year plan announced by Hitler last night was an absurdity and that this organization viewed the latest political developments with scepticism and reserve."[34]

German assurances provided little comfort for Sackett, who remained not only skeptical but fearful about the future. His analysis of the nature of the Hitler government was a reflection of his inability to fathom the extremes to which the Nazis were capable of going. But he was not the only one to misjudge them. Throughout the history of the Hitler movement there was a tendency to underestimate the Nazis.[35] Sackett was misled

32 Klieforth to State, 31 January 1933, FRUS, 1933, 2: 184.
33 Circular of the State Secretary, 30 January 1933, *Documents on German Foreign Policy*, Series C, 1: 1–2.
34 Klieforth to State, 2 February 1933, FRUS, 1933, 2: 186.
35 Karl Dietrich Bracher, *The German Dictatorship*, 199.

because of several fundamental assumptions he held, which colored and confused his analysis.

He had always believed that the Nazis were incapable of governing Germany, and in this respect he was right. The Nazi party was so devoid of high-quality leadership that Hitler had to rely on the existing bureaucracy and its supporting social elite to operate the machinery of government.[36] It followed, therefore, that the Nazis could not succeed in office. Sackett always thought of Hitler and the Nazis as a short-term threat. What he feared was that the Communists would move in to pick up the pieces after their failure. It was his consistent hope and belief that Brüning would be the one to step in to clean up the Nazi mess.

Despite the lack of quality Nazi leadership, Hitler was able to co-opt enough support to sustain the government. Meanwhile he would rely on his dogged determination and belief in his own destiny to control Germany. Although the Nazis lacked the kind of leaders who could govern, the party was quite efficient. Louis Lochner, chief of the Associated Press bureau in Berlin, attested to the party's superb organization. In an age before the computer, the journalist wrote that the party files would be the envy of a detective agency. Party officials could find every Nazi baker in Germany "within a few moments."[37] General inability to recognize the underlying efficiency of the party was part of the reason that Hitler and the Nazis were regularly underrated as a political entity. More attention was paid to the extravagant claims and, as Gordon put it, "hare-brained" schemes than to the sound organization of the party. Secretary Stimson was misled into believing that the Nazis were really "not so much a party as a protest." The party, he wrote, "lacked organization and was made up of many discordant elements and had no coherent or logical policy."[38]

It was failure in understanding Hitler that led Sackett to believe that Nazis' choice of cabinet positions reflected their inability to govern. For Sackett, the offices they accepted emphasized their lack of serious purpose. The Nazis, the ambassador reported, "have taken charge of the purely political and administrative departments of the Government, leaving to others those ministries in which constructive work requires unpopular measures." Having Frick as Reich minister of the interior and Göring in charge of the Prussian Ministry of the Interior were portrayed as "political plums." Sackett ignored the importance of Nazi control over the police in both the Reich and by far the largest German state. He noted that Frick and Göring did have control over the police, as well as the civil service, schools, universities, and other educational institutions. He stressed that their positions gave them a monopoly of political patronage, but he failed

36 Stachura, *Gregor Strasser and the Rise of Nazism*, 118.
37 Manuscript, "First Article," Munich (AP), about March 1931, Lochner Papers; Metcalfe, 1933, 53.
38 Stimson Diary, 31 January 1933.

to see the critical importance of controlling the police power.[39] Sackett thought that stressing control of the police was a way of shirking duty and a refusal to face up to the real problems of government.

Sackett failed to understand Hitler's drive for naked power. Like Papen and Hugenberg, who made the Hitler government possible, he believed that Hitler was hemmed in and isolated by those who brought him into office; that his authority was severely circumscribed. Like most Americans, the ambassador firmly believed that the real tasks of governing were in the arena of economics and finance. Although Hitler had the constitutional authority to set government policy, Sackett regarded Papen and Hugenberg as the real power. In all matters concerning "fundamental and vitally important national problems," the two men were the "guiding spirits." Hugenberg had undertaken the "greatest responsibility" and assumed "gigantic" tasks. He was "practically economic dictator." In the definitive area of economics, "Hugenberg rather than Hitler will be the decisive factor." Otherwise, more responsible elements of the government would be required to do the real work of governing.[40]

When Hitler found he could not get Center party support for an enabling act that would give him authority to govern without the Reichstag, he decided to dissolve the parliament and scheduled new elections for March 5.[41] Hitler, who had avoided the prospect of new elections, was emboldened to call for a new test at the polls with his advantageous position as chancellor. The government parties expected to poll more than 50 percent of the votes, giving them control of the Reichstag.[42] However, Hitler and Hugenberg were now at loggerheads, according to Sackett. All the cabinet had in common was "a fanatic chauvinism coupled with a common hatred of democratic government and the parliamentary system." The Nazis had the advantage in purging administrative positions of democratic and republican influences. They were acting with "an avidity and swiftness" that Germans had never before witnessed. Most of the dismissed officials were replaced by Nazis, with far fewer positions going to the Nationalists, "who naturally resent a Nazi monopoly of political patronage." The competition between Hitler and Hugenberg was so intense that they tended to slight the problems of governing and concentrated on winning the forthcoming elections. Hugenberg observed Hitler's campaigning "with manifest alarm." The Nazi was electioneering in a fashion to strengthen his party's position rather than for the benefit of the government.[43]

Much to Sackett's delight Brüning entered the picture again. Like Papen,

39 Sackett to State, 13 February 1933, FRUS, 1933, 2: 188–189.   40 Ibid.
41 Klieforth to State, 1 February 1933, 862.00/2893; Rudolf Morsey, "Hitlers verhandlung mit der Zentrumsführung am 31. Januar 1933," VJZG 182–194.
42 Klieforth to State, 1 February 1933, 862.00/2893.
43 Sackett to State, 13 February 1933, FRUS, 1933, 2: 189–190.

the former chancellor undoubtedly believed he could control Hitler, and Sackett obviously agreed that he could. Hugenberg was alarmed that the Nazis would increase their vote, enabling Hitler to govern with the two Catholic parties. That would put Brüning back into a pivotal position and leave the Nationalists out in the cold. To avert that disaster, Hugenberg combined his Nationalists with the Stahlhelm and Papen to evoke images of Germany's imperial past. They campaigned as the "Kampfblock-Schwarz-Weiss-Rot," evoking the image of Wilhelmine Germany with the imperial colors black, white, and red. Hugenberg, Papen, and Stahlhelm leader Franz Seldte were the standard-bearers. The consensus was that the government would not win a majority in the Reichstag. Therefore, Sackett claimed, Brüning would play a critical role. It was, he wrote, an "open secret" that Hitler preferred to collaborate with the Catholic parties rather than Hugenberg. Brüning had informed Sackett, in strict confidence, "that he felt he could personally work with Hitler" but had some reservations regarding his lieutenants. The former chancellor probably had a coalition in mind, in which the two Catholic parties would replace Hugenberg and the Nationalists in the cabinet.[44]

The Hitler government had asked that the Reichstag be dissolved so the Nazis and Nationalists could take advantage of the wave of enthusiasm among their followers. With the government in their hands, and with control of the radio, they expected to win a majority of the votes.[45] Aware of Hitler's proclivity for showmanship, Sackett stressed that the Nazis were doing all they could "to keep alive the flame of enthusiasm kindled by their cleverly-staged torch procession in the Wilhelmstrasse" on the night Hitler had "seized power." Immediately after the Reichstag was dissolved, Hitler broadcast a manifesto, which was a "clever piece of political agitation." Sackett called it an appeal to the emotions rather than an enunciation of policy; it was meant to show Hitler's followers that he was "prepared to do big things." A vague four-year plan was announced and a clearer plan for obligatory labor service, which was an astute means of maintaining the Storm Troopers at government expense.[46]

The welter of political parties was being reduced to two opposing forces, combinations that had very little in common except opposition to the other grouping. Sackett saw Germany dividing into two "hostile camps of approximately equal numerical strength and equally heterogeneous elements." One group was composed of such disparate elements as the "monarchistic, ultra-capitalist" Hugenberg Nationalists, and Hitler's "pseudo-socialistic Nazis." The other group was composed of "pious

44 Sackett to State, 13 February 1933, FRUS, 1933, 2: 190, and 862.00/2914, the confidential portion of the despatch not published; Stimson, Memorandum of a Conversation with Prittwitz, 12 February 1933, Stimson Papers, 162: 578.
45 Klieforth to State, 1 February 1933, 862.00/2893.
46 Sackett to State, 6 February 1933, 862.00/2903.

Catholics, champions of democracy, and Communists."[47] On the one hand were Hitler, Hugenberg, Papen, and Seldte. The opposition, unfortunately for it, was less identifiable by its leadership, with the exception of Brüning. They were the Catholic parties, the Social Democrats, and their bitterest enemies, the Communists, arrayed in opposition rather than in alliance against Hitler.

Sackett characterized the contest for control of Germany as "a most bitter political" campaign, conducted under "extraordinary circumstances." The Nazis practically had monopoly control of the radio, which they used to campaign for themselves, not the government. Göring used the Prussian police to suppress Communist and Socialist meetings, demonstrations, and their press. An emergency decree made it difficult for new parties to enter the lists. Sackett speculated that it was designed to prevent Gregor Strasser from entering the campaign with a ticket of his own. The American thought it would take "prophetic vision" to predict the outcome of the election. No one knew "what surprises the Nazis may still spring in the final days of the campaign." Hitler had been unable to make any inroads into the labor parties of the Left, which he had set out to destroy. Socialist losses were absorbed by "the more radical Communists." The middle-class parties, with the exception of the two Catholic parties, were all but destroyed. Sackett thought Hitler had two options left open to him: either to "resort to unfair methods" to keep the opposition away from polling places, or to concentrate on winning the vote of "the large army of voters" who so far had failed to cast a ballot. Hitler needed a record vote to have a chance for a majority.[48]

Hitler did both. To speak of "unfair methods" was an underestimation of Nazi capability. Hitler and his followers went beyond anything imaginable for people such as Sackett who were accustomed to genteel anti-Semitism and explainable, pardonable unfairness. Hitler would shock the political world again and again, and then they would be surprised to find out about his latest enormity. As the election approached, Sackett stated that "Nazi terrorism" guaranteed that the vote would not be a "free expression of the will of the people." The opposition press was muzzled, leaving people without reliable sources of news that gave "rise to disquieting rumors." The only factual accounts of what was happening in Germany were in the foreign press. Almost 150 newspapers were suppressed, most of them Socialist and Communist, with a few Center party papers closed down. Republican officials were being purged, especially in Prussia. Non-Nazis in the cabinet were alarmed when they learned that Nazis were taking over administrative positions as republican sympathizers were removed. Sackett wrote that the Nazis now dominated the police, and almost all were former military officers "of the daring type."[49]

47 Ibid.　　48 Sackett to State, 7 February 1933, 862.00/2902.
49 Sackett to State, 16, 23, 27 February 1933, FRUS, 1933, 2: 191, 198, 199–200.

The Storm Troopers and Stahlhelm were now part of the police force, wearing their own uniforms with white armbands signifying that they were "Auxiliary Police." Sackett was alarmed at the "employment of young men imbued with fanatical political ideas as special policemen"; it was a situation, he wrote, that "augurs no good." He was especially dismayed at Göring's "recent extraordinary instruction to the Prussian police to treat political organizations opposed to the parties in power as enemies of the state." The Nazi threatened to discipline any police officers who failed "to make liberal use of their firearms."[50] If further assurance were needed that the Weimar Republic was dead, Sackett reported that the Nationalists joined the Nazis in asserting that they intended to remain in power regardless of the outcome of the elections. Rumor had it that they intended to violate the constitution if they failed to win a majority in the election.[51]

The Reichstag fire ended any uncertainty Sackett had about the extremes the Nazis would go to in trying to achieve full control of the nation. On the night of February 27 the building housing the Reichstag went up in flames. The Nazis responded with swiftness and a severity that again passed the bounds of what most people considered acceptable conduct. Sackett reported that the fire was the pretext the Nazis needed for further "repressive measures against political opponents." The provisions of the Weimar constitution, amounting to the German bill of rights, were suspended. Sackett declared that the political campaign was over for the parties of the Left. After the fire, their participation in the election campaign was reduced to "a farce." The Social Democrats were "so completely muzzled that outwardly at least they have ceased to exist." Nazi banners, posters, Storm Troopers, parades, mass meetings, and control of the radio with daily broadcasts by Nazi leaders created "the impression that there is only one large party in Germany."[52]

The Nazis used the fire as the justification to destroy the Communist and Socialist parties. A Dutch Communist was arrested in the Reichstag building and accused of setting the fire. Sackett maintained that it was merely another "pretext for a new drastic decree against the Communist party." After the orders were issued, Göring "ordered a wholesale arrest of Communist deputies in the Reichstag and the Prussian Diet." The Storm Troopers and the Stahlhelm veterans, who were called up to meet the manufactured crisis, also arrested "prominent pacifists, journalists, authors, educators and lawyers who defended Communists in political trials, and a number of Social Democrats." Göring boasted that two thousand persons were imprisoned in Rhineland and Westphalia alone.[53]

50 Sackett to State, 25 February 1933, 862.00/2915.
51 Sackett to State, 23 and 27 February 1933, FRUS, 1933, 2: 198, 200.
52 Sackett to State, 14 March, enclosing 3 March 1933, FRUS, 1933, 2: 201–203; the despatch, delayed to avoid an open pouch, was sent later by courier pouch, 862.00/2935.
53 Sackett to State, 3 March 1933, FRUS, 1933, 2: 201–202.

Sackett quickly dismissed Göring's attempt to link Social Democrats to the fire. Just as adamantly he doubted that the Communists had anything to do with it. Furthermore, he contended that they had little to gain from such an act of terrorism, but he was also certain that it would be used against them, and that it had "propaganda value" for the Nazis. Many believed, he wrote, but were afraid to say, that the Dutchman arrested was an "*agent provocateur*, or that he acted on his own initiative without the knowledge" of the Communist party. In a remarkable defense of that party, Sackett went on at great length to explain that the Communists were not associated with such overt acts of violence. He wrote that they did not "resort to anarchist methods with which Bolshevists in the United States and other countries are usually identified." He explained further that such acts as political murders and assassinations had, in the past, been "committed by Right radicals." He was sure that simply accusing the Communists accelerated "the advent of a purely Fascist regime in Germany."[54]

The American ambassador caught the essence of the Reichstag fire question – its consequences were of far greater import than the issue of who started it. After he had drawn his own conclusions, Sackett met with Rumbold and French Ambassador François-Poncet. The three diplomats agreed that the German Communist party did not set the fire, nor was it implicated in any way. All three were inclined to the view that it was a "provocative action" by some Nazi organization to which the Nazi party leadership was not privy.[55] Subsequent scholarship leans toward the view expressed by the three diplomats. There is still debate on the issue, but many concede that the fire was set by a special organized group of Nazis.[56]

The Reichstag fire gave Hitler the opportunity he wanted to suspend civil rights and rig the Reichstag elections in his favor. Sackett was convinced that the election was certainly not going to be an expression of the will of the German people. Aside from the government parties, only the Center and the State parties were allowed to campaign and hold meetings. Nazi tactics of intimidation and especially the condoning of violence guaranteed them a successful election. Writing of the Nazi leadership, Sackett called them "past masters of propaganda" who were able "to stir up the country to a pitch comparable only to war-time hysteria." Nazis and their symbols appeared to be everywhere. Tension, excitement, apprehension, seemed pervasive. The ambassador wrote that the "enthusiasm of the growing Nazi following knows no bounds, while the rest of the population – intimidated and nervous – is awaiting the week-end with anxiety and misgivings."[57]

54 Sackett to State, 28 February, 862.00/2916, and 3 March 1933, FRUS, 1933, 2: 202–203.
55 Rumbold to Simon, 2 March 1933, DBFP, 4: 437.
56 Craig, *Germany, 1866–1945*, 573–574n12.
57 Sackett to State, FRUS, 1933, 2: 202–203.

Violence was anticipated on election day, March 5, but Sackett reported there were very few significant outbreaks. Polling places were heavily guarded to prevent disorders; Hitler wanted his triumph to be legitimate. The election campaign puzzled Sackett. The Nazis had everything in their favor, but where would they get additional votes? The middle parties had already been effectively wiped out. Sackett reported Hitler had set out to destroy the Left, but he had not been able to win support from Social Democratic ranks. Socialist losses had meant Communist gains. The ambassador correctly guessed that if the Nazis were to experience an increase in voting strength, it would have to come from that section of the population which did not normally vote.[58]

Hitler had to be disappointed in the results. It was the highest voter turnout on record, with 39.3 million people voting, 88.5 percent of those eligible. Sackett was correct in his estimation of where the Nazis would win new votes. After studying the returns, he claimed that "about four million persons who usually stay away from the polls must have voted this time for the Nazi party."[59] The ambassador reported an "unprecedented victory," for the Nazis, but not as large as one would expect "in view of the advantages in their favor." The Nazis polled 17.2 million votes and won 288 seats in a 647 seat Reichstag, and 44 percent of the vote. This was far from a majority, but with the Nationalist vote of 3.1 million, and 52 seats, the governing parties together had a majority of 52 percent. Hugenberg had made a "poor showing," with the same number of seats as in the previous Reichstag, but with the larger total of deputies, it represented a decline. The Catholic parties held their own. But the Center with 74 seats and the Bavarian People's party with 18 seats had lost their pivotal position. Still, their vote was needed if Hitler was to get the enabling legislation he needed to govern without the Reichstag by means of an enabling act.[60]

In spite of the intimidation, and the "ruthless prohibition of all Marxist newspapers and campaign activities," Sackett was pleased to report that the Socialists suffered minimal losses – only one seat. On the other hand, the Communists "suffered substantial losses" of more than a million votes. Opposition to the Nazis was evaporating at an alarming rate with "intimidation of a large section of the population by the Brown Army." Bavaria, its government weakened, was no longer a center of opposition to Hitler or his cabinet.[61]

The Nazis had clear sailing toward their goal of single-party control of the nation. Sackett began to see that he had not discerned the realities of power. Those who he had expected to virtually run the government –

58 Sackett to State, 7 February 1933, 862.00/2902.
59 Sackett to State, 9 March 1933, FRUS, 2: 207.
60 Sackett to State, 6 March 1933, 862.00/2918.   61 Ibid.

Papen, Hugenberg, and the Stahlhelm, partners in the Harzburg Front that brought Hitler into power – were now disappearing into oblivion.[62]

Despatches from the American embassy were unrelieved in reporting Nazi acts of violence and their swift usurpation of the coecive forces of the state. Hugenberg and his Nationalist party expected a dominant role for themselves in the New Germany. Sackett reported that they now "realize that they will have little to say in the Third Reich and this realization mars the rejoicing over the decisive defeat of democracy in Germany." Hitler, he said, could now pursue a "uniform policy" throughout the Reich, unhampered by state governments.

The ambassador was amazed "that an anti-democratic party, with avowed dictatorial aspirations, has managed to obtain power by means of the secret ballot, which constitutes the very foundation of democracy." Hitler's victory was unprecedented. "Democracy in Germany has received a blow from which it may never recover." The nation was "submerged under a huge Nazi wave. The much heralded Third Reich has become a reality. What form this Third Reich will finally take is not yet clear in these critical days of political confusion and uncertainty."[63]

The embassy chancery in Berlin was busy with conjecture about Germany's future. Speculation ranged from guesses that the monarchy would be restored, drawing from the analogy with Fascist Italy, to wishful thinking about Brüning's chances for a comeback. Leon Dominian, consul general in Stuttgart, drew on his experience in Italy when Mussolini came to power to illustrate the similarities. Fighting and street brawls, suppression of civil liberties, the squelching of a free press, the ouster from office of anyone who was not an enthusiastic supporter of the regime, all happened in 1921 Italy, parallel with events in Germany. Dominian was appalled by "Fascist bravoes" in their Storm Trooper uniforms "going about in groups of four or five, with arrogant and swaggering attitude" every day, but especially on Sundays and holidays. Bands of Nazis, in party-owned trucks, traveled from village to village, "entering the homes of private citizens" to determine whether or not they were Nazis, of if there were any Jews in the house.

Dominian suspected that the general "intimidating and terrorizing attitude," so "minutely" similar to what happened in Italy, might be the result of "coaching from Italian masters." The consular officer believed that any people who, in the twentieth century, had submitted to the rule of the Kaiser were "unlikely to oppose another militarist government" such as the Nazis were organizing. Allowances would need to be made for the differences between Germany and Italy, but he believed one could

62 Sackett to State, 13 February, 20 March and Gordon to State, 3 April 1933, 462.00 R296/5750, 862.00/2938 and 2950.
63 Sackett to State, 9 March 1933, FRUS, 1933, 2: 207–209.

expect the Germans to follow suit with the Italian Fascists "in the field of colonial expansion."[64] He warned of the revival of a pre-1914 mentality, hostility to democracy, a restoration of the monarchy, the "Prussian Spirit," and "prewar methods of aggressively disturbing the political structure of Europe with the aim of territorial aggrandizement and the subjugation of non-Germanic peoples."[65]

Sackett warned that a revival of the idea of monarchy could not be ignored. Anticipating a political crisis after the March elections, royalists were looking forward to a restoration. While in Prussia the question was which Hohenzollern would best fit the bill, the Bavarians were ready to restore their own throne. A Wittelsbach was preferred to either a Hohenzollern or "a Nazi dictatorial regime." A small group of legitimists favored the return of the Kaiser, but there was little chance of that happening. Meanwhile, the ex-crown prince kept himself in the public eye, hoping to win popular support. To that end, he appeared in full uniform at the state-sponsored funeral for a Storm Trooper killed on the day Hitler was named chancellor. For their part, the Nazis favored the ex-crown prince's son. But they refused to take a clear stand on the issue of restoration. Sackett pointed out that the Nazis' interest was in the "reorganization of the Reich along Fascist lines with or without a monarch as the nominal head."[66]

Americans had a hard time accepting the reality of the Hitler regime. Many continued to hope that Brüning would save the day. Others looked for a moderate Hitler to emerge and take control of the wilder Nazi elements. Sackett frequently alluded to a comeback by the former chancellor. Americans persisted in their high estimation of Brüning, and their belief that he had a future in German politics. Norman Davis, talking with French Premier Édouard Daladier, Marriner, and Allen Dulles, believed that Hitler was "contemplating" giving Brüning the Foreign Ministry to ward off foreign complaints about Jewish persecution and the violence in Germany.[67]

The idea of Brüning's return would persist even through World War II. Messersmith, talking with the former chancellor in 1937, referred to him as "one of the greatest living Germans" and as "the man best fitted to head the Government which most good Germans hope will succeed the present one."[68] Charles Dawes confided to Brüning that democracy and

---

64 Dominian to State, 21 February 1933, FRUS, 1933, 2: 193–198.
65 Dominian to State, 1 March 1933, 862.00/2927.
66 Sackett to State, 27 February 1933, 862.00/2922.
67 Davis, Memorandum of a Conversation with Daladier, Marriner, and Dulles, 5 April 1933, Box 9, Norman Davis Papers.
68 Messersmith, Memorandum of a Conversation with Brüning, 27 December 1937, 762.00/153. Schleicher thought of bringing Brüning into his government, Fromm, *Blood and Banquets*, 67.

peace in Europe could have been saved if only the chancellor's plans for peace and disarmament had been accepted six years earlier.[69] In 1945, Hoover wrote to Stimson, then secretary of war, that Brüning, living in the United States at the time, was being harassed by the Federal Bureau of Investigation. His mail had been opened and his telephone tapped. Hoover insisted he should be left alone, not only because of the fine work he accomplished in the past, but because of the future, in which he would emerge again as "an important personality" in Europe.[70]

The longing for the past, and wishful thinking about the future, were submerged in the whirlpool of ferocity that inundated the American diplomats in Germany. Report after report depicted a nation given to violence. Descriptions of "terrorist activities" by Storm Troopers against individuals and trade unions were daily reading in the embassy chancery. The accounts came from consular officials and other sources. The Nazi flag now appeared everywhere, over all public buildings, while the republican red, black, and gold flag was nowhere to be seen. A presidential decree ordered that henceforth the Nazi flag should fly side by side with the old imperial flag of black, white, and red, until national colors were legislated. Sackett saw it as just another sign of Nazi dominance of the German landscape.[71]

American diplomats opened up a flood of correspondence to the State Department on Nazi persecution of Jews. Attacks on Jews, on people who "looked Jewish," and on Jewish property became the order of the day. Storm Troopers roamed the streets of German cities, intimidating the public and committing acts of violence, while the regular police were either "powerless or reluctant" to intervene. The "Brown Army" forced the closing of Jewish-owned department and chain stores all over Germany, while in Berlin they stood in front of stores, intimidating the public, insisting that they buy "only German goods and in non-Jewish stores."[72] As the attacks spread to American citizens the State Department began to take notice. Stimson, who would continue in a state of disbelief, "was disinclined to lend credence" to reports that the entire Jewish population of Germany was faced with "a campaign of murder" which was about to begin.[73]

The later failure of the United States to come to the aid of Jews can be attributed in some degree to the inability of diplomats and others to fathom the depths of Nazi racism. In response to Stimson's urgent cable asking for an explanation of what was happening, Sackett reported that the attacks on Jews could be understood as stemming "from the heat of the recent

69 Dawes to Brüning, 10 October 1938, Box 221, Dawes Papers.
70 Hoover to Stimson, 27 June 1945, Post–presidential Papers, Individuals, Stimson, Henry L., HHPL.
71 Sackett to State, 10 and 13 March 1933, 862.00/2921 and 2923.
72 Sackett to State, 10 March 1933, 862.00/2921.
73 Stimson to Sackett, 3 March 1933, FRUS, 1933, 2: 320.

election campaign." An even less credible interpretation of what was happening in Germany, at least from a more recent perspective, was the conviction that Hitler would intervene to restrain the violence of his followers. It was a widely held view, and not only among Americans, that Hitler was a moderate surrounded by radicals. When Hitler asked his Storm Troopers "to maintain law and order, to avoid molesting foreigners," to stop interrupting businesses or creating "possibly embarrassing international incidents," Sackett had good reason to believe that he could and would restore order. Not only was there "good discipline generally" among Nazis,[74] the ambassador had reported numerous instances of Hitler bringing his followers into line under his authority.

Hitler went on the radio to admonish his supporters to "abstain from all physical violence" against political opponents. They were not to interfere with businesses but to exercise "iron discipline" and take satisfaction from knowing that "the Nazi victory was so great that personal revenge could not be tolerated."[75] The admonition to Nazis, demanding restraint on their part, was believable to Americans. Messersmith pointed out that attacks on American Jews had been halted under the direction of Göring after Hitler issued the order. The consul general, who would later be among the most knowledgeable critics of Nazi Germany, claimed that the fears of many were unfounded.

Messersmith had been relegated to a less public position than he would have liked by Gordon's disdain for consular officials. Now, with a new administration in Washington, he meant to demonstrate how well consular officers could do with political reporting.[76] It was his contention that Hitler's adherents had gotten out of hand, but it was unlikely that Hitler would lose control. Like so many others, he thought, at the time, that Hitler would have nothing to do with such lawlessness, which was conceived to be part of the activity of the radical wing of the party. Messersmith said two factors needed to be understood to comprehend what was going on in Germany. First was sole and complete Nazi control of the nation, not only of the central government, but of states and municipalities, down to the communes. Second, order was "completely reestablished in a comparatively short time." Police authority was restored and the situation was "completely in hand" with "no organized or unorganized minorities" capable of challenging Nazi authority.[77]

Although uncontrolled violence was halted, it was because of Hitler's interest in maintaining control of his party. At the same time, he engineered the systematic removal of Jews from public life. Jews were now being expelled from positions in the government at every level, from the Reich

74 Sackett to State, 11 March 1933, FRUS, 1933, 2: 322.
75 Sackett to State, 13 March 1933, 862.00/2923.
76 Stiller, *George S. Messersmith*, 35.
77 Messersmith to State, 21 March 1933, FRUS, 1933, 2: 323.

to the state, provincial, and communal governmemts. They were dismissed from administrative, executive, and even judicial positions. In some cases they were removed from private sector employment, especially in the legal professions and the entertainment fields. Gordon feared that the removals would extend to the medical and scientific fields, and that Jewish students might "encounter serious obstacles." The chargé surmised that some caution would need to be exercised by those Nazis "who are directing this anti-Semitic purge." He explained that many prominent businessmen "and practically all of the important bankers are Jews," which might require more prudence on the part of the Nazis.[78]

The State Department was inundated by letters and telegrams protesting the campaign against Jews in Germany. Americans were outraged by Nazi conduct and demanded that their government do something about it. The new administration of Franklin Roosevelt was faced with the problem of how to respond to widespread demands for action. Secretary of State Cordell Hull asked Gordon for help. The department, he appealed, was "under heavy pressure to make representations in their behalf to the German Government." He was convinced that outside interference in such matters accomplished little and usually worsened matters. The chargé replied that he agreed. American intervention would only feed recriminations against the false "atrocity propaganda" the Germans insisted was emanating from the United States. The Nazi press had just embarked on a crusade against the "campaign of calumny" aimed at Germany from foreign sources; the principal complaint was against Americans. Gordon had a solution for the problem. Hitler, he wrote, would welcome any help in restoring order, even if it were only indirect. The Nazi leader was head of the forces of moderation in his party and would be perceptibly strengthened if the United States would take the line of "expressing confidence in Hitler's determination to restore peaceful and normal conditions emphasizing what a great place he will achieve in the estimation of the world if he is able to bring it about."[79]

Gordon appealed for understanding on the part of the U.S. government. American leadership should be aware that "a far-reaching revolution has actually taken place." Circumstances were such that even under ideal conditions it would take time "before a state of equilibrium can be reestablished." Physical violence had diminished and it probably would extend to the campaign against Jews before long. The persistent theme of an internal struggle among Nazi leaders was reasserted. A "violent radical

78 Gordon to State, 23 March 1933, FRUS, 1933, 2: 328–239.
79 Hull to Gordon, 24 March 1933, Gordon to Hull, 25 March 1933, FRUS, 1933, 2: 330–331; State Department files are overflowing with letters and telegrams of concern about the treatment of Jews in Germany; State Department concern is illustrated in the sample of diplomatic exchanges in the section on "Persecution of Jews in Germany," FRUS, 1933, 2: 320–365.

wing" led by Goebbels and Göring was opposed by the moderates, led by Hitler. The radicals were favored by a long-standing campaign of "anti-Semitic hatred and revenge" fostered by Hitler himself. Unless the Storm Troopers and others were given some outlet for the passions generated by Hitler, the party was destined for serious internal trouble. The moderates, in Gordon's view, were favored because "of those considerations which appeal to all civilized and reasonable people." That consideration was reinforced by the realization that the outside world was certain to react if the state of "uncontrolled terrorism" was allowed to go on. Still, Gordon feared that the Communists might be outlawed, giving Hitler a "legal majority" in the Reichstag which would eliminate the restraining influence of the Nationalist party.[80]

Ambassador Sackett was in the final days of his mission. The reports issuing from the American embassy in Berlin painted a picture of unrelieved gloom.[81] The ambassador was tired and despondent. Bella Fromm, the social and diplomatic reporter, was at the Sacketts' after the Reichstag fire. She remarked that he "is too disappointed about the failure of the Hoover plan and deeply displeased with German domestic politics."[82] He had presided over an exceptionally difficult diplomatic post, beset by heightened and prolonged pressures.[83] He was ready to leave Berlin. As a Hoover appointee, he would be expected to resign when Roosevelt assumed the presidency. Sackett had confided in Castle that he hoped the president would accept his resignation promptly. The domestic political situation in Germany "has taken such a turn and has created such a break with the past, that it is of great importance that the new Ambassador begin his ministry at the earliest possible moment." Uncertainty was prevalent in Germany, and he believed "we may look for most anything, but I have the feeling that whatever may happen Germany is looking forward to a continued Hitler regime." He cautioned against naming anyone of Jewish heritage because anti-Semitism was "one of the tenets" of Nazism.[84]

As was customary, Sackett submitted his resignation to the new president on inauguration day, March 4, 1933, to be effective that day or as soon as convenient. Personal matters commanded his attention and he expressed the desire to be relieved of his assignment "at an early opportunity." Nearly two weeks later the Roosevelt administration responded with an acceptance. The ambassador's resignation was "to be effective upon the date of your departure for the United States or on the date of the

80 Gordon to State, 23 March 1933, FRUS, 1933, 2: 328–330.
81 See Sackett to State, 10, 21, 24 March 1933, FRUS, 1933, 2: 210–214.
82 Fromm, *Blood and Banquets*, 76.
83 See Division of Foreign Service Personnel to Hugh Cumming, Hull's secretary, 14 September, and William E. Dodd to Roosevelt, 1 September 1933, Official File 523: Dodd, William E., FDRL.
84 Sackett to Castle, 13 February 1933, Castle Papers.

presentation of your letter of recall, whichever may first occur."[85] Sackett received the customary eulogy from Papen, but not from Hitler, and was warmly received by Hindenburg. With his wife he departed in a reserved railway carriage, with one compartment filled with gifts and flowers, while a flock of diplomats gathered at the station to see them off.[86] It was March 22, the day before the intimidated and subservient Reichstag, with Brüning's help, passed the Enabling Act that paved the way for Hitler's legal dictatorship.

Taken ill with an attack of influenza, by an ironic twist of fate, Sackett decided to take the cure at Vichy, France. Interviewed by the press, he emphasized the importance of the World Economic Conference in London. Still thinking in terms of the aspirations of his friend Heinrich Brüning, he predicted that the future would depend upon the "freedom and voice" Germany was given at that critical meeting. If equality were denied to Germany, it could lead to a "bitter international struggle" that would be "scarcely less ruinous to the world at large than the war itself." He expressed his firm belief that economics lay, as it always had, at the base of a nation's politics. Most of the political dangers could be overcome "if there is a wise treatment" of Europe's economic problems. The "political revolution" in Germany could be "attributed first of all to economic conditions."[87]

Sackett called for "a suspension of judgment" on what was happening in Germany. When he left Berlin, he felt that the "phase of physical demonstration was over." There were no further reports of anti-Jewish activity and it appeared that the "period of incidents" was past. He cautioned against using these episodes as the basis for a general condemnation of the Hitler government. Such a mistake could lead to "a real anti-Semitic movement in Germany." Again, he rationalized the extremes of Nazi behavior by attributing it to the excess of zeal flowing from the intensity of the party's election campaign. It was always difficult, he said, to prevent early intemperate activity by such partisans. Sackett declined to comment on Hitler or the Nazi movement except to express his regret at the disappearance of a free press and democracy in Germany.[88]

At best, Sackett was seeing through a glass darkly. His official despatches revealed that he feared the worst from Hitler's dictatorship. From the very beginning he singled out Hitler and the Nazi party as the principal danger to the Weimar Republic and to the peace of Europe. He still held out hope that the World Economic Conference, for which he worked so hard and

85 Sackett to Roosevelt and Roosevelt to Sackett, 4 and 17 March 1933, Official File 321: Sackett, Frederic M., FDRL.
86 Fromm, *Blood and Banquets*, 93; the diplomatic reporter's chronology and detail cannot be trusted, but she usually captured the color and general tenor of events.
87 *New York Times*, 29 March 1933, clipping in the Filson Club.
88 *New York Times*, 29 March 1933.

so long, could solve Germany's domestic problems, and bring peace to Europe. His relentless efforts to help Brüning went far beyond those of any other diplomat and were carried out with a diligence that surpassed the intentions of his own government. It seems clear enough that regardless of his best efforts, nothing could be done to save Brüning or the Weimar Republic. Sackett foresaw the disaster for democracy in Germany. His inability to divine the future of Nazi Germany was a failure he shared with most of the world's leaders, who until the end of the Third Reich were unable to comprehend the enormity of the Hitler regime.

Sackett might have found some solace in the fact that six months after Hitler was named chancellor, Ambassador William E. Dodd, his successor, was unable to make an accurate assessment of the immediate future. The new ambassador wrote Roosevelt that it was not possible to determine whether the Hitler regime would "take a more liberal or a more ruthless direction." It was his guess that the government would "take a more moderate course." Roosevelt was pleased that Dodd did not "seem quite as pessimistic as some other people."[89] Like so many others, Sackett believed that the responsibilities of power would soften the Hitler government. Later, in October 1933, he wrote Hoover that the methods of the political revolution in Germany were "tragic," but he believed that "the sobering effects of the responsibility of power ... will gradually work an improvement of recent conditions. My correspondents indicate the more conservative elements are becoming more active already."[90]

Sackett returned to Louisville and again took up his familiar interests in the coal industry in a variety of executive capacities. He conducted his business affairs in the offices of the Louisville law firm of Bruce and Bullitt and spent much of his time at his farm near Lexington. There the former senator and diplomat was able to devote himself to two of his greatest loves – agriculture and horses, which he continued to enjoy until his death of a heart attack while visiting Baltimore on May 18, 1941.[91]

---

89 Dodd to Roosevelt, 30 July 1933, Official File 523: Dodd, William E., FDRL.
90 Sackett to Hoover, 5 October 1933, Post-presidential Papers – Individuals, Sackett, F. M., HHPL.
91 *New York Times*, 19 May 1941.

Conclusion

FROM THE TIME he arrived in Berlin to the date of his departure from Germany, Ambassador Sackett expressed his concern that the Weimar Republic was in danger. Very early in his mission he detected a problem in American policy. It was the intention of the United States to support political stability and economic prosperity in Europe. The means adopted to achieve that goal was to support republican government in Germany with a policy of loans and investments. Committed to the Weimar Republic, the United States relied on the private sector to achieve its goal. Although he was without experience in diplomacy, Sackett was a seasoned veteran in business and finance, which enabled him quickly to understand that American loan policy to Germany was a source of potential trouble for both nations. Sackett was confronted with the loan issue soon after he arrived in Berlin when he learned that American bankers were organizing a major loan to the German government. Without hesitation, Sackett criticized the loan as unnecessary and undesirable. He opposed the loan and informed the U.S. government that the Germans should be forced to deal with their domestic fiscal problems with their own resources; such loans only helped to postpone the consequences of German failure to address their pressing domestic financial problems. It was that inability to put their financial house in order that Sackett saw as the fundamental problem faced by the Germans.

Although the U.S. government resisted a direct and significant commitment to Germany, Sackett intervened to elicit a more active role from the Hoover administration. The ambassador had lost patience with and faith in the corporatist system and attempted to influence his government to shift its emphasis away from American private sector loans to the Germans. His initial suggestion for solving the problem was to advise the Germans to convert their short-term obligations into long-term ones. It was his belief that his proposal could be accomplished if the Germans sold their securities outside New York and other financial centers and instead offered them to the American hinterland. He persisted in offering that counsel to the Germans, but soon came to the conclusion that the problem ranged far beyond Germany's short-term indebtedness. The problem was so serious that Sackett thought it threatened the very existence of the Weimar Republic. The ambassador finally came to believe that only an international conference of all the major powers was adequate to address the complex problem of intergovernmental debt.

Sackett thought the situation had become critical when after the September 1930 Reichstag elections George Murnane, acting from the private sector, arranged another major loan for the Germans, this time with the political purpose of supporting the Brüning government. Murnane feared the consequences if Hitler came into power, and he was able to convince American and European financiers that it was prudent to support Brüning. But Sackett demurred, warning the U.S. government that loans to Germany were excessive and that the whole system was being overdone. The ambassador thought that the private sector was acting in an irresponsible way. Sackett consulted with Brüning about Germany's financial condition and together they decided that an international conference of heads of state was the best way to address the issue. Such a conference would have to deal with more than short-term loans; it would need to confront the broader problems of war debts and reparations. Sackett and Brüning agreed that the Americans, led by President Hoover, were the only people with the prestige and authority to convene a meeting of that importance, and, of course, the only power that could annul the war debts.

Sackett placed a great deal of faith in the efficacy of an international economic conference and shared Brüning's enthusiasm for the idea. From Brüning's perspective it was an excellent opening to an effective agreement regarding German overborrowing and, most importantly, it provided an opportunity for a final settlement of the reparations issue. For Sackett such a conference was the best way yet devised to deal with the international financial problems that were a major cause of the depression, and at the same time it gave him a chance to come to Brüning's rescue.

Sackett believed it was mandatory that the U.S. government intervene to prevent an international financial emergency. Leaders in business and finance soon came to agree with him, but the Hoover administration was slow to respond. When, in 1931, the financial crisis struck, Sackett was in Washington and played a significant role in the development of the Hoover Moratorium. Even then the United States acted with minimal assistance; the government neither had the will nor did it believe it had the power to intervene decisively. Sackett urged the government to help resolve the German crisis by opening the negotiation of the war debts and reparations issues. Although he was able to broach the subject with the president and secretary of state, Sackett was unable to make any progress to that end.

Beyond that, Sackett with American and foreign diplomats in Berlin,

Paris, London, and Washington did everything they believed they could to support the Weimar Republic. Among the Americans, until 1931, the initiative was left in the hands of the private sector, which had intervened with significant loans in support of the postwar reparations settlement. The French and British governments were active participants in that financial policy. But when the prospects for profits virtually disappeared with the deepening depression, financiers and bankers no longer had the power or the authority to respond to events in Germany beyond what they could do to save their investments. The enormous might of American finance proved inadequate to cope with the crisis, and American private sector leaders joined with Sackett in calling for the assistance of the U.S. government.

The private talks he had with Brüning opened the way to the most outstanding feature of Sackett's mission in Germany: the extraordinary relationship he established with the German chancellor. A strong personal and political friendship was cemented in the December 1930 meeting in which both men saw the need for an international economic conference. Beginning with those talks, Sackett did everything in his power to help Brüning to achieve German foreign policy goals. After he induced the U.S. government to intervene he went beyond his instructions in his efforts to help Brüning and then invented ways of his own to assist his friend.

Sackett was able to use a personal relationship with President Hoover to gain his attention and get him to act. The ambassador was convinced of the importance of the government's taking an active role in the resolution of the developing emergency in international finance. In a long, personal letter, he warned of the dangers faced by the Brüning government; the situation was so serious, he argued, that only intervention by the United States could avert the impending crisis. Hoover responded favorably, but a series of unfortunate and fortuitous events intervened to delay action in convening a conference.

While he waited for the president to take the initiative to call a meeting of heads of state, Sackett persisted in spreading the word about the dangerous financial situation in Germany. Alarmed by what he perceived to be an impending financial breakdown, he wanted to alert the Hoover administration to the perilous state of affairs in Germany, but thought it necessary to keep the matter within official government circles. He believed the private sector was responsible for the crisis and feared that alerting the bankers and financiers might lead to an even greater disaster. Sackett reported that some major American banks had nearly 50 percent of their capital loaned to Germany. The amounts were so great, he warned, that they could be neither recalled nor renewed without great danger to the American financial community. Further revealing his lack of faith in the corporatist system, he feared that if the seriousness of the situation became public, there would be a call on loans and a withdrawal of funds, which could precipitate an economic disaster for the United States and Europe, and would almost certainly destroy the Weimar Republic.

The plan for an international economic conference stirred British interest in such a meeting, as that country was moving toward the conviction that the cycle of reparations and war debts should be brought to an end. When British Ambassador Rumbold queried Sackett about the probability of President Hoover's calling a major conference, the American could not offer any assurances. Disheartened, but not despairing of action from his government, Sackett took advantage of an already planned vacation in the United States. He wanted to bring the plight of the Brüning government and the danger to the financial world to the attention of Hoover and Stimson in person. Meanwhile, Sackett took advantage of British interest, working in concert with his boyhood friend Oswald Garrison Villard. They were able to influence like-minded Britons in and out of the government to help Brüning. The result was the conference at Chequers where Brüning was able to discuss German financial distress with Prime Minister MacDonald, who then urged the U.S. government to act.

When the financial crisis struck, the Americans intervened with what they believed to be massive government intervention with the Hoover Moratorium. But the assistance turned out to be minimal; the government neither had the will nor did it believe it had the power to intervene decisively. Principal American bankers and financiers agreed it was necessary for the government to play a decisive role, and along with Sackett attempted to stimulate greater involvement by the Hoover administration. Influenced by Sackett, and later by many others, Hoover understood the need for greater participation in the crisis by the organs of government. The result was that with the Hoover Moratorium the United States acted with greater force to solve a problem in international finance than ever before.

Sackett advised that one way to help resolve the German crisis was to negotiate the war debts and reparations issue, a policy Brüning urged on the American ambassador; but that resolution of the crisis was unlikely considering American attitudes toward war debts and the French stance on reparations. Given such an impasse, there was very little that could be done.

Nevertheless, American diplomats did everything they believed they could to support the Weimar Republic. Until 1931, the initiative was left in the hands of the private sector, which intervened with significant loans in support of the postwar reparations settlement. But advancing more money to Germany enabled it to defer the consequences of domestic fiscal policy and to make relatively painless reparations payments until the world economy had reached crisis proportions. The postwar settlement was allowed to fester without resolution, feeding the climate of opposition in Germany. Although it is unlikely that the reparations issue could have been settled short of a crisis, the powers were never required to face the real repercussions because of American money. The three loans organized by George Murnane in 1930 enabled the Germans to delay the arrival of the day of reckoning. In each case, Sackett saw the loans as unusual and uncalled-for, allowing the Germans to carry on as if there were no problem.

In the Weimar years, the United States placed inordinate faith in the private sector's ability to resolve political problems with financial means. American leadership believed that by converting reparations payments into a commercial obligation they had taken the issue out of politics. That unrealistic position was worsened by the failure to acknowledge the political nature of the loans to Germany. Far from being closer in tune with the general public than politicians and bureaucrats, which was a basic tenet of the corporatist system, the financiers seriously misunderstood the attitude of the German people. There was no disguising the fact that Germany was paying reparations whether converted into a business matter or not.

American presidents are influenced by their perception of what public opinion will accept. President Hoover was convinced that the American public would not accept cancellation of war debts owed to the United States. That made it difficult to find an alternative to the cycle of American loans to Germany to pay reparations, and reparations to the Entente Allies to pay war debts to the United States. When American loans were involuntarily removed from the cycle, the system was bound to collapse. Rather than face that reality and resolve the issue, as Sackett advised, the United States stood by while at Lausanne the European powers effectively annuled the system. Then in London, in June 1933, the United States refused to cooperate in an attempt to create a new international system. The World Economic Conference, which Sackett hoped would accomplish that very goal, was a failure. It had the support of neither the Hoover nor the Roosevelt administration.

When in 1931 the U.S. government intervened with the Hoover Moratorium, that too proved to be insufficient. It did not help Brüning. It provided only very short-term assistance and deprived the German of the domestic credit he could have won by declaring a moratorium himself. In addition, the one-year postponement of debt also delayed any action the chancellor might have been able to take.

With heavy investment in Germany, one school of thought would have it that the United States exercised enormous influence.[1] On the contrary, American money was hostage to the Germans who, including Brüning, used the United States for all they could get without ever conceding anything of importance. All Brüning offered in return for the help extended to him was his continuance in office and further demands. American assistance proved to be irrelevant when Brüning was forced to resign. The United

1 For example, Link, *Die Amerikanische Stabilisierungspolitik in Deutschland*, 502–503.

States did not even have the clout to force Hindenburg to abandon his pet hobby, the pocket battleships. The United States was not only not the preponderant power in Europe, it is difficult to see it even as a dominant power. The British and French both courted American political cooperation but were put off, which left the European powers to fend for themselves.

In spite of everything Sackett did, United States efforts to bolster Brüning and impede Hitler's climb to power were minimal. Although there were direct attempts to assist Brüning, Americans did not respond explicitly to Hitler but, rather, to the conditions that made his popularity possible. Today, when diplomacy, intelligence activity, and covert operations are closely tied together, it nearly passes credulity to realize that the United States did not even contemplate action. Neither political nor military means were marshaled to help the Weimar Republic and thwart Hitler. American diplomats even avoided contact with the Nazis for almost two years after Hitler became a central figure in German politics. When Ambassador Sackett made his only attempt to meet Hitler, it was done furtively and with apologies to both his own and the German government.

Rather than exercise power, the United States was little more than a bystander in the events played out in Germany. Sackett agreed with the firm American belief that economic involvement would help sustain republican ideology. Although he did urge more political involvement in his recommendations for intervention, he was unable to persuade his government to act. For all practical purposes, when the political-economic-ideological crisis struck the German nation, the Americans were unable to project their national strength to remedy the situation in their favor. The United States failed to translate its economic strength into political clout. If the dollar were to be used to implement American foreign policy in Europe, it needed to be backed by American military and diplomatic determination.[2] Although, with Sackett's prodding, American leadership perceived a threat to American strategic interests, they were unable and unwilling to act. The Americans simply abandoned the field, leaving Germany to its fate, while the private sector acted almost alone, but only to salvage what they could of their financial and economic investments.

Economic well-being was accepted as the key to solving the political problems that beset Germany. To this end Sackett counseled United States support for the leadership and policies of Heinrich Brüning that were considered the most likely avenues to economic and political stability in Germany and hence in all of Europe. Although Brüning did not act decisively to end the depression, and instituted what Sackett characterized as a "veiled dictatorship," his policies were acceptable to the United States. The economic and political implications of the domestic program of the "Hunger

2 See Brian McKercher, "Reaching for the Brass Ring: The Recent Historiography of Interwar American Foreign Relations," 565–598, esp. 584–586.

Chancellor" were lost to the Americans in a fog of commitment to the efficacy of money to achieve desired ends.

If, as suggested, the United States "could have tried to give greater understanding, support, and encouragement to the moderate forces in the Weimar Republic,"[3] then Ambassador Sackett gave all he could. With Sackett's encouragement, the United States was willing to concede to Brüning the customs union with Austria, the reduction of reparations, equality in armaments, and a revision of the Polish Corridor among other things. All the concessions were seen as desirable in themselves, but also as a means of thwarting Hitler and the Nazis. The American position fostered revisionism in Germany without taking any direct action to facilitate that revision.

With profitable investment drying up in Germany, the private sector intervention diminished and the public sector began to play a larger role.[4] Whereas the Lausanne Conference was a strategy to resolve the tangled web of war debts and reparations, the disarmament conference at Geneva was meant to settle the issue of Germany's power status. At Lausanne, Papen was able to reap the harvest sown by Sackett and Brüning. The European powers effectively annuled the war debts issue by directly tying them to a reparations schedule that in effect ended both problems. At Geneva, French preoccupation with their security against German aggression annoyed Americans. In cooperation with the British, the Americans wanted to convince the French that they should make concessions to Germany. The Anglo-Americans were willing to see Germany rearm and expected France to accept that approach to European peace based on the belief that Brüning offered the best hope for an acceptable solution for all parties concerned.

For too long, American policy revolved around the person of Heinrich Brüning. There was no German policy but, rather, a Brüning policy, a deceptively easy relationship. As the disarmament conference clearly demonstrates, the Americans, seconded by the British, were willing to make significant concessions to the Center party leader, concessions they refused to extend to his successor. Franz von Papen was taken to be a symbol of what was wrong with Germany. The United States had been committed to a head of government when the proper relationship was state to state, not person to person. When Brüning was removed from office, Americans would not give to Germany what it was eager to give to the Center party leader.

Americans misread Brüning's intentions, and Ambassador Sackett was partly responsible. The American was aware that Brüning was attempting

3 Kennan, *American Diplomacy*, 79.
4 On the reduced role played by the private sector after 1931, especially in the early New Deal years, see Erdmann, "Mining for the Corporatist Synthesis," 196–200.

to win back everything Germany had lost at Versailles, from territorial revision, to rearmament and the reacquisition of colonies. Sackett made a realistic assessment of the chancellor's intentions when he was in office, but found the same goals unacceptable when sought, first by Papen, then by Hitler. Sackett and the Hoover administration were able to overlook the possible dangers in Brüning's goals partly because they perceived him as the one person who could solve Germany's economic problems. In addition, they persisted in their belief that the German was a democrat and a republican. He was neither. An advocate of a constitutional monarchy, Brüning abided by the Weimar Constitution until such time as he could establish a regency to make way for a restoration of the Hohenzollern dynasty.

Some seasoned diplomats in the State Department began to see Sackett as too pro-German. The ambassador was bold in taking initiatives and making promises to Brüning; they felt he was too optimistic in evaluating the chancellor's ability to succeed. Sackett, some thought, believed so much in Brüning that he might be crippled in his analysis of his friend and blind to his faults. But, importantly, neither Hoover nor Stimson shared those views. They valued Sackett's appraisals of the situation in Germany and were as deeply committed to Brüning as the ambassador was. That was particularly the case with Stimson, who was much influenced by the ambassador. The president and secretary of state were willing to heed Sackett's advice and responded by doing all they felt was possible to help the German chancellor.

In spite of all the assistance the Americans gave to Brüning, he consistently refused to offer concessions in return for advantages gained. He and his government irritated Americans and the British as well by an unfailing refusal to offer thanks for favors received. The more he was helped, the more the German asked in his drive to achieve German national goals. Brüning and his government knew that the Americans and British were acting according to national policy that was dependent on a strong Germany. There were no thanks necessary to governments carrying out their own policy interests.

It might well have been possible for Brüning to push an expansionist foreign policy without the outbreak of a major war resulting. As one authority maintains, "Weimar foreign policy provided opportunities for advancing and defending national interests without automatically threatening the rest of Europe."[5] Brüning's approach won the support of the United States and Great Britain. Given that backing, the German could have won French agreement. One can conceive of a series of compromises in which Germany, France, and Poland could settle territorial and power relationships. However, Brüning's foreign policy goals became irrelevant.

5 See John Hiden, *The Baltic States and Weimar Ostpolitik*, x.

When he failed to win Harzburg Front support to extend President Hindenburg's term of office without an election, Brüning's days were numbered. To his credit, Sackett realized how important the Social Democratic party was to the survival of the Weimar Republic and the Brüning government. Sackett believed it was that dependence on Socialist support which spelled the doom of Brüning and the republic. The ambassador realized that none of the power brokers in Germany were willing to continue a system dependent on Socialists and that they were even willing to accept a Hitler as an alternative to a welfare state.

The conservative lawyer-businessman from Kentucky not only expressed his unfailing admiration for the Socialist party and its leaders, he attributed Brüning's fall to the intrigues of large landowners and industrialists who took advantage of discontent among army officers disturbed by the chancellor's reliance on trade unions and Socialists for support. Sackett believed that Brüning's resignation was an event of major historical importance and took the time to outline a chronology of events that had led to his friend's decision and foreshadowed the collapse of the Weimar Republic.

Sackett was stunned by Brüning's resignation. It took all the personal meaning out of his mission. He refused to accept the Papen government as anything more than a disaster for Germany. He shifted his relationship with the German government to one of stiff formality and waited for it to rectify the mistake of naming Papen chancellor. He expected the German people to come to their senses and call Brüning back into office. Sackett recognized that the new cabinet was not unlike Brüning's "veiled dictatorship," and he deplored Papen's move toward monarchy, still unaware that his friend entertained just such purposes. Like Sackett, the U.S. government suffered such a sense of loss with Brüning's resignation that it affected policy. Stimson severely cut the budget for the disarmament delegation at Geneva and gave up hope that anything of significance was likely to happen there or at Lausanne.

When he was chancellor, Brüning continued to pursue his foreign policy even in the face of strong American opposition, further evidence of the lack of American power in influencing events in Germany. The chancellor pursued his goals even after he exasperated Sackett with his refusal to grant concessions to anyone, and after he upset Hoover with his demands for more help even on the heels of the moratorium. Hoover believed the German was undermining the impact of this holiday in the payment of intergovernmental debts. But Brüning was able to persist in spite of American opposition because he believed he had command of the one issue that would rally support for him – communism.

Sackett encouraged Brüning in the belief that communism was the single threat that could get the attention of the American government. When the chancellor thought he had gone too far in using the Red Scare, Sackett went him one better and exaggerated the danger to the extent of completely discounting the threat Hitler and the Nazis posed to the republic. Moreover, Sackett was personally responsible for misleading Hoover, Stimson, and the State Department in stressing the danger to Germany of communism rather than the Nazis. It became common currency in the State Department to view the Nazis as no more than an instrument of German policy that enabled them to threaten and alarm foreign governments into granting Germany concessions.

Sackett's inordinate fear of communism was just an extreme case of that fear among almost all political and business leaders in the West. In his official reports Sackett emphasized the dangers of Hitler and the Nazis to the Weimar Republic, although in his more important personal correspondence with Hoover and Stimson he accentuated his personal view that communism constituted the principal danger. Beginning with his first official reports after he arrived in Berlin as ambassador, and continuing until the end of his mission, Sackett unfailingly expressed his apprehension about the possibility of a Hitler government. It is likely that the ambassador used the communist threat at times because he thought it was the most effective way to get the attention of the Hoover administration.

Although Sackett continued to see communism as the ultimate beneficiary of the collapse of the Weimar Republic, to his credit, when confronted by continued Nazi success, he began to focus more on Hitler and the Nazis. The possibility of Hitler's success in the presidential elections and Wiley's return to Berlin were instrumental in prompting him to learn more about the Nazis. It was then that he met Göring, Goebbels, and even Hitler. He did not think Hitler had the qualities necessary to govern Germany – he saw him as a rabble-rouser and a demagogue incapable of exercising the authority needed to cope with the complexity of government.

Sackett's direct relationship with President Hoover and with Secretary of State Stimson gave him the opportunity to influence policy. He had some success, for example, during the financial crisis of 1931 and in urging a call for a World Economic Conference. But he wasted his knowledge of Hitler and the Nazi party. Much of what he reported was relegated to the category of what one clerk told to another. Instead of emphasizing the danger of Hitler and the Nazis, he used the personal authority he developed in fruitless warnings of the dangers of communism. It was easy for Americans to grasp the dangers of the Red Menace; comprehending Hitler proved to be a more difficult problem.

When Sackett did use a "Hitler threat," it was merely to get the attention of the U.S. government after he had worn out the Red Scare tactic. But rather than using this threat in a meaningful way, Sackett merely indicated that the radicalism represented by Hitler could be foisted on Europe as a "drastic dose of medicine" by Brüning. Sackett withdrew the thought immediately but left the impression that the United States and the European powers should come to their senses and grant Brüning his foreign policy goals or something extreme was likely to happen.

By stressing communism in his correspondence with Hoover, Sackett contributed to the failure of the United States to act more decisively in European affairs. Strongly reluctant to intercede in European politics, the United States was unlikely to be moved by the familiar, long-term fear of communism, which was perceived as a domestic problem rather than as a threat of war. It is possible, even if not likely, that Sackett could have moved the Hoover administration to action regarding the war debts issue had he emphasized the danger of warfare in Europe that a Hitler government threatened.

In his official despatches Sackett did refer to the Nazis as a warlike party, but he did not think that Germany posed an immediate threat of war until Papen became chancellor. It was then he saw Germany as a danger to the peace of Europe with or without Hitler. It was Sackett's perception that Papen was moving toward militarism and monarchy that raised the ambassador's consciousness in the matter of potential war.

Sackett and his staff were alarmed at the mood of many Germans. There was a nationalistic core of opposition to the Weimar Republic, which did not augur well for the future of democracy in Germany. Sackett identified that center of nationalist sentiment with the Nazi movement, but he emphasized a distinction between the Nazi party and the Nazi movement. The Nazi party was essentially negative in its approach, in his view, with a vague and opportunistic program. The Nazis simply promised to eliminate everything they considered undesirable and replace it with a regenerated, purely National Socialist state. Sackett described the Nazi movement as composed of nationalistic Germans who were idealistic and enthusiastic to the point of fanaticism. His analysis of Hitler's intentions and Nazi party activity was excellent for the most part,[6] and by the summer of 1932 he had the full attention of the U.S. government. No better evidence attests to that interest than the near panic that set in when Sackett failed to report on Hitler's meeting with Hindenburg in August 1932.

Sackett was convinced that the Nazi movement could and would be used. He was, however, not convinced that Hitler was the man to take advantage of it – a view shared by many German leaders who hoped they

6 Historians disagree on the effectiveness of Sackett's political reporting. Arnold Offner, *The Origins of the Second World War*, 50, writes that "Sackett proved to be a very poor analyst of the political scene, but this did not dissuade him from encouraging American investment in Germany and from becoming a sympathetic, if sometimes indiscreet, spokesman for the German Government in its battle to end reparations." Jesse Stiller, *George S. Messersmith*, 33–34, disagrees. Referring to events after Hitler became chancellor, he writes that "Ambassador Sackett had kept Washington well informed on these critical developments." In fairness, it should be noted that neither scholar focused on Sackett, both being concerned with the period after Hitler became chancellor.

would be beneficiaries. The Reichswehr, Brüning, and Schleicher were among those who aspired to divert Hitler and win the support of the Nazi movement. For a time Joseph Goebbels thought he could assume control, and some, including Sackett and Schleicher, thought Gregor Strasser could capture it by splitting the Nazi party.

Under Brüning's influence the American believed that the movement could be won over with a patriotic program such as ending reparations payments, acquiring lost territory, and rearming Germany. Brüning convinced Sackett that he could either win over the movement or control it by working with and controlling Hitler.

At first Sackett thought that Brüning could accomplish those very ends. When Brüning failed, Sackett lost hope that the movement could be controlled by anyone but Hitler. The American diplomat's outlook was improved when in the July 1932 Reichstag elections Hitler failed to win a majority. Sackett estimated that the Nazis had reached the maximum strength they could hope for. He believed there was only the remotest of possibilities that Hitler could form a majority government.

Sackett was almost gleeful in reporting the decline of Hitler and the Nazis when they suffered defeat in the November 1932 elections. He believed that the Nazi party had passed its peak and was slowly disintegrating, and proclaimed that Hitler's chances for forming a majority cabinet were shattered; the Third Reich was now only a distant, even unlikely, prospect. Sackett shared the view of many at the time, including many Nazis, that Hitler's all-or-nothing tactic to win control of the government had failed. Since Brüning had convinced Sackett that the Nazi movement could be won over, the ambassador was ready for someone to complete the task.

Sackett and Brüning were among the many who believed that Hitler could not maintain control of such a large and amorphous force as the Nazi movement. Even after Hitler had been handed the chancellorship, Sackett was convinced that he and his party would fail. The ambassador feared above all that the German Communist party would inherit the anti-Weimar movement in the wake of Nazi failure. For their part, the Communists agreed. Their strategy was to wait for Hitler to come to power so that they could pick up the pieces. The American capitalists feared, and the Soviet Communists hoped, that Nazism was but a brief episode in the coming communist revolution in Germany.

It was an urgent matter for Sackett that Germany find a leader who could be trusted to reinvigorate the Weimar Republic. The German electorate had turned radical with a majority voting for the Communists and Nazis combined. The Weimar Republic was in danger of dissolution, and in the ambassador's estimation, only a figure of Brüning's stature could win the support of the radical electorate. In a desperate search for a solution for the republic and democracy in Germany, Sackett found his champion in General Kurt von Schleicher.

When General Schleicher became chancellor, Sackett divested himself of all reservations he had concerning the military politician. Earlier, Sackett had not been favorably impressed by the general, but now as Schleicher began to form a government, the American saw more than hope, he saw the salvation for the republic. As the conservative American diplomat observed Schleicher's attempt to establish a broad base of support he was pleased to find that the general wanted to extend his backing to include the trade unions and the Socialists. More than anything else, Sackett was gladdened by the enemies the political general made, especially politicians of the ilk of Alfred Hugenberg.

When Schleicher attempted to broaden his support to include a section of the Nazi party, Sackett was delighted. He now placed all his hopes for the survival of the republic in the general's ability to win the backing of Gregor Strasser, split the Nazi party, and capture the vote of the Nazi movement. The American ambassador, as so many others, was lulled into believing that the Weimar Republic had won a reprieve with the proposed alliance of Schleicher and dissident Nazis. They were shocked and dismayed that the moribund Harzburg Front had been able to rescue Hitler from what they thought would be oblivion.

German politics had been quiet over the holiday season and Sackett, with many others, was happy that Schleicher seemed to be making progress toward a stable government. When Hitler was named chancellor, Sackett thought it important to account for such an unhappy sequel to what he thought was a satisfactory political settlement. Again, the conservative Republican politician attributed Hitler's success to the intrigues of the Nationalist party and their reactionary allies, including large landowners, who were upset that Schleicher courted socialists and organized labor, and favored social welfare policies.

It was difficult for Sackett to accept the reality of the Hitler government. He found consolation in what he believed to be the Nazi's eventual undoing. When Hitler left the finance and economic ministries in the hands of the Hugenberg Nationalists and experts, Sackett thought it would soon be over for the new chancellor. Even while acknowledging that the Nazis had taken control of the police in the Reich and Prussia, Sackett was sure that Hitler would fail. By leaving money matters in the control of others, the Nazis confirmed his belief that they were incapable of governing Germany. The real reins of power were not in Nazi hands. Hitler would fail and, the American ambassador thought, the door would again be opened for Brüning's return.

Sackett was appalled by Hitler's government. His reports were an unrelieved account of Nazi violence and acts of anti-Semitism, and he was in a state of disbelief. Sackett, with his trusted colleagues British Ambassador Horace Rumbold and his French counterpart André François-Poncet, agreed it was Nazis who had set the Reichstag fire and used it as a pretext for suspending civil liberties and jailing their political opponents. They could not believe what was happening. The American diplomats in Berlin attibuted the violence to the enthusiasm of the Nazis and their Storm Troopers, who were releasing their pent-up emotions. They believed that Hitler, who appeared as the moderate in the midst of the radicalism that surrounded them, would calm down his followers. Sackett hoped that what he was witnessing was an aberration that would go away with time and took some consolation in the fact that although Hitler had everything going for him in the March 1933 elections, he still was unable to win a majority of the electorate's votes. The ambassador tried to put the best face on events and hoped for a better future.

Neither Sackett nor the world's statesmen, not even the German people, were sure about what the Hitler government held out for the future. Hitler had not yet fully developed his public persona. It took time for him to form the role he played as leader of the German people. He had established some of the symbols that would guide his regime, but very few had been clarified.[7] The large minority of Germans who voted for him in 1933 were expressing their frustration with the economic and political failures of the Weimar Republic. Sackett saw the Nazis as just the most radical and impatient of the republic's opponents. He judged most of Germany's grievances to be legitimate.

Still, Sackett was disappointed to the point of despondency when Hitler became chancellor. He was uncertain about the consequences that could be expected, but he knew they were all unwelcome. The creation of a dictatorship and a National Socialist state was certain; Sackett was impressed by "Hitler's dogged determination to rule alone." But by promising everything, the Nazis had committed themselves to nothing. Hitler pursued power with a will and determination hard to understand. When power was achieved, he had the opportunity to move in any of a number of directions. The United States was willing to support significant change. It was not Germany's desire to upset the Versailles Treaty that bothered Americans. Above all, it was the Nazi style and methods that they found reprehensible. In Germany, Hitler was accepted in 1933 by the traditional German power base – not as an alternative to Brüning or even to Papen, but as a less desirable equivalent. To them, Hitler's liability was that although he would pursue the same policies, he would bring with him people who were socially, as well as politically, undesirable. Moreover, he was shown to be willing to use force to achieve his ends.

That conclusion was easily drawn by Sackett from the violent record of Hitler's private army. Nazi Storm Troopers first appeared as near comic figures to American diplomats. The image was of an overblown troop of Boy Scouts, as Gordon put it. That initial impression was transformed into

---

7 Ian Kershaw, *The "Hitler Myth": Image and Reality in the Third Reich*, 2–3.

fear and repugnance as the Nazis grew in numbers and in success. Their physical violence alarmed Americans and contributed to the perception that the Nazis were a band of thugs rather than a serious political party capable of governing in a parliamentary system. Once Hitler achieved his goal of governing Germany, Sackett was convinced that one of two paths would open. Either Hitler would be an abject failure, or the responsibilities of power would moderate his leadership and the tone and methods of his party. No one at the time could have been aware not only that Hitler would succeed, but that his style and methods would take a turn toward a violence beyond the experience of the statesmen who dealt with the problems of Hitler's rise to power.

Bibliography

The literature on the Weimar Republic and Hitler's rise to power is enormous. A helpful introduction is Peter D. Stachura, *The Weimar Era and Hitler, 1918–1933: A Critical Bibliography* (Oxford, Clio Press, 1977). The works cited in the following bibliography played a direct role in writing this monograph. The author is indebted to many others whose labors helped to form his views.

Manuscript collections

Bernard M. Baruch Papers, Princeton University.
Nicholas Murray Butler Papers, Columbia University.
William R. Castle Diary, Harvard University.
William R. Castle Papers, Herbert Hoover Presidential Library.
Norman Davis Papers, Library of Congress.
Charles G. Dawes Papers, Northwestern University.
John Foster Dulles Papers, Princeton University.
Federal Reserve Bank of New York.
Herbert Feis Papers, Library of Congress.
Jerome Frank Papers, Yale University.
Felix Frankfurter Papers, Library of Congress.
Hugh Gibson Papers, Hoover Institution on War, Revolution and Peace, Stanford University.
Alexander Gumberg Papers, State Historical Society of Wisconsin.
George L. Harrison Papers, Columbia University.
Herbert Hoover Papers, Herbert Hoover Presidential Library.
Louis P. Lochner Papers, State Historical Society of Wisconsin.
J. Theodore Marriner Papers and Diary, Columbia University.
George S. Messersmith Papers, University of Delaware.
J. Pierrepont Moffat Papers and Diary, Harvard University.
DeWitt C. Poole Papers, State Historical Society of Wisconsin.
Frederic M. Sackett Papers, Filson Club, Louisville, and University of Kentucky.
Jacob Gould Schurman Papers, Cornell University.
General George Simonds Papers, Library of Congress.
Henry L. Stimson Papers and Diary, Yale University.
Oswald Garrison Villard Papers, Harvard University.
John Cooper Wiley Papers, Franklin D. Roosevelt Presidential Library.
Hugh R. Wilson Papers, Herbert Hoover Presidential Library.

Unpublished official documents

Manuscripts housed in the U.S. National Archives, Washington, D.C.

German Foreign Ministry Records (Microfilm, T-120 series)
Alte Reichskanzlei
Auswärtiges Amt
Büro des Reichsministers
Büro des Staatssekretärs

U.S. Department of State, General Records, Record Group 59.
U.S. Department of War, Military Intelligence Division, Military Attaché Reports.

Public Record Office, London

British Foreign Office, United States Correspondence, 1930–1937, Foreign Office Collection 371, General Correspondence, Political (Microfilm, Center for Research Libraries, Chicago).
The British Treasury, "Economic Depression and International Finance, 1916–1943," Selected from Pro Class T172, Part 1, "International Financial Situation and Policy, 1916–1943" (Microfilm, Center for Research Libraries, Chicago).

Correspondence (diplomats and others)

Thomas W. Bullitt, attorney, Louisville, Kentucky.
William C. Bullitt, diplomat, Washington, D.C.
Dean Charles B. Burdick, historian, San Jose State University, San Jose, California.
C. E. Cotting, Lee Higginson Corporation, Boston.
Herbert Feis, State Department Economic Adviser, 1931–1943, York, Maine.
George Kennan, Language Officer, Berlin 1929–1931, Princeton, New Jersey.
Alfred W. Klieforth, First Secretary, Berlin, 1929–1933, San Diego, California.
Marion McVitty, Sackett's niece, New York.
George Murnane, Lee, Higginson partner, New York.
Edgar F. Racey, Lee, Higginson & Co., 1927–1932, Columbus, Ohio.

Published official documents

Akten zur deutschen auswärtigen Politik, 1918–1945, aus dem Archiv des auswärtigen Amts, Hans Rothfels et al., eds. Göttingen; Vandenhoeck & Ruprecht, 1966– , Serie B. 1925–1933.
British Documents on Foreign Affairs: Reports and Papers from the Confidential Print, Kenneth Bourne and D. Cameron Watt, eds.
  Series C, *North America, 1919–1939*, D. K. Adams, ed.
  Series F, *Europe, 1919–1939*, Christopher Seton-Watson, ed.
  Series J, *The League of Nations*, Peter J. Beck, ed.
Documents on British Foreign Policy, 1919–1939, E. L. Woodward and Rohan Butler, eds. London: His Majesty's Stationery Office, 1946– , Second Series.
Documents on German Foreign Policy, 1918–1945, Raymond J. Sonntag, John W. Wheeler-Bennett, Maurice Baumont et al., eds. Washington, D.C.: Government Printing Office/London, His Majesty's Stationery Office, 1949– .

U.S. Department of Commerce, *The United States in the World Economy: The International Transactions of the United States During the Interwar Period*. Washington, D.C.: Government Printing Office, 1943.

U.S. Department of State, *Instructions to Diplomatic Officers*.

U.S. Department of State, *Papers Relating to the Foreign Relations of the United States*. Washington, D.C.: Government Printing Office, 1861– .

U.S. Senate, Finance Committee, *Hearings*, 72nd Congress, 1st Session, "Sale of Foreign Bonds or Securities in the United States."

U.S. Senate, Sub-Committee on Banking and Currency, *Hearings*, 72nd Congress, 2nd Session, "Stock Exchange Practices," Part 4, "Kreuger and Toll."

Memoirs, diaries, personal accounts

Norman H. Baynes, ed., *The Speeches of Adolf Hitler, April 1922–August 1939*, 4 vols. New York: Gordon Press [1942].

Heinrich Brüning, "Ein Brief," *Deutsche Rundschau*, 70 (July 1947): 1–22.

Memoiren, 1918–1934. Stuttgart, Deutsche Verlags-Anstalt, 1970.

"The Statesman," in Robert B. Heywood, ed., *The Works of the Mind*. Chicago: University of Chicago Press, 1966 [1947].

Maude Parker Child, *The Social Side of Diplomatic Life*. Indianapolis: Bobbs-Merrill, 1925.

Julius Curtius, *Sechs Jahre Minister der deutschen Republik*. Heidelberg: Carl Winter, Universitätsverlag, 1948.

Charles G. Dawes, *Journal as Ambassador to Great Britain*. New York: Macmillan, 1939.

Martha Dodd, *Through Embassy Eyes*. Garden City, NY: Garden City Publishing, 1940.

William E. Dodd, Jr., and Martha Dodd, eds., *Ambassador Dodd's Diary, 1933–1938*. New York: Harcourt, Brace, 1941.

Walter Evans Edge, *A Jerseyman's Journal: Fifty Years of American Business and Politics*. Princeton: Princeton University Press, 1948.

André François-Poncet, *The Fateful Years: Memoirs of A French Ambassador in Berlin, 1931–1938*, translated by Jacques Le Clerq. New York, Howard Fertig, 1972 [1946].

Elke Fröhlich, ed., *Die Tagebücher von Joseph Goebbels, Sämtliche Fragment*, Part 1. München: K. G. Saur, 1987.

Bella Fromm, *Blood and Banquets: A Berlin Social Diary*. Garden City, NY: Garden City Publishing, 1944.

Adolf Hitler, *Mein Kampf*. New York: Reynal & Hitchcock, 1940.

Hitler's Secret Conversations, 1941–1944. New York: Octagon Books, 1972 [1953].

Calvin Hoover, *Memoirs of Capitalism, Communism and Nazism*. Durham, NC: Duke University Press, 1965.

Herbert Hoover, *The Memoirs of Herbert Hoover*, 3 vols. 2: *The Cabinet and the Presidency*; 3: *The Great Depression*. New York: Macmillan, 1952.

Sir David Kelly, *The Ruling Few, or the Human Background to Diplomacy*. London: Hollis & Carter, n.d. [c. 1952].

Louis P. Lochner, *Always the Unexpected: A Book of Reminiscences*. New York: Macmillan, 1956.

Herbert Hoover and Germany. New York: Macmillan, 1960.

What About Germany? New York: Dodd, Mead, 1942.

Kurt G. W. Ludecke, *I Knew Hitler: The Story of a Nazi Who Escaped the Blood Purge*. London: Jarrolds, 1938.

Hans Luther, *Vor dem Abgrund, 1930–1933, Reichsbankspräsident in Krisenzeiten*. Berlin: Propyläen Verlag, 1964.

Raymond Moley, *After Seven Years*. New York: Harper & Brothers, 1939.

William Starr Myers and Walter H. Newton, *The Hoover Administration: A Documented Narrative*. New York: Scribner, 1936.

Friedrich von Prittwitz und Gaffron, *Zwischen Petersburg und Washington: Ein Diplomatenleben*. München: Isar Verlag, 1952.

Hermann Pünder, *Politik in der Reichskanzlei: Aufzeichnungen aus den Jahren 1929–1932*. Stuttgart: Deutsche Verlags-Anstalt, 1961.

Hjalmar Schacht, *76 Jahre meines Lebens*. Bad Wörishofen, Germany: Kindler & Schiermeyer Verlag, 1953.

Hans Schlange-Schöningen, *Am Tage Danach*. Hamburg: Hammerich & Lesser, 1946.

Lutz Graf Schwerin von Krosigk, *Es geschah in Deutschland: Menschenbilder unseres Jahrhunderts*, 3rd edition. Tübingen and Stuttgart: Rainer Wunderlich Verlag Hermann Leins, 1952.

Henry L. Stimson and McGeorge Bundy, *On Active Service in Peace and War*. New York: Harper & Brothers, 1948.

Lewis L. Strauss, *Men and Decisions*. New York: Doubleday, 1962.

Gottfried Reinhold Treviranus, *Das Ende von Weimar: Heinrich Brüning und seine Zeit*. Düsseldorf/Wien: Econ-Verlag, 1968.

Robert Vansittart, *The Mist Procession: The Autobiography of Lord Vansittart*. London: Hutchinson, 1958.

Ray L. Wilbur and Arthur M. Hyde, *The Hoover Policies*. New York: Scribner, 1937.

Newspapers and other periodicals

Berliner Tageblatt und Handels-Zeitung
Business Week
Current History
Literary Digest
Louisville Courier-Journal
Louisville Herald
Louisville Herald-Express
Louisville Herald-Post
Louisville Post
Louisville Times
Moody's Investors Service
The Nation
New York Times
Outlook and Independent

Providence Journal
Saturday Evening Post
Times Literary Supplement

Secondary accounts: books, articles, theses, and dissertations

David Abraham, *The Collapse of the Weimar Republic: Political Economy and Crisis.* Princeton: Princeton University Press, 1981, and 2nd edition, New York: Holmes & Meier, 1986.

Siegfried Bahne, "Die Kommunistische Partei Deutshlands," in Erich Matthias and Rudolf Morsey, eds., *Das Ende der Parteien 1933.* Düsseldorf: Droste Verlag, 1960.

Edward W. Bennett, *German Rearmament and the West, 1932–1933.* Princeton: Princeton University Press, 1979.

Germany and the Diplomacy of the Financial Crisis, 1931. Cambridge, MA: Harvard University Press, 1962.

Moritz J. Bonn, *Wandering Scholar.* New York: John Day, 1948.

Karl Dietrich Bracher, *Die Auflösung der Weimarer Republik: Eine Studie zum Problem des Machtverfalls in der Demokratie,* 4th edition. Schwarzwald, Germany: Ring-Verlag, 1964.

The German Dictatorship: The Origins, Structure, and Effects of National Socialism, translated by Jean Steinberg. New York: Praeger, 1970.

Joseph Brandes, *Herbert Hoover and Economic Diplomacy: Department of Commerce Policy, 1921–1928.* Pittsburgh: University of Pittsburgh Press, 1962.

Martin Broszat, *Hitler and the Collapse of Weimar Germany,* translated and with a Foreword by V. R. Berghahn. Leamington Spa, UK · Berg, 1987 [1984]

Peter H. Buckingham, *America Sees Red, Anti-Communism in America, 1870s to 1980s: A Guide to Issues and References.* Claremont, CA: Regian Books, 1988.

Alan Bullock, *Hitler: A Study in Tyranny,* 2nd edition. New York: Harper & Row, 1962.

Charles B. Burdick, *An American Island in Hitler's Reich: The Bad Nauheim Internment.* Menlo Park, CA: Markgraf Publications Group, 1987.

Kathleen Burk, "Diplomacy and the Private Banker: The Case of the House of Morgan," in Gustav Schmidt, ed., *Konstellationen Internationaler Politik, 1924–1932, Politische und wirtschaftliche Faktoren in den Beziehungen zwishen West Europa und den Vereinigten Staaten.* Bochum, Germany: Studienverlag Brockmeyer, 1983.

Bernard V. Burke, "American Diplomats and Hitler's Rise to Power, 1930–1933: The Mission of Ambassador Sackett." Ph.D. dissertation, University of Washington, 1966.

"American Economic Diplomacy and the Weimar Republic, *Mid-America,* 54 (October 1972): 211–233.

"Senator and Diplomat: The Public Career of Frederic M. Sackett, *The Filson Club History Quarterly,* 61 (April 1987): 185–216.

David Carlton, *MacDonald Versus Henderson: The Foreign Policy of the Second Labour Government.* London: Macmillan, 1970.

Edward Hallett Carr, *German-Soviet Relations Between the Two World Wars, 1919–1939.* Baltimore: Johns Hopkins University Press, 1951.

John M. Carroll, "Owen D. Young and German Reparations: The Diplomacy of an Enlightened Businessman," in Kenneth Paul Jones, ed., *U.S. Diplomats in Europe, 1919–1941.*

F. L. Carsten, *Britain and the Weimar Republic: The British Documents.* London: Batsford Academic and Educational, 1984.

The Reichswehr and Politics, 1918–1933. Oxford, Clarendon Press, 1966.

Werner Conze, "Die Krise des Partienstaates in Deutschland 1929/30," *Historische Zeitschrift*, 178 (1954): 47–83.

"Zum Sturz Brünings," *Vierteljahrshefte für Zeitgeschichte*, 1 (1953): 261–288.

Frank Costigliola, *Awkward Dominion: American Political, Economic, and Cultural Relations with Europe, 1919–1933.* Ithaca, NY: Cornell University Press, 1984.

"John B. Stetson, Jr. and Poland: The Diplomacy of a Prophet Scorned," in Kenneth Paul Jones, ed., *U.S. Diplomats in Europe, 1919–1941.*

Gordon A. Craig, *The Politics of the Prussian Army, 1640–1945.* New York: Oxford University Press, 1956.

Germany, 1866–1945. New York: Oxford University Press, 1978.

Gordon A. Craig and Alexander L. George, *Force and Statecraft: Diplomatic Problems of Our Time*, 2nd edition. New York: Oxford University Press, 1990.

Charles Cutter, "The American Yiddish Daily Press Reaction to the Rise of Nazism, 1930–1939." Ph.D. dissertation, Ohio State University, 1979.

Robert Dallek, *Democrat and Diplomat: The Life of William E. Dodd.* New York: Oxford University Press, 1968.

Alexander DeConde, *Half Bitter, Half Sweet: An Excursion into Italian-American History.* New York: Scribner, 1971.

Lawrence Dennis, "'Sold' on Foreign Bonds," *New Republic*, 65 (November-December 1930): 8–11, 38–41, 65–68, 93–97, 131–134.

Sander A. Diamond, *Herr Hitler, Amerikas Diplomaten, Washington und der Untergang Weimars.* Düsseldorf: Droste Verlag, 1985.

John P. Diggins, *Mussolini and Fascism: The View From America.* Princeton: Princeton University Press, 1972.

David Dilks, ed., *Retreat From Power: Studies in Britain's Foreign Policy of the Twentieth Century*, 2 Vols. London: Macmillan, 1981.

Theodore Dreiser et al., *Harlan Miners Speak: Report on Terrorism in the Kentucky Coal Fields, Prepared by Members of the National Committee for the Defense of Political Prisoners.* New York, 1932.

John Foster Dulles, "Our Foreign Loan Policy," *Foreign Affairs*, 5 (October 1926): 33–48.

Jean-Baptiste Duroselle, *France and the United States: From the Beginnings to the Present*, translated by Derek Coltman. Chicago: University of Chicago Press, 1978.

Modris Eksteins, "War, Memory, and Politics: The Fate of the Film *All Quiet on the Western Front*," *Central European History*, 13 (March 1980): 60–82.

Fritz T. Epstein, "Germany and the United States: Basic Patterns of Conflict and Understanding," in George L. Anderson, ed., *Issues and Conflicts: Studies in Twentieth Century American Diplomacy.* Lawrence: University of Kansas Press, 1959, 284–314.

Andrew P. N. Erdmann, "Mining for the Corporatist Synthesis: Gold in American Foreign Economic Policy, 1931–1936, *Diplomatic History*, 17 (Spring 1993): 171–200.

Theodor Eschenburg, "The Role of Personality in the Crisis of the Weimar Republic: Hindenburg, Brüning, Groener, Schleicher," in Hajo Holborn, ed., *Republic to Reich*.

Erich Eyck, *A History of the Weimar Republic*, translated by Harlan P. Hanson and Robert G. L. Waite, vol. 2 of 2 vols. Cambridge MA: Harvard University Press, 1963.

Martin L. Fausold, *The Presidency of Herbert C. Hoover*. Lawrence: University Press of Kansas, 1985.

Martin L. Fausold and George T. Mazuzan, eds., *The Hoover Presidency: A Reappraisal*. Albany: State University of New York Press, 1974.

Herbert Feis, *The Diplomacy of the Dollar, First Era, 1919–1932*. Baltimore: Johns Hopkins University Press, 1950.

1933: Characters in Crisis. Boston: Little, Brown, 1966.

John H. Fenton, *Politics in the Border States*. New Orleans: Hauser Press, 1957.

Robert H. Ferrell, *American Diplomacy in the Great Depression: Hoover-Stimson Foreign Policy, 1929–1933*. New Haven: Yale University Press, 1957.

Robert H. Ferrell, ed., *Frank B. Kellogg, Henry L. Stimson*, vol. 11 of Ferrell, ed., *The American Secretaries of State and Their Diplomacy*. New York: Cooper Square, 1963.

Joachim C. Fest, *Hitler*, translated by Richard and Clara Winston. New York: Harcourt Brace Jovanovich, 1974.

Glenn Finch, "The Election of United States Senators in Kentucky: The Beckham Period," *The Filson Club History Quarterly*, 44 (January 1970): 38 30.

"The Election of United States Senators in Kentucky: The Cooper Period," *The Filson Club History Quarterly*, 46 (April 1972): 161–178.

Conan Fischer, *Stormtroopers: A Social, Economic and Ideological Analysis, 1929–1935*. London: George Allen & Unwin, 1983.

Frank Freidel, *Franklin D. Roosevelt: Launching the New Deal*. Boston: Little, Brown, 1973.

Martin Gilbert, *The Roots of Appeasement*. New York: New American Library, 1966.

Sir Horace Rumbold: Portrait of a Diplomat, 1869–1941. London: Heinemann, 1973.

Winfried Glashagen, "Die Reparationspolitik Heinrich Brünings 1930–1931, Studien zum wirtschafts- und aussenpolitischen Entscheidungsprozess in der Auflösungsphase der Weimarer Republik," 2 vols. Ph.D. dissertation, Bonn University, 1980.

Ellis W. Hawley, *The Great War and the Search for a Modern Order: A History of the American People and Their Institutions*. New York: St. Martin's Press, 1979.

"Herbert Hoover and American Corporatism, 1929–1933," in Martin L. Fausold and George T. Mazuzan, eds., *The Hoover Presidency: A Reappraisal*, 101–119.

John L. Heineman, *Hitler's First Foreign Minister: Constantin Freiherr von Neurath, Diplomat and Statesman*. Berkeley: University of California Press, 1979.

George Bernard Hermann, "American Journalistic Perceptions of the Death of Weimar Germany: January 1932 – March 1933." Ph.D. dissertation, Carnegie-Mellon University, 1979.

John Hiden, *The Baltic States and Weimar Ostpolitik.* Cambridge: Cambridge University Press, 1987.

Godfrey Hodgson, *The Colonel: The Life and Wars of Henry Stimson, 1867–1950.* New York: Knopf, 1990.

Richard Hofstadter, *The American Political Tradition, and the Men Who Made It.* New York: Vintage Books, 1961.

Michael J. Hogan, "Corporatism," in Michael J. Hogan and Thomas G. Paterson, eds., *Explaining the History of American Foreign Relations.* Cambridge: Cambridge University Press, 1991.

Informal Entente: The Private Structure of Cooperation in Anglo-American Economic Diplomacy, 1918–1928. Columbia: University of Missouri Press, 1977.

"Thomas W. Lamont and European Recovery: The Diplomacy of Privatism in a Corporatist Age," in Kenneth Paul Jones, *U.S. Diplomats in Europe, 1919–1941.*

Hajo Holborn, ed., *Republic to Reich: The Making of the Nazi Revolution, Ten Essays.* New York: Pantheon Books, 1972.

Jon Jacobson, *Locarno Diplomacy: Germany and the West, 1925–1929.* Princeton: Princeton University Press, 1972.

Klaus Jaitner, "Deutschland, Brüning und die Formulierung der britischen Aussenpolitik Mai 1930 bis Juni 1932, *Vierteljahrshefte für Zeitgeschichte,* 28 (1980): 440–486.

Harold James, *The German Slump, Politics and Economics, 1924–1936.* Oxford: Oxford University Press, 1986.

Malcolm E. Jewell and Everett W. Cunningham, *Kentucky Politics.* Lexington: University of Kentucky Press, 1968.

Manfred Jonas, *The United States and Germany: A Diplomatic History.* Ithaca, NY: Cornell University Press, 1984.

Kenneth Paul Jones, "Alanson B. Houghton and the Ruhr Crisis: The Diplomacy of Power and Morality," in Kenneth Paul Jones, ed., *U.S. Diplomats in Europe, 1919–1941.*

Kenneth Paul Jones, ed., *U.S. Diplomats in Europe, 1919–1941.* Santa Barbara, CA: ABC-Clio, 1981.

David E. Kaiser, *Economic Diplomacy and the Origins of the Second World War: Germany, Britain, France, and Eastern Europe, 1930–1939.* Princeton: Princeton University Press, 1980.

Walter H. Kaufmann, *Monarchism in the Weimar Republic.* New York: Bookman Associates, 1953.

George F. Kennan, *American Diplomacy, 1900–1950.* Chicago: University of Chicago Press, 1951.

Ian Kershaw, *The "Hitler Myth": Image and Reality in the Third Reich.* New York: Oxford University Press, 1987.

Charles P. Kindleberger, *Manias, Panics, and Crashes: A History of Financial Crises.* New York: Basic Books, 1978.

Fritz Klein, "Zur Vorbereitung der faschistischen Diktatur durch die deutsche

Grossbourgeoisie (1929–1932), *Zeitschrift für Geschichtswissenschaft*, 1 (1953): 872–904.

Jürgen Baron von Kruedener, *Economic Crisis and Political Collapse: The Weimar Republic 1924–1933*. New York: Berg, 1990.

Robert R. Kuczynski, *Bankers' Profits From German Loans*. Washington, D.C.: The Brookings Institution, 1932.

Marshall M. Lee and Wolfgang Michalka, *German Foreign Policy, 1919–1933: Continuity or Break?* Leamington Spa, U.K.: Berg, 1987.

Melvyn P. Leffler, *The Elusive Quest: America's Pursuit of European Stability and French Security, 1919–1933*. Chapel Hill: University of North Carolina Press, 1979.

Werner Link, *Die amerikanische Stabilisierungspolitik in Deutschland, 1921–1932*. Düsseldorf: Droste Verlag, 1970.

Douglas Little, "Antibolshevism and American Foreign Policy, 1919–1939: The Diplomacy of Self Delusion," *American Quarterly*, 35 (1983): 376–390.

Charles S. Maier, *Recasting Bourgeois Europe: Stabilization in France, Germany, and Italy in the Decade After World War I*. Princeton: Princeton University Press, 1975.

Sally Marks, *The Illusion of Peace: International Relations in Europe, 1918–1933*. New York: St. Martin's Press, 1976.

Erich Matthias, "Social Democracy and the Power in the State," in *The Road to Dictatorship*, translated by Lawrence Wilson. London: Oswald Wolff, 1964.

Forrest McDonald, *Insull*. Chicago: University of Chicago Press, 1962.

Brian McKercher, "Reaching for the Brass Ring: The Recent Historiography of Interwar American Foreign Relations, *Diplomatic History*, 15 (Fall 1991): 565–598.

William C. McNeil, *American Money and the Weimar Republic: Economics and Politics on the Eve of the Great Depression*. New York: Columbia University Press, 1986.

Norton Medlicott, "Britain and Germany: The Search for Agreement, 1930–1937," in David Dilks, ed., *Retreat From Power: Studies in Britain's Foreign Policy of the Twentieth Century*, 1: 78–101.

Philip Metcalfe, *1933*. New York: Harper & Row, 1988.

Richard Hemmig Meyer, *Banker's Diplomacy: Monetary Stabilization in the Twenties*. New York: Columbia University Press, 1970.

D. E. Moggridge, "Policy in the Crises of 1920 and 1929," in Charles P. Kindleberger and Jean-Pierre Laffargue, eds., *Financial Crises, Theory, History, and Policy*. Cambridge: Cambridge University Press, 1982.

Rudolf Morsey, "Hitlers Verhandlungen mit der Zentrumsführung am 31. Januar 1933," *Vierteljahrshefte für Zeitgeschichte*, 9 (1961): 182–194.

"Zur Geschichte des 'Preussenschlags' am 20. Juli 1932," *Vierteljahrshefte für Zeitgeschichte*, 9 (1961): 430–439.

Harold G. Moulton and Leo Pasvolsky, *World War Debt Settlements*. New York: Macmillan, 1926.

War Debts and World Prosperity. New York: The Brookings Institution, 1932.

Heinrich Muth, "Agrarpolitik und Parteipolitik im Frühjahr 1932," in Ferdinand A. Hermens and Theodor Schieder, eds., *Staat, Wirtschaft und Politik in der Weimarer Republik: Festschrift für Heinrich Brüning*. Berlin: Duncker & Humblot, 1967.

Jeanette P. Nichols, "Roosevelt's Monetary Diplomacy in 1933," *American Historical Review*, 56 (January 1951): 295–317.

J. Noakes and G. Pridham, eds., *Nazism, 1919–1945: A History in Documents and Eyewitness Accounts*, 2 vols. New York: Schocken Books, 1983. Vol. 1: *The Nazi Party, State and Society, 1919–1939*.

Arnold A. Offner, *The Origins of the Second World War: American Foreign Policy and World Politics, 1917–1941*. New York: Praeger, 1975.

Anne Orde, "The Origins of the German-Austrian Customs Union Affair of 1931," *Central European History*, 13 (March 1980): 34–59.

Dietrich Orlow, *The History of the Nazi Party: 1919–1933*. Pittsburgh: University of Pittsburgh Press, 1969.

Thomas G. Paterson, *Meeting the Communist Threat, Truman to Reagan*. New York: Oxford University Press, 1988.

John Ed Pearce, *Divide and Dissent: Kentucky Politics, 1930–1933*. Lexington: University Press of Kentucky, 1987.

Neal Pease, "The United States and the Polish Boundaries, 1931: An American Attempt to Revise the Polish Corridor," *The Polish Review*, 27 (1982): 122–137.

Gaines Post Jr., *The Civil-Military Fabric of Weimar Foreign Policy*. Princeton: Princeton University Press, 1973.

Frederic L. Propas, "Creating a Hard Line Toward Russia: The Training of State Department Soviet Experts, 1927–1937," *Diplomatic History*, 8 (Summer 1984): 209–226.

James Warren Prothro, *The Dollar Decade: Business Ideas in the 1920s*. Baton Rouge: Louisiana State University Press, 1954.

Joachim Remak, "Two German Views of the United States: Hitler and His Diplomats," *World Affairs Quarterly*, 28 (April 1957): 25–35.

Norman Rose, *Vansittart: Study of a Diplomat*. New York: Holmes & Meier, 1978.

Emily S. Rosenberg, *Spreading the American Dream: American Economic and Cultural Expansion, 1890–1945*. New York: Hill & Wang, 1982.

David F. Schmitz, *The United States and Fascist Italy, 1922–1940*. Chapel Hill: University of North Carolina Press, 1988.

David Schoenbaum, *Hitler's Social Revolution: Class and Status in Germany 1933–1939*. Garden City, NY: Doubleday, 1966.

Robert D. Schulzinger, "Complaints, Self-justification, and Analysis: The Historiography of American Foreign Relations Since 1969," *Diplomatic History*, 15 (Spring 1991): 245–264.

Klaus Schwabe, "The United States and the Weimar Republic: A 'Special Relationship' That Failed," in Frank Trommler and Joseph McVeigh, eds., *America and the Germans*.

Robert Shaplen, *Kreuger, Genius and Swindler*. New York: Knopf, 1960.

Frank H. Simonds, *Can Europe Keep the Peace?* New York: Harper & Brothers, 1931.

Peter D. Stachura, *Gregor Strasser and the Rise of Nazism*. London: George Allen & Unwin, 1983.

"Introduction: Weimar, National Socialism and Historians," in Peter D. Stachura, ed., *The Nazi Machtergreifung*. London: George Allen & Unwin, 1983.

Ronald Steel, *Walter Lippmann and the American Century*. Boston: Little, Brown, 1980.

Jesse H. Stiller, *George S. Messersmith, Diplomat of Democracy*. Chapel Hill: University of North Carolina Press, 1987.

Graham H. Stuart, *American Diplomatic and Consular Practice*. New York: D. Appleton-Century, 1936.

John M. Thompson, *Russia, Bolshevism, and the Versailles Peace*. Princeton: Princeton University Press, 1966.

Helga Timm, *Die deutsche Sozialpolitik und der Bruch der Grossen Koalition im März 1930*. Düsseldorf: Droste Verlag, 1952.

George Brown Tindall, *The Emergence of the New South, 1913–1945*. Baton Rouge: Louisiana State University Press, 1967.

The Ethnic Southerners. Baton Rouge: Louisiana State University Press, 1976.

Frank Trommler and Joseph McVeigh, eds., *America and the Germans: An Assessment of a Three-Hundred-Year History*, 2 vols. Vol. 2: *The Relationship in the Twentieth Century*. Philadelphia: University of Pennsylvania Press, 1985.

Henry Ashby Turner, Jr., *German Big Business and the Rise of Hitler*. New York: Oxford University Press, 1985.

Oswald Garrison Villard, *The German Phoenix: The Story of the Republic*. New York: Harrison Smith & Robert Haas, 1933.

Thilo Vogelsang, *Reichswehr, Staat und NSDAP, Beiträge zur deutschen Geschichte 1930–1932*. Stuttgart: Deutsche Verlags-Anstalt, 1962.

"Zur Politik Schleichers gegenüber der NSDAP 1932," *Vierteljahrshefte für Zeitgeschichte*, 6 (1958): 86–118.

Lisa Walker, "Anti-Bolshevism and the Advent of Mussolini and Hitler: Anglo-American Diplomatic Perceptions, 1922–1933." Master's thesis, Portland State University, 1993.

Harris Gaylord Warren, *Herbert Hoover and the Great Depression*. New York: Oxford University Press, 1959.

Gerhard L. Weinberg, "From Confrontation to Cooperation: Germany and the United States, 1933–1939," in Frank Trommler and Joseph McVeigh, eds. *America and the Germans*.

"Hitler's Image of the United States," *American Historical Review*, 69 (July 1964): 1006–1021.

John W. Wheeler-Bennett, *The Nemesis of Power: The German Army in Politics, 1918–1945*. London: Macmillan, 1954.

Wooden Titan: Hindenburg in Twenty Years of German History, 1914–1934. London: Archon Books, 1936.

Joan Hoff Wilson, *American Business and Foreign Policy*. Lexington: University Press of Kentucky, 1971.

Herbert Hoover, Forgotten Progressive. Boston: Little, Brown, 1975.

"A Reevaluation of Herbert Hoover's Foreign Policy," in Martin L. Fausold and George T. Mazuzan, *The Hoover Presidency: A Reappraisal*, 164–186.

Index

All Quiet on the Western Front, 102–4
anti-Semitism, 84, 94, 104, 166, 168, 170,
    188–9, 286, 295–6, 310
Armour, Norman, U.S. chargé, Paris, 227
Article 48, Weimar constitution, 60–1, 63,
    65, 74, 82, 83, 90, 200

Bank for International Settlements, 50, 85,
    92, 128–9
Baruch, Bernard M., U.S. financier, 131,
    133, 156
Bavaria, 38, 193, 199, 238, 257, 289, 291
Bessinge disarmament talks, 204–6, 210,
    216–19, 222
Boal, Pierre de Lagarde, U.S. diplomat, 153,
    169, 187–8, 190, 214, 234, 245
bolshevism, *see* communist threat
Borah, William E., U.S. senator, 70
Braun, Otto, Prussian minister-president,
    98
Brüning, Heinrich, German chancellor,
    53–5, 60–6, 74, 80–5, 90–3,
    100–3, 108, 113, 135, 141, 150,
    154, 158–9, 170, 177, 180, 185–6,
    194, 197–8, 202, 208, 215–18,
    237, 246, 252, 255–6, 259,
    261, 263, 283–4, 291–2, 296–7,
    299–300, 302–7
  and armaments, 174, 176, 181, 196,
    204–6
  and communism, 95, 109, 150–3,
    155–6, 158, 161, 306
  and customs union, 125–6, 136, 143
  and depression, 149–50
  described, 99, 215, 226
  and economic conference, 106, 108–11,
    116–22, 125
  and financial crisis, 123, 125, 131–6,
    145, 147–8, 149–50
  and Hindenburg, 175, 232–3
  and Hitler, 63–4, 91, 102, 104–5,
    172–4, 178–80, 194–6
  and letter from Sackett, 217–24
  and monarchy, 104–5, 150, 181, 196,
    234

and pocket battleships, 126, 137–8,
    140–1, 148
  and presidential election, 173, 175–6,
    181, 190, 196
  and resignation, 225–32
Bullitt, William C., U.S. diplomat, 184
Bülow, Bernhard von, state secretary,
    Germany Foreign Ministry, 118,
    141, 205, 223, 278–9, 282

Carpenter, Col. Edward, U.S. military
    attaché, Berlin, 154, 156
Carr, Wilbur J., U.S. assistant secretary of
    state, 44
Carter, John, U.S. diplomat, 258
Castle, William R., assistant, later
    undersecretary of state, 1, 15–16,
    20, 74, 132, 135, 149, 152, 178–9,
    183, 209, 235, 244–6, 249, 252, 295
  and communism, 153, 248, 260
  and moratorium, 139–40, 144–7
  and pocket battleship, 137–8, 140
Cecil, Lord Robert, British diplomat, 155,
    165
Chamberlain, Neville, British chancellor of
    the exchequer, 121
Claudel, Paul, French ambassador to the
    U.S., 133
communist threat (*see also* Brüning
    and communism; Sackett and
    communism), 55–9, 109, 111,
    152–5, 157, 179–80, 235, 242–3,
    248, 258, 269, 306–7
Coolidge, Calvin, 32, 35
corporatism, 33, 42–3, 46–8, 50–1, 93–4,
    108, 113–15, 130, 167, 251, 302
Cotton, Joseph P., undersecretary of state,
    20, 51, 112, 121, 251
Craigie, Robert L., British diplomat, 116
Curtius, Julius, German foreign minister,
    22, 68–70, 103, 105–8, 117–18,
    131, 135–6, 140–1, 143, 146–7,
    153, 155, 176–7
customs union, 125–6, 128, 135, 140–2,
    304

Danubian confederation, 208–10, 212
Davis, Norman, U.S. disarmament delegate,
    211–12, 216–19, 222, 250, 291
Dawes, Charles G., U.S. ambassador,
    London, 33, 116, 122, 124, 130,
    291
Dawes Plan, 33–5
de Haas, Walter, chief, American section,
    German Foreign Ministry, 21, 50,
    68
Dieckhoff, Hans, German diplomat, 176
Dietrich, Hermann, German vice-chancellor
    and minister of finance, 229
Dillon, Read and Company, 45
disarmament, 3, 41, 70, 86, 105, 108,
    110, 120, 137–8, 140–1, 143–4,
    149, 151, 154, 157, 159, 173, 188,
    216–19
Disarmament Conference, Geneva, 176,
    181, 196, 199, 202–7, 210–11,
    217–19, 220–2, 227, 234, 237,
    255, 304, 306
Dodd, Martha, 73–4
Dodd, William E., U.S. ambassador, Berlin,
    1933–1937, 72, 290
Dolbeare, Frederic, U.S. disarmament
    delegate, 217–19, 221, 223
Dominian, Leon, U.S. consul general,
    Stuttgart, 290–1
Duesterberg, Theodor, Stahlhelm
    presidential candidate, 181–2
Dulles, Allen, U.S. disarmament delegation
    legal adviser, 213, 291
Dulles, John Foster, U.S government
    consultant, 85–6, 131, 209

Edge, Walter E., U.S. ambassador, Paris,
    115, 137–8, 177, 199, 208, 221

fascism, 166–70, 188, 290–1
Feis, Herbert, State Department economic
    adviser, 47, 129, 132, 168, 170–1,
    207, 220, 237–8, 273
financial crisis, 127–9, 144–6, 153, 156
Fischer, Louis, journalist, 155–6
Flandin, Pierre-Etienne, French finance
    minister, 165, 208
foreign loan policy, 43–5
France, 1, 3, 4, 28–32, 34–6, 41, 49–50,
    69–70, 85–6, 97, 113, 115,
    118–19, 122, 149, 169, 175–9,
    185, 188, 199–200, 202, 208, 211,
    215–16, 219, 234, 261, 300–1,
    304–5
    and disarmament conference, 202–7,
    212–13, 218–22
    and Hoover Moratorium, 128–9, 131,
    122–40, 142–4

François-Poncet, André, French
    ambassador, Berlin, 188, 220–1,
    288, 310
Frankfurter, Felix, Harvard law professor,
    47, 273
Fraser, Leon, bank official, 85
Frick, Wilhelm, Nazi Reichstag deputy,
    105, 160–1, 163, 264, 267, 269,
    281–3
Fromm, Bella, Berlin social reporter, 295

Garrett, John W., U.S. ambassador, Rome,
    250
Gibson, Hugh R., U.S. ambassador,
    Brussels, disarmament delegate, 130,
    211–12, 214, 216–19, 221–3, 227
Gilbert, S. Parker, agent general for
    reparations, 33, 44, 49–50
Goebbels, Joseph, Nazi official, 161–3,
    165, 172, 180, 187–90, 195, 200,
    248, 253, 264, 267, 269, 295, 307,
    309
Gordon, George Anderson, U.S. counselor
    of embassy, Berlin, 1, 71n9, 71–4,
    86, 90–2, 97, 126, 171, 176,
    183–4, 187, 239, 244–6, 252, 257,
    260, 273, 293–4, 311
    and communism, 81–2, 157, 164,
    239–40
    on Hitler, 80–1, 89–90, 163–5, 272,
    276–7, 294
    and Nazis (*see also* Stennes revolt),
    73, 78–9, 86–7, 91–2, 101, 160,
    163–5, 237, 239, 245–6, 258–9,
    272, 277, 283, 295
    and Reichstag elections, 74–5, 77–81,
    260–1
    and Reichswehr, 87–9, 240–1
    and Social Democrats, 91, 98, 261
Göring, Hermann, Nazi official, 1, 163,
    172, 184, 187–9, 254–5, 264, 267,
    270, 281, 283, 286–7, 295, 307
Grandi, Dino, Italian foreign minister, 204,
    206
Great Coalition, 27, 54, 62, 64
Groener, Gen. Wilhelm, Reichswehr
    minister, 62, 89, 174–5, 198–201,
    214–15, 228–9
Gumberg, Alexander, 155

Hammerstein-Equord, Gen. Kurt von,
    Reichswehr commander, 87–9, 200,
    229, 271
Harding, Warren G., 32
Harlan County strike, 25–6, 125, 250
Harrison, George L., governor, Federal
    Reserve Bank of New York, 50, 85,
    108, 133, 227

Harzburg Front, 173, 181–2, 280–1, 290, 306, 310
Henderson, Arthur, British foreign secretary, 118–19, 121, 135, 140–1
Herriot, Édouard, French premiere, 34, 213, 216–19, 221–3, 266
Hindenburg, Col. Oskar von, 228
Hindenburg, Field Marshal Paul von, 22, 38, 62–3, 80, 126, 132–3, 154, 158, 172–3, 198–200, 214, 223–4, 228–34, 245–7, 253–7, 261–6, 270, 272–3, 277–82, 296, 306
  and Papen, 225, 252
  and pocket battleships, 136, 140–1, 303
  and presidential elections, 173, 175–6, 181, 190–3, 196
Hitler, Adolf, 26, 36–9, 60, 75–7, 80–1, 84–5, 123, 155, 158–9, 161–3, 167–71, 173–4, 179–80, 183, 185–7, 196, 198–201, 203, 212–13, 222, 233–4, 236, 239, 241–2, 245, 247, 252, 259, 261–5, 267, 270, 272, 274, 278, 284, 299, 303, 305, 307, 310
  as chancellor, 276–86, 289–90, 293–5
  and financial support, 79, 81, 170, 185, 193, 230, 234, 240, 256, 259–60, 277
  and presidential elections, 182, 190–3, 196
Hoesch, Leopold von, German ambassador, Paris, 138
Hohenzollerns, 62, 103, 174, 181, 193, 234–5, 240, 257–8, 261, 291, 305
Hoover, Herbert Clark, 1, 15, 32–3, 94, 114–15, 123–4, 137, 149, 151, 176, 207, 209, 244, 249–51, 257, 260, 274, 292, 297, 300–2, 305–8
  and disarmament, 204, 218–20
  and economic conference, 108–9, 112, 114, 117–18, 121–2, 274–5
  and financial crisis, 127–34, 138–9, 144–7
  as secretary of commerce, 43–4, 167
Hoover Moratorium, 123–4, 132–8, 143–4, 151, 154, 176, 299, 301–2, 306
Houghton, Alanson, U.S. diplomat, 32, 152
Hugenberg, Alfred, Nationalist party leader, 36–9, 60, 136, 173–5, 193, 198, 215, 241, 252, 254–5, 258, 261–3, 267–9, 279–81, 284–6, 289–90, 310
Hughes, Charles Evans, 32–3, 152
Hull, Cordell, 294

Insull, Samuel, Chicago utilities man, 13–14, 46

Jewish concerns, 84, 94, 104, 168, 188, 243, 261, 276, 279, 290–6

Kelley, Robert F., State Department, chief, Eastern European desk, 58, 153
Kellogg, Frank B., 35, 44, 107–12, 118
Kennan, George F., quoted, 2, 71, 184
Kiep, Otto, German diplomat, 48, 74–5
Klieforth, Alfred, first secretary, Berlin [misspelled Kliefoth consistently in State Department correspondence], 169, 185–6, 229, 232, 273, 276–7, 279–82
Klots, Allen T., Stimson's aide, 157–8, 167
Kreuger, Ivar, Swedish financier, 45–7, 210, 278
Kuh, Frederick, United Press bureau chief, Berlin, 155
Kühlental, Col. Erich, chief, Intelligence Section, German General Staff, 87–9

Lamont, Thomas, J.P. Morgan partner, 35, 51, 130, 220
Lausanne Conference, 176, 178, 181, 196–7, 209, 215, 217–18, 220–3, 227–8, 230, 236, 251–2, 302, 304, 306
League of Nations, 28, 110, 128–9, 209, 213–14, 278
Lee, Higginson and Co., 45–6, 48–51, 84, 92–3, 114–15
Leitner, Rudolf, German chargé, Washington, 137, 153
Lindsay, Ronald, British ambassador, Washington, 220
Lippmann, Walter, U.S. newspaper columnist, 154
Locarno, treaties of, 34–5
Lochner, Louis, Associate Press bureau chief, Berlin, 283
London Economic Conference, see World Economic Conference, London
Luther, Hans, Reichsbank president, 108, 113

MacArthur, Gen. Douglas, U.S. army chief of staff, 207, 256
MacDonald, Ramsay, British prime minister, 34, 117–18, 120, 132, 135, 180, 204–7, 210, 217, 301
McGarrah, Gates, director, Bank for International Settlements, 85–6

Marcks, Maj. Erich, German press chief, 280
Marriner, J. Theodore, U.S. diplomat, 74, 226, 256, 291
Mayer, Ferdinand, U.S. disarmament delegate, 211–12
Meissner, Otto, Hindenburg's secretary, 228, 264–5, 269
Mellon, Andrew D., U.S. secretary of treasury, 43–4, 114–15, 129–30, 132, 138
Messersmith, George S., consul general, Berlin, 1, 70–3, 147, 157, 184, 291, 293
Meyer, Eugene, governor, Federal Reserve Board, 132, 147, 175
Miller, Douglas, U.S. diplomat, Berlin, 187
Mills, Ogden, U.S. undersecretary of treasury, 130–3, 139, 144
Moffat, J. Pierrepont, U.S. diplomat, 147, 218, 234, 244–6, 258, 260–1, 273, 276
Moody's Investors Service, 52–3
Morgan, J. Pierrepont, Jr., U.S. banker, 32, 35, 130
Morgan, J. P. and Co., 34, 49
Morrow, Dwight, U.S. senator, 129–32
Mowrer, Edgar Ansel, U.S. reporter, Berlin, 167
Müller, Hermann, German chancellor, 45, 54–5
Murnane, George, partner in Lee, Higginson and Co., 45–6, 49–50, 84–5, 92, 113–14, 299, 301
Mussolini, Benito, 154, 166–7, 169–71, 250, 262, 290

Nadolny, Rudolf, German disarmament delegate, 234
Nazi movement, 38, 101–2, 155, 164, 187, 191, 202, 225, 241, 247, 253, 256, 258, 296, 308–9
Nazi party, 36, 39, 75–8, 80, 83, 100–2, 109, 136, 158, 165–6, 169, 173–4, 178–80, 187–8, 202, 214–15, 308
Nazis and Communists, 58–9, 78, 83–4, 98, 136, 148, 149, 154–5, 158, 165–6, 180, 195, 236, 238, 259–61, 270, 279, 309
Neurath, Konstantin von, German foreign minister, 232–3, 281–2
New Plan, *see* Young Plan
Newton, Basil, British chargé, Berlin, 135–6, 141–2
Newton, Walter, Hoover's secretary, 250
Norman, Montagu, governor, Bank of England, 154

occupation of Germany, 29–31, 35
Oldenburg-Januschau, Elard von, Nationalist Reichstag deputy, 231
organized labor, German, 168, 170–1, 229–30, 238–9, 248, 256, 265–6, 268, 272, 280, 282, 286, 292, 306, 310
Osthilfe program (Eastern aid), 63, 231

Papen, Franz von, German chancellor, 173, 225, 227, 233–40, 242–3, 246–7, 251–7, 259, 261–3, 265, 267–8, 276–81, 284–6, 289–90, 304–6, 308
Planck, Erwin, secretary Reichschancellery, 228, 231, 279
pocket battleships, 126, 135–7, 140–2, 146
Polish Corridor, 2, 28–9, 68–70, 185, 212–14, 222, 228, 304
Poole, DeWitt C., counselor of embassy, Berlin, 20
Prussia, 98, 198–200, 203, 214, 234, 238, 243, 254, 266, 270, 272, 283, 286–7, 291, 310
Prussian Diet elections, 192–4, 196, 200, 213, 219
Pünder, Hermann, secretary, Reichschancellery, 200

Reichstag fire, 287–8, 295, 310
Reichswehr, 3, 62, 82, 88–9, 101, 103, 140–1, 154, 174, 202, 214–16, 233, 240, 247, 252, 309
reparations, German, 3, 4, 28–36, 38, 41, 44, 49–53, 83, 96, 104–8, 110, 113, 115, 117–34, 137, 142, 145, 149–51, 159, 165, 173–81, 185–6, 188, 196, 209, 215, 218–22, 251–2, 257, 299–302, 304, 309
repudiation of debt, fear of, 53, 78–9, 82–3, 96, 106, 159, 170–1, 178, 185–6, 188, 191, 257
Robbins, Warren, American diplomat, 152
Robsion, John M., Kentucky congressman, 14, 17–18, 66, 75
Röhm, Ernst, Storm Troop chief of staff, 160, 163, 174, 259
Roosevelt, Franklin D., 250, 274–5, 294–5, 297
Roosevelt, Theodore, 167
Rumbold, Horace, British ambassador, Berlin, 91–2, 105–6, 119–21, 124–6, 147–8, 177, 183, 200, 218, 222, 245, 279, 288, 301, 310

Sackett, Frederic Moseley, Jr., 1–3, 72–3,
79, 81–3, 96–8, 104, 159, 176,
200–1, 208, 218, 259, 264,
269–70, 278, 295–7
appointment as ambassador, 17–21
and Brüning, 4, 59–61, 63–7, 90, 95,
102–3, 105–6, 108, 110–11, 138,
141, 143–4, 146, 161, 172, 175–6,
178–80, 197, 206–7, 214, 217,
252, 254, 269, 285, 290–1, 296–7,
301, 303–4, 306, 309
and Brüning's resignation, 225,
227–32, 245, 249
and communism, 25–6, 55–9, 109,
111, 156–8, 172, 179–80, 195–6,
242, 262, 269, 288, 306–8
and corporatism, 49–50, 53, 251, 298,
300
and customs union, 126–7, 130, 136,
141–2
and Danubian confederation, 208–11
describes Brüning, 99, 215
early career, 9–13
and economic conference (*see also*
World Economic Conference,
London), 4, 106, 109–12, 114–22,
249, 274–5, 299–300, 302
and financial crisis, 123–4, 127,
129–30, 133–6, 139, 146–7
and Gordon, 72
and Hitler, 4–6, 8–9, 60, 83, 99–100,
102, 109–11, 148, 172, 174,
178–80, 185–7, 189–95, 236–7,
240, 243–4, 247–0, 252–3, 256,
262–5, 267, 270–1, 274, 281–6,
289–90, 293, 296–7, 304, 307–12
and letter for Brüning, 217–24
and loans to Germany, 41–2, 47, 50,
106, 112–15, 298, 300, 302
and Messersmith, 70–1
and Nazi anti-Semitism, 59, 286, 292–5
and Nazi party split, 258, 266–8, 270,
279, 309–10
and Nazis, 6, 55–60, 63–4, 66, 100,
109–11, 159–60, 164–5, 172,
183, 199, 202, 237, 252–4, 270–2,
287–9, 295, 308
as new ambassador, 21–5, 40, 54–5
and Papen, 233, 235–8, 242–3, 252,
255, 308
and pocket battleships, 137–8, 140–2
and Polish Corridor, 68–70
and Reichstag elections, 74–5, 241,
289, 309, 311
and Reichstag fire, 287–8, 310
and reparations, 41, 178, 210, 257
and Schleicher, 7, 248, 261, 263,
265–70, 274, 309–10

as senator, 11–15
and Social Democrats, 7, 54–5, 57–8,
64, 66, 98, 169–71, 194, 230,
238, 241–3, 248, 254–5, 266, 272,
287–9, 306, 310
and Storm Troopers, 201, 240, 243,
253–4
and Gregor Strasser, 270–3, 279
and Treaty of Versailles, 68–70
and World Power Conference, 13–14
Sackett, Olive Speed, 10, 23
Sampson, Flem D., Kentucky governor,
14–15, 19, 26
Schacht, Hjalmar H. G., 45, 49, 114–15,
154, 173, 185, 282
Schäffer, Hans, secretary, German Finance
Ministry, 113
Schleicher, General Kurt von, German
chancellor, 62–3, 97, 174, 214–15,
225, 228–30, 233, 239, 247–8,
253, 256, 259, 261, 264
as chancellor, 263–73, 276–81, 309–10
Schröder, Baron Kurt von, Cologne
banker, 276–7
Schurman, Jacob Gould, U.S. ambassador,
Berlin, 16, 37–9, 56, 153
Seeckt, Gen. Hans von, Reichswehr
commander, 101
Seldte, Franz, Stahlhelm leader, 181,
285–6
Severing, Karl, Prussian interior minister,
98, 200
Simon, Sir John, British foreign secretary,
273
Simonds, Gen. George, U.S. disarmament
delegate, 207, 307
Smoot-Hawley tariff, 128
Soviet Union, 111, 153, 158, 188–9,
202–3, 281
Stauss, Emil Georg von, Berlin banker,
185
Stennes revolt, 161–5, 267, 271
Stimson, Henry Lewis, U.S. secretary of
state, 1, 52,70, 94, 97–8, 175–6,
190, 208–9, 233–5, 238, 257, 260,
265, 275, 283, 292, 301, 307
and Brüning, 145–6, 157–8, 167–8,
305
and disarmament, 204–6, 211, 217,
219, 221, 227
and financial crisis, 127, 130–1, 133,
138–40, 145, 149
and Japan, 207
on Sackett, 146–7
Storm Troops, 81, 89, 160–3, 171, 173,
185, 198–202, 214, 228, 237–40,
243, 253–4, 258, 267, 285, 287,
292–3, 295, 311

Strasser, Gregor, 36, 105, 180, 215, 259, 264, 266–72, 277–9, 286, 309–10

Strauss, Lewis L., New York banker, 165–6, 168

Stresemann, Gustav, German chancellor, foreign minister, 31–2, 34, 213–17

Tardieu, André, French premier, 204, 206, 208–10, 212–14, 216, 218, 221

Thälmann, Ernst, Communist presidential candidate, 232

Thompson, G. H., British diplomat, 116

Thyssen, Fritz, industrialist, Hitler supporter, 277

Treviranus, Gottfried, cabinet minister, 115, 219, 229

Vansittart, Robert, permanent undersecretary, British Foreign Office, 142, 148, 149n1

Versailles, Treaty of, 3, 28–30, 34, 36, 68–70, 78, 86, 98, 104–5, 126, 140, 150, 185, 205–6, 213, 237, 246, 257, 261, 311

Villard, Oswald Garrison, editor *The Nation*, 115–18, 120, 251, 301

war debts owed the United States, 4, 28, 30, 32–6, 44, 52, 115, 117, 119–22, 124, 128–30, 132, 145, 148, 151, 159, 188, 209, 252, 275, 299, 301–2, 304, 308

Weimar Coalition, 27, 194

Wiggin, Albert H., New York banker, 115

Wiley, John Cooper, counselor of embassy, Berlin, 1, 20, 171, 182–4, 200, 245, 307
    and communism, 55, 57–8, 183
    and Hitler, 189
    and Nazis, 57, 182–3, 187–90
    and Social Democrats, 56–8

Wilhelm II, 231

Willert, Arthur, British diplomat, 116

Wilson, Hugh, U.S. minister, Switzerland, 165, 212, 216, 218–19

Wittelsbachs, 257, 291

Wolf, Otto, Hitler supporter, 277

Wooley, Mary, U.S. disarmament delgate, 227

World Economic Conference, London, 249–52, 273–5, 296, 302, 307

World Power Conference, Berlin, 10–13

Wuest, Lt. Col., U.S. military attaché, Berlin, 240–1

Young, Owen D., U.S. industrialist, 33, 35, 115, 154

Young Plan, 28, 35, 49–50, 98, 106, 119, 127, 173

Zetkin, Clara, Communist Reichstag deputy, 253